THE CAMBRIDGE COMPANION TO BRITISH POSTMODERN FICTION

Postmodern modes of writing have contributed to a rich tradition of innovative and memorable British fiction in the period stretching from the late twentieth century to the present day. Postmodernism has been dismissed as introspective or ahistorical, but its British incarnation demonstrates how compassionate, political, and socially conscious it can be. This volume provides fresh, accessible readings of the most influential examples of postmodern British fiction, and work by more recent, post-millennial writers working in its slipstream. It plots its emergence, reassesses its highpoint in the 1980s and 1990s, and delineates its legacy in the twenty-first century. A valuable resource for students, researchers, and the general reader, this *Companion* provides powerful critical frameworks to understand its geographies; its relationship to North American postmodernism; its renovation of literary forms such as the romance, speculative fiction, and the historical novel; and its vibrant engagements with race, gender, sexuality, and questions of national identity.

BRAN NICOL is Professor of English Literature at the University of Surrey. His many publications include *The Cambridge Introduction to Postmodern Fiction* (2009), *Postmodernism and the Contemporary Novel: A Reader* (2002), *Stalking* (2006), *The Private Eye* (2013), and a co-authored biography (with Emmanuelle Fantin) of Jean Baudrillard (2025).

A complete list of books in the series is at the back of the book.

THE CAMBRIDGE COMPANION TO BRITISH POSTMODERN FICTION

EDITED BY
BRAN NICOL
University of Surrey

Shaftesbury Road, Cambridge CB2 8EA, United Kingdom

One Liberty Plaza, 20th Floor, New York, NY 10006, USA

477 Williamstown Road, Port Melbourne, VIC 3207, Australia

314–321, 3rd Floor, Plot 3, Splendor Forum, Jasola District Centre,
New Delhi – 110025, India

103 Penang Road, #05–06/07, Visioncrest Commercial, Singapore 238467

Cambridge University Press is part of Cambridge University Press & Assessment,
a department of the University of Cambridge.

We share the University's mission to contribute to society through the pursuit of
education, learning and research at the highest international levels of excellence.

www.cambridge.org
Information on this title: www.cambridge.org/9781009585873
DOI: 10.1017/9781009585903

© Cambridge University Press & Assessment 2025

This publication is in copyright. Subject to statutory exception and to the provisions
of relevant collective licensing agreements, no reproduction of any part may take
place without the written permission of Cambridge University Press & Assessment.

When citing this work, please include a reference to the DOI 10.1017/9781009585903

First published 2025

Cover image: Interior of Judge Business School in Cambridge, UK. Photo: marinuse – England /
Alamy Stock Photo

A catalogue record for this publication is available from the British Library

A Cataloging-in-Publication data record for this book is available from the Library of Congress

ISBN 978-1-009-58587-3 Hardback
ISBN 978-1-009-58589-7 Paperback

Cambridge University Press & Assessment has no responsibility for the persistence
or accuracy of URLs for external or third-party internet websites referred to in this
publication and does not guarantee that any content on such websites is, or will remain,
accurate or appropriate.

For EU product safety concerns, contact us at Calle de José Abascal, 56, 1°, 28003 Madrid, Spain,
or email eugpsr@cambridge.org

Contents

List of Contributors		*page* vii
Chronology		xi
Acknowledgements		xx
	Introduction: British Postmodern Fiction Bran Nicol	1
1	The Politics of Postmodern British Fiction Hywel Dix	18
2	British Postmodern Fiction and the Rise of 'Declinism' Graham Matthews	33
3	Postmodern British Fiction and the Postcolonial Graham MacPhee	49
4	The Geographies of British Postmodern Fiction Neal Alexander	66
5	Transatlantic Fictions Stephen J. Burn	82
6	The Scottish Postmodern Novel? Stefanie Lehner	97
7	Outside Postmodernism: B. S. Johnson Before, During, and After Glyn White	113
8	The Recovery of Genre in Contemporary British Fiction: Return of the Romance Suzanne Keen	129

9 Alternative Realisms: Speculation, Magic, and Miracle
  in British Postmodern Fiction   144
  Andrew Tate

10 'Queer' Postmodernism? British Gay and Lesbian Fiction   159
  Kate Haffey

11 Black British and British Asian Fiction: Postmodernism
  and Beyond   174
  Kristian Shaw

12 History and the British Novel After Postmodernism   191
  Alison Lee

13 Neo-Victorian Fiction   206
  Patricia Pulham

14 The End of Postmodernism?   224
  Bran Nicol

15 British Fiction Beyond Postmodernism   240
  Nick Bentley

16 Postmodern British Fiction: Then and Now   255
  Hans Bertens

Further Reading   272
Index   278

Contributors

NEAL ALEXANDER is Senior Lecturer in twentieth-century literature at Aberystwyth University. He is the author of two books, *Late Modernism and the Poetics of Place* (2022) and *Ciaran Carson: Space, Place, Writing* (2010). With David Cooper, he is co-editor of *The Routledge Handbook of Literary Geographies* (2024) and *Poetry & Geography* (2013); and with James Moran, co-editor of *Regional Modernisms* (2013).

NICK BENTLEY is Reader in English literature at Keele University. He is the author of numerous journal articles, book chapters, and books including *Youth Subcultures in Postwar and Contemporary Fiction* (2025), *Contemporary British Fiction: A Reader's Guide to the Essential Criticism* (2018), *Martin Amis* (2015), *Contemporary British Fiction* (2008), and *Radical Fictions: The English Novel in the 1950s* (2007). He is co-editor of *The 2000s: A Decade of Contemporary British Fiction* (2015), *The 2010s: A Decade of Contemporary British Fiction* (2018), and *Teenage Dreams: Youth Subcultures in Fiction, Film and Other Media* (2018).

HANS BERTENS is Emeritus Professor of comparative literature, Utrecht University, The Netherlands, and past President (2013–16) of the International Comparative Literature Association. He has published in Dutch and in English, with his main interests being American literature, postmodernism, and literary theory. His English-language books include *The Idea of the Postmodern: A History* (1995), *Contemporary American Crime Fiction* (2001; with Theo D'haen), *American Literature: A History* (2013; again with Theo D'haen), and *Literary Theory: The Basics* (4th revised edition 2024).

STEPHEN J. BURN is Head of English literature at the University of Glasgow, and the author or editor of eight books, the most recent of which is *The Encyclopedia of Contemporary American Fiction: 1980–2020* (2022, with Patrick O'Donnell and Lesley Larkin).

HYWEL DIX is Professor of English at Bournemouth University. He has published extensively on the relationship between literature, culture, and political change in contemporary Britain, most notably in *Postmodern Fiction and the Break-Up of Britain* (2010), *After Raymond Williams: Cultural Materialism and the Break-Up of Britain* (2nd edition, 2013), *Multicultural Narratives: Traces and Perspectives*, co-edited with Mustafa Kirca (2018), and *Compatriots or Competitors? Welsh, Scottish, English and Northern Irish Writing and Brexit in Comparative Contexts* (2022). His wider research interests include modern and contemporary literature, critical cultural theory, authorial careers, and autofiction. His monograph about literary careers entitled *The Late-Career Novelist* was published in 2017 and an edited collection of essays on *Autofiction in English* was published by Palgrave in 2018. He has also completed a study entitled *Autofiction and Cultural Memory* with Routledge (2022).

KATE HAFFEY is Professor of English at the University of Mary Washington in the department of English and Linguistics and serves as an affiliated faculty of the Women's, Gender, and Sexuality Studies programme. Her areas of expertise include twentieth and twenty-first-century literature, feminism, and queer theory. She is the author of the monograph *Literary Modernism, Queer Temporality: Eddies in Time* (2019), and her work has appeared in *Narrative*, *ASAP/J*, as well as in edited collections. She is currently serving on the editorial board of *Women's Studies Quarterly* (*WSQ*). Her more recent work has turned toward ecocriticism, posthumanism, and science studies in the humanities.

SUZANNE KEEN writes about narrative empathy and the impact of immersion reading. Her books include *Thomas Hardy's Brains* (2014), *Empathy and the Novel* (2007), *Romances of the Archive in Contemporary British Fiction* (2001), *Victorian Renovations of the Novel* (1998), and the recent collection of her essays in *Empathy and Reading: Affect, Impact, and the Co-Creating Reader* (2022). Between 2012 and 2018 she co-edited (with Emma Parker) the Oxford University Press journal *Contemporary Women's Writing*. She serves as Professor of English at Scripps College.

ALISON LEE teaches in the departments of English and Writing Studies and Gender, Sexuality and Women's Studies at Western University. Her current research is a comparative study of nineteenth-century decadence and twentieth-century postmodernism as critical methodologies for reading contemporary neoliberal discourses. Articles have appeared in *Cahiers victoriens et édouardiens*, *Volupté*, *Contemporary Literature*, and the *Journal of Modern Literature*.

STEFANIE LEHNER is Senior Lecturer in Irish literature at Queen's University, Belfast, and Fellow at the Senator George J. Mitchell Institute for Global Peace, Security and Justice (QUB). Her current research explores the role of the arts, specifically performance, in conflict transformation processes, with a focus on the Northern Irish context. She also researches on the politics and ethics of representation in contemporary Scottish and Irish writing. She is author of *Subaltern Ethics in Contemporary Scottish and Irish Literature* (2011) and co-author of *Sounding Conflict: From Resistance to Reconciliation* (2023).

GRAHAM MACPHEE is an Honorary Research Fellow at the University of Manchester. He is the author of *Postwar British Literature and Postcolonial Studies* (2011) and *The Architecture of the Visible* (2002), as well as essays on modernism, twentieth-century British literature, and critical theory. He has edited journal special issues on 'Arendt, Politics, and Culture' and 'The Banalization of War' (co-edited with Angela Naimou) and he is co-editor (with Prem Poddar) of *Empire and After: Englishness in Postcolonial Perspective* (2007). He is working on a study of the right-wing public intellectual and politician Enoch Powell.

GRAHAM MATTHEWS is Associate Professor in English and Provost's Chair in medical humanities at Nanyang Technological University. He is the author of two monographs and over thirty articles and chapters on contemporary literature in journals such as *Modern Fiction Studies*, *Textual Practice*, *English*, *English Studies*, *Literature & Medicine*, *Literature & History*, *Configurations*, and *Critique*. His current research projects include an interdisciplinary and cross-sector engagement with culture and mental health stigma in Singapore, and a book-length study of medicine in mid-century British literature.

BRAN NICOL is Professor of English Literature at the University of Surrey. His many publications include *The Cambridge Introduction to Postmodern Fiction* (2009), *Postmodernism and the Contemporary Novel: A Reader* (2002), *Stalking* (2006), *The Private Eye* (2013), and a co-authored biography (with Emmanuelle Fantin) of Jean Baudrillard (2025).

PATRICIA PULHAM is Professor of Victorian Literature at the University of Surrey, where she is Head of the School of Arts, Humanities and Creative Industries. Her books include a co-edited collection (with Rosario Arias), *Haunting and Spectrality in Neo-Victorian Fiction* (2009), and her monograph *The Sculptural Body in Victorian Literature: Encrypted Sexualities* (2020). She is currently President of the British Association for Victorian Studies (BAVS).

KRISTIAN SHAW is Associate Professor in English literature at the University of Lincoln. He is the author of *Cosmopolitanism in Twenty-First Century Fiction* (2017) and *Brexlit: British Literature and the European Project* (2021). He is the co-editor of *Hari Kunzru: Twenty-First Century Perspectives* (2023, winner of the BACLS Edited Collection Prize), *Kazuo Ishiguro: Twenty-First Century Perspectives* (2023), and the forthcoming *Routledge Handbook to Literature and Globalization* (Routledge).

ANDREW TATE is Professor in literature, religion, and aesthetics at Lancaster University. His work focuses on the intersections between literature, theology, and aesthetics. His numerous publications include the books *Contemporary Fiction and Christianity* (2008), *The New Atheist Novel* (2010, co-authored with Arthur Bradley), and *Apocalyptic Fiction* (2017).

GLYN WHITE is Senior Lecturer in twentieth-century literature and culture at the University of Salford. His publications include *Reading the Graphic Surface: The Presence of the Book in Prose Fiction* (2005), *Re-Reading B. S. Johnson* (co-edited with Philip Tew, 2007), 'The Sadism of the Author or the Masochism of the Reader?' in Julia Jordan and Martin Ryle's collection *B. S. Johnson and Post-War Literature: The Possibilities of the Avant-Garde* (2014), pp. 153–66, and 'Not the Last Word on the Sixties Avant-Garde: An Afterword', in Kate Mitchell and Nonia Williams' *British Avant-Garde Fiction of the 1960s* (2019), pp. 248–61.

Chronology

DATE	EVENTS	LITERATURE
1948	British Nationality Act: citizens from the British Commonwealth permitted to gain British passports and work in the United Kingdom	
1957		Muriel Spark, *The Comforters*
1959		Publication in English and one volume of Samuel Beckett's *Trilogy*: *Molloy, Malone Dies, The Unnamable*
1960	Landmark obscenity case over D. H. Lawrence's *Lady Chatterley's Lover* ends in the acquittal of Penguin Books	
1962		Doris Lessing, *The Golden Notebook* Anthony Burgess, *A Clockwork Orange*
1963	Kenya gains independence (from Britain) US President John F. Kennedy assassinated	
1964		B. S. Johnson, *Albert Angelo* Anthony Burgess, *Nothing Like the Sun*
1965		John Fowles, *The Magus*
1967	Sexual Offences Act (following the Wolfenden Report of 1957), decriminalises private homosexual acts in England and Wales between men aged over twenty-one The 'Summer of Love'; Beatles release *Sergeant Pepper's Lonely Hearts Club Band*	Roland Barthes, 'The Death of the Author' Ngũgĩ wa Thiong'o, *A Grain of Wheat*

1968	Commonwealth Immigrants' Act: controls rate of inflow into UK of those holding UK passports who have no substantial connection with the United Kingdom Student-led protests in France nearly bring down French government	Christine Brooke-Rose, *Between*
1969	United States land men on the moon	John Fowles, *The French Lieutenant's Woman* Brigid Brophy, *In Transit: An Heroi-Cyclic Novel*
1970	Gay Liberation Front meets for the first time at the London School of Economics	Muriel Spark, *The Driver's Seat* J. G. Ballard, *The Atrocity Exhibition*
1972	First British Gay Pride rally Launch of *Gay News*, fortnightly newspaper	Angela Carter, *The Infernal Desire Machines of Doctor Hoffman*
1973	Global oil crisis: the result of Arab OAPEC oil embargo against nations supporting Israel during Yom Kippur War	J. G. Farrell, *The Siege of Krishnapur* J. G. Ballard, *Crash* B. S. Johnson, *Christie Malry's Own Double-Entry* Thomas Pynchon, *Gravity's Rainbow*
1974	Conservative government introduces 'three-day week' to combat inflation, conserve energy, and cap wages for coal-industry workers Resignation of US President Richard Nixon following Watergate Scandal (1972–4)	J. G. Ballard, *Concrete Island* Anthony Burgess, *The Napoleon Symphony*
1975		J. G. Ballard, *High-Rise* Maureen Duffy, *Capital* Christine Brooke-Rose, *Thru*
1978	International Lesbian and Gay Association founded Birth of first test-tube baby	Raymond Williams, *Volunteers*
1979	Scottish devolution referendum: majority in favour but total voters represent only 32.9 per cent of registered electorate: devolution not introduced Conservative government elected, led by Margaret Thatcher as Prime Minister First Sony Walkman released in the UK	Angela Carter, *The Bloody Chamber* Jean-François Lyotard, *The Postmodern Condition*

1980	Homosexuality decriminalised in Scotland	Julian Barnes, *Metroland*
1981	Beginning of the Aids epidemic in the UK Assassination of Egyptian President Anwar Sadat	Alasdair Gray, *Lanark: A Life in 4 Books* Salman Rushdie, *Midnight's Children* (awarded that year's Booker Prize)
1982	Homosexuality decriminalised in Northern Ireland Falklands war with Argentina	
1983		Peter Ackroyd, *The Last Testament of Oscar Wilde* Graham Swift, *Waterland* Jean Baudrillard, *Simulations*
1984	Beginning of twelve-month coal miners' strike UK unemployment reaches record high of 3.3 million First Virgin Atlantic flight	Martin Amis, *Money: A Suicide Note* Angela Carter, *Nights at the Circus*
1985	Mikhail Gorbachev becomes premier of the Soviet Union British geneticist Sir Alec Jeffreys develops technique used in DNA profiling Accidental shooting of Cherry Groce in Brixton sparks riots in Brixton, Tottenham, and Peckham in London First mobile phone call in the UK made	Jeanette Winterson, *Oranges Are Not the Only Fruit* Peter Ackroyd, *Hawksmoor*
1986	Chernobyl nuclear disaster, Ukraine (then part of the Soviet Union)	
1987		Jeanette Winterson, *The Passion* William Owen Roberts, *Y Pla* Ian McEwan, *The Child in Time* Penelope Lively, *Moon Tiger* Iain Sinclair, *White Chappell, Scarlet Tracings* Peter Ackroyd, *Chatterton* Brian McHale, *Postmodernist Fiction*

Year	Events	Publications
1988	Local Government Act includes Clause 28, stating that local authorities must not promote 'homosexuality as a pretended family relationship' Lockerbie bombing kills 270 'Young British Artists' begin to exhibit work together	Alan Hollinghurst, *The Swimming Pool Library* Salman Rushdie, *The Satanic Verses* Doris Lessing, *The Fifth Child* Michael Moorcock, *Mother London* Linda Hutcheon, *A Poetics of Postmodernism*
1989	Fall of the Berlin Wall Tiananmen Square massacre in Beijing, China Iran's Ayatollah Khomeini issues a 'fatwa', sentencing to death Salman Rushdie and others involved in the publication of *The Satanic Verses*; Iran breaks off diplomatic relations with Britain.	Janice Galloway, *The Trick Is to Keep Breathing* Jeanette Winterson, *Sexing the Cherry* Kazuo Ishiguro, *The Remains of the Day* Martin Amis, *London Fields*
1990	End of Cold War: over nineteen months in 1990–91, fifteen member states of the Soviet Union declare independence; East and West Germany reunified PM Margaret Thatcher resigns as Conservative Party leader, and is replaced by John Major, who becomes Prime Minister Beginning of Gulf War as Iraq invades Kuwait Nelson Mandela freed from prison	Hanif Kureishi, *The Buddha of Suburbia* Judith Butler, *Gender Trouble* A. S. Byatt, *Possession*
1991	'The End of Postmodernism: New Directions' conference, University of Stuttgart, featuring Malcolm Bradbury, Raymond Federman, William Gass, and John Barth Dial-up internet becomes available	Martin Amis, *Time's Arrow* Jeanette Winterson, *Written on the Body* Christine Brooke-Rose, *Textermination* Angela Carter, *Wise Children* Fredric Jameson, *Postmodernism, or, The Cultural Logic of Late Capitalism*
1992	Economic recession in the UK triggered by 'Black Wednesday' (16 September), when UK forced to drop out of Europe's Exchange Rate Mechanism Department of National Heritage founded John Major elected Prime Minster	Jim Crace, *Arcadia* Angela Carter, *Wise Children* Adam Thorpe, *Ulverton* Alasdair Gray, *Poor Things* Malcolm Bradbury, *Doctor Criminale*

1993	Turkish translator of Rushdie's *Satanic Verses* escapes after being targeted in hotel arson attack in Sivas, Turkey – thirty-seven people are killed; Rushdie's Norwegian publisher, William Nygaard, shot and seriously wounded in Oslo Downing Street Agreement signed Provisional IRA carry out two bomb attacks in Warrington killing two and injuring fifty-six; IRA truck bomb kills one and wounds forty-four in Bishopsgate, London	Irvine Welsh, *Trainspotting* Vikram Seth, *A Suitable Boy* Booker of Bookers Prize (25th Anniversary prize) awarded to Salman Rushdie, *Midnight's Children*
1994	End of apartheid in South Africa Launch of Netscape Navigator, the first commercially successful web browser GMO foods go on sale IRA announce ceasefire	James Kelman, *How Late It Was, How Late* awarded Booker Prize – Kelman gives controversial acceptance speech about language, nationality, and cultural identity which anticipates later concerns about decolonisation and self-determination
1995	Establishment of the World Trade Organization Amazon.com launched (initially as online bookstore)	Hanif Kureishi, *The Black Album* A. L. Kennedy, *So I Am Glad*
1996	Dolly the sheep cloned in Scotland IRA ends ceasefire; detonates large bomb in London's Docklands, killing two	Geoff Ryman, *253* David Foster Wallace, *Infinite Jest*
1997	Referendums in Scotland and Wales result in establishment of Scottish Parliament and National Assembly for Wales Election of Labour government under Prime Minister Tony Blair Princess Diana dies in car crash	Mihangel Morgan, *Melog* Bernardine Evaristo, *Lara* Ali Smith, *Like*
1998	Google founded in California, US Good Friday agreement signed advancing the Northern Ireland peace process	Paul Magrs, *Could It Be Magic?* Sarah Waters, *Tipping the Velvet* Jackie Kay, *Trumpet* Julian Barnes, *England, England* China Miéville, *King Rat* Christine Brooke-Rose, *Next*

Year	Events	Literature
1999	Scottish Parliament founded Introduction of the single currency, the Euro, as the official currency of eleven of the fifteen EU Member States (and 'virtual currency' for commercial and financial transactions only in the UK) SMS texts are able to be sent across different networks	David Mitchell, *Ghostwritten*
2000	Vladimir Putin elected President of Russia Opening of Tate Modern, London Millennium Dome, London, opened First series of *Big Brother* airs on Channel 4 IRA car bomb explodes outside BBC's London headquarters	Zadie Smith, *White Teeth*
2001	Terrorist attack on the Twin Towers in New York, USA, on 11 September ('9/11') Wikipedia launched	Ali Smith, *Hotel World* David Mitchell, *number9dream*
2002	Euro enters circulation as coins and banknotes in Europe	Sarah Waters, *Fingersmith* Zadie Smith, *The Autograph Man* Hari Kunzru, *The Impressionist* Nicola Barker, *Behindlings* Caryl Phillips, *A Distant Shore*
2003	Clause 28 of the Local Government Act 1988 repealed US and British invasion of Iraq in response to 9/11 Millions in the UK march in protest against the Iraq war Completion of the human genome project	Shena Mackay, *Heligoland* Monica Ali, *Brick Lane*
2004	Launch of Facebook and MySpace The beginning of Web 2.0, internet's 'second generation', increasing interactivity and connectivity	Suhayl Saadi, *Psychoraag* Alan Hollinghurst, *The Line of Beauty* Hari Kunzru, *Transmission* David Mitchell, *Cloud Atlas* Nadeem Aslam, *Maps for Lost Lovers* Andrea Levy, *Small Island*

2005	Bombings in London on 7 July (known as '7/7'): 52 people killed and more than 700 injured following explosions on Underground trains and bus in Tavistock Square Launch of YouTube Gender Recognition Act comes into effect	Ian McEwan, *Saturday* Tom McCarthy, *Remainder* Kazuo Ishiguro, *Never Let Me Go* Ali Smith, *The Accidental* Caryl Phillips, *Dancing in the Dark* Bernardine Evaristo, *Soul Tourists* Zadie Smith, *On Beauty*
2006	Launch of Twitter	Gautam Malkani, *Londonstani*
2007	Start of Global Financial Crisis Apple introduces the iPhone Release of Amazon's Kindle	
2008	Global Financial Crisis hits Britain Barack Obama elected US President	Jhumpa Lahiri, *Unaccustomed Earth* Bernardine Evaristo, *Blonde Roots* Rushdie's *Midnight's Children* named as 'Best of the Booker [Prize]' award
2009		China Miéville, *The City & the City*
2010	Election of coalition government between Conservative and Liberal Democrats, with David Cameron (Conservative) as Prime Minister and Nick Clegg (Liberal Democrats) as Deputy Prime Minister Arab Spring (widespread protests in Arab countries)	Tom McCarthy, *C* Andrea Levy, *The Long Song*
2011	End of Iraq war Osama Bin Laden assassinated by US special forces in Pakistan	Hari Kunzru, *Gods Without Men* Sunjeev Sahota, *Ours Are the Streets* Julian Barnes, *The Sense of an Ending*
2012	Discovery of Higgs Bosun, a fundamental particle	Zadie Smith, *NW* James Kelman, *Mo Said She Was Quirky* Tom McCarthy, *Men in Space* John Lanchester, *Capital* Jeanette Winterson, *Why Be Happy When You Can Be Normal?* Will Self, *Umbrella*

2013	The Marriage (Same Sex Couples) Act comes into effect	Zadie Smith, *The Embassy of Cambodia*
2014	The word 'selfie' is added to the OED	Ali Smith, *How to be Both* Will Self, *Shark* Booker Prize opened to global authors provided their work is in English and published in the UK David Mitchell, *The Bone Clocks*
2015	David Cameron (Conservative) elected Prime Minister Beginning of European Migrant Crisis: 1.3 million people request asylum	Jeanette Winterson, *The Gap of Time* 'What [in the World] was Postmodernism?' Symposium, University of Otago, New Zealand.
2015		Tom McCarthy, *Satin Island* Kazuo Ishiguro, *The Buried Giant*
2016	UK European Union membership referendum: majority (52 per cent) votes to leave the European Union	Launch of the Man Booker International Prize
2017	UK General Election: governing Conservative Party loses small overall majority and forms minority government (with 'confidence and supply' agreement with Democratic Unionist Party of Northern Ireland); Theresa May elected PM Donald J. Trump elected President of the US Streams and downloads of music, film, and TV overtake physical sales for first time #MeToo movement Grenfell Tower fire in London kills seventy-one	Kazuo Ishiguro wins Nobel Prize
2019	23 May: final European Parliament elections in the UK held prior to the withdrawal of the UK from the European Union	
2020	The withdrawal of the UK from the European Union ('Brexit') officially takes place at 23:00 GMT on 31 January	

2021		Kazuo Ishiguro, *Klara and the Sun*
2022	Salman Rushdie stabbed multiple times at public lecture in New York, US	
2023		Salman Rushdie, *Victory City*

Acknowledgements

I'd like to thank Ray Ryan at Cambridge University Press for his encouragement and guidance, all the contributors to this volume for their chapters, their patience, and unflagging co-operative spirit, the excellent team overseeing its production (Nicola Chapman, Reshma Venkatachalapathy, and Helen Kitto), and Tricia for her tireless support, keen critical eye – and everything else besides.

Introduction
British Postmodern Fiction
Bran Nicol

In May 2018 Historic England announced that it was listing seventeen postmodern buildings. These included a trading estate in Slough, a business park in Gloucestershire, four London docklands housing schemes, as well as buildings with more obvious historical significance such as the Thematic House in London, designed in the late 1970s by the architectural historian and postmodernist theorist Charles Jencks. Historic England's chief executive explained that '[p]ostmodern architecture brought fun and colour to our streets' and the buildings were 'scarce survivals of a really influential period of British architecture'.[1] The buildings rejected the functionalist ethos of modernist architecture, privileging instead aesthetic freedom over utility and a 'self-conscious' acknowledgement, through visual clues (e.g., the resemblance of an Isle of Dogs canalside housing scheme to both a vast coal conveyor and the bridge of a ship echoing the area's industrial and colonial past), that they *are* buildings, constructions which complement their particular surroundings, as well as belonging to a national architectural tradition. The occasion gave a stamp of respectability to an aesthetic style which had once seemed controversial to many – academics and public alike – and represented to some merely pointless introspective artistic indulgence. It acknowledged postmodernism as an official part of Britain's architectural history. But it also suggested implicitly that where postmodernism was once synonymous with the contemporary moment, it was now firmly in the past, a historic period.

Postmodern British fiction is also distinguished by its self-conscious commentary on Britain's history and literary traditions and its advertising of its own status *as* fiction, and is thus similarly valuable and influential. Classic examples such as John Fowles's *The French Lieutenant's Woman* (1969) or Salman Rushdie's *Midnight's Children* (1981) use disruptive authorial interventions and the manipulation of historical records to ensure readers reflect, respectively, on the ideology behind the realist novel and the British colonial history of India. But it is harder simply to confine British postmodernism to the past in the manner of listing historical buildings, or even in the way we do with other literary periods that have been surpassed, such as the Early Modern or Victorian periods. It is also more difficult to recognise the multiplicity of varieties of postmodern fiction than it is for an observer to identify postmodern architecture, with its clear visual styles.

The literary theorist Brian McHale has noted that, because of the 'historicity encoded in the very term "postmodernism"' postmodernism was from the very beginning 'self-conscious about its identity as a period, conscious of its own historicity'.[2] In one obvious way (though not in others, as we shall see) his statement applies less to British postmodernism than its American counterpart. Postmodern American writers such as William Gass, John Barth, or Raymond Federman were keen to theorise and historicise their literary practice and published essays about postmodernism and their own practice. While there are some notable exceptions in British writing, such as the novelist Gilbert Adair and his collection *The Postmodernist Always Rings Twice*[3] or the 1995 piece 'What Was Postmodernism?' by the academic and novelist Malcolm Bradbury,[4] this self-historicising was not the norm in relation to British postmodernism, even by literary critics. Even amongst the mass of material published on postmodernism by scholars and theorists over the past few decades, for all the significance of British fiction in the overall debate about postmodernism, and despite the prevalence of noted British critics and thinkers contributing to this debate (such as Christopher Norris, Terry Eagleton, Patricia Waugh, and David Harvey), it remains under-historicised and under-theorised. Apart from three books published in the 1990s, Alison Lee's *Realism and Power: Postmodern British Fiction*,[5] Theo D'haen's and Hans Bertens's *British Postmodern Fiction*,[6] and Bertens and Douwe Fokkema's *International Postmodernism: Theory and Literary Practice*,[7] no book-length study on this topic has appeared – until the one you are reading now.

This Cambridge Companion makes the case not just for postmodernism as an important and distinctive moment in British literary history, but as a paradigm that continues to make sense of some prominent currents within twentieth- and twenty-first century British fiction. It is true that the currency of the term postmodernism has diminished over the past couple of decades in academic spheres, perhaps especially in Britain (arguably unlike the United States), as new theoretical frames have emerged to explain contemporary literary production. Yet the analysis of contemporary fiction can still benefit from assessing the legacy of postmodernism, as a formation that attempted to make sense of cultural responses to the social, economic, and political factors that were prevalent in the last century and are either still at work now or have shaped our current moment. It is also by no means clear that we have actually moved beyond postmodernity – rather than merely advancing into a later incarnation of it.

Some of the issues that dominate cultural thought now, at the time of writing, such as climate change, digital culture, the role of media in producing 'post-truth' politics, the pre-eminence of China or the Middle East petrostates as powerful global economic and cultural forces, the Russian invasion of Ukraine, or the rise of far-right politics and authoritarian regimes in regions throughout the world, were not evident, or at least not as pressing, during the highpoint of the postmodern debate in the 1980s and 1990s. But it would not be stretching things too far to claim that these phenomena and their effects might still productively be analysed through the lens of postmodernism. The most obvious context is the late-capitalist or neoliberal system – never too far from postmodern analyses – which still presides over every aspect of life in most regions in the world and which, by definition, always expands and absorbs new developments, innovating and renovating, making obsolete what has been superseded, in order to ensure financial accumulation and power for a small percentage of the population, the wealthiest or the most fortunate. Another still-relevant factor is the creation of the knowledge economy and its dependence on what the philosopher Jean-François Lyotard once called 'metanarratives' to legitimate power.[8]

The same is true of the cultural response to such developments in our global socio-cultural formation which, although they have mutated and been re-fashioned, are familiar to anyone studying postmodernism in the 1980s and 1990s. The continued predominance of pastiche or repetition in cultural production, such as endlessly repeated movie franchises, re-makings of classic films or TV shows, or the production of retro-sounding popular music, still seems to spring from the fact that the culture industry is trapped in the kind of late-capitalist or neoliberal logic exposed by theorists of the postmodern like Fredric Jameson or Mark Fisher, where there is no ability to challenge the system and no need to because everything is driven by the impetus to generate revenue.[9] Continuing with genres or franchises which have proven successful guarantees more success; there is no incentive to innovate nor to break the mould. The disbelief in metanarratives or shared official 'truth' can also provide a context for the alarming rise of conspiracy thinking in the twenty-first century, widespread convictions about the pervasiveness of 'fake news', and the proliferation of non-mainstream media outlets, accessed often via social media platforms, which produce a multiplicity of what Lyotard termed 'petits récits' (or 'little stories', the opposite to the metanarrative).

However, the aim of this collection is not to argue for the continued relevance of these late-twentieth-century theoretical frames, nor to revive previous methods of analysing literature and 'apply' them to contemporary examples. Postmodernism was always a fluid and flexible term, especially when it came to literature, and as much as this could be a disadvantage (as it made it difficult to condense the various understandings of postmodernism and postmodernity into one coherent overall definition) the advantage is that its flexibility allows fresh perspectives to be taken on board. Postmodernism in Britain was never as prominent as a literary phenomenon as it was in the United States from the mid-1960s to the late 1990s, where – spearheaded by a range of high-profile writers such as William Burroughs, Vladimir Nabokov, John Barth, Robert Coover, Donald Barthelme, Kurt Vonnegut, William Gaddis, Thomas Pynchon, Ishmael Reed, Toni Morrison, Kathy Acker, Don DeLillo, and latterly, David Foster Wallace and Dave Eggers – it seemed like an expression of a broader 1960s/1970s counter-cultural spirit. The work of such writers is characterised by the deployment of quite radical metafictional techniques – that is, ones unignorable by the reader, and disruptive to the reading experience – such as the creation of fragmented and distorted narratives, disrupted temporality, an indeterminacy of 'meaning', an irrepressible ironic spirit, and a fondness for intertextuality, pastiche, and parody.

While similar stylistic features can be found in many British texts in the same period, and indeed from the 2000s to the present day (as many of the contributions in this Companion will show), it is not simply the use of self-reflexive technical features which distinguishes postmodernism in British fiction. Rather it is a more thematic, perhaps even a different tonal, preoccupation with the instability of historicity and temporality, and the importance of ethics and morality, which dovetails with counterparts to the impulse we find dominant in American writing to expose the effects of late-capitalism, to challenge normative social categories, and to counter prevailing metanarratives. The preoccupation with history – both in its general sense as discourses which explain people and nations today, and with British history and its imperialist past, in particular – is arguably more significant in British postmodernism than the desire to expand the possibilities of the novel.

As in the North American literary tradition there is undoubtedly a canon of 'classic' postmodern British writers working principally in a similar period, the 1960s to 1990s: John Fowles, Angela Carter, Martin Amis, Hanif Kureishi, Salman Rushdie, Jeanette Winterson, Julian Barnes, Graham Swift, and A. S. Byatt, amongst others. Fresh readings of work produced by these writers are included in many of the chapters in this Companion. But many more pages are devoted to examples of a wealth of innovative and diverse fiction by a younger generation of British writers published in the first decade and a half of the twenty-first century, authors such as Monica Ali, Nicola Barker, Jonathan Coe, Bernardine Evaristo, Maggie Gee, Allan Hollinghurst, Hari Kunzru, Andrea Levy, Toby Litt, Tom McCarthy, David Mitchell, China Miéville, Will Self, Ali Smith, and Zadie Smith. Fiction by these post-millennial writers can usefully be regarded as being caught up in the slipstream of postmodernism – grappling with similar issues to those which preoccupied late twentieth-century British writers, but in a changed context, which has led them to modify or reject recognisably postmodern perspectives and narrative techniques, and means that interpreting them requires a new set of reading strategies and emphases.

Towards a History of British Postmodern Fiction

Brian McHale's *Cambridge Introduction to Postmodernism* (2015) includes a useful general history of postmodern literature which can function as a basis for a more specifically British one.[10] He divides postmodernism into four phases. The first is the early period, dated from 1966 to 1973, or the 'onset' of postmodernism, as he calls it (echoing, perhaps unintentionally, the connotations of postmodernism as an affliction or a 'condition' which were present in much of the debate during the 1980s and 1990s),[11] when literature of this time in the United States was bursting with innovation and avant-gardism in a way which connected to movements within the counter-culture generally in the 1960s and the opening-up of American society and culture to voices from the margins. This period is followed by 'peak' postmodernism, its high-water mark, which lasts from around 1973 (a landmark year in North American writing, given the publication of Thomas Pynchon's *Gravity's Rainbow*) until the late 1980s. The third phase McHale identifies is a short transitional period from 1989 to 2001 – or from the end of the Cold War to the attack on the Twin Towers in New York – which he terms 'the interregnum' (after the transitional period in British history from 1649 to 1660 when the nation was uniquely under short-lived republican rule). History itself seemed to lack direction or to be 'multi-directional' in this period,[12] and despite the impatience towards postmodernism expressed in American fiction of the 1990s (most notably by that decade's defining US figure, David Foster Wallace) '[p]ostmodern modes of expression seemed particularly well adapted to capture the decade's volatility and multidirectionality'.[13]

Because he is unconvinced that this interregnum period constitutes a distinctly different 'post-postmodernist' phase, McHale posits a fourth stage: the 'aftermath' of postmodernism. Where normally the years after a literary period would, by definition, not be a part of that period, the need to consider postmodernism's own 'post' is a reflection both of the strangeness of the 'interregnum' period – a transitional phase without it being clear what was being transitioned *to* – and a broader scepticism about time, history, and consequently the very nature of beginnings and aftermaths, which is an integral part of the postmodern mindset.

A comparable history of British postmodern fiction would work more or less along the same lines. However, the distinction between any interregnum-type transitional moment and postmodernism's 'aftermath' is more blurred than it is in the United States, as many of the chapters in this Companion will show. This is why we should divide British postmodernism into just three successive phases:

1. late modernism/early postmodernism;
2. peak postmodernism;
3. late postmodernism/post-postmodernism.

Britain's 'onset' period lasted longer than America's, from the 1960s until 1981, because it took longer for British postmodernism to become a significant and noticeable presence in the modern British literary landscape. This period would therefore best be understood as more like a twenty-year incubation (to pick up McHale's ailment analogy), during which time the staples of North American postmodern writing (self-reflexivity, ideas about history and temporality, experiments with genre, etc.), began to emerge in British fiction though not yet with the kind of frequency with which they would feature in the 1980s and 1990s. Early British postmodernism encompasses the 1960s and 1970s, though it might be dated back to around 1957, when Muriel Spark's *The Comforters*, an early work of metafiction (part uncanny ghost story, part comic meditation on the business of creating character) appears. Doris Lessing's *The Golden Notebook* (1962) interweaves different narratives to self-consciously explore the function of storytelling in human lives and also to advance a powerful feminist critique. Fowles's *The French Lieutenant's Woman*, published in 1969, is the first example of a postmodern historical novel, or what became known as a 'historiographic metafiction'. J. G. Ballard's 1960s and 1970s novels meditate the effects of a culture of the image. The 1960s and 1970s is also characterised by a late flowering of modernism which co-existed with the exuberance, playfulness, and indulgence in narrative associated with postmodernism – no doubt influenced by the publication in English and in one volume of the late-modernist/proto-postmodernist Samuel Beckett's *Trilogy* in 1959. Writers like B. S. Johnson, John Berger, Christine Brooke-Rose, Brigid Brophy, Anthony Burgess, Alan Burns, Wilson Harris, and Ann Quin combined in their work a modernist fascination with language with a self-conscious playfulness that amounted to something recognisably different from 'high' modernism.

Britain's 'peak' postmodern period in fiction also spans the 1980s and 1990s (stretching perhaps to the first decade of the twenty-first century). Observable in these decades is both a noticeable departure from modernism and a kind of reconciliation with the potential of realism (not found in American fiction to the same degree) – as well as a fascination with how we construct and interpret history. Two broader social and political factors contributed significantly to the rise of a specifically British postmodern fiction in these 'peak' decades. The first is the richly diverse and multicultural society much of Britain had become by the 1980s as a result of its distinctive patterns of immigration over the previous few decades (following the 1948 British Nationality Act, intended to ease the nationwide labour shortage). This saw, first, the arrival of citizens from the West Indies (especially from Jamaica and Trinidad and Tobago), South Asia, and Cyprus, and then, in the late 1950s and 1960s, migrants from India, East and West Pakistan, Nigeria, and Ghana. The shift in the composition of Britain's population led inevitably to rising tensions and increased racism, but the presence of so many people from different cultures radically transformed the nation's art and popular culture. New voices emerged from immigrant communities, and there was a receptive readership for work published in English which reflected the multicultural British experience or presented life in other countries. Many of the prominent novelists in the period from the 1960s to the 1980s who were either UK-based or born in the UK include Doris Lessing, Jean Rhys, Salman Rushdie, V. S. Naipaul, Buchi Emecheta, and Hanif Kureishi. While not all of these were postmodern writers (though Lessing, Rushdie, and Kureishi certainly would be considered as such), the spirit of British multiculturalism was in tune with that of postmodernism: it was inclusive, embraced diverse influences (e.g., the narrative technique of Rushdie's *Midnight's Children* echoes the 'spirals' and 'loops' of Indian oral narrative forms),[14] and chimed with the postmodern spirit of contesting and challenging an authoritarian, nationalist view of the world and the nation.

The second factor was a more antagonist one, a force which worked against this spirit of liberation and dissent: the Conservative government which came to power on 4 May 1979, making its leader Margaret Thatcher Prime Minister of the United Kingdom. Thatcher herself was a hugely divisive figure, and her authoritarian personality, her apparent philistinism, and her belief in a kind of social atomism, outraged many British artists, writers, and producers of popular culture. As Kureishi put it some years later, Thatcher 'actively hated culture, as she recognised that it was a form of dissent'.[15] Her approach to policy (deregulating finance, reducing inflation, favouring flexible labour markets, disempowering trades unions, privatising industries and utilities companies, and cutting arts funding) was continued by successive Conservative governments until the late 1990s, Thatcher herself being replaced by John Major in 1990. The result was that many cultural practitioners felt that Britain had by then been turned irrevocably into a deeply polarised, functionalist, and nakedly individualist society.

However one natural consequence of the antagonism created by this reshaping of society was an energetic mobilising of the forces of dissent in popular music, alternative comedy, fashion, the arts, and literature. It seems no accident that the early 1980s saw the publication of a rich stream of impressive British novels, as if unleashed by an urgent need to respond to this new socio-political atmosphere. In 1981, for example, an extraordinarily accomplished Booker Prize shortlist featured three postmodern novels, *Midnight's Children* (which won), Muriel Spark's *Loitering with Intent*, and D. M. Thomas's *The White Hotel*, as well as *The Comfort of Strangers*, by Ian McEwan, a writer whose work was subsequently regarded as relating more tangentially to postmodernism.[16]

As the inclusion of McEwan in the oppositional category shows, postmodernism was not the only mode of literary dissent. Diran Adebayo and Courttia Newland also each wrote late 1990s realist novels which mounted a critique of Thatcherite social policies.[17] Nor was postmodern British fiction uniformly shaped by the Britain Thatcher had made. As an inherently pan-Western phenomenon, postmodernism was equally created by global factors such as the intensification of third-stage or 'late' capitalism or neoliberalism, the growth of the knowledge economy, and globalisation. Yet postmodernism was undoubtedly part of the spirit of the 1980s and 1990s in the United Kingdom, and many of the most prominent postmodern British writers either emerged during this time (figures such as Kureishi, Rushdie, Winterson, Barnes, Thomas, A. L. Kennedy, and Will Self), or rose to special prominence (Martin Amis, Malcolm Bradbury, David Lodge, Doris Lessing, Angela Carter, J. G. Ballard, Muriel Spark, and A. S. Byatt).

It is in this 'peak' phase of British postmodernism that North American theorists in the late 1980s and early 1990s turned their attention to the works of British fiction which were reinventing the historical novel.[18] Linda Hutcheon's influential category, historiographic metafiction, referred to novels which directed the kind of metafictive self-reflexivity which was distinctively postmodern (a feature of works of early postmodernism such as Johnson's *Christy Malry's Own Double-Entry* or Lessing's *The Golden Notebook*) towards a recreation and interrogation of historical events and periods in the manner of the historical novel.

Hutcheon's analysis was – especially viewed now, in retrospect – somewhat monolithic. It was unable to draw fully on what would have been a powerful tool in its theoretical armoury, postcolonial theory, because this discourse was not fully to emerge until the 1990s, after Hutcheon's studies appeared. Yet in her classification Hutcheon does identify and define what McHale later described as 'perhaps *the* characteristic genre' of postmodernism,[19] and the majority of significant British postmodern writers in this peak period produced important examples of it. As well as Rushdie's *Midnight's Children* and Thomas's *The White Hotel*, there were Jeanette Winterson's *The Passion* (1987) and *Sexing the Cherry* (1989), Julian Barnes's *Flaubert's Parrot* (1984) and *A History of the World in 10½ Chapters* (1989), Graham Swift's *Waterland* (1983), Peter Ackroyd's *Hawksmoor* (1985) and *Chatterton* (1987), Jim Crace's *The Gift of Stones* (1988), Rose Tremain's *Restoration* (1989), A. S. Byatt's *Possession* (1990), Lawrence Norfolk's *Lemprière's Dictionary* (1991), Barry Unsworth's *Sacred Hunger* (1992), Matthew Kneale's *English Passengers* (2000), A. S. Byatt's *The Biographer's Tale* (2000), and Sarah Waters's *Fingersmith* (2002).

Postmodern historical fictions were by no means the only notable postmodern works published in British fiction's peak postmodern period. Other important self-reflexive narratives about contemporary existence appeared, such as Alasdair Gray's *Lanark* (1981), Martin Amis's *Money: A Suicide Note* (1984), Nigel Williams's *Star Turn* (1985), Bruce Chatwin's *Utz* (1988), and Kureishi's *The Buddha of Suburbia* (1990). But the 1980s undoubtedly heralds a significant 'historical turn' in theories of postmodern art and literature, and postmodern fiction as a dominant type of literature in Britain.

The third phase of British postmodernism, the necessarily indistinct 'late postmodern/post-postmodern' stage, may be dated from the turn of the millennium until the present. It is in this period that work published by the prodigious twenty-first-century writers I listed above appears, as well as later novels by authors whose output spans both the 'peak' and 'post' periods of postmodernism, such as Rushdie, Barnes, Amis, Peter Ackroyd, and Kazuo Ishiguro. Post-millennial fiction can usefully be regarded as being caught up in the slipstream of postmodernism – grappling with similar issues to those which preoccupied late twentieth-century British writers, but in a changed context, which led them to modify or reject recognisably postmodern perspectives and narrative techniques, and means that interpreting them requires a new set of reading strategies and emphases.

This is merely an outline of a history of postmodern British fiction, intended as a 'road map' for readers as they navigate through the chapters which follow. Specific stages and key historical moments will be fleshed-out and coloured-in these contributions. I have not included in this sketch an extensive summary of the varieties of post-postmodern fiction produced in the capacious third 'aftermath' zone of postmodernism. This is partly because it now constitutes a stretch of time longer than the peak postmodern period and contains such a rich diversity of subjects, techniques, and approaches, but it is also because this 'aftermath' space is the one inhabited by the contributors to this collection. Even when reassessing classic postmodern British fictions from the 1960s to the 1990s, the chapters in this collection explore what postmodernism is to us *now* – and this is in fact a way of helping readers understand what postmodernism *was*. In this way this Companion maintains a sense of the continued innovation and dynamism of postmodern British fiction rather than attempting to fix it – like Historic England's roster of postmodern buildings – in any kind of frozen, official, historical 'list'.

Outline of Chapters

The first three chapters of this book are devoted to three of the most important and wide-ranging contexts which help us to understand a specifically postmodern British fiction: politics, history, and postcoloniality/decolonisation. In Chapter 1, Hywel Dix provides a materialist analysis of the emergence of British postmodern fictional techniques which engages critically with Fredric Jameson's famous argument that postmodernism amounts – purely and simply – to the 'cultural logic of late capitalism'.[20] From the outset, Dix argues, supporting his discussion with discussions of numerous examples of fiction from Fowles, Spark, and Ballard to McEwan and Barnes, the formal features of British postmodern fiction were geared towards political critique, especially the portrayal of class struggle, precarity, and working class life, rather than expanding the possibilities of fiction. This is followed by Graham Matthews's chapter 'British Postmodern Fiction and the Myth of Decline', which makes the case that an integral part of postmodernism as it developed in Britain was the need to grapple with a pervasive pessimism about the nation's diminishing capacity to be a financial, technological, and cultural centre. Postmodern fiction, Matthews shows (as evidenced by alternative readings of Fowles, Swift, and Barnes, as well as analyses of novels by Spark, Lessing, Ballard, Penelope Lively, and Ishiguro) offers a way out of the trap created by this myth by portraying alternatives to 'the grounded universe' which 'declinist' myths purport to describe. Chapter 3, Graham MacPhee's 'Postmodern British Fiction and the Postcolonial', provides a rigorous assessment of what two dominant 'master-theoretical' terms, the postmodern and the postcolonial, add to each other, now that they have passed their moments of prime valence – but also explains why the processes they describe need to be kept separate. Looking back from our current vantage point, MacPhee argues, we can see that what is at stake is not whether British postmodern fiction can be read as embodying the postcolonial but how, in the post-imperial world of the twenty-first century, British fiction can reimagine not just the conception of postmodernism by drawing on the lessons of postcolonialism, but Britishness, too.

Chapters 4 to 6 examine specifically British postmodern understandings of the complexity of Britain's perceptions of its own geography and its relation to those of other nations. Neal Alexander's chapter 'The Geographies of British Postmodern Fiction' surveys literary approaches to the distinctive urban and regional spaces of Britain's geography, both real and imagined, and casts new light on a wide range of writers from the 1960s to the 1990s: Christine Brooke-Rose, Brigid Brophy, J. G. Ballard, Maureen Duffy, Michael Moorcock, Iain Sinclair, Zadie Smith, Jeanette Winterson, Angela Carter, Alasdair Gray, Peter Ackroyd, Salman Rushdie, Hanif Kureishi, Julian Barnes, and Adam Thorpe. He contends that geography is more than a prominent theme in British postmodern fiction but a key driving force behind its innovations in form, style and narrative technique. Stephen J. Burn's chapter, 'Transatlantic Fictions' (Chapter 5) provides a detailed analysis of the inter-relationship between the British and American postmodern traditions, concentrating in particular on how twenty-first-century novels by Hari Kunzru, Tom McCarthy, David Mitchell, and Zadie Smith engage with postmodern 'precursor' texts (such as Martin Amis's *Money*) to imagine British and American national spaces as 'overlapping zones' in our globalised reality. Rather than staging an oppositional comparison of the two traditions (a repeated move, as Burn shows, in the theory and criticism of postmodern literature) he insists that the story of postmodernism in British fiction is really about the dissolution of transatlantic binaries.

A regional focus is also central to Stefanie Lehner's chapter (6) which examines the extent to which the discourse about postmodernism has informed conceptions of Scottish literary fiction since the 1980s. The critical reception to works by Scottish novelists such as Alasdair Gray, Muriel Spark, and A. L. Kennedy is why Scotland has a chapter of its own in this Companion, though it is important to note here that of course other British regional traditions (Dix covers Welsh postmodern fiction in his chapter) can be identified. Lehner shows how work by the Scottish writers James Kelman, Janice Galloway, Irvine Welsh, and Suhayl Saadi avoid what she characterises as a particular postmodern trap, of opting for an empty celebration of multiculturalism rather than confronting unflinchingly the real inequalities of race, class, gender, and nation.

In Chapter 7, Glyn White provides an in-depth and authoritative study of B. S. Johnson, a singular and highly representative figure in the history of British postmodernism, the most fêted writer to emerge from that 'early' period in the 1960s where avant-garde writing influenced by modernism provided a departure point for newly postmodern approaches – and, tellingly, as White explains, an author not co-opted into the postmodern 'canon' until the twenty-first century. In a complementary discussion to that of Dix in Chapter 1, White identifies a distinctive 'double-coding' in Johnson's fiction and his sense of his mission as a writer: his anxieties are postmodern ones, and aspects of his literary response appear to be postmodern, but his novels never lose their urgent social realist drive to examine how to respond to the forces of class, education, conformity, death, decay, and old age in mid-century Britain.

White's chapter is followed by a sequence of six chapters which each place in the spotlight ways in which British postmodern fiction has renovated or expanded specific modes of writing (genre fiction, speculative fiction, the historical novel), and how it has depicted racial and sexual identities which have become progressively less marginal in British culture and society in the years from 'peak' to 'post' postmodernism. The first of this sequence is Suzanne Keen's chapter on the 'return of the romance' in

British fiction (Chapter 8), which explores the use of genre by postmodern writers, focusing in particular on one prominent case study: romance. A standard assumption in postmodern criticism was that postmodern fiction 'deploys' genre, but Keen proposes we should turn this formulation around and recognise that, on the contrary, popular fiction has developed in the late twentieth- and early twenty-first centuries by using postmodernism. Postmodern fiction might even, by this account, be regarded as a mutation of popular fiction, the result of its forms being taken up by 'literary' writers. The postmodern facility with incorporating and blending genres (as illustrated by Byatt's novel *Possession*), Keen argues, paved the way for the diversification of contemporary fiction, as can be evidenced by considering work by more recent authors, such as Hilary Mantel and China Miéville.

A complementary analysis is provided in the next chapter, Andrew Tate's 'Alternative Realisms' (Chapter 9), which examines the postmodern capacity for co-opting, expanding, or even bypassing realism by ranging across other modes of fiction, such as gothic, fantasy, carnival, or myth – modes which were once called 'fabulation'[21] and are now more commonly referred to as 'speculative fiction'. Tate shows how distinctively postmodern alternative realisms continue to flourish in the early twenty-first century by drawing on fiction by David Mitchell, Ali Smith, and Kazuo Ishiguro. The ability of this work to evoke a 'plurality of worlds', he argues, continues the postmodern impetus to convey a distrust of authoritarianism by preserving a sense of the sublime.

Many of the key postmodern writers in Britain, such as Jeanette Winterson, Hanif Kureishi, and Alan Hollinghurst, were also writers of 'queer' fiction – fiction that combined a carnivalesque depiction of queer sexuality with postmodern technique. Kate Haffey's chapter on gay and lesbian postmodern fiction in Britain (Chapter 10) explores the interface between 'queer' theory, which emerged in the 1990s, and postmodernism. Postmodern literary practice, with its glorying in the ephemeral, the fluid, and the contradictory, and its delight in performativity, is naturally in keeping with the spirit of queer theory and its mission to liberate identities dismissed as marginal or non-normative in some spheres of politics and society. Haffey argues that where late-twentieth-century queer writers took on the task of exposing and challenging homophobic discourses that sought to demonise and deny queer desire (often in direct response to very real circumstances, such as the aftermath of the decriminalisation of homosexuality in Britain in 1967 and the Aids epidemic in the 1980s), the twenty-first century has become distinguished by an increasing 'homonormativity'. This does not mark the end of hostile queer-eradicating discourses, of course, but means that at least these are challenged by an empowering counter-narrative contributed to by the postmodern writers noted above, along with novels by Paul Magrs and Sarah Waters, whose fiction Haffey also considers.

Kristian Shaw's 'Black British and British Asian Fiction' (Chapter 11) offers a nuanced perspective on the idea – invoked by a number of chapters in this Companion – that peak postmodernism achieved some important 'ground-clearing' work in opening-up new possibilities for fiction and helping readers understand the conditions of contemporary reality, but inevitably, as society and literature continued to change, needed to be superseded by a new incarnation. He explains that postmodern writing, and the work of British Asian authors such as Salman Rushdie and Hanif Kureishi in particular, contributed powerfully to the transformation of British literature into a genuinely multicultural phenomenon, only for the advent of new writing by a much more expansive range of Black British and British Asian writers to be so richly varied that the postmodern paradigm could no longer fully account for it. Shaw develops this case through an analysis of the fiction of Hari Kunzru, Bernardine Evaristo, and Zadie Smith, writers who self-consciously adopt some postmodern perspectives and adapt others to rewrite historical struggle and racial hierarchy in a way which is ultimately more in tune with the 'ethno-political power' articulated in postcolonial theory than with earlier postmodern theory.

Alison Lee's 'History and the British Novel After Postmodernism' (Chapter 12) demonstrates, through readings of novels which can be regarded as the descendants of classic 1980s and 1990s postmodern historical fiction (Hilary Mantel's *Wolf Hall* (2009), Ali Smith's *How to Be Both* (2014), Jeanette Winterson's *The Gap of Time* (2015), and David Mitchell's *The Bone Clocks* (2014)), that post-millennial fiction exhibits a distinctively twenty-first-century ease with the dual understanding that the present is always historical but that the historical record is always already constructed and unreliable. Historiographic metafiction helped make this awareness possible. However, the lessons it taught readers about conflicting and competing histories is now such a part of everyday existence due to the role played by technology and social media in twenty-first-century life, that the postmodern historical novel has naturally evolved. In a complementary analysis in the next chapter (Chapter 13), Patricia Pulham examines a specific kind of historical novel which has its roots in historiographic metafiction: neo-Victorian fiction. A peculiar temporal dislocation presides over this genre, she argues. It emerged from the peak postmodern period (two of its most classic examples are Fowles's *The French Lieutenant's Woman* and Byatt's

Possession), has continued to be produced by post-postmodern writers such as Sarah Waters, and also – to complicate things further – figures as a 'gateway' back into Victorian literature. A disruption of history is therefore encoded in its very generic features. Though denigrated by some because of its 'marketplace' successes and the fact it can seem mere pastiche, Pulham argues that its multi-temporality enables the neo-Victorian novel to focus on social injustices or prejudices about marginalised racial and sexual identities which were occluded from or validated in Victorian fiction, brought out by postmodernism, and challenged powerfully in recent decades.

At the heart of the final three chapters is the idea which is now something of a critical consensus: that postmodernism is over, and we are now in either an as-yet unnamed new phase or a modified, extended 'post-postmodern' period. My own chapter, 'The End of Postmodernism?' (Chapter 14) expands on the point I referred to above, about postmodernism's self-consciousness of its own historicity, and considers first why critics and theorists were so keen, especially in the first decade of the twenty-first century, to declare postmodernism over, and, second, what this means for a society which – due to advances in digital technology – now widely shares a similar uncertainty about the historicity of its own period. The chapter examines some key examples of fiction from the same early-century 'aftermath' period (Ali Smith's *The Accidental*, David Mitchell's *Cloud Atlas*, and Kazuo Ishiguro's *Never Let Me Go*) which convey a kind of historical 'out-of-time-ness', one which implies the postmodern has, like a ghost, both ended and continued.

Nick Bentley's 'British Fiction Beyond Postmodernism' (Chapter 15) provides a thoughtful and valuable assessment of the 'ethical turn' taken by postmodern writers during the new millennium. Bentley considers how those writers who span postmodernism's 'peak' and 'post' periods (such as Martin Amis, Julian Barnes, A. S. Byatt, Kazuo Ishiguro, Ian McEwan, Salman Rushdie, Will Self, and Jeanette Winterson) and also the newer generation of post-millennial writers (such as David Mitchell, Nicola Barker, Ali Smith, Monica Ali, and Andrea Levy) engage in a dialogue with postmodernism, combining recognisably self-reflexive postmodern elements with a revival of realist and modernist techniques. The scepticism about totalising narratives which defined postmodernism meant, Bentley contends, that the discourse effectively implied that moral decision-making could be delayed or circumvented. In the twenty-first century, however, propelled by a new understanding of the politics of identity, race, and ethnicity, fiction after postmodernism feels a responsibility to respond to this urgency.

The last chapter in this Companion, Chapter 16, is Hans Bertens's overview of seven decades of postmodern British fiction, 'Postmodern British Fiction: Then and Now'. The chapter is both an authoritative taking-stock of what British postmodernism was and is in terms of its stylistic features and how it differs from European and American traditions, and an argument – delivered through re-readings of classic postmodern works, such as Graham Swift's *Waterland* and Julian Barnes's *Flaubert's Parrot*, and Martin Amis's *Money* as well as more recent works by Nicola Barker and David Mitchell – that claims about the shift from postmodernism to post-postmodernism in British fiction are founded on a misleading caricature of early and peak postmodernism being more radical and nihilistic than they actually were. Though formally more conservative and later to flourish than other traditions, postmodern British fiction (and the contributions to this Companion would support Bertens's view overall) was always humane, compassionate, and conscious of moral responsibility, and this means that what is often deemed post-postmodern was in fact always already postmodern.

Notes

1. Catherine Croft, 'Postmodern Architecture is Making History – and About Time', *The Guardian*, 14 May 2018: www.theguardian.com/commentisfree/2018/may/14/postmodern-architecture-listing-historic-england-brutalism.
2. Brian McHale, 'What Was Postmodernism?' ('Fictions Present' thread of Electronic Book Review, 20/12/2007) [unpaginated]: https://electronicbookreview.com/essay/what-was-postmodernism/.
3. Gilbert Adair, *The Postmodernist Always Rings Twice: Reflections on Culture in the 90s* (London: Fourth Estate, 1992).
4. Malcolm Bradbury, 'What Was Postmodernism? The Arts in and After the Cold War', *International Affairs (Royal Institute of International Affairs 1944–)* (October, 1995), pp. 763–74, p. 771.
5. Alison Lee, *Realism and Power: Postmodern British Fiction* (London: Routledge, 1990).
6. Theo D'haen and Hans Bertens, eds., *British Postmodern Fiction* (Amsterdam: Ropodi, 1993).
7. Hans Bertens and Douwe Fokkema, eds., *International Postmodernism: Theory and Literary Practice* (Amsterdam: John Benjamins, 1997).
8. Jean-François Lyotard, *The Postmodern Condition: A Report on Knowledge*, trans. Geoff Bennington and Brian Massumi (Minneapolis, Minnesota: University of Minnesota Press, 1984).
9. Fredric Jameson, *Postmodernism, or the Logic of Late Capitalism* (London: Verso, 1991); Mark Fisher, *Capitalist Realism* (Winchester: Zero Books, 2009).

10. Brian McHale, *The Cambridge Introduction to Postmodernism* (Cambridge University Press, 2015). See also Brian McHale and Len Platt, eds., *The Cambridge History of Postmodern Literature* (Cambridge University Press, 2016).
11. Bran Nicol, *The Cambridge Introduction to Postmodern Fiction* (Cambridge University Press, 2009).
12. McHale, *Introduction*, p. 7.
13. Ibid., p. 126.
14. Salman Rushdie, '*Midnight's Children* and *Shame*: An Interview', *Kunapipi* 7:1 (1985), pp. 1–19.
15. Hanif Kureishi, 'Margaret Thatcher: Acceptable in the 80s?', *The Guardian*, 11 April 2009: www.theguardian.com/books/2009/apr/11/thatcher-and-the-arts.
16. Alastair Cormack, 'Postmodernism and the Ethics of Fiction in *Atonement*', in Sebastian Groes, ed., *Ian McEwan: Contemporary Critical Perspectives*, 2nd ed. (London: Bloomsbury, 2013), pp. 70–82.
17. Diran Adebayo, *Some Kind of Black* (London: Abacus, 1997) and Courttia Newland, *Society Within* (London: Abacus, 1999).
18. Linda Hutcheon, *A Poetics of Postmodernism* (New York: Routledge, 1988); Lee, *Realism and Power*; Susana Onega, 'British Historiographic Metafiction in the 1980s', in D'haen and Bertens, *British Postmodern Fiction*, pp. 47–61.
19. Brian McHale, 'History Itself? or, The Romance of Postmodernism', *Contemporary Literature* 44.1 (2003), pp. 151–61, p. 151.
20. Fredric Jameson, *Postmodernism, or the Logic of Late Capitalism* (London: Verso, 1991).
21. Robert Scholes, *Fabulation and Metafiction* (Chicago, Illinois: University of Illinois Press, 1979).

CHAPTER I

The Politics of Postmodern British Fiction
Hywel Dix

The Cultural Logic of Late Capitalism

Studies of postmodernism often begin with Fredric Jameson's famous suggestion that postmodernism embodies the cultural logic of late capitalism. The overall thrust of this suggestion has been that postmodernism is a movement that privileges aesthetic attributes and ludic qualities over serious forms of political and sociological commitment. For this reason, critics of postmodernism have seen it as a frivolous movement, lacking critical perspective.[1] According to their thinking, postmodernism represents a stage in the history of cultural production during which the gap between consumerism and culture, or between capitalism and art, has been effectively diminished so that the capacity for art to provide critical commentary on capitalism is compromised and undermined.

It is significant that this argument was developed by Jameson in 1990, at a time when the Cold War was coming to an end and when division of the world into the spheres of influence of two global ideologies, capitalism and communism, was also ending. With the end of the Cold War, the latter disappeared so that capitalism started to have a truly global reach. With no competing ideology to restrain capitalism, the critical distance between politics and economics on the one hand, and art and culture on the other, disappeared and art instead became even more thoroughly implicated in capitalism and consumer culture than it ever had been: hence the Jamesonian argument that postmodernism is tantamount to the cultural logic of late capitalism.

That argument is not inaccurate, but it is incomplete in the case of British postmodern fiction, where writers were often more concerned with ethics than aesthetics so that their work retains an important critical dimension with regard to the dominant ideology. In other words, British postmodern fiction is not primarily defined by its formally experimental textual properties but by its capacity to generate critical perspectives with regard to postmodern society.

In fact British postmodernism unfolded in three phases: a gradual emergence characterised by slowly increasing textual experimentation in the 1960s and 1970s; a phase of genuinely critical postmodern writing characterised by a high level of fictional critique of the political and economic order in the 1980s and 1990s; and a third period up to about 2012, by which point both the techniques and ideas associated with postmodern literature had become so commonplace that they could no longer be considered radically oppositional.

The Emergence of Postmodernism in Britain

The emergence in Britain of a type of fiction that can properly be categorised as postmodern is difficult to date with precision. In the United States, the McCarthyite purges of the 1950s, the Cold War period, and the Vietnam War generated a strong early sense of political disillusionment which was registered in the experimental style of such major works as Ray Bradbury's *Fahrenheit 451* (1954), William Burroughs's *Naked Lunch* (1959), Kurt Vonnegut's *Slaughterhouse-Five* (1969), and Thomas Pynchon's *Gravity's Rainbow* (1973). Social unrest in societies as diverse as Argentina, Italy, and France is also an important context in which the formal experiments of postmodern writers such as Jose Luis Borges, Italo Calvino, and Georges Perec should be understood.

In Britain, by contrast, the kind of writing that became dominant during the 1950s and 1960s was of a light, comedic nature. Kingsley Amis's *Lucky Jim* (1954) and John Wain's *The Contenders* (1958) are mischievous rather than radical in their portrayal of social snobbery and class pretence. John Braine's *Room at the Top* (1959) and David Storey's *This Sporting Life* (1960) are heavier and more serious in tone, but like many of the novels of the period they too lack formal experimentation and generate a surprisingly 'conservative interpretation' of the social conflicts of the period.[2] As the 1950s gave way to the 1960s, there was no direct equivalent in Britain of a generation of American writers directly influenced by Vietnam. Moreover, the waves of popular protests that spilled onto the streets of European capitals throughout 1968 created only delayed ripples on the campuses of British universities and the literary imagination in Britain at the time was, initially, correspondingly tame.[3] Instead, what emerged was a gradual willingness on the part of British writers to engage in increasing degrees of formal innovation, combined with an equally gradual search for new themes.

One of the earliest postmodern writers in Britain, and one who was influenced by events and schools of thought in mainland Europe, was John Fowles. Fowles's 1965 novel *The Magus* might seem on the surface somewhat too esoteric to be considered really politically challenging. When read against the context of the then-dominant strain in British writing, however, it begins to appear more innovative. The novel combines a sense of escapism with a portrayal of a fundamentally unequal power dynamic in a series of challenging philosophical dialogues. Nicholas Urfe is drawn into a manipulative relationship with the Greek estate owner Maurice Conchis, whose power games and recreation of increasingly horrifying historical and mythical tableaux plunge Urfe into an existential crisis. This combination, if not a major break with existing literary themes and forms, nevertheless reveals a commitment to extending them. A similar portrayal of mental and emotional manipulation takes place in Muriel Spark's 1970 novella *The Driver's Seat*, where the main female character Lise appears to commit suicide by tempting a patient recently released from an asylum into killing her.

After *The Magus*, Fowles's next published novel was *The French Lieutenant's Woman* (1969), a work that is commonly cited as one of the starting points for British postmodernism because of its use of 'historiographic metafiction'.[4] Although the plot of the novel takes place in the nineteenth century, its characters and narrator are given occasional access to a twentieth-century consciousness and idiom. The disparity of outlook between the two periods in a form where both are nevertheless deployed represents a significant break from the techniques associated with realism. The use of historiographic metafiction is also a significant technical innovation in J. G. Farrell's novel *The Siege of Krishnapur* (1973), a novel that portrays the 1857 Indian Mutiny against British Imperial rule and parodies contemporary British reaction to it. Like Fowles, Farrell evokes a figural twentieth-century consciousness by using a narrator who occasionally intervenes in the narrative, and characterisation and dialogue that are otherwise confined to the nineteenth century. By this means Farrell makes an imaginative leap between the India of the 1850s and the Britain of the 1970s and undermines the heroic manner in which the ideology of imperialism had previously been portrayed.

By the mid-1970s, for the first time since World War II Britain was involved in a series of economic crises. A global scarcity of oil in 1973 had had the effect of pushing up the price of coal and driving up inflation.

Edward Heath's Conservative government adopted a number of policies to combat this inflation, most notably a cap on wages for workers in the coal industry and the introduction in 1974 of the 'three-day week', aimed at conserving coal reserves by specifying that businesses could only use electricity on three days per week and within a specified maximum level of consumption. Since neither the wage cap for the coal workers nor the restriction of energy use applied to either private enterprise or private homes, the overall feeling created by the Heath government was one of conscious class warfare. When Farrell endows his characters of the 1850s with the language and ideas more typical of the 1970s in *The Siege of Krishnapur* he also implicitly makes the former resonate more strongly with the latter in order to mock and subvert the dominant assumptions of the privileged ruling elites of both periods.

Gayatri Spivak has dated the start of postmodernism to 1971, when a number of firms trading on the American stock exchange pooled their technological resources to create the combined Securities Industries Automation Corporation, thus bringing communications technology and economic activity into a close alliance.[5] In Britain, the response to economic turbulence is portrayed explicitly in J. G. Ballard's novel *High-Rise* (1975), a novel that conforms to the influential argument made by architect Charles Jencks that postmodernism is a movement which fundamentally rethinks how cultural constructions of space affect social relationships.[6] The action of *High-Rise* is located entirely within a luxury forty-storey London apartment complex, the spatial organisation of which signifies a form of social hierarchy. But as petty wars break out among the tower's richest residents and their bourgeois counterparts on the lower floors, they revert to an atavistic, tribal state. As their relationships cease to function, so too does the building: the electricity, water, and air conditioning all start to fail. It is hard not to interpret this portrayal of a stratified society at war with itself as its lights go out as Ballard's critical comment on the three-day week in microcosm.

A year before the publication of *High Rise*, Muriel Spark had lightly parodied the Richard Nixon of the Vietnam War and the Watergate scandal in her novella *The Abbess of Crewe* (1974), transplanting the drama from the White House to a girls' convent. For the most part however, it is the sense of economic crisis that we find in *High-Rise* rather than the Cold War, or Vietnam, or the popular protests of 1968 in Europe that provide an important context for understanding the development of postmodern fiction in Britain, which thus occurred somewhat more belatedly than in other countries. The sense in Britain of capitalist class warfare gave rise to a new suspicion of political and economic leaders, which in turn is registered in the fiction in a whole series of portrayals that would become more formally experimental over time. Indeed, a further number of economic crises throughout the 1980s, 1990s, and early twenty-first century were to provide a significant stimulus for that experimentation.

The Pathologies of Political Economy

One of the most prominent British writers to combine political and cultural criticism with writing fiction during the 1970s was the Welsh intellectual Raymond Williams. The many major contributions that he made to literary research emphasised that aesthetic judgements are underpinned by political ideologies, which, if read against the grain, can allow for a greater range of perspectives (especially those of class, feminism, and postcolonial societies) than had previously been acknowledged in critical practice. Thus Williams's work was committed to the democratisation of culture. A further implication of that process was the possibility of overcoming the dividing line between high art and popular culture. Popular genres such as crime and romance started to receive greater scholarly attention as a result.[7]

Breaking down the distinction between 'high' art and popular culture is one of the common features of postmodern writing and was practised by writers including Angela Carter, David Peace, and China Miéville, often in direct contradistinction to the minority and extremely intellectual forms of modernism that we find in Eliot, Joyce, Pound, and others.[8] But Williams himself did not share this enthusiasm for postmodernism and in fact used the term wholly negatively. This is because although the intellectual rigour of modernism appealed only to a narrow readership, he equated modernist aesthetics with a revolutionary avant-gardism and hence with a radical political sensibility. Like Jameson, he then saw postmodernism as a cultural form that represented the decline of modernism's own radical political potential and its incorporation into an unequal capitalist social order.[9]

Despite his suspicions of the word, though, Tony Pinkney has argued that Williams's fictional practice represents a gradual embracing of the form and techniques associated with postmodernism.[10] His *Volunteers* (1978) draws on many of the techniques that have been described as postmodern: it is written in a popular generic form, a thriller, and uses the investigation not so much to posit final answers (like a conventional whodunnit) as to raise questions about the existing capitalist order. By juxtaposing the violence used to break a current industrial strike with historic violence in colonial Kenya the novel moves between two periods in the same way Farrell does in *The Siege of Krishnapur*. Although Williams does not make the same use of historiographic metafiction as Farrell had done, he introduces a different innovative technique, setting *The Volunteers* in a then-imagined future in which political autonomy had been devolved from Westminster to Wales (which did not happen historically until after the Welsh referendum of 1997, the same year that Mihangel Morgan published his novel *Melog*, which along with William Owen Roberts's work of historiographic metafiction *Y Pla* [*Pestilence*] represent the most successful instances of postmodern fiction in Welsh).

A fictive critique of the political order was a significant component of British postmodern fiction at its peak, during its second phase in the 1980s and 1990s. For example, an under-recognised feature of Graham Swift's *Waterland* (1983) is that the backdrop to its teacher-narrator Tom Crick's professional crisis is the onslaught made by the Conservative central government on the Labour-held Greater London Council under Thatcherism. This onslaught was made in the name of standardisation, and would result in the introduction of a national curriculum in education for the first time by the end of the decade. In the novel it threatens the school's – and Crick's – autonomy, and hence his ability to cultivate among his students the capacity to think critically about the political order. So although much critical discussion of *Waterland* emphasises Swift's playful use of metafiction, situating the novel in the social and political context in which it intervened shows that it is not only an instance of postmodern self-indulgent play, but of opening a critical perspective on the world in which it was written.

This dual capacity to deploy innovative textual forms on the one hand while also connecting them to a developing critical consciousness on the other was a key component of British postmodern writing of the 1980s and 1990s. Martin Amis's *Money* (1984) represents an extremely unflattering parody of greed and unchecked consumption at the highest levels of metropolitan society in the Thatcherite world. Margaret Thatcher herself is caricatured openly in Ian McEwan's early work, *The Child in Time* (1987) as well as Salman Rushdie's *Satanic Verses* (1988). *The Child in Time* renders more explicit what was only implied in Swift's *Waterland*: the connection between the dominant ideology of the period and political attempts to prevent education from being used to promote what Paulo Freire calls a critical 'political consciousness'.[11] In the society McEwan portrays the aggressive, individualist economic policies of the government have given rise to a large, disenfranchised economic underclass of people so powerless and dispossessed that they are not even permitted to beg unless granted licences. The intersection between educational policies that restrict criticism of the government and an economic policy that creates widespread economic inequality and so makes it necessary to criticise in the first place is emphasised when a homeless woman freezes to death.

At the heart of *The Child in Time* is a juxtaposition between two characters: the children's writer Stephen Lewis, whose daughter had been abducted from a supermarket some years earlier, and his publisher, the politician Charles Darke. The political and commercial pressures to which Darke is subject are made manifest in a peculiar form of pathology that causes him to become more and more childlike over time. His death, like that of the homeless woman, is caused by overexposure to the elements but is embraced voluntarily in the orchard of his country estate. His regression to the woodland and the amniotic quality of the snow that engulfs him make his death feel like a return to an earth-like womb. The ordinary everyday reality that McEwan portrays is undermined by the intrusion of an uncanny element that defies simple realism. This is significant because so much of the dominant ideology in western capitalist societies in the period in question depended on a logic of linear progress, endless onward development, and economic growth. McEwan reverses this logic when he makes Darke grow backwards. As with Swift's use of metafiction, this eruption of the uncanny is not merely an instance of ludic postmodernism for its own sake because the resulting feeling of absurdity makes it possible to interrogate the dominant political ideology of the time.

The idea of economics and politics as forms of pathology that McEwan portrays in *The Child in Time* is common in British postmodern writing of the second phase, the 1980s and 1990s, as writers suggested that the corruption of power and the politics of greed were poisoning British society. For example, Jim Crace's *Arcadia* (1992) is a poetic novel that draws on a number of Jungian character 'archetypes' which elevate the text onto a transcendental plain from which the capitalist at its heart, Victor, can be both observed and critiqued. Although Victor is exposed as a ruthless exploiter of working people, he sets up two memorials to his mother: a fashionable new mall on the site of Covent Garden; and a statue of her holding him when he was a baby. Thus the statue he installs cements his role as eternal child rather than self-made man. Despite the fulfilment of his financial and material aspirations he is reduced to the same pathological status as McEwan's politician. What is memorialised is the pathology, not the material gain. The textual innovation of writing a poetic novel is not merely an aesthetic strategy that retreats from questions of politics and ideology, but enables critical engagement with them.

A third example of the pathologies of corrupt politicians and toxic economics is Julian Barnes's 1998 novel, *England, England*, a novel in which the megalomaniac tycoon Sir Jack Pitman creates a microcosm of the nation on the Isle of Wight. This portrayal of a theme-park version of England based on iconic buildings such as Wembley Stadium, Big Ben, and Harrods is Barnes's most explicit fictional representation of a Baudrillardian simulacrum, that is, a copy that supersedes its original.[12] In doing so it raises philosophical questions about the relationship between reality and representation, questions which are not specific to postmodernism but which, in postmodern societies, have been rendered more pressing by the preponderance of new media. *England, England* follows the logic of the simulacrum because when Pitman dies actors are commissioned to perform his role so that he passes into the folklore of the place and becomes one of the legendary figures people come to the park to visit. The representation surpasses the subject it represents and this can be considered paradigmatic of media cultures in postmodern society.

England, England was published in 1998, the year of the introduction of the Euro for electronic transactions in parts of Europe and the year after Wales and Scotland voted in favour of devolution in the referenda of 1997. Barnes harnesses both these political contexts to his representation of a picture-postcard England, which is given a sharp ironic twist by the counter-examples they provide. The financial success of Sir Jack's project is portrayed as leading to an increase in the value of shares in his company in a way that undermines Britain's public finances, thereby threatening the very structure of British society. In this way, Barnes alludes also to the economic recession that had dominated Britain's economy earlier in the 1990s, and in particular to Black Wednesday (16 September 1992), when the United Kingdom had been forced to drop out of Europe's Exchange Rate Mechanism, at a cost to the British treasury that has been variously estimated between three and thirty billion pounds.

One of the most prominent members of the cabinet at the time of Black Wednesday was David Mellor, who had been Chief Secretary to the Treasury before becoming Secretary of State in the Department of National Heritage. These two government departments are explicitly parodied in *England, England* through the novel's portrayal both of a major blow to the treasury's fortunes and of the concept of a theme park based on icons of England's national culture. Mellor ended up resigning from government office after a number of newspaper allegations that he had had an affair with an actress, Antonia de Sancha. Mellor himself is not directly parodied in the novel, but the combination of sexual fantasy with politics and economics specifically within the 'heritage' industries suggests that Barnes subjects such activities to fictional pastiche. They are also an indication of a further series of emerging and related elements of Britain's postmodern culture in its next phase, specifically voyeurism, celebrity status, and Debord's society of the spectacle, which in turn began to be represented in postmodern fiction.[13]

From Critical Postmodernism to Celebrity Culture

Raymond Williams had noted as early as 1974 that Britain was a thoroughly 'dramatised' society – both because its members watched more drama (via television) than ever and because television treated drama as a private, solitary activity, as opposed to a public, communal one, and hence militated against developing networks of solidarity in opposition to the ideologies of capitalism.[14] It also invited viewers to conduct their ordinary lives as if they were characters in a drama, and implicit in this dramatisation of daily life was the potential to break down the distinction between the 'performers' and the 'audience'. So-called reality television, certain forms of game show, and certain confessional genres emerged as a logical result of this process.

In a sense, Angela Carter's last novel *Wise Children* (1991) can be read as an elegy to earlier forms of drama such as pantomime and music hall that declined as a result of television. Nora and Dora Chance are seventy-five-year-old dancers attending the hundredth birthday of their uncle Peregrine, the brother of a Shakespearean actor, Melchior Hazard. Perry's grandson Tristan, by contrast, has abandoned the stage and the variety hall altogether and presents a television game show. The careers of these different generations thus embody the transition between different forms of media that was accelerated by the growth of postmodernism in a media-saturated society. But Carter's novel avoids lapsing into simple nostalgia and primarily through the technique of magical realism revivifies both the older cultural forms and the new. Rupert Thomson also finds a new and innovative way of imagining the dramatisation of society in his novel *The Insult* (1996), where following a gunshot wound the main character is able to receive television signals directly into his mind and thus finds that his daily experience of the world is framed as if it were a live broadcast. Like Barnes in *England, England*, Thomson would go on to allegorise the perceived 'break-up' of Britain that was implicit in Scottish and Welsh votes for political autonomy in his subsequent work, *Divided Kingdom* (2005).[15]

A more sinister representation of the society of the spectacle is generated in Tim Lott's novel *The Seymour Tapes* (2005), where the concept of spectacle is transformed into both surveillance and voyeurism. It is a latter-day Othello in which a middle-class man becomes convinced that his wife is having an extramarital affair and installs secret cameras to observe her behaviour. It is also a portrayal of a psycho-sexual power game (like Fowles's *The Magus*) in which the husband himself is drawn into a sexual relationship with the woman who supplied him with the surveillance equipment, before being murdered by her. From here, different kinds of textual object rapidly multiply: the text hints that the story of the Seymour murder has already been separately – and widely – reported in the tabloid media, a film documentary, and on various television news bulletins. These narratives are presented as salacious and designed purely to satisfy a stupefied mass audience's hunger for blood and scandal, thereby justifying the need for a true and accurate account, which the novel posits but does not provide.

The perception of an ill-informed population lusting only after tales of sex and violence was widely cultivated in Britain by the print and televisual media coverage of such events as the murder of two year-old James Bulger in 1993; the shooting of news reporter Jill Dando outside her home in London in 1999; the marriage of football player David Beckham and singer Victoria Adams also in 1999; the release of a 'sex tape' featuring the wealthy American heiress Paris Hilton in 2003; and the divorce of the actors Brad Pitt and Jennifer Aniston in 2005. We cannot say for certain that Lott had any of these specific news stories in mind when writing *The Seymour Tapes*, but we can say that they are the general kind of media event that he portrays in composite form. What is satirised is not so much the idea of an ill-informed population craving such stories, but the media moguls who create that desire among their readers.

Since the society of the spectacle offers to convert important events into passive entertainment, it diminishes the critical distance between the world and the way it is represented. The loss of this critical distance then makes it difficult to perform fictive critique of the dominant ideology, and in fact this lack of criticality is commonly identified as a weakness of certain kinds of postmodernism.[16] This squeezing out of the critical space has accelerated since the turn of the century, bringing British postmodernism into its third phase, and was particularly evident in British fiction written in the aftermath of the 2008 worldwide banking crisis.

For example, Amanda Craig's 2009 novel *Hearts and Minds* is set in London between the terrorist attacks of 2005 and the banking crisis of 2008 and portrays a failed attempt to assassinate a fictional Prime Minister at a party hosted by a lifestyle magazine, the *Rambler*. The *Rambler*'s proprietor Roger Trench had bought it from the bankrupted estate of a disgraced former media magnate, Max de Monde. But although these figures are apparent lampoons of the wealthy businessmen Rupert Murdoch and Conrad Black, the identification between Craig's fictional characters and the public figures on whom she based them is too explicit. It results in those real-world figures being reduced to 'characters' in a novel so that they seem like pantomime villains rather than real-world agents involved in the generation of financial inequality and therefore not genuinely harmful to the collective welfare of the society in question. This compromises the efficacy of its critique.

Sebastian Faulks came across a similar challenge in *A Week in December* (2009), a condition-of-England novel that explicitly satirises the principal antagonists in the banking crisis that followed the collapse of Lehman Brothers in the USA and Northern Rock in the UK. Faulks depicts an antihero, John Veals, who successfully short-circuits thousands of mortgages and almost brings down a bank on whom so many people's homes depend that the government is forced to intervene to protect them. Veals very closely resembles unscrupulous financiers such as Nick Leeson (who had earlier bankrupted Barings Bank) and Fred Goodwin who presided over the largest financial loss in the history of British banking at the Royal Bank of Scotland in 2008. This means that *A Week in December*, like *Hearts and Minds*, portrays too closely the world it purports to fictionalise. Lacking the loose, free, and associative qualities of pastiche in favour of the more precise and specified targets of parody, it loses the ability to imagine the world differently. In other words, whereas Fredric Jameson famously favoured parody over pastiche because he felt that the former was more critical than the latter,[17] British postmodern writers who have used the allusive properties of pastiche have generated a more effective critical practice than those whose parodies have let their subjects off the hook.

The capacity to do this has diminished over time in the face of the continual shrinking of the public space and the absorption of all aspects of cultural production into the political and economic mainstream from where, by definition, it cannot be critical of it. Thus although Rose Tremain more innovatively portrayed the effects of the financial crash among eastern European immigrants in London in *The Road Home* (2007), the dominant tone in the final phase of British postmodern fiction is characterised overall by this loss of criticality. Two further examples of this process are John Lanchester's *Capital* (2012) and David Mitchell's *The*

Bone Clocks (2014). In its portrayal of artists and celebrities alongside bankers and millionaires, *Capital* replicates the structure of *A Week in December* almost exactly. In *The Bone Clocks*, which is a highly imaginative world-building work of speculative fiction, Mitchell portrays a 'bad-boy' novelist (modelled on Martin Amis) collecting a literary prize from a businessman and television celebrity who is equally explicitly modelled on the entrepreneur and government 'Enterprise Champion' Lord Alan Sugar. Whereas the earlier novels by McEwan, Crace, and Barnes portrayed generic tycoon-figures without making a precise connection to any single real-world model in order to semi-fictionalise the world they portrayed, Mitchell portrays no generic tycoon in the abstract, but the empirically existing tycoon, Lord Alan Sugar. The result is that despite Mitchell's attempt to bring a critical ethical perspective into the novel the fictive critique of the financial world collapses in the face of a harsh reassertion of the existing economic order.

One important reason for this disappearance of critique is that the neoliberal economic order that had already started to develop during the years of New Labour restructuring (1997–2010), and that was dramatically accelerated by the 2008 financial crash, more strongly polarised the distinction between the extremely wealthy and the rest of the population. At the same time, because wealthy corporations control the overwhelming majority of print and broadcast media, their owners have been very successful in cultivating media images of themselves as 'celebrities' rather than as bankers. During the really creative phase of British postmodernism, in response to a number of political and economic challenges, writers presented exploitive commercial and financial leaders as pathologically flawed in all sorts of innovative and dynamic ways. During the final phase, by contrast, the stranglehold of corporations and powerful individuals over the bulk of the wealth has become so strong that they have been able to make a number of incursions into the domains of popular culture where they present themselves as television 'personalities', thereby legitimising their economic practices. Alan Sugar's long-running 'reality' TV show *The Apprentice* is a good example. That this representation of bankers and businesspeople as celebrity versions of themselves who can be made to appear benign has carried over into forms of fiction underlines the extent to which the reassertion of neoliberal economics has become the dominant mode of thinking in British society. In the aftermath of Brexit, with successive Prime Ministers pursuing global free trade arrangements with a number of other countries, neoliberalism has become even more solidified and spaces for dissent to it have been eroded even further.

The Precariat and the Politics of Uncertainty

With the extension of neoliberal economics in Britain there has come a systematic introduction of political measures that exacerbate financial inequality and disproportionately affect the poor. These include a rolling back of employees' rights; new legislation aimed at ensuring the majority of working people will have to work for longer hours and until later in life; a dramatic reduction in state welfare provision; a reduction in the equality of access to education, especially at university level; a significant reduction in legal aid; and an onslaught against the National Health Service. All of these have the effect of reasserting the primacy of a socio-economic elite and a political order that exists mainly to safeguard the minority interests of its members. It has also been accompanied by the rise of a new class in Britain, a class that Guy Standing refers to as the *precariat* because its members exist in an ongoing and fundamental state of economic precariousness, surviving on narrow financial margins and subject to the imposition on their lives of the arbitrary forces of wealth and power beyond their control.[18]

The representation of this class in fiction represents the last gasp of British postmodernism. Thus Marina Lewycka fictionalises the aftermath of the 2008 banking crash in *Various Pets Alive and Dead* (2012) by portraying a young man who drops out of a PhD in mathematics at Cambridge to take a lucrative job with a city bank. He keeps this secret from his politically idealistic parents who, having grown up in a socialist commune, would feel betrayed by his decision. Although in the end Serge has a change of heart and resigns from his job, this comes about as a result of the plot's deflection into romance and leaves the economic structure represented by the bank unscathed. This deflection contrasts with Shena Mackay's earlier representation of a commune in *Heligoland* (2003), a novel that combines realism with fable and hence can be considered critically postmodern. In a comic subplot, Serge suspects his boss at the bank is visiting a prostitute for exotic sex games. When it transpires that the woman is a colonic irrigation nurse rather than a prostitute, the banking structure is implicitly vindicated from any impropriety or exploitation. Where *England, England* portrayed the tycoon's addiction to prostitution as a pathological component of his desire for economic domination, *Various Pets Alive and Dead* reduces the audience's expectation for pathology into humour. Between publication of the two novels in 1998 and 2012 the strength of global capitalism was so strongly reasserted that even in fiction the capacity to imagine alternatives became weaker.

The precariat, whom Lewycka keeps in the background of *Various Pets Alive and Dead*, are more fully represented in two other novels published in 2012, Zadie Smith's *NW* and James Kelman's *Mo Said She Was Quirky*. In *NW* Smith portrays an aspiring footballer who, having failed a trial for a London club, drifts into unemployment and commits a murder. He confides in a female barrister who had grown up on the same run-down North London estate as him, and who takes legal aid cases as a means of staying close to her working-class roots. Kelman's *Mo Said She Was Quirky* is a portrayal of a woman who works in an all-night casino and uses the metaphor of the luck of the draw to build a powerful and ironic portrayal of political disempowerment among a class of people who have, for complex economic and political reasons, lost control of their own destiny.

NW and *Mo Said She Was Quirky* are both more formally experimental than *Various Pets Alive and Dead*. This implies that just as the emergence of postmodernism in Britain is difficult to date precisely, so too there is no single moment at which it came to an end. It would be more accurate to suggest that the general process by which the values of a political-economic elite have become entrenched coincides with a gradual decline in a really creative and critical postmodern fictional practice. In general, the most innovative portrayals of the precariat, and hence the most creative and critical forms of fiction in Britain since 2008, are no longer expressed in the conventions of postmodernism, but in such emerging areas as neo-modernism, digi-modernism, or post-humanism.[19] At its peak postmodern writing was able to imagine a sense of critical distance from the political and economic order in Britain, but as that order has become strongly reasserted it has incorporated the most challenging elements of postmodernism into its own logic in a way that causes postmodernism to yield the floor. This means that the qualities of dynamism, experimentalism, and critique that defined British postmodernism at an earlier stage have subsequently migrated into other new and still emerging fictional forms.

Notes

1. See Chris Harman, 'History, Myth and Marxism' in *Essays on Historical Materialism*, ed. John Rees (London: Bookmarks, 1998), pp. 9–23.
2. Alan Sinfield, *Literature, Politics and Culture in Postwar Britain* (London: Continuum, 1997), p. 92.
3. Gerd-Rainer Horn, *The Spirit of '68: Rebellion in Western Europe and North America, 1956–76* (Oxford University Press, 2008), p. 235.
4. Linda Hutcheon, *The Politics of Postmodernism* (London: Routledge, 1988).

5. Gayatri Spivak, *In Other Worlds: Essays on Cultural Politics* (London: Routledge, 1988), p. 170.
6. Charles Jencks, *What Is Post-Modernism?* (London: Academy Editions, 1996), pp. 6–8.
7. See Raymond Williams, 'Culture is Ordinary' (1958) reprinted in his *Resources of Hope* ed. Robin Gable (London: Verso, 1989); and *The Long Revolution* (London: Chatto and Windus, 1961).
8. See Andreas Huyssen, *After the Great Divide: Modernism, Mass Culture, Postmodernism* (Bloomington: Indiana University Press, 1986), p. 143.
9. See Raymond Williams, 'When was Modernism?' in his *Politics of Modernism: Against the New Conformists* (London: Verso, 1989), p. 35.
10. Tony Pinkney, *Raymond Williams* (Bridgend: Seren, 1995), p. 70.
11. Paulo Freire, 'Education for Critical Consciousness' in *The Paulo Freire Reader* ed. Ana Maria Araújo Freire and Donaldo Macedo (London: Bloomsbury Academic, 2013), pp. 80–94.
12. Jean Baudrillard, 'The Precession of Simulacra' in his *Simulacra and Simulation* trans. Sheila F. Glaser (Ann Arbor: University of Michigan Press, 1994), pp. 1–42.
13. Guy Debord, *The Society of the Spectacle* trans. Donald Nicholson-Smith (London: Rebel Press, 1992). First published 1967.
14. See Raymond Williams, 'Drama in a Dramatized Society' in his *Writing in Society* (London: Verso, 1985), pp. 11–21.
15. See Tom Nairn, *The Break-Up of Britain: Crisis and Neo-Nationalism* (London: New Left Books, 1977); and Hywel Dix, *Postmodern Fiction and the Break-Up of Britain* (London: Continuum, 2010).
16. See Aijaz Ahmad, *In Theory: Classes, Nations, Literatures* (Oxford University Press, 1992), p. 33.
17. Fredric Jameson, *Postmodernism: Or the Cultural Logic of Late Capitalism* (Durham, North Carolina: Duke University Press, 1990), p. 25.
18. See Guy Standing, *The Precariat: The New Dangerous Class* (London: Bloomsbury Academic, 2011).
19. See Siân Adiseshiah and Rupert Hildyard (eds.), *Twenty-First Century Fiction: What Happens Now* (Basingstoke: Palgrave Macmillan, 2013).

CHAPTER 2

British Postmodern Fiction and the Rise of 'Declinism'

Graham Matthews

Introduction

Since the mid-1990s, the idea of national economic decline has shifted from an incontrovertible fact to something to be treated with scepticism. There exists a long tradition of characterising Britain by its lack of enthusiasm for science, the indifference of government to commerce, and the low status of research and development, industry, and engineering. This perception was encouraged throughout the second half of the twentieth century by political scientists, economists, columnists, and historians who drew on 'decline' as an interpretative framework despite the many disagreements about its meaning, evidence, causes, and remedies. Consequently, the history of 'declinism' – the idea or, in the Barthesian sense, the myth of decline – and the notion of an embattled national identity is deeply embedded in British postmodern fiction. British politicians across the spectrum, from Harold Wilson to Margaret Thatcher, capitalised on the negative perception of Britain's technology and industry and employed narratives of decline as a major component of election strategies that drew upon equal parts nostalgia for a halcyon time that never really existed and contemporary anxieties about status, economics, and national pride. Concerns about national and economic decline have occupied an important role in British culture to the extent that debates about immigration, sovereignty, and the economy relative to European nations shaped the 2016 United Kingdom European Union membership referendum. This chapter asks how British postmodern authors responded to this atmosphere of impoverishment and historical failure.

British decline is relative rather than absolute. Although Britain's 'share of world manufactured exports had indeed declined from 22 per cent in 1950 to 16 per cent in 1960', as David Kynaston notes, 'the British economy's annual rate of growth between 1957 and 1965 would be 3.2 per cent, the most impressive rate since the 1860s'.[1]

It is true that the British economy grew more slowly than the world economy during the second half of the twentieth century, but it is also true that there was an enormous improvement in living conditions, standards of education, military power, and healthcare. British citizens saw broadening democratisation in society and culture as well as substantial and prolonged growth in output, income, and national wealth. British innovation and technical training have been stronger than generally believed, and the economy, with a few brief exceptions such as the recession in 1979–81, grew substantially by a few percentage points each year. In his 1993 presidential address to the Economic History Society, Barry Supple discussed Britain's putative economic decline over the past century and challenged 'the assumption that things are going from bad to worse, when so much evidence suggests that they are going from not so bad to something somewhat better'.[2] David Cannadine claims that changes over the second half of the twentieth century were 'emphatically for the better rather than visibly for the worse'.[3] Nevertheless, as the cultural critic Stuart Hall notes, 'the idea of decline is very deeply embedded in British culture and it underwrites the debate in Europe too'.[4] Britain was defined by change, transformation, and a more diverse and inclusive culture rather than decline.

Declinist claims of a failure in economic growth are highly qualified; based on selective evidence, the claims tend to entirely ignore contrary viewpoints and are ultimately rooted in the assumption of disdain for science, technology, and expertise within British society. But as David Edgerton concludes in *Warfare State* (2005), if this disdain truly existed in British society then declinist writers would not have garnered such an enthusiastic and popular reception.[5] Jim Tomlinson argues first, that 'declinism' is an ideology that is both popular and largely unquestioned; second, that the notion of a '100-year decline' is a retrospective judgement; and third, that declinism 'has not taken a constant form, but rather has been reinvented periodically in relation to differing current concerns'.[6]

The rise of declinism coincides with the supersession of modernism in literary studies. Most accounts of postmodernism view it as a selective intensification of tendencies within modernism rather than an abrupt caesura, marking off a break with the past. For instance, Brian McHale identifies a shift from the dominant tendency of the modernist novel – with its concern with epistemological questions to do with knowledge and interpretation – to the postmodern concern with ontology, the philosophy of being, and the construction of worlds. He states: 'an ontology is a description of *a* universe, not of *the* universe; that is, it may describe *any* universe, potentially a *plurality* of universes'.[7] In other words, postmodern fiction does not seek a grounding for the universe but offers the opportunity to describe alternative universes. It is therefore able to recognise and mitigate against 'declinist' myths that purport to describe the grounded universe. Entities can change their ontological status through history as real things become myths and belief systems are eroded to the extent that mythological entities become fictions. In this light, fiction offers the only honest ontology when it foregrounds its status as fiction. The chief challenge to the shifting dominant argument comes from the postface added to the 1982 edition of Ihab Hassan's *The Dismemberment of Orpheus* which places modernism in opposition to postmodernism. The former is associated with authoritarian logocentrism while the latter is described in terms of dispersal, displacement, indeterminacy, exhaustion, and absence – all terms which bear an elective affinity with the thematic tropes of decline. Steven Connor detects in Hassan's argument the claim that 'the excesses of disintegration are the guarantee of authentic speech' and an analogous impetus appears to have inspired the work of both British postmodern writers and the early declinist historians.[8] Unlike other national postmodern traditions, novels by writers as diverse as Muriel Spark, John Fowles, B. S. Johnson, Doris Lessing, Graham Swift, and Julian Barnes are united by a concern with national decline and the loss of confidence in Britain's role as a financial, technological, and cultural centre.

Three reinventions of the myth of decline coincide with the changing thematic and stylistic concerns of British postmodern fiction. At midcentury, British postmodern writers such as Spark, Fowles, and Johnson engaged in formal metafictional experimentation to question the relationship between authors, texts, and readers; these texts evince a subtle shift in the cultural dominant from epistemological questions of self and identity towards more expansive questions concerning the construction of worlds. The theme of decline was incorporated into novels such as *The Comforters* (1957), *The Magus* (1966), and *Albert Angelo* (1964) in which alienated individuals are rendered analogous to the state of the nation. In the 1970s and 1980s, declinism entered the political mainstream and British postmodern writing underwent what Suzanne Keen refers to as the 'historical turn'.[9] A new generation of British postmodern novelists sought to problematise the relationship between historical fact and experiential event and inaugurated a shift from portraying decline to presenting declinism as a historiographic narrative. Finally, the late 1980s and 1990s saw the emergence of a strand of British postmodern fiction that explicitly thematised declinism and sought to problematise what had become a pernicious myth. In *The Remains of the Day* (1989), Kazuo Ishiguro anticipated the work of revisionist histories that systematically debunked the declinist myth while Julian Barnes's *England, England* (1998) dramatised the potentially devastating outcomes of belief in declinism. Accordingly, the periodic reinvention of the decline myth parallels the development of British postmodern fiction – from concentrating on formal experiments in reflexivity to the production of historiographic metafiction, and finally to a heightened socio-political sensibility.

The Birth of Declinism

At mid-century, British postmodern fiction tended to subordinate character and plot to the creation of autonomous worlds, not through the production of fantasy, but by refusing to suppress its own part in the making of the fiction. Linda Hutcheon's influential account of metafiction, *Narcissistic Narrative* (1980), identifies novels that 'thematize and actualize the very processes undertaken by both writer and reader'.[10] These texts displayed a rising critical awareness and self-consciousness and sought to close the gap between high culture and mass culture by complicating generic integrity. Muriel Spark incorporated elements of detective and spy fiction, B. S. Johnson foregrounded working-class voices, and John Fowles engaged in generic mixing. Foregrounding a text's own status as fiction emphasises the figure of the author, the act of writing, and narrative conventions in a way that signals a shift in the cultural dominant from epistemology to ontology. Consequently, the personal introspection and dissolution of the integrity of the self, characteristic of modernist texts, was mapped onto broader world-building narratives of national decline.

In *Albert Angelo*, the post-existential fate of B. S. Johnson's semi-autobiographical protagonist is coupled to that of the nation through a scene in which he comments on his shambolic environs: 'I enjoy it decadent and decaying, decrepit, like my state, London's state, England's state, man's state, the human condition'.[11] Despite being a qualified architect, Albert must earn a living as a socially marginalised supply teacher at a series of inner-London schools. Having recently separated from his girlfriend, Albert foregrounds his resentment and seeks redemption through an appeal to authenticity. During the fourth chapter titled 'dissolution', the author seemingly tires of the fictionality of his narrative and directly addresses the reader in an effort to declare his dedication to truth by identifying the lies that comprise the preceding narrative. This intrusion signals a parallel between the increasingly downtrodden schoolteacher, the failed architect, and the vocation of the poet or the novelist who finds him or herself increasingly cast out from society and bound to the imperative of function over aesthetics by the strictures of economic necessity: 'So it's nothing to you that I am rabbeting on about being a poet and having to earn a living in other ways: but what about your own sector of the human condition then? Eh? Eh? Eh eh eh!'[12] The intrusive narrator makes a direct address to the reader that conflates the personal with the political and ties the suffering of an individual to the decline of the nation. This theme was to become increasingly common as the century progressed.

Muriel Spark's postwar novels contain several allusions to national decline. In *Robinson* (1958), the island, named after Defoe's *Robinson Crusoe* (1719), is inexorably sinking into the sea as an allegory for the British Isles sinking into decline. *The Ballad of Peckham Rye* (1960) depicts a modern suburb whose inhabitants are assailed by the disaffection and estrangement typical of the workforce in postwar Britain. However, it was in *The Comforters*, which exhibits postmodernist characteristics such as metafictional tropes, challenges to generic integrity, and self-reflexive questioning, that Spark had begun her critical engagement with decline. The novel presents a bucolic image of England that incorporates pastiches of the smuggling tale, detective fiction, and the conversion narrative alongside a metafictional conceit whereby the central character, Caroline Rose, experiences a series of hallucinations in which she hears the very novel she is in being written by a figure she calls the Typing Ghost. Throughout the narrative, various characters come to believe in fantastic scenarios with absolute conviction, thereby reflecting the novel's central theme about the construction of narrative and the kind of truth told by fiction. Among Caroline's 'comforters' is the Baron, a naturalised British citizen who originally came from the Belgian Congo and condemns the decline of English values: 'the Baron was rather scrupulous about his English observances and confident that he had the English idea, so that his contempt for the English, their intellect, their manners, arose from a vexation that they did not conform better to the idea'.[13] The Baron has modelled his persona on the stereotypical notion of the English gentleman, a figure that was increasingly subject to simplistic scapegoating by declinist historians. Spark's Baron is shown to adhere, unconvincingly, to a cultural stereotype commonly seen in declinist arguments that British society was run by gentleman amateurs uninterested in science, technology, and progress.

John Fowles's *The Magus* portrays British values as lacklustre and exhausted in a manner that reflects the work of two major figures in the emerging declinist literature: Andrew Shonfield and Michael Shanks delivered left-wing critiques of class divisions that emphasised economic decline and the marginalisation of experts, industrialists, and scientists in governmental and administrative positions.[14] The 1963 edition of *Encounter* magazine titled 'Suicide of a Nation?' blamed Britain's putative economic 'decline' on the prevailing culture – the editor, Arthur Koestler, excoriated the 'cult of amateurishness' among the governing elites – and presented the nation as nurturing a long-standing hostility to mercantilism and engineering.[15] The novel tells the story of Nicholas Urfe who, having been educated at Oxford in the Arts, finds himself ill-equipped to pursue a career in banking, commerce, or industry and consequently becomes disillusioned with the newly professionalised and unpoetic Britain. Nicholas exiles himself to the Lord Byron school on the Greek island of Phraxos where, in marked contrast with his homeland, pupils are 'ruthlessly pragmatic' and care 'nothing for literature, and everything for science'.[16] There he encounters the enigmatic trickster Maurice Conchis who, through a series of masques known as the 'godgame', teaches him that reality is composed of a series of appearances and that no single appearance is necessary. In imparting to Nicholas the value of scepticism and uncertainty and by continually frustrating Nicholas's attempts to seek a concrete reality behind appearances, the novel dramatises the means by which national mythologies, such as declinism, are constructed yet taken for truth.

Early postmodern novels by Spark, Johnson, and Fowles employ metafictional devices to foreground the novel's status as fiction and present a shift in the cultural dominant from epistemological to ontological questions. The false starts, interruptions, and digressions of Johnson's *Albert Angelo* foreground the novel's fictionalising function and, similarly, Spark's *The Comforters* presents an author who has found their way into the text, thereby opening questions of authorship and the process of reading. Meanwhile, Fowles's *The Magus* depicts a series of complex psychological games that blur the distinction between fiction and reality. British postmodern fiction employs various strategies to foreground the ontological structure of text and world, and in the process they problematise the apparatus of myth making and complicate the emergent narrative of national decline.

Reversing Decline as Political Discourse

Declinism became widespread during the economic downturn in the 1970s, which saw rising inflation and unemployment, despite tight limits to the growth potential of the economy and other west European countries being subject to parallel constraints. The discourse of 'reversing decline' burgeoned under the Thatcher government where it was deployed in political debates that were increasingly removed from economic reality. Thatcher harnessed the narrative of national decline to a broader critique of the permissive society of the 1960s and espoused Victorian values such as thrift, sobriety, patriotism, and independence, without referencing Victorian vices. She argued that national decline was producing an enfeebling and insidious state of mind that had weakened the entrepreneurial spirit that had previously made Britain great. Her cabinet were influenced by polemical yet immensely popular declinist accounts that criticised Britain's anti-industrial spirit and the nation's anti-technological and anti-scientific elite.[17]

British postmodern fiction in the 1980s and early 1990s typically combined historical novels with metafictional tropes. John Brannigan writes that 'on or around 1980, historical fiction changed. A new generation of novelists emerged in Britain whose work became characterised by its self-reflexive, critical engagement both with the nature and with the very possibility of historical knowledge'.[18] Linda Hutcheon dubbed this form 'historiographic metafiction' and argued that this genre acknowledged that 'both history and fiction are discourses'.[19] Novels by Graham Swift, John le Carré, and Penelope Lively depict historical events that are then subjected to distortion, falsification, and self-conscious fictionalisation. Together they indicate that we can only learn about history through narrative and, by extension, that novels 'expose the fictionality of history itself'.[20] Hayden White also challenged the notion that history could be objective and described historiography as explanations structured through argument, plotting, and ideology: 'history is no less a form of fiction than the novel is a form of historical representation'.[21] Postmodern novels highlight the links between fiction and historical reality by 'visibly contradicting the public record of "official" history; by flaunting anachronisms; and by integrating history and the fantastic'.[22] Consequently, novelists rehearsed the myth of decline in order to implicitly deconstruct it by problematising all monolithic myth-making apparatus. Rather than a direct rebuttal that would constitute a straightforward counter-narrative, the text exhorts readers to exercise their critical faculties and interrogate the naturalised myths of the present. Consequently, British postmodern fiction in the 1970s and 1980s did not simply depict decline as a historical fact but declinism as a discourse.

Doris Lessing's *The Fifth Child* (1988) charts the lives of Harriet and David Lovatt, an upper-middle-class couple who desire a large family. All is well until the birth of the fifth, Ben, who is viewed by the family as a monstrous, insatiable, and aggressive child. Ben's arrival ruptures the previously happy family and is paralleled by anxieties about wider social and moral decline:

> Brutal incidents and crimes, once shocking everyone, were now commonplace ... The house next door had been burgled three times ... At the end of the road there was a telephone box that had been vandalised so often the authorities had given up: it stood unusable.[23]

The national allegory is extended by references to the family home as a 'kingdom' that protects the children from the storms of the world, and David's stepmother's description of the house as 'gloomy and detestable, like England'.[24] The novel ironises the couple's conservative outlook and Thatcher's triumphalist rhetoric of renewal in the face of insidious moral, social, and economic decline at the moment that David's career falters and his friends are made redundant. Consequently, the novel subtly satirises declinism and anticipates the growing problem of political polarisation: 'it seemed that two peoples lived in England, not one – enemies, hating each other, who could not hear what the other said'.[25]

In a similar vein, Angela Carter, writing in *New Society* in 1983, comments on the rising fashion for the 'aesthetic of poverty' that 'makes you look like the victim of a catastrophe'.[26] Carter notes that this violent visual language both heightens and naturalises the culture of decline and blurs the distinction between the genuinely impoverished and cultural elites. In a separate article published a year earlier, Carter comments on the self-mythologising tendencies of the English and seeks to debunk the stereotype of the comic toff promulgated by declinists. She also criticises the comedic value attached to 'the British worker' presented in the media as the *non-worker*: 'As a national symbol – if adopted by democratic consent – this Schweik-like, fiddling shirker, who treasures the right to strike above rubies, would make a most appealing one'.[27] The figure of the 'shirker' reaffirmed right-wing arguments of moral and economic decline and placed them squarely at the feet of a lack of entrepreneurial or industrial spirit within the English working class. Although Lessing and Carter do not call into question Britain's putative decline, they challenge the ways in which declinist myths and stereotypes were utilised by right-wing politicians and the popular media to promote deregulation and privatisation, and to marginalise working class voices.

Graham Swift's *Waterland* (1983) offers one of the most nuanced representations of British decline that provides a fictionalised retelling of the myth while simultaneously problematising it. The narrator, Tom Crick, details the rise and fall of his ancestors' business empire originating with the farmer and maltster Josiah Atkinson in 1751, the development of a commercial monopoly under the auspices of his son, William Atkinson, through to the drainage and land reclamation of the titular Fens by Thomas Atkinson, followed by a steady decline from 1875 to the present. The fate of the Atkinson business empire is directly correlative to the narrative of Britain's decline as presented by the Thatcher administration. The national allegory is reinforced when, for bringing prosperity to the town of Norfolk, Thomas Atkinson is named the 'living emblem of the spirit of Albion' while the work of his sons is presented not only as an advance in commerce and engineering but as a series of improvements to the region's infrastructure, the welfare of the population and the sustenance of the community.[28] These achievements are anachronistically presented in terms reminiscent of Thatcher's conflation of enterprise with national glory: 'proof that all private interest is subsumed by the National Interest and all private empires do but pay tribute to the Empire of Great Britain'.[29] Despite his best efforts, Tom's history of the Atkinson family is interspersed with speculative and fantastical elements that are themselves indicative of the ways in which mythologies coalesce around the unknown, even when the subject matter is quotidian and impersonal. Tom's narrative of entrepreneurism and industrial innovation is compelling, especially when set against the flat and dismal landscape of the present-day Fens, and this in turn is indicative of the appeal of the myth of decline. The portrayal of a fall from greatness evokes nostalgia for a distant past and, as Tom's later reflections on history suggest, can be harnessed by the politics of the present.

Towards the novel's conclusion, Tom reflects on his own predicament as a history teacher whose discipline has been struck from the curriculum. Witnessing first-hand the destroyed German cities in 1946 brought home to him the fragility of civilisation. Reflecting on the nuclear threat in the 1980s, Tom states: 'I don't know if things were better or worse than they were in the year nought. There are myths of progress, myths of decline'.[30] Rather than arbitrating between competing or contradictory versions of the past, Tom makes the more radical gesture of questioning the exactitude of official histories. While ostensibly attempting to construct a purposive linear history, his narrative is persistently complicated by the intrusion of cyclical myths, superstitions, and folktales.

Swift's novel highlights the disparity between national mythologies and the economic reality and this scepticism towards history became a recurrent theme in British postmodern fiction. John le Carré's metafictional novel, *A Perfect Spy* (1986), charts the mental and moral dissolution of Magnus Pym, a British intelligence officer, following the betrayal of his country. Holed up in a nondescript English boarding house, Pym writes about a life spent role-playing, planting insinuations, and creating false identities, paralleled by the narrative itself, which is revealed to be contradictory and unreliable. Viewed through the lens of decline, the novel becomes a reminder that hopes for the future are often merely nostalgic longings for a lost, imagined past. Penelope Lively rehearses similar themes in *Moon Tiger* (1987). Claudia Hampton, a famous historian who lies dying in a hospital, painstakingly creates a mosaic of her past life and times, attempting to reconcile her memories of the past with events in world history. Nevertheless, historical evidence rarely rests easily with her recollections and so the novel provides yet another example of a British postmodern writer seeking to undermine the certitude of historical narrative rather than directly offering a counter-narrative to declinism. Although writers such as Lively, Swift, and Carter lacked the empirical evidence that would enable them to directly challenge declinism, their growing scepticism towards declinist narratives was made manifest by their embrace of fragmentation, paradox, and pastiche. The 'historical turn' inaugurated a development from a variety of literary self-reflexivity that dwelt on the relationship between author, text, and reader to a robust engagement with the construction of historical narratives. These texts constitute 'a resistance to old certainties about what happened and why' that is receptive to uncertainty, contingency, subjectivity, and the multiplicity of 'truth'.[31] British postmodern fiction's challenge to objectivity and monolithic interpretations of the world, coupled with the recognition that our world is one possibility among many, problematised the narrative of decline.

Debunking Declinism

The mid-1990s saw the rise of revisionist histories — all histories revise our understanding of the past — that systematically debunked the declinist myth, spearheaded by the economic historian David Edgerton. He argued that most of the historical accounts of British science and technology since

1870 suffer from a 'double inversion of historical reality: one of time and one of space'.[32] First, although British technology and manufacturing industries had been presented as contracting, this was a period of expansion. Second, other countries were viewed as more technologically advanced than Britain. Yet even at its peak, Britain was never primarily an industrial or manufacturing nation but had always possessed a highly efficient economy based on commerce, finance, and services. As W. D. Rubinstein notes, 'what is so often seen as Britain's industrial decline or collapse can be seen, with greater accuracy, as a transfer of resources and entrepreneurial energies into other forms of business life'.[33] Accordingly, the culture was far less hostile to capitalism, liberalism, and modernity than other west European nations. Furthermore, the popularity of declinism across nearly all sections of society suggested that science, technology, and industry were far from being out of favour. In Andrew Gamble's words, 'there clearly has not been anything approaching an absolute economic decline'.[34] Barry Supple commented in 1993 that the 'economic and political debate has come to be dominated by the idea that Britain is in such serious decline that it is heading for national ruin' while noting that this *idea* of decline was spread through political and popular images that distorted economic reality.[35]

As the myth of decline met with a robust response from professional historians, a new wave of British postmodern novelists explicitly thematised it within their texts. These novels presented a national mood of loss and regret that highlights the dangers of nostalgia for an illusory past. Kazuo Ishiguro's *The Remains of the Day* and Julian Barnes's *England, England* challenge the authenticity of history and memory and explicitly critique the myth of decline. Whereas Ishiguro delivers a subtle reproach to traditionalism, heritage, and nostalgia, Barnes employs elements of satire and farce to critique the production of national myths.

In *The Remains of the Day*, the narrator's assumptions and blind spots when reminiscing about the past highlight the ways in which memory is distorted by nostalgia. David James calls the novel a 'postmodern period piece' that appropriates features of the novel of manners to draw attention to the challenges attendant on evaluating a culture from within.[36] The novel presents the recollections of Stevens, a country-house butler who stands as an emblem for traditional English values at a time when they appear to be in a period of decline. Throughout his life, he has unquestioningly upheld his duty to serve his master, Lord Darlington, who he presents as standing at the centre of world affairs, yet it is revealed that he is an aristocratic fascist who hosts Nazi sympathisers. Darlington's fall is interpreted by the butler as emblematic of British decline when he selectively quotes Mr Lewis, an American politician, who denounces Lord Darlington as 'an amateur ... and international affairs today are no longer for gentleman amateurs'.[37] Lewis's comments echo declinist accounts that claimed that British society marginalised professionals and experts and stymied meritocracy. Stevens's emotional detachment mirrors his disavowal of his master's politics and a series of gaps and errors in his account alert the reader that he is an unreliable narrator performing the role of the dutiful and neutral servant. As Kathleen Wall notes, the novel is preoccupied with 'unreliability at the level of both content and form, and the consequent saturation of the text with indicators of unreliability, reveals the means that an author has at his disposal for speaking silently to the implied reader'.[38] Stevens delivers a narrative of decline of traditional values and is nostalgic for an idealised version of the past that obfuscates fascist politics. Despite initially appearing to be a straightforward historical novel, through Stevens's unreliable narration, *The Remains of the Day* is revealed to be a historiographic metafiction that catalyses re-evaluation of the past in the light of the present. As Linda Hutcheon argues, 'what postmodernism does ... is confront and contest any modernist discarding *or* recuperating of the past in the name of the future' thereby refusing transcendent or timeless meanings.[39] The butler is nostalgic for a misremembered past as a golden time of tradition and order, while disavowing his master's fascist sympathies. Ishiguro's novel reveals that the nostalgia mode is ineluctably linked to a politics of decline because it stimulates belief in an idealised past that never really existed. Postmodern contestation encourages the reader to question how we come to that past by evaluating the mediating narrative.

Throughout his oeuvre, Julian Barnes manifests his preoccupation with the mutability of memory and the ways in which it both colours and is coloured by the present. Rather than trying to locate an absolute or essential truth, Barnes presents the mechanisms by which individuals come to believe in ideologically determined truths and mistake contingency for necessity. *England, England* presents a vision of Britain that has been superseded by a heritage theme park called England, England situated on the Isle of Wight. While the theme park prospers, 'Old England' exits the European Union (EU), in a manner that anticipates the result of the 2016 UK European Union membership referendum, and steadily regresses into an agrarian society devoid of international political influence.

Barnes's novel portrays the deleterious effects of unregulated commercialisation alongside the moral, political, cultural, and militaristic changes that would take place in the event of an absolute economic decline. Sir Jack Pitman is a larger-than-life businessman confronted with the claim that Britain is in irrevocable decline: 'there are some people out there ... who think it's our job, our particular geopolitical function, to act as an emblem of decline, a moral and economic scarecrow'.[40] Pitman's belief in the nation's status as a faded economic power results in revivalist dreams and he proposes to rebrand the nation as a tourist haven by relocating all of its cultural icons to the newly purchased Isle of Wight. By flattening out a series of British icons such as Shakespeare, Queen Victoria, the Industrial Revolution, and afternoon tea into easily consumable form, Pitman merges the typically non-fungible spheres of cultural capital and economic capital; one consequence of this is that a professor of history is hired not in order to preserve historical accuracy or to educate visitors to the island but to devise strategies to make them feel less ignorant. Pitman's sweeping commodification of British culture dramatises the declinist ideal of unfettered entrepreneurism and satirises the economic priorities of the Department of National Heritage established in 1992.

In interview, Barnes points out the disparity between national mythologies and the economic reality: 'England as a functioning country is comparatively rich and healthy; many elements of society are comparatively happy. That may be the state of England; but, whether it is or not, what is the idea of England?'[41] In the final section of *England, England* titled 'Anglia', Barnes portrays 'a time of vertiginous decline' for the mainland that has discarded the politics of renewal and abandoned 'the long-agreed goals of the nation – economic growth, political influence, military capacity and moral superiority'.[42] The economy judders to a halt, mass depopulation takes place, Scotland and Wales opportunistically expand their territory, the Channel Islands are annexed by France, ties with the EU are gradually eroded, and after negotiating with 'such obstinate irrationality that they were eventually paid to depart', exit the EU entirely.[43] This drastic decision anticipates the 2016 Referendum and results in the erection of a trade barrier against the world, the prohibition of foreign ownership of land, and the dissolution of the military. The now-isolated country devolves into a self-sustaining set of rural communities divided into provinces based upon the kingdoms of the Anglo-Saxon heptarchy. While earlier British postmodern novels had questioned the construction of historical narratives, Barnes's portrayal of Anglia directly opposes the arguments of the declinist historians that Britain had previously been an industrial and entrepreneurial powerhouse that had sunk into decline due to the valorisation of art and culture, tradition and history over the needs of science, technology, and engineering. In Barnes's depiction, it is the very subsumption of British culture and tradition to the profit motive and the professionalisation of previously symbolic roles such as the monarchy that results in a genuine decline. Nevertheless, *England, England* ends on an ambivalent note as Martha Cochrane, one of the chief architects of the theme park, retires to a hamlet in Anglia where, surrounded by spurious folk myths and half-remembered countryside ceremonies, she decides to live out the rest of her days. Martha's retirement can be interpreted as either a rejection of the entrepreneurial spirit of England, England in favour of a return to a rural idyll or alternatively it could suggest that she has come to terms with the notion that 'authenticity' is ineluctably rooted in artifice. No matter which interpretation the reader chooses, declinism is revealed to be a pernicious fiction. Barnes's examination of the dynamics of truth and memory, coupled with his engagement with the nature of belief rather than simply the belief itself, allows for a sophisticated critique of a declinism that is cultural rather than economic, and that for half a century has preyed on and manipulated fears and anxieties about sovereignty and the nation.

Notes

1. David Kynaston, *Modernity Britain, 1957–62* (London: Bloomsbury, 2015), pp. 490–1.
2. Barry Supple, 'Fear of Failing: Economic History and the Decline of Britain' in Peter Clarke and Clive Trebilcock (eds.), *Understanding Decline: Perceptions and Realities of British Economic Performance* (Cambridge: Cambridge University Press, 1997), p. 9.
3. David Cannadine, 'Apocalypse When? British Politicians and British "Decline" in the Twentieth Century' in Peter Clarke and Clive Trebilcock (eds.), *Understanding Decline: Perceptions and Realities of British Economic Performance* (Cambridge: Cambridge University Press, 1997), p. 261.
4. Stuart Hall, 'Interview' in *Rethinking British Decline*, ed. Richard English and Michael Kenny (Basingstoke: Macmillan, 2000), p. 109.
5. David Edgerton, *Warfare State: Britain, 1920–1970* (Cambridge: Cambridge University Press, 2005).
6. Jim Tomlinson, 'Inventing "Decline": The Falling Behind of the British Economy in the Postwar Years', *Economic History Review* XLIX.4 (1996), p. 731.
7. Brian McHale, *Postmodernist Fiction* (London: Routledge, 1987), p. 27.
8. Steven Connor, *Postmodernist Culture: An Introduction to Theories of the Contemporary*. 2nd ed. (London: Blackwell, 1997), p. 120.
9. Suzanne Keen, *Romances of the Archive in Contemporary British Fiction* (Toronto: University of Toronto Press, 2001), p. 167.

10. Linda Hutcheon, *Narcissistic Narrative: The Metafictional Paradox* (Waterloo, Ontario: Wilfred Laurier University Press, 1980), p. 45.
11. Bryan Stanley Johnson, *Albert Angelo* (New York: New Directions, 1987), p. 116.
12. Johnson, p. 169.
13. Muriel Spark, *The Comforters* (New York: New Directions, 2014), p. 81.
14. Andrew Shonfield, *British Economic Policy Since the War* (Harmondsworth: Penguin, 1958); Michael Shanks, *The Stagnant Society* (Harmondsworth: Penguin, 1961).
15. Arthur Koestler, 'Introduction: The Lion and the Ostrich', *Encounter* (1963), p. 8.
16. John Fowles, The Magus (London: Vintage, 2004), p. 51.
17. Correlli Barnett, *The Audit of War: The Illusion and Reality of Britain as a Great Nation* (Basingstoke: Macmillan, 1986); Martin J. Wiener, *English Culture and the Decline of the Industrial Spirit, 1850–1980* (Cambridge: Cambridge University Press, 1981).
18. John Brannigan, 'The Novel as History' in *British and Irish Fiction Since 1940*, ed. Peter Boxall and Bryan Cheyette (Oxford: Oxford University Press, 2016), p. 243.
19. Linda Hutcheon, *Poetics of Postmodernism: History, Theory, Fiction* (London: Routledge, 2003), p. 4.
20. Connor, p. 132.
21. Hayden White, *Tropics of Discourse: Essays in Cultural Criticism* (Baltimore, Maryland: Johns Hopkins University Press, 1978), p. 122.
22. McHale, p. 90.
23. Doris Lessing, *The Fifth Child* (New York: Vintage, 1989), p. 22.
24. Ibid., p. 13.
25. Ibid., p. 22.
26. Angela Carter, *Shaking a Leg: Collected Journalism and Writings* (London: Vintage, 1998), p. 162.
27. Ibid., p. 232.
28. Graham Swift, *Waterland* (London: Picador, 2008), p. 77.
29. Ibid., p. 77.
30. Ibid., p. 240.
31. Martha Tuck Rozett, *Constructing a World: Shakespeare's England and the New Historical Fiction* (Albany: SUNY Press, 2003), p. 2.
32. David Edgerton, *Science, Technology and the British Industrial 'Decline', 1870–1970* (Cambridge: Cambridge University Press, 1996), p. 3.
33. W. D. Rubinstein, *Capitalism, Culture and Economic Decline in Britain, 1750–1990* (London: Routledge, 2015), p. 24.
34. Andrew Gamble, 'Theories and Explanations of British Decline' in *Rethinking British Decline*, ed. Richard English and Michael Kenny (Basingstoke: Macmillan, 2000), p. 3.
35. Supple, p. 9.

36. David James, 'Decentring Englishness' in *British and Irish Fiction since 1940*, ed. Peter Boxall and Bryan Cheyette (Oxford: Oxford University Press, 2016), p. 435.
37. Kazuo Ishiguro, *The Remains of the Day* (London: Faber & Faber, 2015), p. 122.
38. Kathleen Wall. '*The Remains of the Day* and Its Challenges to Theories of Unreliable Narration', *Journal of Narrative Technique* 24.2 (1994), p. 38.
39. Hutcheon, *Poetics of Postmodernism*, p. 19.
40. Julian Barnes, *England, England* (London: Vintage, 2008), p. 39.
41. Shusha Guppy, 'Julian Barnes, The Art of Fiction No. 165'. *The Paris Review* (Winter 2000), p. 74.
42. Barnes, p. 251, p. 253.
43. Ibid., p. 253.

CHAPTER 3

Postmodern British Fiction and the Postcolonial
Graham MacPhee

Weaponising Uncertainty

How does fiction deal with the history and legacy of colonialism when located in a nation-state that leveraged its empire to gain a privileged position in the postimperial world order? Does postmodernism as a literary practice and a mode of thought offer specific innovations, resources, or insights – or presage particular weaknesses, absences, or pitfalls when it comes to understanding how the United Kingdom has come to terms with its imperial past?

The terms 'postcolonial' and 'postmodern' have had a curiously proximate yet distanced relationship in Britain. They rose to literary and academic prominence at about the same time in the late 1980s, appearing to fuse seamlessly in the writing of Salman Rushdie, who won the Booker of Bookers prize in 1994. Rushdie's influential novels *Midnight's Children* (1981) and *The Satanic Verses* (1988) were widely seen to have mapped the concerns of postmodernist high theory onto the cultural experience of migrants from former colonies and the predicament of cultural identity in the aftermath of decolonisation. For such a prominent theorist as Homi Bhabha, the answer to my opening questions was quite clear: postmodernism was to be 'rename[d]' – or substantiated – 'from the position of the postcolonial'. According to Bhabha, postmodernism was not simply an internal question of 'the failures of logocentrism' (or the pitfalls of understanding language as a reliable expression of external reality) but rather articulated an epochal cultural shift '[d]riven by the subaltern history of the margins of modernity'.[1]

The connection between fiction and postmodern theory was widely influenced by Jean-François Lyotard's short theoretical text *The Postmodern Condition*, first published in English in 1984.[2] Here Lyotard sees Western modernity as having been dominated by 'grand narrative[s]' or 'metanarrative[s]' such as nationalism, human emancipation, Marxism, or the progressive realisation of intellectual speculation itself. He claims that such metanarratives – often called 'master narratives' – are necessarily committed to 'cultural imperialism', 'universality', the 'notion of progress', and the 'project of totalisation', through which they seek to legitimate knowledge and prescribe social 'norms'.³ In contrast, he sees in postmodern culture the emergence of 'the little narrative [*petit récit*]' as a mode of political orientation incommensurable with grand narrative, which he describes as a localised articulation of 'undecidables, the limits of precise control, conflicts characterised by incomplete information, "*fracta*", catastrophes, and pragmatic paradoxes'. Such little or micro-narratives are seen to foster a perpetual dissensus and so are understood by Lyotard to provide an alternative 'idea and practice of justice' to oppose grand narratives and technical systematicity.⁴

Yet at the same time, for many of the key proponents of postcolonial studies based in Britain, such as Benita Parry and Neil Lazarus, the assimilation of postcolonial literature to postmodernism imposed an exclusive cosmopolitan canon that marginalised authors engaged in ongoing struggles within the postcolonial nation or against neocolonial exploitation, especially those not writing in English. Moreover, such a 'postmodern postcolonial' was seen as effectively dissolving historical purchase and political orientation by reducing literary interpretation to the play of signifiers associated with deconstruction.⁵ As postcolonial critics, committed to the critique of imperialism and the neoliberal globalisation it bequeathed, Parry and Lazarus might argue that postmodernism functions to promote Western concerns over genuinely non-Eurocentric cultures and perspectives and to sideline real-world struggles within the neoliberal world system.

The first two decades of the twenty-first century put a new twist on the close but antagonistic relationship between the postmodern and the postcolonial. Despite their apparently entrenched status by the end of the 1990s, both terms quietly fell out of favour in the decades following the US and British invasion of Iraq in 2003. However, their diminished visibility has followed diverging trajectories in the culture wars that have characterised the intellectual dominance of neoliberalism. Postmodernism's epistemological scepticism (although often not named as such) has been weaponised by corporate apologists and the radical right.⁶ Meanwhile, the study of colonialism and its legacies has become the target of 'anti-woke' discourse and university cuts.⁷

A sense of what is at stake for fiction in a British context can be dramatised by taking a brief look at Ian McEwan's 2005 novel *Saturday*.

Set on 15 February 2003, the day of global protest against the impending US and British invasion of Iraq, the novel presses a postmodern hostility towards grand narrative into the service of what might be taken as a postcolonial critique of Western ignorance of the complexities of non-Western societies. As the protagonist, neurosurgeon Henry Perowne, observes the anti-war protestors gathering in London, the melee of people and placards suggests to him a 'cloying self-regard'.[8] 'None of [the demonstrators] . . . even knows much about [Iraq] at all', he muses, noting that while he has 'followed closely' the actions of Saddam Hussein's regime, '[i]t's likely most of them barely registered the massacres in Kurdish Iraq, or in the Shi'ite south'.[9] Postmodern scepticism, it seems, dovetails with an understanding of the gap between Western solipsism and an uncertain world which cannot be reduced to comfortable moral certainties: 'Perowne can't feel, as the marchers probably can, that they have an exclusive hold on moral discernment'.[10] 'It's not a visionary age', he concludes, offering instead the postmodern prescription: 'No more big ideas. The world must improve, if at all, by tiny steps'.[11]

Thus the novel seeks to puncture what might be seen as the certainties of 'metanarrative' – the 'big ideas' and the future pathways they imply: the progressive expansion of international law and justice, say, or a humanistic vision of responsibility and solidarity. Against these, the novel endorses an engagement with the local and palpable – something like Lyotard's 'little narratives' or *petits récits* – as signified by Perowne's unmediated grasp of physiological ailments through his own direct impressions rather than moral frameworks or conceptual schemes. In the denouement, this localised diagnostic aesthesis is explicitly identified with the literary when the villain, Baxter, is disarmed by a reading of Matthew Arnold's poem 'Dover Beach'. And we quickly learn that Baxter's disjointed mental state is due to the medical condition Perowne had earlier diagnosed. Thus, Perowne's untheorised impressionism is identified with postmodern *petit récit* in the shape of what he judges to be the poem's localised 'plea to be true to one another' in the face of its rejection of the 'sea of faith'.[12]

Yet the novel's choreography of local certainty and futural uncertainty trips up. Although Perowne insists we are fated to suffer uncertainty – 'It's a future no one can read'[13] – in extrapolating from genetic code to individual character, Perowne affirms that 'It is written'[14] and that 'Your future is fixed and easily foretold'.[15] In fact, this futural certainty extends beyond the local to the social order with which he identifies: 'He doesn't doubt that in years to come, the [genetic] coding mechanism will be known ... he knows it will come, the secret will be revealed, as long as the scientists and the institutions remain in place.'[16]

The commitment to the local, to the little narratives, is not a neutral or nonideological stance but implies a commitment to *what is*, the status quo of 'institutions' that must 'remain in place'. Equally, although action orientated to achieving different outcomes is cast as the violent projection of knowledge onto a future that is unknowable, eschewing such action also implies and imposes a quasi-certain future. Where the current social order is structured by hierarchies and inequalities, the absence of consciously directed action means that those hierarchies and inequalities will intensify and multiply themselves, generating a new dispensation that will resemble the present but in more exaggerated forms. Not changing anything doesn't mean nothing changes: it just means that the scope of change is narrowed and locked within the parameters of what already is.

This commitment to a certain social order can be glimpsed across the novel, for example in its unproblematic valorisation of Matthew Arnold's poem, which projects its threatening uncertainty beyond England's shores to the wider world of the non-Western. But it is most evident in Perowne's inaccurate and imperious characterisation of the London demonstration. In fact, at the protest in February 2003 many demonstrators vocally denounced Saddam's human rights abuses but argued that the histories of colonialism and its aftermath suggested that Western military intervention would bring much greater suffering[17] – as indeed was the case.[18] Sadly, under neoliberal globalisation the future is *not so uncertain*.

Postmodernism claims an ethical and political force through its refusal to restrict future possibility within grand narratives, a claim based on the rejection of frameworks said to be anchored in the fixity of 'essence', 'origin', 'authenticity', or 'the real'. Its identification with the postcolonial might be seen simply as a matter of materialising or historically embedding such theoretical claims. But in McEwan's novel, the dissolution of master narrative in favour of extrapolating the certainties of the local becomes a way of evaporating the histories of colonialism, decolonisation, and neoliberal globalisation, and thereby of misrecognising the implication of the contemporary within them.

This leaves us with a different set of questions than we began with. It's not simply about how a British 'postmodern fiction' might align with or embody the 'postcolonial'; but rather, about how fiction associated with this postimperial polity might inscribe colonial and postcolonial histories so as to reimagine what we take as 'British' and 'postmodern' in ways that allow for *different possible futures*.

To address these questions, I turn to Ngũgĩ wa Thiong'o's *A Grain of Wheat*, first published in 1967. The novel is widely categorised as 'postcolonial fiction' but is not generally seen as 'postmodernist' nor indeed as an example of 'British' literature, given that its author is Kenyan and subsequently chose to write in Gikuyu. In fact, Ngũgĩ was born a British subject in Kenya Colony, and the book was written between 1964 and 1966 when he was studying at the University of Leeds in the north of England – that is, during the decade that saw the publication of many of the groundbreaking early texts of the British and American postmodernist canon. Equally, it exhibits a concern with some of the key issues associated with postmodernism, from intertextuality and the fictionalisation of historical events, through questions of identity and truth, to the problem of narrating collective meaning. The point is not to argue for a redefinition of the novel as either straightforwardly 'postmodernist' or 'British', but to explore a liminal case that interrogates each of these ways of talking about the fiction of the period.

Entwining Master and Micro Narrative

A Grain of Wheat is set in the Gikuyu village of Thabai in the days leading up to the celebration of Kenya's independence from Britain – or *Uhuru* (freedom) in Swahili – on 12 December 1963. However, the novel's present is overshadowed by the events of the 'Kenyan Emergency' (1952–60), the near-genocidal suppression of a popular uprising by the Gikuyu and their allies in the Kenya Land and Freedom Army, which British propaganda called the 'Mau Mau'. The impending Independence Day is troubled in the novel by two converging plotlines: the search for the traitor who handed over the charismatic nationalist fighter Kihika to the British for execution; and the community's attempt to persuade a former inmate of the British detention camps, Mugo, to act as the main speaker for the Uhuru celebrations. The villagers perceive Mugo as the spiritual heir of the nationalist struggle embodied by the dead Kihika because of his silent and apparently stoical withdrawal from everyday village life, which they take as a sign of the moral fortitude engendered by his heroic suffering under British torture. Seen as the latest in an unbroken line of warriors and anticolonial resistance heroes, his presence at the moment of decolonisation is felt to affirm the continuity of Gikuyu culture from the precolonial past into the postcolonial future. Mugo's public confession that he was Kihika's betrayer therefore comes as a shattering blow to the story of national liberation and Gikuyu identity, signalling a deep unease about the political prospects of the new postcolonial state.

At the same time, the collective drama of Uhuru is interlaced with more personal and individualised stories that stretch back through the years of the Emergency to the immediate postwar years, primarily focusing on a number of villagers but also including members of the white colonial administration. Central here is the figure of Kihika's sister, Mumbi, and the two rivals who pursue her, Gikonyo and Karanja. Although Mumbi chooses Gikonyo as her husband, Karanja uses his position as a government collaborator to pressurise her into a single sexual encounter while Gikonyo is in detention, and the resulting child poisons Gikonyo against his wife.

The prominent Kenyan scholar Simon Gikandi translates the novel's narrative construction into the key postmodern concepts of grand narrative and the *petits récits* by way of the terms 'allegory' and 'irony', elements that are seen as operating concurrently through the novel. Allegory is understood as 'the figure that valorises the authority of ideals', specifically in this case the ideals of political and cultural nationalism, and so underpins the 'grand' or 'foundational narrative of postcoloniality'.[19] Irony is understood as 'the figure that calls such ideals into question' and, like postmodernism's micro-narratives, 'deconstruct[s] key allegorical moments in the narrative'.[20] But crucially, Gikandi does not treat these terms as a static opposition but demonstrates how they are implicated in one another and so work together dynamically – how they are in fact always entwined.

Gikandi sees allegory operating in a number of ways through the text: in instances where the narrator or the village community recount the history of resistance against British colonialism and its connection to Gikuyu tradition and beliefs; in the figure of Kihika, both in terms of his own statements and in his meaning for the community; and in the echoes of Gikuyu tradition involved in the naming of key characters: Mugo's name recalls the anti-colonial prophet Mugo wa Kibiro, while the pairing of Mumbi and Gikonyo suggests the legendary parents of the Gikuyu people, Mumbi and Gikuyu.[21] Such moments are ironised, Gikandi argues, through Ngũgĩ's skilful deployment of the novel form, which inhabits a messy world of prosaic experience and employs complex, individualised characterisation that cannot remain penned within the clean lines of allegory's ideals. Most obviously, Mugo's status as hero is undermined by the narrative revelation of his subjective motivations: unhappy, isolated and self-obsessed, he betrays Kihika out of a mixture of weakness, resentment, and selfishness, while his subsequent reticence and supposed stoicism reflect his existential collapse in facing the consequences of his actions. But set against the allegorical dimension of the novel – its figuring of the metanarrative of anticolonial resistance and liberation – this individualised characterisation *takes on a collective and political meaning*. For it is the community that misrecognises Mugo as hero and writes him into the narrative of resistance and liberation as 'the signifier of their authentic temporal destiny'.[22] This means that allegory and irony are not opposed but entwined and dependent on one another. As Gikandi writes, through national allegory 'the act of narration [functions] as the process by which our knowledge of the colonial past is established as a precondition for establishing a postcolonial future';[23] but at the same time the ironisation of national allegory shows 'that the narrative of the future' is always 'haunted by repressed histories'.[24] Irony does not erase allegory so much as modulate, reinterpret, and renew it.

Crucially, then, Gikandi sees in Ngũgĩ's novel a different way of reading the relationship between master and micro narrative. Although novelistic characterisation and plot work to ironise allegory, this does not mean that the aspiration for national liberation – 'the great historic promise of nationalism'[25] – is rejected. Rather, irony *sustains* the promise of national liberation by acknowledging that the historical reality of decolonisation has fallen far short, producing instead 'cultures and subjects ... held hostage to the colonial past they work so hard to transcend'.[26] 'Ironizing history does not abrogate it',[27] Gikandi writes, arguing that 'the purpose of irony' for Ngũgĩ 'is to secure the allegorical narrative of national independence at a time when its ideals are threatened at their foundations'.[28]

In the remaining part of this chapter, I seek to extend and develop Gikandi's insight – that *A Grain of Wheat* offers a different way of configuring the relationship between master and micro narrative in the light of colonialism's historical legacy. This reading teases out the historical shifts in late imperial ideology figured by the novel in its central British character, John Thompson. But it also reveals a wider potential for narrative in the pivotal role of the most prominent female African character, Mumbi. Taking these two figures together helps us to see how the novel's reconfiguration of postmodern concepts emerges from the historical predicament of the end of empire *and* the dynamics of anticolonial resistance.

Unmastering Imperial Ideology

A key step in mapping the postcolonial onto the postmodern has involved identifying the continuity of imperial ideology as a master narrative of progress, taking shape in the eighteenth and nineteenth centuries as the discourse of the 'civilising mission' and persisting through the period of decolonisation to underpin the cultural nationalism of the postcolonial nation.[29] In Kwame Anthony Appiah's words, what joins the '*post-*' of postcolonialism to 'that of postmodernism' is that both 'challeng[e] earlier legitimating narratives' – of imperial rule and anticolonial nationalism as well as logocentrism.[30]

The 'civilising mission' was a widely held set of assumptions in Europe that justified empire as a project of 'civilising' non-European populations judged to be more 'primitive' in terms of culture, moral values, religious beliefs, norms of behaviour, and intellectual achievement. It implies a linear grand narrative of civilisational development: in its British iteration, the pinnacle or normative endpoint was occupied by 'British civilisation', while non-European cultures were ranked according to their supposed proximity to or distance from the British model. This vision implies a single line of progress for all cultures, which were expected to ascend a kind of civilisational ladder from the depths of 'savagery' to the heights of intellectual sophistication, aesthetic refinement, and moral cultivation.[31] Imperial control over other societies was justified as a form of tutelage: colonial rule was a kind of society-wide 'education' aimed at transforming the 'primitive' into the 'civilised'.[32] That is, the master narrative of empire was – at least as public ideological justification – primarily *cultural*: about the cultivation of human capacities, values, and beliefs, rather than being based on, say, economic advantage, power politics, or national prestige.

However, recent scholarship on British imperial self-understanding tends to complicate this monolithic picture, indicating that belief in the civilising mission had begun to fray by the end of the nineteenth century and, after World War II, was transformed by the new geopolitical realities of US hegemony. It is possible to pick out two pivotal shifts, although these were much messier, more uneven, and less all-encompassing in reality than a schematic summary might suggest.

The first shift involves deemphasising the 'civilising' project in favour of a more pragmatic justification of empire through its capacity to manage cultural differences and maintain geopolitical order. Karuna Mantena shows how in response to major rebellions in India, Jamaica, and elsewhere during the nineteenth century there was an increasing 'repudiation of central assumptions and imperatives underlying the "civilising mission"' by many key ideologues of empire, from Henry Maine in India and Lord Cromer in Egypt to Lord Lugard in sub-Saharan Africa.[33] 'In place of the universalist project of civilisation, which believed at its core in the possibility of assimilating and modernising native peoples', she observes, 'a new emphasis on the potentially insurmountable differences between peoples came to the fore'.[34] The 'collapse of the liberal model and its moral vision' significantly reengineered the master narrative of progress which has retrospectively underpinned the alignment of 'postmodern' and 'postcolonial'.[35] Rather than imposing a linear story of universal progress that 'native' societies were meant to follow, each 'native society' was seen as a discrete 'functional whole' which operated in its own terms.[36] Such societies were not to be 'aggressively modernised' but instead 'inserted into the institutional dynamics of imperial power'.[37] That is, imperial legitimation depended less on a grand narrative of *cultural superiority* – even if it still lurked in the background – and more on a localised appeal to 'facts on the ground', the effective management of culturally divergent societies. The master narrative of 'civilisation' was supplemented by a mastery of local certainties, the pragmatic capacity to negotiate micro-narratives of cultural difference within an over-arching geopolitical order.

Mantena's account helps us to understand a second, startlingly rapid ideological shift which occurred in the late colonial period after World War II, when US global dominance incorporated European imperial structures whilst maintaining the new rhetoric and institutions of international law. With the emergence of powerful national liberation movements across the colonial world and the defeat of Nazism, the 'civilising mission' and the claims for racial superiority which it had enabled were simply no longer tenable. As Suke Wolton describes it, this period saw the emergence of a syncretic Anglo-American discourse that sought to establish 'a new moral language to express legitimate authority' without appealing to 'the language of white race superiority'.[38] Instead, 'control and administration' were authorised by 'a new language of development'.[39]

The postwar discourse of 'development' introduced an alternative blanket characterization better able to incorporate cultural difference (albeit in decidedly limited ways): namely, a conception of progress based not on cultural 'advancement' but on acceptance of 'Free World' economic, financial, legal, and bureaucratic institutions. Non-European societies were no longer to 'evolve' over time under European tutelage, so that one day in the distant future they would *become* modern. Rather, the achievement of modernity was a matter of acceding to institutions judged to be modern, that is to say, compatible with a globalising American capitalism. All societies were *potentially* modern *right now*, regardless of (at least some) cultural differences – so long as they accepted Western institutions and insertion into the US-led world system.

In British terms, this meant that those colonial populations that adopted the transitional institutions introduced during the late colonial period were judged to be modern – to be at least for bureaucratic purposes functionally 'British'. As Wolton explains, although never fully implemented, 'the new plan was that colonial people would receive the same assistance that British people were about to receive with the building of the new welfare state' since, at least on the level of public policy, all British subjects were now conceived of as the same.[40] But this also meant that instances of non-comformity, resistance, or rebellion were no longer to be registered according to the metanarrative of civilisation: as the expression of evolutionary cultural differences, of an inherent or residual 'savagery' that was understandable, predictable, and negotiable, if dangerous. Rather, such expressions signified an internal rupture *within* the simultaneous modernity of Britishness itself, a threat that was as unknowable and unpredictable as it was unnegotiable. As British subjects, rebels were no longer 'savages' but had become, in the official discourse of the Emergency, *terrorists*.

No More Big Ideas . . . and Terror

The implications of this ideological history are subtly dramatised in *A Grain of Wheat*'s figuring of its central British character, John Thompson. Formerly the up-and-coming District Officer responsible for Kihika's execution, his career has crashed as a result of his involvement in the events at Rira Camp, the novel's thinly veiled rendering of the historical Hola Camp. On 3 March 1959, eleven detainees at Hola were beaten to death and elaborate attempts at a cover-up were subsequently exposed at the inquest. After persistent questioning in the British House of Commons, the killings and the cover-up both received international media attention, and the name of Hola briefly became a byword for what were perceived in mainstream British public opinion as the 'excesses' of colonial rule in Africa.[41]

The novel's account of Thompson's intellectual trajectory offers a shrewd assessment of late colonial ideology. At Oxford Thompson had become enthused by the discourse of the 'civilising mission' – or the 'British Mission in the World' as he calls it – which he identifies with the spreading of 'the three principles basic to the Western Mind: i.e. the principle of Reason, of Order and of Measure'. But he subsequently undergoes a moment of epiphany: 'In a flash' he makes a 'great discovery' which reveals to him Britain's future global destiny. On the strength of meeting two elite, Western-educated Africans, Thompson concludes they are 'no different from the British': 'Where was the irrationality, inconsistency and superstition so characteristic of the African and Oriental races?'[42] Translated into the language of individual disposition or 'attitude', the myriad complexity of the world becomes neatly resolvable into the certainty of the local: 'to be English', Thompson now believes, 'was basically an attitude of mind: it was a way of looking at life, at human relationships, at the just ordering of human society'.[43] And because shared, this localised certainty can then be scaled up to the geopolitical: his 'great moral idea' is to '[t]ransform the British Empire into one nation', a single globe-spanning polity 'embracing peoples of all colours and creeds, based on the just proposition that all men were created equal'.[44] Reduced to Thompson's own 'attitude of mind' – and significantly, echoing the individualised language of the United States' Declaration of Independence – there's no need to appeal to grand narratives of civilisation or insurmountable cultural differences: colonial subjects are already British, already modern, and already share 'our' social and political aspirations – if only they knew it.

Superficially Thompson's 'postimperial' aesthesis may sound benign, ostensibly swapping the master narrative of cultural superiority for an acceptance of the palpable and immediately felt certainties of the local. But although invested in immediacy, his vision depends on the normativity generated by past paradigms of progress – even while this normativity is submerged in the banality of the local as the intuitive British 'attitude of mind'.[45] The effect of this collapsing and conflating of scales – of local and global, particular and universal, master and micro – is to reduce the world to the coordinates of banal consciousness ('attitude of mind') while grossly inflating that consciousness so as to become normative for everyone.

Ngũgĩ's novel is painfully aware of the terrifying consequences of this particular configuration of master and micro narrative. The anticolonial resistance that pervades the novel demonstrates that not all colonial people behave as 'modern British subjects' are supposed to, nor do they share Thompson's solipsistic vision. 'Was it not possible', Thompson muses, 'to reorientate people into this way of life?'[46] The Emergency regime in Kenya did indeed hit upon such a method of 'reorientation'. In the massive network of detention camps known euphemistically as the 'pipeline', detainees were broken down physically and mentally through hard labour, summary beatings, and the most appalling torture, and so forced to renounce the collective politics of anti-imperial resistance.[47]

Thompson is haunted by the memory of his experience at Rira, the fictionalised Hola Camp, but in a sense that is precisely limited. He is not troubled by the ghosts of the dead, for guilt would require a sense of his own responsibility for others: in his mind the extrajudicial killings are rendered simply as 'a little beating and eleven detainees died'.[48] What haunts him rather is the always imminent collapse of his own 'dignity'.[49] His sense of self is sustained by the prestige and authority of a militarised power structure, and so is intensely vulnerable because always at the mercy of its changing strategic and tactical priorities. Inhabiting an inflated subjectivity whose ambition is to get 'to the top',[50] Thompson struggles throughout the novel to suppress the painful awareness that he 'might not be indispensable after all'.[51] The combination of exorbitant ambition and gnawing vulnerability blots out the world around him, rendering him incapable of communicating with his wife, Margery – and still less, of meaningfully understanding the plight of the African detainees.

Ngũgĩ's portrait of Thompson, it might be said, is remarkably restrained. He is neither a monster nor an archetype; or to borrow from Hannah Arendt's account of Adolf Eichmann, he is 'not Iago and not Macbeth'.[52] Yet in the context of the organised camp system, which was designed by the Emergency regime to break popular resistance by isolating and traumatising the target population, Thompson's failure to register a world beyond his own hypertrophied but fragile subjectivity enables his casual participation in terror.

Local to Global and Back Again: Storytelling, Social Texture, and Switching Scales

However, *A Grain of Wheat* also shows another way that master and micro narratives can be related, one that recognises storytelling's embeddedness in the world and opens up rather than closes down different possible futures. This alternative is embodied in concentrated form in the extended story that Mumbi recounts to Mugo in chapter nine and which prompts him to confess his betrayal publicly, so bringing about the novel's denouement. Mumbi's story weaves together an extraordinary range of different narrative scales: from the intimate history of her own feelings and her relationship with Gikonyo; through her family history, the public execution of her brother Kihika, Karanja's rise as a collaborator, and the moment of their sexual encounter; to the history of the destruction of the village and the collective political aspiration for national liberation and *Uhuru*.

Yet this is not the banal telescoping of scales, the conflation of self and world, displayed by Thompson; for Mumbi's narration is mediated through social texture, the network of affiliations, responsibilities, and duties that bind us to and separate us from our shared world.⁵³ Strikingly, Mumbi's storytelling relates – rather than opposing – public and private, the allegorical and the novelistic, grand narrative and *petits récits*. Speaking of the capacity to 'look into the future and see great things', she recounts how

> It was there . . . when my brother talked. My heart travelled with his words. I dreamt of sacrifice to save so many people. And although sometimes I feared, I wanted those days to come. Even when I got married, the dream did not die. I longed to make my husband happy, yes, but I also prepared to stand by him when the time came . . . If danger came and he fell, he would fall into my arms and I would bring him safely home to myself.⁵⁴

The impact which Mumbi's storytelling has on Mugo helps to underline what is at stake. 'Previously', he relates,

> he had liked to see events in his life as isolated. Things had been fated to happen at different moments. One had no choice in anything . . . He did not, then, tire his mind by trying to connect what went before with what followed after. Numbed, he ran without thinking of the road, its origin or its end.⁵⁵

But now 'Mumbi's story had cracked open his dulled inside and released imprisoned thoughts and feelings'.⁵⁶ Instead of heedlessly running down the road of what is given without thought to 'origin or . . . end', this different configuration of narrative possibility enables Mugo to take responsibility – at least in this moment – for his own actions and his place in the world.

Mumbi's localised narratives – of love and despair, acquiescence and resistance – make sense only in the larger narratives of colonial domination and political nationalism. But in turn, her *petits récits* reorder the terms of the grand narratives of Gikuyi identity and postcolonial independence, as the novel makes clear in Gikonyo's final realisation of the need to revise the patriarchal tradition associated with the legendary Mumbi: 'in future he would reckon with her feelings, her thoughts, her desires – a new Mumbi'.⁵⁷ Thus, while the novel questions the singular drive and fixity of metanarrative, it does not reject the connectivity, evaluative capacity, or futural scope of such narrativisation per se. Nor does it place its faith exclusively in *petits récits*, the micro-narratives of the local and the granular. In showing how such local stories make sense only in relation to broader narratives – however revisable and renegotiable they may need to be – the novel gestures to a more complex interplay of narrative genres that exceeds postmodernism's opposition between the grand narrative as ineluctably totalising and the freedom said to lie in *petits récits*.

Beyond Us? Seeing and Unseeing

A Grain of Wheat is significant here because it asks us to rethink the postmodern and the postcolonial together within the aftermath of decolonisation. Kwame Anthony Appiah's claim that the '*post-*' of the postcolonial is 'like that of postmodernism' because it 'challenges earlier legitimating narratives' begs the question as to whether those legitimating narratives were, in the period of decolonisation, still organised through such a stark opposition between master and micro narrative.[58] And here the novel's neglected British dimension becomes important. If we follow Mantena's account of the 'collapse of the liberal model and its moral vision'[59] and the consequent complication of the legitimating narratives of global authority traced by Wolton, then the enormous wager placed upon the deconstructive disruption of the coherence and unity of grand narrative may prove to have been dangerously misplaced. In fusing the postmodern and the postcolonial, the tendency has been to homogenise and unify Western discourse retrospectively on the model of the universality and perdurance of law. But as Hannah Arendt notes ironically, '[w]hen Europe in all earnest began to prescribe its "laws" to all other continents, it so happened that she herself had already lost her belief in them'. As the novel demonstrates, Britain not only exported the discourses of civilisation and race but also – *under the impact of anticolonial resistance* – what Arendt terms 'its processes of disintegration'.[60] Moreover, the novel demonstrates that different narrative possibilities become available in the process of decolonisation, potentials that cannot be hermetically defined as 'British', but which emerge through the plurality engendered by empire.

These insights are not merely historical but bear on the contemporary if we attend to the way in which narrative organises perception. As the narrative voice of *A Grain of Wheat* presciently asks, 'Why ... did the incident at Rira camp capture the imagination of the world? For there were other camps, bigger, scattered all over Kenya, from the Manda Islands in the Indian Ocean to the Magata Islands in Lake Victoria'.[61] Late colonial violence, this question implies, was made amenable to Western opinion not so much through the unifying vista of the discourse of civilisation, but by a localisation and fragmentation of vision that occluded the systematicity of the camp regime within a new configuration of global authority – as much by the micro-narrative of a single excess easily rectified as by the master narrative of Western superiority. Without narrative connection, particulars do not tell 'little stories' that are liberatory or ethically responsible but rather counsel resignation to the unequal disposition of power and resources bequeathed by empire.⁶² In McEwan's *Saturday* this reduction of perception to the scope of micro-narrative returns: 'No more big ideas'.⁶³ Yet the invasion of Iraq was not primarily sold to the British public through grand narratives and 'big ideas', but by way of immediacy – the evidence that, apparently, we could see right before our eyes.

Notes

1. Homi Bhabha, *The Location of Culture* (London: Routledge, 2004), p. 252.
2. Jean-François Lyotard, *The Postmodern Condition: A Report on Knowledge* (Manchester: Manchester University Press, 1984).
3. Ibid., p. 27, p. 30, p. 34, pp. 30–31.
4. Ibid., p. 60, p. 65, p. 66.
5. See for example Benita Parry, 'Problems in Current Theories of Colonial Discourse', *Oxford Literary Review* 9.1 (1987), pp. 27–58; and Neil Lazarus, 'Doubting the New World Order: Marxism and Postmodernist Social Theory', *Differences* 3.3 (1991), pp. 94–138.
6. See Erik M. Conway and Naomi Oreskes, *Merchants of Doubt: How a Handful of Scientists Obscured the Truth on Issues from Tobacco Smoke to Global Warming* (London: Bloomsbury, 2012); and Ruth Wodak, *The Politics of Fear: What Right-Wing Populist Discourses Mean* (London: Sage, 2020).
7. See Alan Lester, 'The British Empire in the Culture War: Nigel Biggar's *Colonialism: A Moral Reckoning*', *Journal of Imperial and Commonwealth History* 51.4 (2023), pp. 763–95; and 'The History of Africa and the African Diaspora at the University of Chichester', *Royal Historical Society* (12 September 2023), https://royalhistsoc.org/the-history-of-africa-and-the-african-diaspora-at-the-university-of-chichester/.
8. Ian McEwan, *Saturday* (New York: Anchor, 2005) p. 71. For a more detailed reading of the novel, see Graham MacPhee, *Postwar British Literature and Postcolonial Studies* (Edinburgh: Edinburgh University Press, 2011), pp. 158–61.
9. Ibid., p. 72.
10. Ibid., p. 73.
11. Ibid., p. 74.
12. Ibid., p. 230.
13. Ibid., p. 147.
14. Ibid., p. 217.
15. Ibid., p. 94.
16. Ibid., pp. 262–3.
17. See Dieter Rucht and Joris Verhulst, 'The Framing of Opposition to the War on Iraq' in *The World Says No to War: Demonstrations Against the War on Iraq*, ed. Stefan Walgrave and Dieter Rucht (Minneapolis: University of Minnesota Press, 2010), pp. 241–2, 249; and 'Could War Save the Iraqi People?' *Guardian*, 18 August 2002, www.theguardian.com/news/2002/aug/18/letters.iraq. Photographs of the demonstration show a visible Kurdish

contingent: see Paul Doyle, 'Stop the War in Iraq Demo, London, UK. 15 February 2003', Alamy (image D8R15T, 2003), www.alamy.com/stock-ph oto-stop-the-war-in-iraq-demo-london-uk-15-february-2003–57054196.html.
18. Neta C. Crawford, *Blood and Treasure: United States Budgetary Costs and Human Costs of Twenty Years of War in Iraq and Syria, 2003–2023* (Providence, Rhode Island: Watson Institute, 2023), pp. 1–2.
19. Simon Gikandi, *Ngugi wa Thiongo* (Cambridge University Press, 2000), pp. 107, 119.
20. Ibid., p. 107, p. 110.
21. Brendon Nicholls, *Ngũgĩ wa Thiongo, Gender, and the Ethics of Postcolonial Reading* (London: Routledge, 2016), pp. 101–2.
22. Gikandi, *Ngũgĩ*, p. 110.
23. Ibid., p. 121.
24. Ibid., p. 117.
25. Ibid., p. 101.
26. Ibid., p. 117.
27. Ibid., p. 111.
28. Ibid., p. 112.
29. Bhabha, *Location*, pp. 137, 138, 201.
30. Kwame Anthony Appiah, 'Is the Post- in Postmodernism the Post- in Postcolonial?', *Critical Inquiry* 17 (1991), p. 353. For an alternative account from around this time, see Sumit Sarkar, 'Post-Modernism and the Writing of History', *Studies in History* 15.2 (1999), pp. 293–322.
31. See Edward Burnett Tylor, *Primitive Culture: Researches into the Development of Mythology, Philosophy, Religion, Language, Art, and Custom* (London: Murray [1871] 1920), pp. 21–33.
32. Thomas Metcalf, *Ideologies of the Raj* (Cambridge University Press, 1995), pp. 29–33.
33. Karuna Mantena, *Alibis of Empire: Henry Maine and the Ends of Liberal Imperialism* (Princeton University Press, 2010), p. 2, p. 7.
34. Ibid., pp. 17–18.
35. Ibid., p. 12.
36. Ibid., p. 3.
37. Ibid., p. 2.
38. Suke Wolton, *Lord Hailey, the Colonial Office, and the Politics of Race and Empire in the Second World War: The Loss of White Prestige* (London: Palgrave, 2000), pp. 146, 153.
39. Ibid., p. 146.
40. Ibid., p. 153.
41. Richard Toye, 'Arguing About Hola Camp: The Rhetorical Consequences of a Colonial Massacre', in Martin Thomas and Richard Toye, *Rhetorics of Empire: Languages of Colonial Conflict after 1900* (Manchester University Press, 2017), p. 187. For a fuller account of the deception and propaganda surrounding the camp system in Kenya, see Aoife Duffy, 'Legacies of British

Colonial Violence: Viewing Kenyan Detention Camps through the Hanslope Disclosure', *Law and History Review* 33.3 (2015), pp. 489–542.
42. Ngũgĩ wa Thiongo, *A Grain of Wheat* (London: Penguin, 2002), p. 52.
43. Ibid., p. 53.
44. Ibid., pp. 52–3.
45. Ibid., p. 53.
46. Ibid., p. 53.
47. See Caroline Elkins, *Imperial Reckoning: The Untold Story of Britain's Gulag in Kenya* (New York: Henry Holt, 2005) and David Anderson, *Histories of the Hanged: The Dirty War in Kenya and the End of Empire* (New York: Norton, 2005).
48. Ngũgĩ, *A Grain of Wheat*, p. 46.
49. Ibid., p. 42.
50. Ibid., p. 55.
51. Ibid., p. 48.
52. Hannah Arendt, *Eichmann in Jerusalem: A Report on the Banality of Evil* (New York: Viking, 1964), p. 287. See Graham MacPhee, 'Escape from Responsibility: Ideology and Storytelling in Arendt's *The Origins of Totalitarianism* and Ishiguro's *The Remains of the Day*', *College Literature* 38.1 (2011), pp. 176–201.
53. See Hannah Arendt, *The Origins of Totalitarianism* (San Diego: Harcourt Brace, 1973), p. 293.
54. Ngũgĩ, *A Grain of Wheat*, p. 132.
55. Ibid., p. 167.
56. Ibid., p. 167.
57. Ibid., p. 243.
58. Appiah, 'Is the Post-?', p. 353.
59. Mantena, *Alibis*, p. 121.
60. Hannah Arendt, 'Karl Jaspers: Citizen of the World?' in *Men in Dark Times* (New York: Harvest, 1968), p. 82.
61. Ngũgĩ, *A Grain of Wheat*, p. 127.
62. See Gillian Rose, *Mourning Becomes the Law* (Cambridge: Cambridge University Press, 1996), pp. 5–7.
63. McEwan, *Saturday*, p. 74.

CHAPTER 4

The Geographies of British Postmodern Fiction
Neal Alexander

Space and spatiality assumed a new significance in the era of postmodernity, a significance that is manifest in the cultural forms characteristic of postmodernism. Indeed, we might say that the postmodern condition is premised upon a thoroughgoing alteration in the ways in which space is perceived, experienced, and conceived. According to the geographer David Harvey, postmodernity is best understood in terms of 'an intense phase of time-space compression', ongoing since the 1960s, which has had disruptive effects across all levels of social, economic, and cultural life.[1] Existing social and spatial relations are in the process of reconfiguration as a result of the combined forces of economic globalisation, neo-imperial conflicts, new transport and communications technologies, mass migrations, political devolution, and ecological crisis on a planetary scale.

One consequence of these events has been the revaluation of space as a category of social thought and the corresponding 'spatial turn' in the cultural sphere. Edward Soja argues that the dominance of historicism and its privileging of time and temporality through the nineteenth and early twentieth centuries began to wane by the 1960s, giving way to a more supple and complex understanding of the socio-spatial dialectic, through which social and spatial relations are conceived as 'dialectically inter-reactive, interdependent'.[2] Crucially, whilst Soja hails the reassertion of space in critical social thought, his version of postmodern geography also deconstructs the binary opposition between time and space. Space is not an inert container or backdrop against which temporal events unfold; rather, it is socially produced, 'never primordially given or permanently fixed'.[3] Space is shaped and reshaped by social relations, but it is also what makes such relations possible in the first place. Understanding postmodern spatiality entails thinking time and space together, even as their relative values and expressions in social life are recalibrated. Building on Soja's work, Fredric Jameson argues that space can be considered 'an existential and cultural dominant' for postmodernism and late capitalism, by contrast with its subordinate role in earlier modes of production.[4] And yet Jameson's appraisal of this dominance of space and spatiality in the postmodern condition is deeply ambivalent. For if postmodernism itself entails 'something like a mutation in built space itself' then the 'hyperspace' of postmodernity exceeds our perceptual capacities to map it and to locate ourselves within it, thereby underscoring our fundamental disorientation and disempowerment within the decentred global system of late capitalism to which it corresponds.[5]

This chapter will survey the varied geographies of British postmodern fiction in light of these wider social, historical, and geopolitical contexts. The geographical imagination of British postmodern fiction tends to represent space in terms of events and becoming rather than stasis, emphasising flows of people, energies, and things so that the relationship between identity and location is rendered radically unstable. It also complicates traditional distinctions between the realms of the real and the imagined, the authentic and the simulated. Bertrand Westphal argues that postmodern fiction is characterised by the 'multiplication of visions of reality', chiefly through its invention of parallel or other worlds that challenge any consensus over the meaning of the real.[6] This representational strategy is part of literature's resistance to the effects of determinism, which seeks to reduce or limit the world's capacity for novelty, possibility, fiction. Developing this line of thought further, Robert Tally describes literary texts as 'imaginary maps' engaged in projects of 'literary cartography' that are simultaneously literal and figurative, employing narrative in a dual sense to represent the world and to bring the world into being.[7]

The slippage between real and imagined spaces, or worlds that are at once actual and projected, is particularly evident in postmodern fictions, but it remains a moot point whether such texts are complicit with or critical of the spatial effects of postmodernity. If as Jameson contends, 'the new spatiality implicit in the postmodern' overwhelms our perceptual and cognitive capacities, leaving us fundamentally disorientated, then it is important to ask whether or not postmodern fictions offer any imaginative solutions to the problem of grasping the meshwork of relations and displacements that structure everyday life in late capitalism.[8] In what follows, I will explore the significance of space in British postmodern fiction and describe some of its characteristic, real-and-imagined geographies, focusing in particular upon three kinds of spaces: cities, non-places, and regions. Throughout, I will seek to demonstrate that geography is not merely a prominent theme in British postmodern fictions, but also plays an active role in conditioning these texts' experiments with style, form, and narrative technique.

Real-and-Imagined Places

British postmodern fiction continues and extends modernism's fascination with the city and urban space as a locus of discordant energies and differences. The city is at once a material environment in which to live, work, and move, and a resonant cultural image in its own right, a place constantly bordering on the imaginary or fantastical: a real-and-imagined place. Set during the Napoleonic Wars, Jeanette Winterson's *The Passion* (1987) depicts Venice as an enchanted labyrinth of streets and canals that seem to shape-shift on a daily basis. The reader's guide to this real-and-imagined place is Villanelle, the web-footed daughter of a boatman whose fluid gender and sexuality are in perfect accord with the character of the watery city that is her home. Of course, Villanelle's name – a villanelle is an intricate, nineteen-line poetic form – calls attention to the status of both character and city as textual constructs, and Winterson's lyrical evocation of Venice is also self-consciously metafictional, as Villanelle's meditations make clear: 'In this enchanted city all things seem possible. Time stops. Hearts beat. The laws of the real world are suspended.'[9] Moreover, as the novel's eccentric love story unfolds, real geographical spaces are increasingly perceived in metaphorical terms as psychological or emotional landscapes, 'the cities of the interior that do not lie on any map'.[10]

Something similar might be said of the imaginative voyages that Jordan describes making in Winterson's subsequent novel, *Sexing the Cherry* (1989), which elaborates on the idea of journeys within journeys and worlds within worlds. Jordan is a botanist and explorer, but the stories he tells are not those of British colonial adventure in the New World, instead describing other times and places, 'the hidden life' of his roaming imagination.[11] Jordan's travellers' tales tell of a city in which the words of its citizens persist as clouds or storms of language; a city in which the people live in houses without any floors; a city that is rebuilt in new forms every day; a city that is repeatedly destroyed by the plague of love; and a floating city that has been freed from the laws of gravity. In all of these tales, Winterson's text reveals its debt to Italo Calvino's postmodern novel *Invisible Cities* (1974), in which the explorer Marco Polo describes a series of fabulous and improbable cities that he claims to have visited in his travels.

Where Winterson's representations of space often seem subordinate to her overriding metafictional concern with the nature of story-telling and the power of the creative imagination, a number of her contemporaries examine the relationship between real and imagined places in a more emphatically political manner. Perhaps the strangest and most powerful example is Alasdair Gray's epic *Lanark* (1981), a text that combines elements of social realism, the *Künstlerroman*, science fiction, and the novel of ideas to create a multifaceted vision of the postmodern city. Doubles and doublings proliferate in *Lanark*. One of the text's characteristic effects is to create correspondences between different characters, places, and levels of narrative reality. The novel begins by describing Lanark's arrival in Unthank, a dystopian version of the post-industrial city whose population suffer from a range of disfiguring diseases – dragonhide, mouths, twittering rigour – that are the bodily manifestations of psychological and social illness.[12] Although his initial reaction is to seek to escape from this hellish place, towards the end of the novel Lanark's civic conscience develops in tandem with his understanding of how Unthank is controlled and exploited by the creature, a global 'conspiracy which owns and manipulates everything for profit'.[13]

Embedded within Lanark's narrative is the story of Duncan Thaw, an artist growing up in mid-twentieth-century Glasgow whose preoccupation with the problem of representing a city apparently without imaginative life is a clear example of the novel's metafictional dimension. And yet, Duncan's childhood and adolescence in Glasgow are conveyed, for the most part, in a meticulously observant realist mode that contrasts with the more fantastical, allegorical character of the books featuring Lanark. Formally, Gray's novel frames its realist core with dystopian fantasy, but the numerous parallels and correspondences between Lanark and Thaw, Unthank and Glasgow deconstruct such architectonic oppositions, making it increasingly difficult to distinguish between ego and alter-ego, real places and imagined worlds. What *Lanark* demonstrates with considerable ingenuity is that the material spaces and social structures of the city have a rich and volatile imaginative life, for they both stimulate and are subject to the unconscious desires and fears of their citizens.

The capacity of human desires to produce and imaginatively reconfigure the spaces of the city is given central importance in Angela Carter's *The Infernal Desire Machines of Doctor Hoffman* (1972). Framed as the memoirs of Desiderio, a veteran and hero of 'the Reality War' waged by the poet-physicist Doctor Hoffman against an unnamed South American city, Carter's novel stages an apocalyptic confrontation between the forces of reason and unreason, the Reality Principle and the Pleasure Principle.[14] Hoffman is able to manipulate the fabric of time and space, creating powerful illusions and simulacra by harnessing erotic energies. By unleashing these on the city, he transforms its streets and thoroughfares into an excessive and metamorphic phantasmagoria, a landscape that is minutely responsive to the illicit desires of its beleaguered population: 'Cloud palaces erected themselves then silently toppled to reveal the familiar warehouse beneath them until they were replaced by some fresh audacity. . . . Hardly anything remained the same for more than one second and the city was no longer the conscious production of humanity; it had become the arbitrary realm of dream.'[15]

The city's protector and guardian is the Minister of Determination, whose stolid empiricism renders him immune to the mirages besieging his city; while his nemesis, Doctor Hoffman, is clearly a portrait of the postmodernist author run amok, distorting and refashioning the very nature of reality at will.

Carter's novel is evidently informed by knowledge of psychoanalysis, magic realism, and post-Saussurean linguistics, as well as contemporary theories of simulation and virtual reality. Given Desiderio's anthropomorphic portrait of the colonial city as emphatically commercial, masculine, and bourgeois, the text's Reality War might also be read allegorically as depicting the assault on Western patriarchal capitalism by Second-Wave feminists, left-wing radicals, and postcolonial insurgents. Or, given the inherently mutable, fluid character of the real-and-imagined cityscape, *The Infernal Desire Machines of Doctor Hoffman* might be said to represent the shift in postmodernity from what Manuel Castells calls 'spaces of places' to 'spaces of flows' – flows of capital, commodities, information, and desire.[16]

London Fictions

Carter and Winterson both exemplify something of the outward-looking internationalism characteristic of postmodernism, but the urban imaginary of British postmodern fiction finds its most consistent focus in writing about London. Post-imperial metropolis, world city, central node in the network society of late capitalism: London embodies the new spatiality of postmodernity in its most intense and distinctive forms. At the same time, however, London's dense historical freight and sheer materiality are often thought to be at odds with the deterritorialising forces of postmodern hyper-reality, offering writers a space in which to imagine alternatives to the dominant culture of the present.

One of the most striking features of late-twentieth-century writing about London is the prevalence of a neo-gothic mode in which the city's material and architectural forms are read in terms of their occult significances and mythic resonance. The seminal text in this regard is Iain Sinclair's *Lud Heat* (1975), a hybrid assemblage of prose and verse that depicts the eight churches built in London by Nicholas Hawksmoor (1661–1736) as occult temples facilitating communication between past and present, the living and the dead: 'A sequence of heated incisions through the membranous time-layer.'[17] In Sinclair's text, the design and placement of Hawksmoor's churches on the map of the city implies some alternative way of reading its spatial complexity, a key or code that can be sensed and intuited but remains ultimately ungraspable. *Lud Heat* also posits a tenuous but suggestive connection between the 'unacknowledged magnetism' of Hawksmoor's churches and the sites of famous murders in central London, including those of the Ratcliffe Highway killer and Jack the Ripper.[18]

This macabre thread linking urban space, ecclesiastical architecture, and ritual murder also informs Sinclair's subsequent novel, *White Chappell, Scarlet Tracings* (1987), which explores the topography of the Ripper killings, and Peter Ackroyd's *Hawksmoor* (1985), a gothic murder-mystery that unfolds its narrative across parallel time frames but consistently locates its action in East London. One narrative strand of Ackroyd's novel is voiced by the architect Nicholas Dyer (loosely modelled on Hawksmoor), whose eccentric church-building projects in eighteenth-century London are conceived as attempts to 'fashion a labyrinth where the dead can give voice once more', confirming the city as a counter-Enlightenment 'Capitol of Darknesse'.[19] The novel's other storyline follows DCS Hawksmoor as he investigates a series of murders at the sites of Dyer's churches in late twentieth-century London and pursues a suspect who may or may not be a ghost. Although Sinclair and Ackroyd both manipulate the generic conventions of gothic and crime fiction in a manner that is informed by postmodern pastiche, it is worth noting that their versions of London gothic coincide closely with the transformation of the capital under Thatcherism in the 1980s. Indeed, Roger Luckhurst has argued that contemporary London gothic should be understood not merely as a knowing reprise of familiar tropes and images but rather as symptomatic of 'that curious mix of tyranny and farce that constitutes London governance'.[20] In which case, the emphasis these texts place upon secret histories and hidden patterns embedded in the city's material fabric can be regarded as an oblique response to the dismantling of London's democratic public sphere in the last decades of the twentieth century.

A related theme in recent London fiction examines the intricate interplay of past and present in the capital, figuring the cityscape as a timescape, a palimpsest of overlaid histories and temporalities. For instance, in Sinclair's *White Chappell*, the narrator's journeys through the city on foot convince him that 'the past is a fiction that absorbs us. It needs no passport, turn the corner and it is with you'; and in *Downriver* (1991) the River Thames is imagined as the river of time itself, a flood of events and voices carrying London's history.[21] Probably the most thorough and formally innovative fictional representation of London as a multilayered timescape is Maureen Duffy's *Capital* (1975), which constructs a fragmentary alternative history of the city, from pre-history to the present, from the perspective of its marginalised and displaced citizens. The novel's central protagonist is Meepers, a homeless war veteran and amateur archaeologist to whom London's past is ever-present in the voices, spirits, and material remains of its 'lively unknown dead'.[22] Meepers's alter-ego is an unnamed university lecturer, whose faith in orthodox historical methods and narratives is gradually eroded by his unsettling encounters with Meepers and by his own personal crisis. Woven into this double-stranded narrative of contemporary London is a sequence of short vignettes depicting scenes from the long durée of the city's history, ranging from Stone Age communities hunting in the Thames Valley to Wat Tyler's Peasant Revolt to the after-effects of the Blitz. Most of these sketches or vignettes are presented from the perspective of ordinary citizens, giving an account of history from below, although some are also overtly fictionalised – such as the tale of the flea that brought the Black Death to London, or the depiction of an androgynous King Elizabeth I surveying Thameside.

To an extent, then, *Capital* can be regarded as an example of historiographic metafiction, because it insistently raises 'the question of how we can come to know the past today'.[23] However, the novel's obsessive concern with history and historiography is itself a function of its geographical imagination, its attempt to fashion a polymorphous image of London through time. This is an ambition that is shared by Michael Moorcock's *Mother London* (1988), in which the eccentric 'urban anthropologist' David Mummery compiles a composite narrative of London histories and myths that is informed by his conception of time as 'like a faceted jewel with an infinity of planes and layers, impossible either to map or to contain'.[24]

In the decades following World War II, as the British Empire entered a phase of terminal decline, London was remade as a post-imperial metropolis, its new multiracial and multicultural reality catalysed by the arrival of hundreds of thousands of immigrants from its former colonies. Indeed, post-imperial London exemplifies Homi Bhabha's claim that 'it is the city which provides the space in which emergent identifications and new social movements of the people are played out'.[25] Several British postmodern fictions have sought to depict London's new status as a transnational space for cultural encounters and inter-racial relationships on a Dickensian scale, most notably Salman Rushdie's *The Satanic Verses* (1989) and Zadie Smith's *White Teeth* (2000).

In Rushdie's novel, London is re-shaped and re-imagined by its central immigrant characters, Saladin Chamcha and Gibreel Farishta, as 'ellowen deeowen' and 'Babylondon', a tropicalised space of cultural and linguistic fusions that is constitutively improper.[26] Transit and transformation are the text's dominant metaphors, affecting both characters and the city itself, which is typically figured as metamorphic and unstable – 'the most protean and chameleon of cities'.[27] Rushdie's exuberant magical realism is harnessed to a critique of racism and xenophobia in British society, for the transmogrifications of Saladin – who grows horns and hooves shortly after arriving in England, and is subjected to police brutality – satirically literalise the media perception of immigrants as dangerous monsters. Nonetheless, and in spite of Britain's draconian immigration laws, London is ultimately figured in *The Satanic Verses* as a fundamentally hospitable city, a space that is open to otherness and difference even against its deepest inclinations.

Smith's *White Teeth* shares Rushdie's conception of London as a city fundamentally reconfigured by its diverse immigrant populations but focuses more consistently upon the confused, hybrid identities of its second-generation immigrants and on tensions within the city's multi-ethnic communities. Set largely in Willesden, North London, and taking the unlikely friendship between Archie Jones and Samad Iqbal as its starting point, the novel also tells the inter-linked stories of their children, Irie Jones, Magid and Millat Iqbal, Londoners of Jamaican and Bengali descent respectively, who oscillate between the poles of enthusiastic assimilation to and angry rejection of Western culture. Where Rushdie's guiding metaphors are those of travel and transformation, Smith emphasises 'involvement' and 'multiplicity' as inevitable consequences of London's (post)colonial history of 'occupation and immigration'; in *White Teeth* it is an inescapable ontological fact that 'the world is Many'.[28] However, the novel also seeks to show that Samad's hypocritical obsession with roots and cultural purity and Millat's attraction to the ideology of Islamic

Non-places and Edgelands

According to one line of thought, the most characteristic spaces of postmodernity are not cities but non-places, those affectless zones of transit and consumption – airports, roadways, retail parks – in which we spend an increasing proportion of our lives. If places can be defined as 'relational, historical, and concerned with identity', writes the anthropologist Marc Augé, then non-places are fundamentally anonymous, indistinctive, and predicated on a social relationship that is solitary and contractual: non-places are 'there to be passed through' rather than inhabited.[29] As I have argued, the geography of British postmodern fiction is predominantly urban or metropolitan, with a particular affinity for the public spaces and material fabric of London, but the peculiar spatial properties of non-places assume significance in a number of experimental novels from the 1960s and 1970s.

Christine Brooke-Rose's *Between* (1968) features a protagonist whose job as a simultaneous translator from French to German means that she spends most of her time in airports, hotels, and conference venues, moving restlessly between locations and languages but never really belonging anywhere. The novel's innovative narrative technique, which conveys the character-narrator's fluid consciousness whilst suppressing first-person pronouns, repeats or recycles passages of description and commentary periodically, creating an effect akin to déjà vu or the disorientations of jet lag. Appropriately for a novel about translation, phrases slur together in non-sequiturs that often pass through several European languages, mimicking the distracted, overstimulated boredom of the narrator's thought-stream and underlining her lack of any identity or agency of her own: 'We merely translate other people's ideas, not to mention platitudes, si-mul-ta-né-ment. No one requires us to have any of our own. We live between ideas, nicht wahr, Siegfried?'[30] Brooke-Rose's protagonist is herself a kind of non-place, little more than a blank space through which the words and ideas of others pass to and fro.

A similar condition of in-between-ness and linguistic anarchy is explored in Brigid Brophy's *In Transit* (1969), which features an ambiguously gendered protagonist who has deliberately stranded herself in an airport departure lounge. In part, her reluctance to board her flight is due to the trauma of her parents' deaths in a plane crash; but she also regards the airport as the quintessential space of the twentieth century, for its consumerist cosmopolitanism accords with her own existential condition of transient un-belonging, being at once 'derooted and derouted'.[31] And yet, while Brophy's narrator appears to celebrate such deracination she also diagnoses its morbid symptoms in the 'linguistic leprosy'[32] from she is suffering, a progressive decay of linguistic meaning that is grotesquely figured in terms of the body's physical disintegration.

Probably the most inventive anatomist of the postmodern geography of non-places is J. G. Ballard, whose novels of the 1970s consistently associate those spaces dominated by automobiles – roadways, overpasses, traffic islands, intersections – with the sexualised violence and psychopathology that is latent in consumer capitalist society. In *The Atrocity Exhibition* (1970), for instance, a post-apocalyptic 'landscape of derelict roadways', concrete plazas, and motorway embankments provides a geometrical analogue for its central protagonist's disordered mental state.[33] This striking correspondence between spatial environment and psychology is developed further in *Crash* (1973), where both the phenomenon of the car crash and the 'technological landscape' of urban motorways are conceived as triggers for a perverse kind of eroticism.[34] The novel's obsessive concerns with sex, death, and celebrity culture are embodied in the figure of Vaughan, disgraced scientist and frustrated actor, who dreams of the deaths of movie stars in automobile crashes of his own engineering. The world of *Crash* is characterised by performances and simulations, 'potent confusions of fiction and reality'[35] in which the characters search for ever more extreme ways to escape the terminal boredom of their suburban lives. What is distinctive and unsettling about Ballard's work is the way in which he succeeds in investing the non-places of highways and flyovers with a sinister glamour and aesthetic appeal while also emphasising their role as sites of profound mental disturbance.

Another variation on this theme can be found in *Concrete Island* (1974), in which the architect Robert Maitland suffers a blow-out on an exit lane of the Westway in North-West London and finds himself marooned on a triangular traffic island between three motorways. A modern Crusoe, Maitland repeatedly tries and fails to escape from this derelict, interstitial space, undergoing both physical and psychological changes before seeking to assert his dominion over the island. Although he catches glimpses of the city from the motorway embankment, Maitland comes to recognise that the island itself is a self-contained space 'sealed off from the world around it' – 'an alien planet abandoned by its inhabitants' – and begins to speculate about the unconscious self-destructive impulses that have cut him off from his former life.[36] As in *Crash* and *The Atrocity Exhibition*, *Concrete Island* finds correspondences or analogies between the non-places of postmodernity and the metaphorical terrain of psychopathology, implying that the external world is intricately but obscurely related to the inner spaces of mental life.

In Ballard's texts, the city's historic role as a focal point or centre has dissipated and his characteristic fictional terrain is the edgelands of London's western suburbs, a displacement of attention that is broadly congruent with his interest in the postmodern spatiality of non-places. Although their residential function is at odds with the characteristic role of non-places as zones of transit, suburbs often display something of the anonymity that characterises such spaces, and their status as commuter belts means that they are closely integrated with networks of roads and railway lines. Dominic Head observes that, in the last decades of the twentieth century, suburbia 'has come to represent the intersection of the domestic and the commercial', and is therefore a symbolically important space in the experience of postmodernity, although it has typically been regarded with ambivalence by British novelists.[37]

Something of this ambivalence is apparent in Julian Barnes's *Metroland* (1980), in which the narrator Christopher Lloyd displays an adolescent disdain for the middle-class inertia of suburban Eastwick, with its rituals of gardening, car-washing, and DIY, but is simultaneously reassured by its 'cosy, controlled rootlessness'.[38] As teenage schoolboys, Christopher and his friend Toni affect a cultured, cosmopolitan Francophilia and youthful idealism that regards art as the most important thing in life. However, following a year in Paris after school, Christopher returns to Metroland and finds himself willingly integrated into the comfortable, complacent world of suburban England. Goaded by Toni over his monogamy and bourgeois values, the adult Christopher paraphrases W. H. Auden by denying the social significance of art and therefore his own adolescent beliefs: 'I just don't see that it makes anything happen'.[39] Although Barnes skilfully maintains a degree of ironic distance from Christopher's viewpoint, the novel ends by posing a fairly stark choice between an idealistic (and possibly self-deluding) commitment to art and the guilty pleasures of conformity.

The narrator of Hanif Kureishi's *The Buddha of Suburbia* (1990), Karim Amir, is initially more consistent in his denunciations of the dull monotony of the South London suburbs in which he has grown up. When his parents' marriage breaks down, Karim adopts an 'itinerant' condition that is in tune with the 1970s zeitgeist of 'general drift and idleness' and eventually makes his escape to the metropolitan centre, which he conceives as a place of boundless excitements and possibilities.[40] While working in London as an actor, however, Karim feels culturally disadvantaged and is made newly aware of the class and racial divides within English society, thereby complicating his enthusiastic identification with London and corresponding rejection of his suburban origins. Moreover, in Kureishi's novel the marginal space of suburbia becomes an unlikely but apposite site for the re-making of Englishness in a post-imperial context.

Regional Postmodernisms

Although the geography of British postmodern fiction as I have described it thus far is broadly urban or ex-urban in nature, several important novels turn to rural or regional landscapes in order to examine the relationships between space and time, fiction and history. Indeed, David James argues that regional cultures and landscapes have a significant place in the geographical imagination of contemporary British fiction, which evokes 'the historical density of such localized settings' but resists 'the compulsion to idealize rural integrity' or sentimentalise place.[41]

A good example of what might be called regional postmodernism is Graham Swift's *Waterland* (1983), a novel that is richly engaged with questions of place and environment, but also highly self-conscious about its own textuality and the various discourses it employs. In some respects, *Waterland* is an exemplary historiographic metafiction: its first-person narrator, Tom Crick, is a history teacher preoccupied not just with events from his own past but also with the ways in which history comes to be understood, interpreted, and transmitted. Moreover, events in the narrative present suggest that he is facing not only the end of history – the history department is due to close as a result of Thatcherite educational policies – but also the end of history, as the spectre of nuclear war threatens to deprive Crick's pupils of a future. However, the stories that Crick begins to tell about his adolescence in the Fens of East Anglia ground historical events in a vividly rendered hybrid geography where land and water, people and place, nature and culture are in constant interaction.

Although *Waterland* interrogates the Enlightenment ideal of history as Progress – 'a well-disciplined and unflagging column marching unswervingly into the future' – Crick also offers his own 'humble model for progress' in the recurrent metaphor of land reclamation.[42] Just as the process of historical inquiry is interminable, so the labour of draining and dredging by which the land of the Fens is won back from its 'natural' watery state is acknowledged to be without end. Moreover, in *Waterland* place and geography are more than merely metaphors for historical processes, for they are shown to have a definite shaping influence upon character, action, and identity. The unrelieved flatness of the Fens, with their huge skies and empty horizons, encourage a characteristically phlegmatic temperament in their inhabitants but also predispose them to imagination and superstition, for this is 'a magical, a miraculous land',[43] raised from the flood by human toil, fertile with stories and fictional potential.

An equally ambitious attempt to grasp the historicity of regional places and landscapes through novelistic form is manifest in Adam Thorpe's *Ulverton* (1992), which tells a series of twelve interlocking stories about the customs, legends, and social life of a village in the Berkshire Downs over the course of more than three centuries. Each chapter or section of the novel is written in a different style, deftly mimicking a variety of oral and written forms, including letters, diary entries, legal depositions, the interior monologue of a farm labourer, and a post-production script for a television documentary. This formal and stylistic diversity is matched by the range of human experience that Thorpe seeks to comprehend in the condensed and fragmented narratives he constructs, from the murder of a soldier returned from Cromwell's Irish campaigns to accounts of the Swing Riots in 1830 and a contemporary clash between village residents, conservationists, and a local property developer.

Although the novel's chronological sequence and many cross-references between the individual chapters help to orientate the reader, the overall impression is of turbulent change and upheaval anchored by the continuities of place and geography. And yet, Thorpe is careful to show that Ulverton itself is inevitably subject to the forces of history, even as it retains (or is perceived to retain) its identity as a traditional English village. For instance, in one chapter an 'improving' farmer holds forth on 'the inestimable advantages of enclosing land' and in the next the Lord of Ulverton House announces his more definite plans to 'inclose the commons'; a fire in 1745 destroys much of the old village but provides work for a generation of carpenters; Ulverton was without a blacksmith for nearly thirty years because of the transportation of rioting workers to Van Dieman's Land; and the encroachment of modernity in the form of motor cars and radio during the 1920s means that the village 'is slowly losing its sense of remoteness'.[44] In an ironic metafictional twist, the novel's final chapter features a cameo by local author 'Adam Thorpe' who presents the melding of 'fact' and 'legends' in his stories of village life as a mode of imaginative resistance to the forces of late capitalist 'development' in the countryside.⁴⁵ In Ulverton, then, Thorpe not only situates his fictional history of rural England in a highly realised human and social geography but also effectively conveys a sense of regional places as 'spatio-temporal events' in which a dialectic of continuity and change is always at work.⁴⁶

Conclusion

This chapter has sought to do no more than chart some of the broad contours and significant landmarks in the geography of British postmodern fiction; a more comprehensive survey lies beyond its scope. Indeed, as Henri Lefebvre remarks, 'any search for space in literary texts will find it everywhere and in every guise: enclosed, described, projected, dreamt of, speculated about'.⁴⁷ The problem is particularly acute in the era of postmodernism, however, in which space assumes the role of an existential and cultural dominant. Certainly, British postmodern fiction reveals a rich variety of geographical imaginations in which the new spatiality of the postmodern is at once projected, described, and interrogated. One of the most common ways in which this occurs is through the creation and exploration of spaces in which the borders between reality and imagination, fiction and history are rendered indistinct. Often, such real-and-imagined spaces are part of an emphatically urban imaginary that foregrounds the social and cultural significance of cities, whether actual or invented.

Within this shared urban imaginary, London remains an important focus of novelistic attention, though it figures in a variety of disparate incarnations: as a neo-gothic city of spectral presences and absences; a timescape in which divergent histories interact; and a post-imperial cosmopolis reshaped by its populations of first- and second-generation immigrants. For some postmodern British novelists, however, the metropolis is itself peripheral, displaced by the proliferation of nonplaces – airports, roadways, shopping malls – in the new global space of postmodernity. Finally, and in spite of the overwhelmingly urban character of postmodern culture, rural landscapes and regional places remain crucial imaginative geographies for several important postmodern British fictions. In all of the texts discussed in this chapter, however, geography matters not merely as setting, theme, or metaphor, but as a shaping context affecting the ways in which the productive work of fiction itself takes place.

Notes

1. David Harvey, *The Condition of Postmodernity: An Enquiry into the Origins of Cultural Change* (Oxford: Basil Blackwell, 1989), p. 284.
2. Edward W. Soja, *Postmodern Geographies: The Reassertion of Space in Critical Social Theory* (London: Verso, 1989), p. 81.
3. Ibid., p. 122.
4. Fredric Jameson, *Postmodernism; or, The Cultural Logic of Late Capitalism* (London: Verso, 1991), p. 365.
5. Ibid., pp. 38–9.
6. Bertrand Westphal, *Geocriticism: Real and Fictional Spaces*, trans., Robert T. Tally Jr. (New York: Palgrave Macmillan, 2011), p. 35.
7. Robert T. Tally Jr., *Spatiality* (Abingdon: Routledge, 2013), p. 42, p. 46.
8. Fredric Jameson, *The Cultural Turn: Selected Writings on the Postmodern 1983–1998* (London: Verso, 1998), p. 49.
9. Jeanette Winterson, *The Passion* (London: Vintage, 1996), p. 76.
10. Ibid., p. 150.
11. Jeanette Winterson, *Sexing the Cherry* (London: Vintage, 1996), p. 10.
12. In Gray's novel, 'mouths' is a disease that causes supernumerary mouths to appear spontaneously on any part of the sufferer's body.
13. Alasdair Gray, *Lanark: A Life in 4 Books* (Edinburgh: Canongate, 2002), p. 410.
14. Angela Carter, *The Infernal Desire Machines of Doctor Hoffman* (Harmondsworth: Penguin, 1982), p. 27.
15. Ibid., p.18.
16. Manuel Castells, *The Rise of the Network Society*, 2nd ed. (Oxford: Blackwell, 2000), pp. 407–59.
17. Iain Sinclair, *Lud Heat and Suicide Bridge* (London: Granta, 1998), p. 16.
18. Ibid., p. 21.
19. Peter Ackroyd, *Hawksmoor* (London: Abacus, 1986), p. 16, p. 47.
20. Roger Luckhurst, 'The Contemporary London Gothic and the Limits of the "Spectral Turn"', *Textual Practice* 16:3 (2002), p. 536.
21. Iain Sinclair, *White Chappell, Scarlet Tracings* (London: Vintage, 1995), p. 63; Iain Sinclair, *Downriver (Or, The Vessels of Wrath): A Narrative in Twelve Tales* (London: Paladin, 1992), p. 304.
22. Maureen Duffy, *Capital* (London: Harvill, 2001), p. 97.
23. Linda Hutcheon, *The Politics of Postmodernism*, 2nd ed. (Abingdon: Routledge, 2002), p. 44.
24. Michael Moorcock, *Mother London* (London: Simon & Schuster, 2000), p. 5, p. 486.
25. Homi K. Bhabha, *The Location of Culture* (Abingdon: Routledge, 2004), p. 243.
26. Salman Rushdie, *The Satanic Verses* (London: Vintage, 2006), p. 37, p. 459.
27. Ibid., p. 201.
28. Zadie Smith, *White Teeth* (London: Penguin, 2001), p. 439, p. 466.

29. Marc Augé, *Non-places: Introduction to an Anthropology of Supermodernity*, trans., John Howe (London: Verso, 1995), pp. 77–8, p. 104.
30. Christine Brooke-Rose, *Between* (London: Michael Joseph, 1968), p. 19.
31. Brigid Brophy, *In Transit: An Heroi-cyclic Novel* (London: Macdonald, 1969), p. 29.
32. Ibid., p. 11.
33. J. G. Ballard, *The Atrocity Exhibition* (London: Harper Collins, 2001), p. 25.
34. J. G. Ballard, *Crash* (London: Vintage, 1995), p. 48.
35. Ibid., p. 111.
36. J. G. Ballard, *Concrete Island* (London: Harper Collins, 2008), p. 13, p. 149.
37. Dominic Head, *The Cambridge Introduction to British Fiction 1950–2000* (Cambridge: Cambridge University Press, 2002), p. 214.
38. Julian Barnes, *Metroland* (London: Picador, 1990), p. 33.
39. Ibid., p. 167.
40. Hanif Kureishi, *The Buddha of Suburbia* (London: Faber, 1990), p. 94, p. 121.
41. David James, *Contemporary British Fiction and the Artistry of Space: Style, Landscape, Perception* (London: Continuum, 2008), p. 48.
42. Graham Swift, *Waterland* (London: Picador, 1992), p. 135, p. 336.
43. Ibid., p. 116.
44. Adam Thorpe, *Ulverton* (London: Vintage, 1998), p. 49, p. 81, p. 115, p. 175, p. 237.
45. Ibid., p. 381.
46. Doreen Massey, *For Space* (London: Sage, 2005), p. 130.
47. Henri Lefebvre, *The Production of Space*, trans., Donald Nicholson-Smith (Oxford: Blackwell, 1991), p. 15.

CHAPTER 5

Transatlantic Fictions

Stephen J. Burn

When the chair of the Booker prize foundation announced in 2013 that the award would be open to writers from around the world, the frailty of British confidence in their own literature was immediately apparent. The American novel, in particular, cast its shadow over the journalistic debate that followed, and even three years later, the *Guardian* could speculate about how poorly British winners would have fared if national restrictions had never been in place. 'Would Graham Swift's *Last Orders* still have won in 1996, the year David Foster Wallace published *Infinite Jest*? How about Ian McEwan's *Amsterdam*, the year Don DeLillo published *Underworld*?' The answer could only be in the negative, at least in mainstream discussion, because these American works exhibited an intimidating 'level of conceptual and stylistic density that British novelists seldom hazard'.[1] Such simple oppositions are always problematic. Not only do they overlook ambitious British texts – Alasdair Gray's *Lanark*, Jeanette Winterson's *Sexing the Cherry*, Lawrence Norfolk's *Lemprière's Dictionary*, Andrew Crumey's *D'Alembert's Principle*, Steven Hall's *The Raw Shark Texts*, and so on – they also betray a somewhat fanciful sense of exactly how often judges' decisions match later evaluations. After all, however highly critics may now rate *Infinite Jest* and *Underworld*, upon publication neither won the National Book Award, the US's major fiction prize. Nevertheless, the opposition they set up between ambitious US fiction and their tamer British counterparts makes most sense as merely the most recent instalment in the long history of seeing American and British fiction in binary terms. In *Dangerous Pilgrimages* (1995), Malcolm Bradbury traces this history, noting that at different times the poles have been labelled new world versus old, motion versus fixity, and technology versus tradition.[2] Yet the story of British postmodern fiction is less about the persistence of such binaries – whether couched in terms of ambition or history – and more about their dissolution, akin to those traced in other contexts by critics such as Paul Giles, Robert Weisbuch, and by the journal *Symbiosis*.

In much more nuanced fashion, and with appropriate caveats about the danger of erecting rigid categories, the texts that canonised postmodern fiction typically followed Bradbury's pattern, by observing national boundaries and marking local variations on either side of the Atlantic. Patricia Waugh's seminal study, *Metafiction* (1984), for instance, worked a sequence of contrasts between British and American postmodernists that follow from her identification of 'a sliding scale of metafictional practices'. At one end of this scale we have works that suggest that since we each adopt different roles in our everyday lives, our social existence is analogous to that of 'characters "playing roles" within fiction'.[3] This is the most muted metafictional act, because its narrative requirements 'can be naturalized ... to fit realist assumptions'.[4] At the scale's other end are more radical works that entirely undermine realist protocols, denying a 'stable tension between "fiction", "dream", "reality"' and so on, as ontological levels multiply without resolution.[5] Waugh clusters British writers, such as Iris Murdoch and Muriel Spark, at the realist end of the spectrum, where metafictional issues 'can be explored thematically, or through macro-structures like plot and narrative voice'.[6] American postmodernists cleave to the scale's opposite end, with John Barth's novels – where 'the metafictional bones are often left obtruding from a very thin human covering'[7] – providing representative examples. Bran Nicol's later study of postmodern fiction maps a similar opposition, albeit with the additional nuance of noting the paradoxical political freight these self-reflexive strategies carry: 'US fiction of the 1960s and 1970s was more concerned than ever with history and politics, yet tended to express this concern – unlike British fiction which reaffirmed its faith in "social realism" – through non-realist modes.'[8]

While there are inevitably counterexamples that suggest exceedingly close affinities in technique and subject matter on either side of the Atlantic –say Angela Carter's and Robert Coover's recycling of folk- and fairy tale materials – both Waugh and Nicol offer persuasive distinctions within the range of fiction they consider. Yet such accounts have a time stamp that necessarily precludes their engagement with both emerging writers and with the way older writers may refine their aesthetic practices as they age. The long arc of John Barth's career, for instance, is marked by a significant late reformulation of his relationship to the codes of realist fiction. Almost thirty years after Waugh's study appeared, Barth has the author/narrator of *Every Third Thought*, George I. Newett, re-read the *Arabian Nights*, and reflect that he finds himself 'impressed this time less by the Special Effects than by the descriptive details of bejewelled palace gates, ugly faces, merchandise for sale by wily merchants in the bazaar. In a word, *texture*.'[9] Newett is not simply a mouthpiece for Barth's theories, yet – from the 1990s onwards – Barth's work counterbalances its stark 'metafictional bones' or 'special effects', with long stretches of relatively conventional narrative, whose texture is rife with 'descriptive details'. As such, Barth prefigures the shift that many critics have noted in US fiction, toward a variegated postmodernism that more obviously accommodates the forms and themes of 'social realism', and that leaves contemporary writers such as Jonathan Franzen or *Manhattan Beach*-era Jennifer Egan looking more like Spark or Murdoch than their American ancestors. Equally (and for good reasons), these accounts tend to focus on what Brian McHale calls 'postmodernism's "peak" period', the movement's emergence out of its incubatory phase in the 1960s, and into the 70s and 80s.[10] Yet beyond those temporal horizons, the boundaries that divide the Anglo-American axis become increasingly permeable, as the gravitational pull of American creative writing professorships alters the cultural geography of British fiction; as the emergence of a 'special relationship' between the two nations intertwines their social, economic, and political fate; and as rapid advances in communication technologies compress global space and flatten local distinctions. This chapter explores the question of what it means for a British novelist to write a postmodern transatlantic novel in an age where economics, institutional reach, and internet technologies, have profoundly changed the meaning of the oceanic divide. The novelistic consequences of such disruptions become clearer when set against changing conceptions of space in the British novel since the nineteenth century.

Martin Amis and the Changing Spaces of the British Novel

In his *Atlas of the European Novel* (1998), Franco Moretti maps the geography of Jane Austen's novels, to suggest that while the starts and ends of her books rely on a condensed micro-England (no 'Lancashire, the North, the industrial revolution', only 'the much older England celebrated by the "estate poems"'),[11] whatever narrative complication her plots require must come from her heroines' contact with more cosmopolitan zones. The messy middles of these novels, then, push the characters into London, Bath, and the seaside, regions where the closed aristocratic world opens up to currents of empire, trade, and speculation. Here her characters might face 'infatuations, scandals, slanders, seductions, elopements' that are harder to imagine in more secure territories.[12] Moving beyond Moretti's example, similar narrative mechanics can be found in the geography of other British texts. Virginia Woolf's *Mrs Dalloway* (1925), for instance, makes the world even smaller: the plot now concentrates its energies on not just a single city, but a single neighbourhood. The reasons for this increasing contraction are partly technological (the emotionally loaded distance between Longbourn and Pemberley loses its narrative weight after the advent of the motor car), and partly indicate changing fashions (Bath's diminished cultural centrality after the rise of coastal resorts). But they also reflect the way that Woolf substitutes geography for character. The world beyond England's borders is no longer conveyed by location, but by characters who act as geographical units: Peter Walsh, lately returned from India, and Septimus's Smith's Italian wife, Lucrezia, link the novel's world with larger national territories, and as they do so, they bridge the gap between the intimate novelistic world of relationships and both the power of international capital, and violent national histories.

While these brief examples ignore the many canonical British texts that do their extensive narrative business on the European or world stage – *Robinson Crusoe*, *Frankenstein*, *Heart of Darkness*, and so on – they do suggest that a certain kind of British novel depends on plot structures that gravitate towards small geographical spaces that tend to be self-contained, but not self-enclosed: that is, because (as Rushdie's Whisky Sisodia notes in *The Satanic Verses*) so much British 'hiss hiss history happened overseas',[13] the larger world tends always to be present somewhere, though its presence is most strongly felt in the text's margins. In these nineteenth- and twentieth-century examples, British space is dominant, and outsiders move within it. In the wake of a sequence of postwar challenges to simplistic conceptions of Britishness – Windrush, the Suez Crisis, and so on – and in the context of the US's emergence as a global superpower, much British postmodern fiction probes fractures in this model. In many ways, Martin Amis's fifth novel, *Money: A Suicide Note* (1984), is not simply illustrative of such fractures, but is the seminal example of how to narrate Britain's changing global geography for writers who published their first books after postmodernism's peak phase.

On one level, Amis's postmodern narrative strategies sit comfortably within the parameters that Waugh sets for British metafiction. Much of John Self's grim humour, for instance, is generated by rapid-fire dialogue whose miscommunications remind us not simply that we're encountering words rather than 'reality', but also that those words can easily slip free from their contexts. Such slippage is easily visible in a typical exchange early in the book, when Goodney explains to Self why one actress will not be available for his movie:

> 'she was date-raped in Bridgehampton by her weekend therapist'.
> 'Date-raped, huh. What kind of deal is that? What, sort of with bananas and stuff?'[14]

Such routines don't simply allow Amis to explore metafictional issues at the level of plot; they also closely parallel his British ancestors' use of homographs to the same effect. Muriel Spark's early story, 'Miss Pinkerton's Apocalypse' (1955), for instance, hinges on identical confusions when an account of a flying saucer mangles tea sets with foreign territories:

> 'That's just it', said Miss Pinkerton. 'Personally, I've been in china for twenty-three years. I recognized the thing immediately.'
> The reporter scribbled and inquired, 'These flying discs appear frequently in China?'[15]

Yet even as Amis works in the British grain, his novel's 'metafictional bones' protrude in the fashion of Waugh's American postmodernism: the stable ontological boundary between real and fictional, in particular, is blurred as Martin Amis wanders through the book, interacting with the narrator, and offering mini-lectures about the finer points of his use of distance and the book's moral economy even as scenes unfold. Beyond its hybrid of British and American postmodern techniques, critics have more generally tracked the novel's transatlantic investments in various ways, with a growing body of scholarship recording the novel's debt to American fictions by Nabokov (Fordham), Heller and Pynchon (Begley), while other scholars have identified the book's repurposing of Amis's non-fiction on US subjects (Brown, Zahare). Such investigations are prompted not just by what Jon Begley calls Amis's 'acute recognition of the contemporary inadequacy of narratives premised upon national circumscription',[16] but more specifically by Joseph Brooker's insistence that the changing political climate meant 'to talk about Britain in the 1980s *was* to talk about the USA'.[17] At a schematic level, Amis manages the necessity of seeing Britishness dialectically with a stereoscopic novelistic structure that oscillates between London and New York. This effectively asks the chapter to do the work in *Money* that the town and the character-from-overseas perform in Austen and Woolf, respectively. Viewed quantitatively, sequestering the overseas narrative in alternating chapters, rather than in a character who might wander in and out of narrative consciousness, commits roughly half the novel to foreign territories: page count alone, then, marks the dwindling dominance of British space compared to Austen's and Woolf's maps. Viewed qualitatively, it reveals more subtle shifts. First, character-world hierarchies are inverted: overseas locations are no longer compressed and introduced into the central character's world in synecdochal form; instead, the central character is stretched between, and at the mercy of, two different geographies. Second, because the spatial and temporal distances between London and New York are mostly elided by the text's staccato jumps between locations, *Money* tends to present both space and time not as extending in linear sequence, but instead as multiply layered phenomena. The consequences of these shifts lie embedded, like a watermark, in the famous opening to the novel's first chapter:

> As my cab pulled off FDR Drive, somewhere in the early Hundreds, a low-slung Tomahawk full of black guys came sharking out of lane and sloped in fast right across our bows. We banked, and hit a deep welt or grapple-ridge in the road: to the sound of a rifle-shot the cab roof ducked down and smacked me on the core of my head. I really didn't need that, I tell you, with my head and face and back and heart hurting a lot all the time anyway, and still drunk and crazed and ghosted from the plane.[18]

That Self is not master of space, freely moving within and acting upon it, is first signalled by the fact that the paragraph begins and ends with him ceding control of movement through space to a cab and to a plane. In case we miss this design, Amis further unseats the character-world binary by empowering the world around Self: he hits a ridge in the road, and space retaliates, as 'the cab roof . . . smack[s]' him on the head. Simple notions of static space are further complicated by contradictory descriptions. The cab hits what is presumably a raised ridge, but it's described in terms of depth not height; the outside of Self's head is hit, yet is described as its 'core'. The passage's historical invocations map a similarly slippery timeframe: the exemplary opening sentence mingles Roosevelt's long presidency, with the arrival of European settlers in the New World (hence the otherwise incongruent ship imagery), and their encounter with Native Americans (the car named Tomahawk) and slavery's legacy (the 'black guys'). None of these historical resonances and their attendant geographies are ordered: they are simply layered or stacked within the passage. FDR next to the tomahawk; the ocean passage with the city. This unsettling of the static coordinates of realist fiction carries with it something of the 'intense phase of time-space compression' that writers such as David Harvey see as the calling card of postmodern life.[19]

Yet it is the novel's specific engagement with one of the era's evolving network technologies of time-space disruption that provides its distinctive edge.

British Postmodernism in the Age of the Network

Money is not the first British fiction to imagine a network society. When *Self* imagines a future Manhattan developing as an 'inverted skyscraper ... crustscraper, corescrapers, a hundred storeys underground' (199), Amis alludes to a key precursor: E. M. Forster's network vision, *The Machine Stops* (1928), where humanity abandons the earth's surface to live in tiered, identical cells that reach deep into the earth. But *Money* may be one of the first British literary fictions to dramatise emerging internet technologies. The modern internet was born, like *Self*, in the 1960s, and was developed out of the packet-switching technologies at the US government's Advanced Research Projects Agency (ARPA). The outcome of this research project, which went live on 1 September 1969, was the so-called ARPANET: a network of interlinked computers, 'with the first four nodes of the network being established at the University of California, Los Angeles, Stanford Research Institute, University of California, Santa Barbara, and University of Utah'.[20] This decentred, horizontal structure with no single command centre provided, as Castells notes, the 'backbone' for the modern internet's evolution[21] and one of its key principles was to eliminate the geographical barrier of distance. As Pynchon glosses it in *Inherent Vice* (2009), 'it's a network of computers ... all connected by phone lines ... Say there's a file they have and you don't, they'll send it right along at fifty thousand characters per second'.[22]

Whether or not Amis was aware of ARPANET's specific history, part of *Money*'s prescience lies in the way it adopts and adapts comparable networks to narrative ends. The entire plot, in fact, is enabled by interlinked computer networks, since Fielding only has sufficient capital to act as Self's antagonist because he is a hacker, who has raised funds by 'riding the software and the memory circuits of banks and conglomerates'.[23] Similarly – and at an equally seminal moment – when the bell tolls on Self's fantasy existence at the Ashbery, the news of his financial doom is simultaneously an account of the network's hidden hold on his existence:

> all America was interflexed by computer processors whose roots spread ever outward from the trunks of skyscrapers until they looped like a web from city to city, sorting, clearing, holding, okaying, denying, denying. Software

America sprawled on a humming grid of linkup and lockout, with display screens and logic boards of credit ratings, debt profiles.[24]

For all that the book's plot depends upon this technology, references to hacking or a looping network of computers are relatively rare in the book, which perhaps explains why *Money* is rarely listed with other early novels about hacking and proto-internet culture. But what makes this passage particularly exemplary of the novel's vision is that it places the network in adjectival relation to space: this is 'Software America', a land whose geographical coordinates have been reconfigured by their relationship to an expanding, 'humming grid'. As the network overcomes distance, with each node sharing the same status as the others, so individual spaces in Amis's novel become layered with others (as in the book's opening passage), and distances between locales are eliminated (as in the book's rapid shuttling between the UK and US). While the book may include few such explicit references to interlinked computer systems, *Money* registers the network's invisible presence by regularly modifying its references to local and national spaces through descriptions that invoke the circulation of electrical signals: a distraught man in a phonebox prompts Self to ask, 'in the cabled tunnels beneath the street ... how much violence was crackling through New York'; an entire borough is characterised by the presence of 'Manhattan static'; while voices from other places enter only through technology, as foreigners 'speak stereo, radio crackle, interference'.[25]

Money is not necessarily an early form of what critics would later call the network novel – a multimedia assemblage whose narrative sprawls beyond the codex, embracing short films, and snatches of audio, in works such as Richard House's *The Kills* (2013) – but the consequences of its engagement with the logic of the early network are far-reaching. Just as ARPANET was assembled by linking together four discrete computer nodes, so *Money* abandons continuity at the level of the chapter, and Amis instead builds chapters by stringing together a sequence of short takes. These subordinate narrative units are often less instalments in an unfolding story than standalone set pieces (on, say, how 'to get good at fighting' [35–36] or riffs on competing voices in Self's head [107–08]), whose accumulation rather than succession creates a larger structure. As is typical of Amis's work, style is a vector of thematic content, and so, a similar network logic infects Amis's sentences. The opening description of Self's arrival in the US, for example, parallels a network structure of equally linked mainframes in its use of paratactic constructions ('with my head and face and back and heart hurting a lot all the time anyway, and still drunk and crazed and ghosted').

Such stylistic choices are closely linked to the novel's networked treatment of space, and especially movement *through* space. Brooker is surely correct to describe 'the kinetic swoop of Amis' opening sentences' as the signature of the novel's first paragraph, but it is a kinesis that moves to stand still.[26] A sequence of interconnected computers creates not a linear path forward, but a loop, and *Money*'s movements parallel such structures. The book's bustling opening results in Self leaving his taxi cab only to get into it once again; movement between the US and the UK in the novel increasingly narrows to the same set of locations, and the same characters begin to populate both locations (Ossie in London, Selina in New York). 'Though travelling nowhere', Self reflects (inadvertently summing up this pattern), 'I have hurtled'.[27] Again, the book's sentences reflect this paradoxically static movement in their tendency to string together multiple (redundant) descriptions for a single object, rather than progressing to the next part of the sentence. Such looping descriptions account for much of the novel's distinct linguistic richness, but also feed into its sense of restless stillness: and so we're told that cabs feature 'taxi-meters, money-clocks'; that Self is 'made up of time lag, culture shock, zone shift'; and that he is surrounded by 'the inanimate, the touchable world'.[28] The static quality of such descriptions is perhaps even clearer when compared to Amis's next novel, *Time's Arrow* (1991), where the sentences are built around repetitions that tend not toward the artful stasis of *Money*'s accumulating synonyms, but rather add new information in a rhythmic fashion that seems designed to capture the relentless, pulsing flow of time: thus doctor's hands are 'so strong, so clean, so aromatic.'[29]

Money – with its list-like clauses and networked set pieces – conceives of America, then, less as Britain's dialectical opposite and more as the site of an emerging network culture, underwritten by electronic corridors and interlinked computer systems, that was collapsing geographical distances. Even as Self marks local differences between the locations ('I like the sky ... in England ... we don't have one'),[30] the book's deeper logic – which structures its sentences, chapters, and total form – reaches toward a temporal and topographical layering that absorbs rather than heightens national polarities. Amis's hybrid of what critics had labelled distinct strands of British and American postmodern metafiction, then, is paralleled by the novel's thoroughgoing sense that new technologies were collapsing transatlantic distances, and the resonance of the book's attention to networks, and reconsideration of space, can be felt through many later postmodern British fictions whose transatlantic affinities have sometimes been overlooked.

In line with the author's own philosophical and theoretical alliances, for instance, critical discussion of Tom McCarthy's work has understandably drawn its reference points from an avant-garde tradition that is typically European and modernist, casting the author as a 'forensic scientist of modernism'.[31] Yet for all McCarthy's clear engagement with Mann, Marinetti, or Musil, these investments are offset by an equally important interrogation of how a writer may proceed after postmodernism's peak phase, and of how American influences might be negotiated in a fashion that closely parallels *Money*'s example. McCarthy's first novel proper, *Men in Space* (2007), for instance, flags its postmodern ancestry in its opening set-piece by catching a character between 'wall-mounted mirrors'. The 'multiplying scene'[32] created here, of course, echoes the proliferating worlds and ontological levels that Waugh describes as the signature of US postmodern metafictions by Barth, Coover, and Pynchon, yet McCarthy's purpose in this novel is not mere repetition, but rather indicates that US postmodernism is one of the author's starting points. What the novel goes on to explore is the American-born movement's critical commodification in Europe, featuring Nick Boardman, a critic who learns that 'the Czechs really like it if you call something *postmodern*, so he called everything he wrote about postmodern' and Joost van Straten who complains that people 'worship postmodernism without really understanding it.'[33] This project, in itself, aligns McCarthy with David Foster Wallace, an American writer who famously framed his earlier work as a conversation and correction to 'the early postmodern writers'.[34] McCarthy, in fact, wrote one of the first essays about *Infinite Jest* – a short piece exploring Wallace's use of machine code[35] – and subtle references to Wallace's work recur in McCarthy's fiction (that *Satin Island*'s Koob-Sassen project need not be secret because it crept 'under the radar by being boring' seems, for instance, to be a deft nod to Wallace's account of the tax code's worst excesses in *The Pale King*, which remain hidden because 'dullness is actually a much more effective shield than is secrecy') .[36]

Yet while it's possible to document the way that McCarthy's negotiation of postmodernism's legacy has absorbed transatlantic influences (and comparable examples could be traced by substituting Pynchon or Faulkner for Wallace), the extent to which his work parallels *Money*'s technical and thematic approaches to the end of national space are also revealing. At a minor level, the disordered and disorienting spatial coordinates introduced in *Money*'s opening paragraph become the routine structures of McCarthy's world: spaces are described in paradoxical terms (thus the trees in *C* '*rise* straight and *inert*');[37] the material world is empowered to act within the books (so *Remainder*'s most elaborate re-enactment unravels not because of human agency, but because 'matter . . . played a blinder');[38] and a sense of static movement becomes a particular obsession of McCarthy's early fiction (here we have not just *Remainder*'s looping re-enactments, and final flight, but also his first book's many suspended 'men in space'). Vitally, this conception of space is closely connected to a conception of networked geography ('I tried to visualize a grid around the earth, a kind of ribbed wire cage . . . weaving the whole terrain into one smooth, articulated network')[39] that infects character descriptions and shapes novelistic structure. Like *Money*'s characters who speak 'radio crackle', McCarthy's networked personalities become synonymous with the technologies that route and deliver information: *Remainder*'s Naz has something 'whirring back behind his eyes'; even more explicitly, in *C* static is the 'sound of thinking', necks emit 'low-frequency radio waves', and eventually Serge culminates this process when he becomes Pylon Man.[40] While *C* does not erect as rigid a pendulum structure as *Money*, its network vision is also predicated on sealing its geographical units into individual chapters: the first five chapters hover around Versoie; chapter six switches to Kloděbrady; London, France, and eventually Egypt follow in episodic sequence.

Zadie Smith's hybrid transatlantic heritage has been much more widely advertised than McCarthy's, and it's tangible as much in her account of writing under the sign of *Gravity's Rainbow*,[41] as in her ongoing engagement with E. M. Forster. Like Amis and McCarthy, Smith's sense of how changing national boundaries have shaped the novel is bound up with the technologies that underwrite the network society. Her most explicit engagement with 'transatlantic communication',[42] for instance, comes in *The Autograph Man* (2002), where the sound of a dial-up connection (enabling in this scene a message to be relayed from the UK to the US) has become so ubiquitous that it needs no direct introduction: 'Alex presses a button and the box of tricks begins to sing. With its screech. With its *jug jug*. With its dirty-bird song. In a few seconds he will be connected to the world.'[43] The embedded allusion to Eliot's *Waste Land* functions as a deft reminder that transatlantic literary connections not only existed before network technologies, but also involved American-born writers repurposing European sources.

The Autograph Man's vision of transatlantic hybrids is comprehensive, and not solely confined to the literary (the Honey Brown aside evokes the UK-US union between Hugh Grant and Divine Brown), yet as the novel's focus oscillates, like *Money*, between London and New York, its themes and techniques often rehearse elements of US postmodern fiction and its aftermath to tell the story of its British-based characters. The book's expansive play with the limits of the printed page (diagrams, varied fonts, text boxes) and especially the way the text overspills its boundaries to invade the dustjacket and paratext, flags Smith's debt to Dave Eggers and *The Believer* coterie. Small scenes replay key moments in earlier US texts: the narrator's reflection that Rubinfine had 'collected things in his life... placing them carefully between you and death' works a variation on the scene late in DeLillo's *White Noise* (1985), where Gladney works through the 'immensity of things' that have collected in his home, and finds in them 'a mortality';[44] Wallace's famous essay about television, self-consciousness, and U.S. fiction—'E Unibus Pluram' (1993)—is the obvious intertext in the novel's opening discourse on Alex-Li's devotion to 'the TV version' of experience, and his origin in 'this generation who watch themselves',[45] but Wallace's example is also more freely diffused within the text (Smith's two text-box pop quizzes, for instance, directly recall Wallace's short fiction, 'Octet' [1999]).

In other contemporary novels, Amis's model undergoes a global expansion beyond the Anglo-American axis, even as the debt to Amis is more flagrantly flagged. David Mitchell's *Ghostwritten* (1999), for instance, advertises its roots in Amis's work both through shared references (the ninth section of Mitchell's novel, like Amis's ninth novel, is titled 'Night Train') and borrowed narrative conceits (the noncorpum that floats through *Ghostwritten* seems to derive from the 'passenger or parasite' that narrates Amis's *Time's Arrow* [1991]).[46] The oscillating trans-Atlantic architecture of Amis's novel, where each subordinate chapter becomes a container of geographic space, similarly underpins Mitchell's cartographic ambitions with the significant difference that Mitchell's stage is global, rather than Anglo-American. Each of *Ghostwritten*'s chapters deals with a different location (ranging from Okinawa, westwards, toward the plot's culmination – heralded, again, by advanced computer network technology – which is described from New York) that is geographically self-contained, but which carries some narrative freight forward from the previous episode. Mitchell's adaptation of *Money*'s design, then, produces a more distributed model that registers the network's expansion beyond Anglo-American accounts.

Hari Kunzru's *Transmission* (2004) similarly depends upon and expands the now familiar 'transatlantic mode of address',[47] but it does so by coordinating London and the US west coast with the Indian subcontinent. The plot's overall arc initially seems to invoke American templates, with a narrative that moves from a tightly packed conspiracy into entropic loose-ends, recalling the logic of a DeLillo novel, and perhaps specifically revising DeLillo's *Mao II* (1991). In this structure, Kunzru's Arjun Mehta stands in for DeLillo's Bill Gray: but where Gray is a novelist, Mehta is a programmer; where Gray disappears in the Middle East, Mehta vanishes by the US-Mexico border. It may not be a coincidence, then, that in Kunzru's novel, the 'period when there was the most noise in the global system' following Arjun's virus 'has come to be known as Greyday'.[48]

But alongside these American invocations, Kunzru also seems to deliberately replay and revise Amis's *Money*. Both novels unfold around the perpetual expense of a movie that will never be completed; both include a London-based character with an unlikely sounding allegorical name (Kunzru's 'paper millionaire'[49] Guy Swift updates Amis's John Self); and both personify money as an agent in its own right (thus Kunzru: 'Money tends to virtuality. It hovers about in the form of promises and conditionalities').[50] What changes in Kunzru – as in McCarthy and Mitchell – is the prominence the network enjoys in the text. While *Transmission* recalls 'the moneyed eighties' as a reference point,[51] its twenty-first-century landscape is one in which network issues that were mostly submerged structural devices in Amis's text become explicit metaphorical chains in Kunzru: the book begins to propose networked connections between characters as the default order of ordinary life ('Did Guy Swift sense some occult connection with the boy on the bus 30,000 feet below?');[52] it offers the network as a model of the cosmos ('Networked nodes winked out of existence like so many extinguished stars');[53] and subtly notes the way we use the same terminology for computer networks and terrorist cells ('Did [Khan] send him through a network of mujahedin safehouses?').[54] This last instance is particularly representative of the way such networked postmodern fictions emerge entangled in questions of power and subversion as they link together disparate geographies. In a logical outgrowth from *Money*'s mixture of Fielding's illegal hacking and the authoritarian power of the banking network to dictate Self's fate, Kunzru's and Mitchell's networked narratives are inextricably linked to questions of terrorism and control.

As the British postmodern novel, then, has absorbed the energies of an American postmodern fiction that was once deemed its polar opposite, it has done so in a triangulated dialogue with the rise of the network society, and the breakdown in our notions of national boundaries. This does not necessarily mean that the old binaries cannot still be found in either country. In Jonathan Franzen's *The Corrections* (2001), for instance, the transatlantic divide is broached in much the way Woolf managed it: that is, through the presence of the alien within. A 'Famous British Author' named Martin (who seems a pointed caricature of Amis) moves amongst the American characters in a distant and alien fashion that serves to shore up national boundaries, securing notions of American sanity in the face of the pompous British ('I suppose that a country that teaches creationism in its schools . . . may be forgiven for believing that baseball does not derive from cricket').[55] Millennial British postmodern fictions by Kunzru, McCarthy, Mitchell, and Smith, by contrast, have followed Amis's example by moving away from this oppositional model, to instead conceive of British and American national spaces as overlapping zones. With this model comes a layered aesthetic (advertised in the titles to Kunru's and Mitchell's novels) that extends the great postmodern tradition of rewriting, as these twenty-first-century authors revise and repurpose the American and British ancestor texts that helped create their ongoing literary network.

Notes

1. Anthony Cummins, 'Hystopia,' *Guardian*, 16 August 2016, www.theguardian.com/books/2016/aug/16/hystopia-david-means-observer-review.
2. Malcolm Bradbury, *Dangerous Pilgrimages* (London: Secker, 1995), p. 7.
3. Patricia Waugh, *Metafiction: The Theory and Practice of Self-Conscious Fiction* (London: Methuen, 1984), pp. 115–16.
4. Ibid., pp. 115–16.
5. Ibid., p. 137.
6. Ibid., pp. 57–8.
7. Ibid., p. 51.
8. Bran Nicol, *The Cambridge Introduction to Postmodern Fiction* (Cambridge University Press, 2009), p. 72.
9. John Barth, *Every Third Thought* (Berkeley: Counterpoint, 2011), p. 158.
10. Brian McHale, *The Cambridge Introduction to Postmodernism* (Cambridge University Press, 2015), p. 65.
11. Franco Moretti, *Atlas of the European Novel* (London: Verso, 1998), p. 13.
12. Ibid., p. 18.
13. Salman Rushdie, *The Satanic Verses* (London: Vintage, 1988), p. 343.
14. Martin Amis, *Money: A Suicide Note* (Harmondsworth: Penguin, 1984), p. 22.
15. Muriel Spark, *The Complete Short Stories* (London: Penguin, 2001), p. 227.
16. Jon Begley, 'Satirizing the Carnival of Postmodern Capitalism', *Contemporary Literature* 45.1 (2004), p. 80.
17. Joseph Brooker, *Literature of the 1980s* (Edinburgh University Press, 2010), p. 6.
18. Martin Amis, *Money* (London: Penguin, 1985), p. 1.
19. David Harvey, *The Condition of Postmodernity* (Cambridge, Massachusetts: Blackwell, 1989), p. 284.

20. Manuel Castells, *The Rise of the Network Society* (Oxford: Blackwell, 2000), pp. 45–6.
21. Ibid., p. 46.
22. Thomas Pynchon, *Inherent Vice* (New York: Penguin, 2009), p. 53.
23. Amis, *Money*, p. 376.
24. Ibid., p. 350.
25. Ibid., p. 19, p. 98, p. 87.
26. Brooker, *Literature of the 1980s*, p. 50.
27. Amis, *Money*, p. 312.
28. Ibid., p. 5, p. 264, p. 313.
29. Martin Amis, *Time's Arrow* (London: Penguin, 1991), p. 11.
30. Amis, *Money*, p. 19.
31. Justus Nieland, 'Dirty Media: Tom McCarthy and the Afterlife of Modernism', *Modern Fiction Studies* 58.3 (2012), p. 570.
32. Tom McCarthy, *Men in Space* (New York: Vintage, 2012), p. 3.
33. Ibid., p. 36, p. 62.
34. Larry McCaffery, 'An Expanded Interview with David Foster Wallace' in Stephen J. Burn (ed.), *Conversations with David Foster Wallace* (Jackson, Mississippi: University Press of Mississippi, 2012), p. 24.
35. Tom McCarthy, 'Rage Against the Machine (But do it in Machine Code)', *Mute* 9 (1998), pp. 52–3.
36. Tom McCarthy, *Satin Island* (London: Cape, 2015), p. 12; David Foster Wallace, *The Pale King* (New York: Little, 2011), p. 83.
37. Tom McCarthy, *C* (New York: Vintage, 2010), p. 3. Emphasis mine.
38. Tom McCarthy, *Remainder*, p. 282.
39. Ibid., p. 38. *C* similarly begins with a character imagining 'a web around the world', p. 16.
40. McCarthy, *Remainder*, p. 87; McCarthy, *C*, p. 79, p. 143.
41. See Zadie Smith, 'This Is How It Feels to Me' *Guardian* (13 October 2001) www.theguardian.com/books/2001/oct/13/fiction.afghanistan.
42. Zadie Smith, *The Autograph Man* (London: Hamilton, 2002), p. 299.
43. Ibid., p. 153.
44. Ibid., p. 200; Don DeLilllo, *White Noise* (New York: Penguin, 1985), p. 262.
45. Smith, *The Autograph Man*, p. 2.
46. Amis, *Time's Arrow*, p. 8.
47. Hari Kunzru, *Transmission* (London: Penguin, 2004), p. 9.
48. Ibid., p. 271.
49. Ibid., p. 12.
50. Ibid., p. 272.
51. Ibid., p. 170.
52. Ibid., p. 12.
53. Ibid., p. 4.
54. Ibid., p. 292.
55. Jonathan Franzen, *The Corrections* (New York: Farrar, 2001), p. 427.

CHAPTER 6

The Scottish Postmodern Novel?

Stefanie Lehner

About half-way through his recently published 'state-of-the-nation' novel, *Caledonian Road* (2024), Andrew O'Hagan offers the following jibe on postmodernism through his protagonist, the Scottish middle-aged art historian-slash-celebrity intellectual, Campbell Flynn: 'That's what they do, the young, thought Campbell. When they hear something funny they say "that's funny" instead of laughing. Maybe that's what postmodernism was in the end: the naming of emotion, as opposed to having it.'[1]

Despite the notable past tense and sense of ending that is suggested by Campbell's reflections – 'that's what postmodernism *was* in the *end*' – its association with 'the young' nonetheless points towards an after-life: postmodernism lingers on and has become something of a legacy that is passed on from one generation to the next; a legacy that we, as readers, as much as Campbell himself, must contemplate and wrestle with – despite, or rather in the face of, the many proclamations of its end or death. This is, then, what this chapter sets out to do: it aims to unpack this legacy by exploring how the discourse of postmodernism has informed conceptions of Scottish literary fiction since the 1980s, and how and if the novels of writers associated with postmodernism can or should be termed postmodern. In other words, it aims to question the implications and aftermath of associating the two terms that form the title of this chapter – or, to put it simply: what do we talk about when we talk about 'The Scottish Postmodern Novel', and what should we perhaps rather talk about? So, let us start with considering those who initially created this category (for, as we shall see in a moment, it was certainly not the novelists themselves). The study of Scottish literature came to consider the relevance of postmodernism rather belatedly.[2] When it did so, approaches fell into two camps: on the one hand, theories of the postmodern were employed to affirm the existence of a distinctively *Scottish* literary tradition that could be considered as 'always already' postmodern. As Cairns Craig contends: 'The characteristics typical of much postmodernist literature ... fit with key elements of the Scottish literary tradition, and do so from long before the invention of "postmodernism" as a critical term.'³ As examples, Craig traces the influence of Hugh MacDiarmid's use of intertextuality, James MacPherson's forged 'translations' of Ossian, and Walter Scott's quasi-'historiographical metafiction' on contemporary Scottish fiction since the 1980s. On the other hand, the language of the postmodern has been evoked for the exact opposite effect: namely to liberate Scottish literature from such restrictive nationalist paradigms. In *Questioning Scotland* (2004), Eleanor Bell draws on the work of Richard Kearney to propose a postnationalist approach to Scottish culture that is specifically indebted to 'the postmodern critiques of the centre' and, by extension, 'of totalitarianism, colonialism and nationalism'. As Kearney suggests: 'The postmodern theory of power puts the "modern" concept of the nation-state into question.'[4] Resonating with Linda Hutcheon's conceptualisation of the postmodern as fundamentally '*ex-centric*', this approach seems specifically apt to capture the reconfigurations of political power through devolution post-1998.[5]

It is, thus, perhaps not surprising that the notion of 'the Scottish postmodern novel' is specifically associated with the experimental fiction that emerged (at least) two decades prior to devolution, which – preceded by Muriel Spark – includes works by writers such as Iain Banks, Janice Galloway, Alasdair Gray, James Kelman, A.L. Kennedy, Frank Kuppner, Emma Tennant, Alan Warner, and Irvine Welsh, amongst others.[6] The historical emergence of this 'new renaissance' has been generally read as filling the political vacuum that was left in the aftermath of the failed 1979 Devolution referendum and the election of the Thatcherite government that same year that left Scotland in a democratic deficit. The new Scottish fiction, thereby, seemed to function for many as the harbinger of a new confidence that, as Scott Hames notes, worked to sponsor 'a conflation of fiction and democracy which figured the novel ... as Scotland's "real" Parliament prior to, and in some sense leading to, the establishment of Holyrood in 1999'.[7] For instance, in 1998 Christopher Whyte suggested that 'in the absence of an elected political authority, the task of representing the nation has been repeatedly devolved to its writers'.[8] In turn, Craig proclaimed that 'the explosion of writing in Scots after 1984 was effectively a devolution of the word, asserting at the level of culture an independence as yet unachieved at the level of politics'.[9]

It is the formal innovations of these new Scottish fictions – their apparent attack on the traditional (realist) form of the novel – that many critics associate with the postmodern. For Mary McGlynn, for instance, it is Kelman's 'embrace of incompletion and fragments, textual experimentation, pastiche, anti-novel, non-story' that positions his works in 'the territory of the postmodern'.[10] In turn, the play between the real and the fantastic in works such as Gray's *Lanark* (1981) and Banks's *The Bridge* (1986), the interlacing metafictional layers of Spark's oeuvre as well as several of Galloway's and Kennedy's fictions (such as Galloway's *The Trick is to Keep Breathing* (1989) or Kennedy's *The Blue Book* (2011)), alongside the decentred voices in Welsh's *Trainspotting* (1993), would indicate an affinity with the 'ontological dominant' of postmodern fiction, as theorised by Brian McHale.[11] As such, Roel Daamen asserts that the work of this generation of writers is involved in 'creating postmodern ontologies that rigorously treat the world as text'.[12]

However, this chapter suggests that a certain circumspection must be brought to bear when reading the fictions of these above-named writers as endorsing endless layers of textualities, or celebrating a seemingly liberating plurality of identities and voices. Whilst there are certainly some works that more unambiguously embrace a postmodern playfulness – Frank Kuppner's intriguing 'novel of another sort' or 'another sort of novel', *A Concussed History of Scotland* (1990), seems a case in point[13] – many of the more well-known and often-cited examples of a putatively Scottish 'postmodern' tradition that includes Gray, Kelman, Galloway, and Welsh, resist and challenge the ideological underpinnings of this new (meta) discourse. From a post-postmodern perspective, it seems thus necessary to detangle these writers' use of literary strategies, which can be labelled postmodern, from their overall commitment to map the concrete social and economic inequalities and divisions that structure the 'postmodern' world in their works. In other words, this chapter proposes that these novels employ postmodern techniques to counter their own apolitical implications with a quasi 'post'-postmodern awareness. This is the legacy that these putatively 'postmodern' Scottish writers have passed on to the new generation of writers emerging in the twenty-first century, such as Ali Smith, Suhayl Saadi, and Jenni Fagan, amongst others.

To elaborate my argument, let me briefly return to *Caledonian Road*. Whilst the novel's stylistic approach to capturing the *Zeitgeist* of contemporary Britain sits in stark contrast to the experimentalism of writers such as Gray, Kelman, Galloway, and Welsh, and comes closer to what James Wood calls 'hysterical realism',[14] Campbell's above reflection contains a crucial insight with regards to approaching the 'postmodernism' of the Scottish novel. For if it satirises Fredric Jameson's notion about postmodernism's 'waning of affect',[15] it also points to a gap between the subjective human response to a trigger ('having' an emotion) and its linguistic representation ('the naming of emotion'); a gap that seems not apparent to his young interlocutor, the trendy gay Danish artist, Carl Friis. This generational awareness of the difference between a direct response and its narrative substitution is, however, important: for it demarcates a specifically 'post'-postmodern perspective on postmodernism's arguably rather problematic tendency to blur the boundary between the real world and our textual representation of it – in other words, the difference between 'fact' and 'fiction'. This insight echoes the epigraph by John Berger to another potentially postmodern Scottish novel, Ali Smith's *The Accidental* (2005), which is elegantly used by Peter Boxall to trace 'a historical difference between the twentieth and the twenty-first centuries'.[16] This epigraph reads: 'Between the experience of living a normal life at this moment on the planet and the public narratives being offered to give a sense to that life, the empty space, the gap, is enormous.'[17] Indeed, despite its initial appearance of the opposite, postmodernism had become such a 'public' discourse that tried to make sense of the experience of living within what Fredric Jameson famously called the 'cultural logic of late capitalism';[18] an experience that was attempted to be captured, and accompanied, by an aesthetics that supposedly celebrated the emancipatory potentials of effacing the distinction between reality and fiction, history and art. However, as Aijaz Ahmad notes, its ultimate effect is that it 'suppresses the very conditions of intelligibility with which the fundamental facts of our time can be theorized'.[19]

Notably, Campbell's reflections appear when Friis commissions him to write a catalogue essay for his forthcoming exhibition, 'A History of Damaged Arts' – that Campbell simply refers to as 'Ruin Art'.[20] As McHale reminds us, echoing Romanticism's fondness thereof, postmodernism displayed a similar fascination with 'fake ruins'.[21] Friss's show, however, displays not fake ruins but artworks damaged by contemporary historical events – including, as Friss tells his admiring audience, 'a stone plinth from Palmyra ... beautifully pocked and splintered, from recent grenade attacks' as well as 'a battered fragment from Alexander Calder's *Bent Propeller*, which was destroyed at the base of the Twin Towers on 9/11'.[22] Hence, rather than suggesting a postmodern approach to historicism, as suggested by Friis ('Art is always history'),[23] 'Ruin Art' stands as an actual reminder of the way in which history – as an external force – imprints itself on art, literalising Jameson's injunction that 'History is what hurts'.[24] This, I suggest, could be taken as the battle-cry of the works of these putative 'postmodern' Scottish novelists, who remain keenly alert to the difference between reality and fiction, and the ways in which history imprints itself on national, classed, gendered, and racial entities and identities, causing various forms of entrapment, dislocation, and confusion associated with the era: and it is this post-postmodern awareness that writers such as O'Hagan and Smith have inherited and developed in different directions.

Accordingly, this chapter traces the origins of this insight in Gray's *Lanark* (1981) by exploring its resistance to all-entrapping textualities, before considering the recalcitrant politics of Kelman's fictions, Galloway's typographical defiance of dominating discursive practices in *The Trick is to Keep Breathing* (1989), and Welsh's critique of postmodern consumption in *Trainspotting* (1993). The chapter concludes by briefly considering the legacy of these writers on Scottish novels in the new millennium, on the basis of Suhayl Saadi's *Psychoraag* (2004) as an example.

Post-Postmodern Mappings in Alasdair Gray's *Lanark*

Alasdair Gray offers an indicative case in point: while his fictions have been repeatedly read through the lens of the postmodern, he himself furiously resisted being associated with this discourse, which he saw as deliberately obscuring unequal power relations and an intelligible understanding of the social whole, and, thereby, the possibility of historical change:

> Postmodernism happened when landlords, businessmen, brokers and bankers who owned the rest of the world had used new technologies to destroy the power of labour unions. Like owners of earlier empires they felt that history had ended because they and their sort could now dominate the world for ever. . . . Critics called their period postmodern to separate it from the modern world . . . when most creative thinkers believed they could improve their community. Postmodernism had no interest in the future, which they expected to be an amusing arrangement of things they already knew.[25]

This passage appositely captures Jameson's notion of the postmodern 'end of temporality' by evoking such dire prophesies as Francis Fukuyama's *The End of History and the Last Man* (1992), which proclaims that there are no alternatives to capitalism. To some extent, this sombre assessment has a distinct resonance with the apocalyptic dystopia of Gray's monumental *Lanark. A Life in 4 Books* (1981), which was seen as a real watershed for the revival of Scottish fiction.

Split into realist and fantasy sections, *Lanark*'s multi-level Russian-doll structure nests a realist *Künstlerroman* about Duncan Thaw as a young artist in Glasgow (Books 1 and 2) within the fantastical-allegorical adventures of a man called Lanark in the dystopian city of Unthank and its related heterocosms (Books 3 and 4). With a Prologue occurring at the end of Book 3 and an Epilogue in the middle of Book 4, this novel deliberately challenges traditional forms of aesthetic unity in terms of progressing time and plot. When we first encounter Lanark, who functions both as a continuation (in the form of a rebirth) and as a double of Thaw, in the opening Book 3 of *Lanark*, he appears as the embodiment of the postmodern condition: his arrival in Unthank, without a name, memory and thereby sense of identity, time, place, or belonging, via a disorientating train journey, symbolises 'the laceration of the Modern'.[26]

As we read on, it transpires that Lanark is not only entrapped in a seemingly timeless system governed by unintelligible power structures but also in layers of textuality. When Lanark escapes together with Rima from the consumerist nightmare of the 'Institute' they take the 'Emergency Exit 3124', which is the exact order of the novel's books, as we are given to read them. Entering an 'intercalendrial zone', which seems to initially offer a reprieve from the restrictions of the former world, they yet remain entrapped in a system of repetitions that offers no apparent meaningful change.[27] As Craig notes, these textual repetitions have a formal analogue in the way in which the novel is 'being littered with cross-references to other works of literature', which are listed, as well as parodied, in the included 'Index of Plagiarisms' that is part of the novel's ironically-placed premature 'Epilogue'. Desperate to find means to save Unthank and expose the injustices of those in power who seek to destroy it, Lanark enters this chapter, towards the end of the novel, through a door that is marked by this title, where he meets his putative author, Nastler. This 'conjuror', who claims a God-like status, informs Lanark that his apparent reality is made solely out of 'Print', over which he, as a character, has no authority or control.[28] This postmodern power play with different ontological levels is resonant of Spark's fiction: for instance, the protagonist of her earliest novel, *The Comforters* (1957), becomes aware of a typewriter recording her thoughts and wonders 'if a writer on another plane of existence was writing a story about us'.[29]

Gray's endeavour in *Lanark* is however the very opposite to Nastler's apparent postmodern intention of 'seducing a living soul into our printed world and trapping it long enough for us to steal the imaginative energy which gives life to us'.[30] Instead, it is concerned with gesturing to gaps beneath its own textual universe: for instance, some of the references in the 'Index of Plagiarisms' point to chapter numbers outside the range of those of the novel itself, while a footnote recognises the book's dependence on a system of production and manual labour, acknowledging the work of 'the compositors employed by Kingsport Press of Kingsport, Tennessee, to typeset this bloody book'.[31] Furthermore, just as Lanark exposes the limits of Nastler's authorial control over his experience (by revealing that he has a son), the novel itself ends by proclaiming the seemingly authoritative limits of its textual cartographies: 'MY MAPS ARE OUT OF DATE ... IT IS TIME TO GO'.[32] In this, the novel, however, invites us to construct our own mental maps, which might negotiate the gap between our own localised perception and a reality and history that transcends our personal experience, in a manner that can be related to Jameson's concept of 'cognitive mapping'. It is exactly through his self-conscious and deliberate use of such 'postmodern' metafictional strategies that Gray exposes and challenges the confining logic of its ideology, which certainly makes him, as Randall Stevenson astutely puts it, 'a post-postmodernist'.[33]

James Kelman's Anti-postmodern Politics

Such a political commitment is also the hallmark of Kelman's work. Like Gray, Kelman has been called 'an exemplary postmodernist'.[34] Yet, he himself has similarly rejected such associations, which, he suggests, 'just show an ignorance of a broader tradition and a lack of wide learning'.[35] In his controversial Booker prize speech for *How Late It Was, How Late* (1994), he positioned his work in a decolonial as well existential tradition.[36] Comparable but also radically different to Gray's *Lanark*, Kelman's fiction is concerned with mapping the experience of a disruptive and alienating 'postmodern condition' that involves the breakdown of traditional working-class solidarities, and its attendant 'incredulity towards metanarratives'.[37] Exposed to labyrinthine power structures and the inequities of late capitalism, his characters yet 'refuse arrest' (to use the titular pun of Craig's essay on Kelman, 'Resisting Arrest'),[38] as in the example of the struggles of Rab Hines against various officials in *The Busconductor Hines* (1984), or are prone to a potential arrest from the actual 'polis': as in *A Disaffection* (1989) in which Patrick Doyle struggles with his own implication in the British educational system; in *How Late It Was, How Late*, Sammy Samuels wakes up blinded by anonymous state forces; and, in the last pages in *You Have to be Careful in the Land of the Free* (2004), Jeremiah Brown faces a 'stolid' cop on his last evening in 'Uhmerka'.

This resistance to any hierarchical governing structures is extended to the level of the narrative and voice, for instance through Kelman's idiosyncratic use of free indirect discourse in his earlier novels, as demonstrated in the opening of *How Late It Was*:

> Ye wake in a corner and stay there hoping yer body will disappear, the thoughts smothering ye; these thoughts; but ye want to remember and face up to things, just something keeps ye from doing it, why can ye no do it; the words filling yer head: then the other words; there's something wrong; there's something far far wrong; ye're no a good man, ye're just no a good man. Edging back into awareness, of where ye are: here, slumped in this corner, with these thoughts filling ye. And oh christ his back was sore; stiff, and the head pounding. He shivered and hunched up his shoulders, shut his eyes, rubbed into the corners with his fingertips; seeing all kinds of spots and lights. Where in the name of fuck . . .[39]

This passage moves from a distanced self-addressing interior monologue to a stream-of-consciousness to a more objective descriptive third-person position, and ends with the character's utterance, presented without any speech markers – all rendered equally in Glaswegian Scots. Such a narrative and linguistic equality between character and narrator, between thought, narration, and speech, could be considered as creating what McHale terms a 'heterarchy'.[40]

Kelman's post-devolutionary fiction – starting with *Translated Accounts* (2001) – is characterised by a move to a more intense and radical style that tests the limits of interior monologue. As Boxall argues, the narrative immediacy of these later fictions can be said to produce an innovative merging of different subject positions, geographies, and temporalities.[41] Boxall offers an example from *You Have to be Careful*, when Jeremiah recounts some advice given to him by his former boss, acknowledging: 'He said it with his ayn accent.'[42] Translating his boss's 'Uhmerkan' accent into his own 'Skarrish',[43] Jeremiah's admission, however, notably foregrounds the politics of representation underpinning his account: rather than presenting his account as reflective of the situation, and thereby as transparent, he points to the gap between the actual speech of this boss and his own retrospectively edited rendering of it. This, I suggest, dissociates, rather than merges, the identities and speaking positions between himself and his American boss.

Jeremiah's translation resonates with the invisible editorial processes underpinning Kelman's *Translated Accounts*. This 'Novel', as its subtitle asserts, is, as with *You Have to be Careful*, set outside Scotland, in the 'somewhere nowhere' of 'an occupied territory or land where a form of martial law appears in operation'.[44] As several critics note, these accounts defy any discernible narrative perspective nor are they locatable in any recognisable social situation. The deliberate foregrounding of their layered mediation in the 'Preface' – not only are they 'transcribed and/or translated into English, not always by persons native to the tongue' but they have also undergone 'editorial control', albeit inefficiently – has been associated with a postmodern 'self-reflexive textuality'.[45] But rather than getting lost in a textualised universe, Kelman's later fiction is, as much as his former work, marked by its commitment to find new forms of representation to map and thereby ultimately to comprehend and critique the violent forces of History that fracture, dislocate, and harm the speaking subject.[46] As much as his characters refuse to be seen as representatives – as one of the voices in *Translated Accounts* puts it: 'you have me in front of your eyes, representative of my country, you have it here, but I am not representative'[47] – his fictions remind us that, as Sammy tells his self-assigned 'rep' Ally: 'There's a difference between repping somebody and fucking being somebody; know what I'm talking about, being somebody'.[48] In resisting controlling narratives, Kelman's fiction enables the emergence of 'being somebody'– not through a removal from a social context but exactly 'from the very violence that has cloven the subject apart'[49] – whilst, at the same time, remaining careful about the dangers of well-meaning allies, such as Ally, or by extensions, the empty promises of liberating discourses, such as postmodernism, whose representational politics ultimately work to reproduce disempowering power dynamics that are devoid of any subversive potential.

Typographical Resistance in Janice Galloway's *The Trick Is to Keep Breathing*

A comparable concern with the way in which discourses determine, define, and confine the human subject is demonstrated in Galloway's fictions, particularly her 1989 novel, *The Trick is to Keep Breathing*. Her textual and typographic experimentation can be related to Gray and Kelman, but, as Glenda Norquay notes, it also owes much to feminist influences, specifically Hélène Cixous's notion of *écriture feminine*.[50] The ways in which her 'deconstructive texts' foreground fragmentation has been furthermore associated with the postmodern, for instance by Carole Jones who notes how her texts 'proliferate into multiple generic forms that disrupt the surface, undermine unity and closure, and deliberately obstruct the reading process'.[51] However, her seemingly 'playful non-standard typography',[52] which includes a variety of typefaces, words in the margins, lists, excerpts from books and magazines, playscripts, and gaps, as well as blank and unnumbered pages, does not imply an intensification of textuality but instead functions as an astute 'commentary upon the ways in which discursive practices determine the materiality' of her characters' lives.[53]

This is exemplified by the oxymoronically named Joy Stone, the protagonist of *The Trick is to Keep Breathing*, who is caught between competing institutional discourses. In her status as the mistress of her recently deceased lover, Michael, she is denied a place to mourn, which is preserved for his wife. Additionally, her illegitimate role almost causes her eviction from the council house into which she moved with Michael before he died, which carries 'his name. Not mine'.[54] Bombarded with stereotypical definitions of femininity, suggested by the women's magazines she consumes, Joy becomes anorexic-bulimic. Yet, her deliberate refusal to allow food to fill her body can be also seen as a refusal to be 'filled' by the discourses that seek to control and define her. This rejection is extended to the text itself which, as Mary McGlynn suggests, can be read as itself 'ejecting what it cannot hold in'.[55]

In this manner, we can understand the ways in which the cultural discourses that surround her, and seek to control her, are not allowed to invade the narrative, as, for instance is the case in a novel such as Eimear McBride's *A Girl Is a Half-formed Thing* (2013).[56] Instead, Galloway's specific use of typographical innovations keeps such dominating discourses notably apart from Joy's own narrative, which is rendered in a first-person diary-like style. For instance, the playscript format is often used to foreground as well as satirise the unequal power dynamics between herself and such controlling interlocutors as her abusive elder sister Myra who hit her as a child; her ex-boyfriend Paul who told her 'he didn't need me for a thing';[57] her boss Tony who forces her to go out on a date that ends with him raping her; and the male representatives of the medical establishment:

DOCTOR Sit. [Pause] So how are things what's new who are you anyway?
PATIENT I'm tired and I still need somebody to talk to. I need to get less angry about everything. I'm going nuts.
DOCTOR Don't tell me how to do my job. Relax. You can talk to me. I made a double appointment so we can have twenty minutes. Go ahead. I'm listening.
PATIENT What can I say that makes sense in twenty minutes?
DOCTOR Try. You're not trying. You're looking for something that doesn't exist, that's why you're not happy. Look at me. I'm under no illusions. That's why I'm in control.[58]

This dialogue does not represent what was actually said but suggests how Joy imagines this interaction; as such, it points to a fissure beneath the textual surface where her real experience resides, which resists representation but nonetheless emerges through the text's gaps and margins. Some of the most poignant examples of this are in the way in which the text visualises her suicide attempt with a blank space, and when it literally abjects her warning thoughts during the rape scene into the very margins of the page.[59] *The Trick is to Keep Breathing* ends with Joy reclaiming her embodied self through the metaphor of learning to swim as 'A little light fiction.'[60] My reading suggests that this does not suggest postmodern conceptions of subjectivity, as in Jones' reading, but rather must be understood in defiance of the discursive practices that have dominated her life.

Postmodern Consumption in Irvine Welsh's *Trainspotting*

Considered, perhaps, as the key Scottish postmodern text, Irvine Welsh's *Trainspotting* (1993) – and even more so its film adaptation – seems to celebrate a liberating postmodern eclecticism in both form and content. Consisting of a heterogenous interplay of different first person accounts, all narrated in their own voice and idiolect, it has been frequently read as 'a collection of loosely related short stories' rather than a novel.[61] Furthermore, the shifting names of the male characters – from the main character, Mark Renton who is mostly referred to as 'Rents' or 'Rent Boy', to his putative mates: Simon David Williamson is called 'Sick Boy'; Daniel Murphy is known as 'Spud'; and Francis Begbie is, behind his back, named 'Franco', 'the General', and 'the Beggar' – suggest the sense of a plural identity. However, as Aaron Kelly argues, these should be rather read as gesturing to a masculine crisis that stems from a breakdown of traditional patriarchal structures, due to the dismantling of heavy industries and large-scale unemployment in the 1980s under Thatcher. Set in what we now consider the postmodern era, it is thus notable that none of the male characters work; instead they are characterised by what they consume, in particular heroin, which provides 'a telling metaphor for the loss of identity in late capitalist consciousness and the putative pleasures and freedoms of consumer society'.[62] Indeed, their consumer choice – as expressed in Renton's famous declaration 'ah choose no tae choose life' – becomes so all-consuming that it becomes potentially lethal.[63] Indeed, the novel is filled with deaths and funerals, as well as references to the undead.

The characters' entrapment in the meaningless, empty, and static world of postmodernity, in which the narratives of modernity that promise progress and movement are no longer available, is encapsulated by the scene set in Leith Central Station. This former train station is now home to the homeless, and it is here that Renton and Begbie meet Begbie's father who fails to recognise his own son yet tells them to 'keep up the trainspotting mind'.[64] This reference to the novel's title is significant – for while it gestures, on the one hand, to the process of finding a vein when injecting heroin, on the other hand, it references the seemingly futile hobby of watching and cataloguing trains, which yet suggests an attempt of mapping: of trying to make sense of a seemingly meaningless and unintelligible system. This, as Kelly rightly notes, can be extrapolated to an endeavour of making sense of the confusions and dislocations of this era.[65]

If Welsh's novel does not, in contrast to the other novels discussed so far, offer his characters any meaningful resistance to the logic of late capitalism, its critique resides in the way in which the novel's last chapter suddenly switches to a third person narration: it details Renton's decision to rip off his mates and start a new life in Amsterdam. Just as the hierarchical framework implied by the omniscient narrator creates distance from Renton's self-serving embrace of individual opportunism, so, too, are we as readers asked to question the ideology behind his decision. For while the novel itself is devoid of pointing to any historical alternatives, it herein retains its recalcitrance to the all-consuming consumer logic of postmodernism.

(D)evolutionary Legacies: Suhayl Saadi's *Psychoraag*

It is this critical awareness towards controlling (meta)narratives that the new generation of Scottish writers, emerging in the twenty-first century, have inherited. This chapter will conclude by briefly considering Suhayl Saadi's *Psychoraag* (2004), which works as an indicative example: his novel develops the formal, stylistic, orthographic, and typographic experimentations associated with the previous generation of novelists. Described by a reviewer as 'not just *Midnight's Children* meets *Trainspotting*',[66] *Psychoraag* indeed bears imprints of the latter novel through a 'breadcrumb trail of references', as Joseph H. Jackson notes.[67] Furthermore, its reimagining of Glasgow and its hallucinatory merging of realism and fantasy, specifically through a Gothic mode, recalls Gray's *Lanark*, whilst its use of an interrupted interior monologue that combines Glaswegian vernacular with fragments of Arabic, Sanskrit, Farsi, Hindi, Urdu, Punjabi, Gaelic, French, and Spanish – collated in an appended 'Glossary' that also contains translations of its Scots words – evokes Kelman's style. Yet, if its hybrid language use and the fact that it has been proclaimed as the 'first Asian-Scottish novel' seems to suggest an unproblematic embrace of a new, post-devolutionary, and putatively postmodern, Scottish multiculturalism, Jackson argues that the novel rejects the notion of 'a celebratory post-racial harmony'.[68] Instead, it proposes the principle of 'Dreaming. Madness. *Junnune*' as a counter to 'obliquely indicated systems of control', in particular, as Jackson notes, 'the British rational organisation of culture and perpetuation of race'.[69] The novel's structure follows Zaf's last night as a DJ, presenting '*The Show of Madness*'.[70] As he gets more and more lost in spatial and temporal disjunctions, reflections, and memories, the narrative reflects his uncertain positioning – again reminiscent of the epistemological uncertainties in the novels of Gray, Kelman, Galloway, and Welsh. As Zaf tells his listeners: 'thur's nae control oan this last episode ae *The Junnune Show*. Or if thur is, then it's beyond me. Madness, music, life.'[71]

Significantly, the novel ends with Zaf drawing out his previously voiced desire to 'redraw all the maps' in a manner comparable to Gray's demand for an imaginary re-mapping of unintelligible and controlling power-structures in *Lanark*. In *Psychoraag*, Zaf's proposal of 'Piscanthropy' – 'whun we aw turn intae fushes' – signals the demand for a utopian egalitarian identity beyond the demarcations of race: 'feel yer skin stre-e-e-tch and turn *silller*'.[72] As Jackson observes, Zaf's suggestion that this would mean a 'move back up the evolutionary scale ae hings', or, indeed, a move back down the devolutionary scale, situates the novel in a post-devolutionary Scottish context as well as in resistance to 'the imperial teleology of civilisational progress', associated with Spencerian rational thought.[73] Moreover, I propose, it is also indicative of the above-traced legacy of resistance to such self-proclaimed evolutionary narratives as postmodernism, whose vacuous celebration of multiculturalism has only proven to obscure the inequalities of race, class, gender, and nation that are inscribed in the historical experience of Zaf – as much as they inform the works of the generation of the putative Scottish 'postmodern' novelists – or shall we simply call them, in the spirit of Stevenson's designation of this title for Gray, already post-postmodernists?

Notes

1. Andrew O'Hagan, *Caledonian Road* (London: Faber and Faber, 2024), p. 266.
2. See Randall Stevenson, 'A Postmodern Scotland' in *Beyond Scotland: New Contexts for Twentieth Century Scottish Literature*, eds. Gerard Carruthers, David Golde and Alistair Renfrew (Amsterdam: Rodopi, 2004), pp. 209–28.
3. Cairns Craig, 'Beyond Reason: Hume, Seth, Macmurray and Scotland's Postmodernity' in *Scotland in Theory*, eds. Eleanor Bell and Gavin Miller (Amsterdam: Rodopi, 2004), pp. 249–83, p. 251.

4. Richard Kearney, *Postnationalist Ireland: Politics, Literature, Philosophy* (London: Routledge, 1997), p. 61.
5. See Linda Hutcheon, *A Poetics of Postmodernism: History, Theory, Fiction*. London: Routledge, 2000), p. 58.
6. See, for instance, Len Platt, 'Celtic Postmodernism: Scotland and the Break Up of Britain', in *The Cambridge History of Postmodern Literature*, eds. Brian McHale and Len Platt (Cambridge University Press, 2016).
7. Scott Hames, 'The New Scottish Renaissance?' in *The Oxford History of the Novel in English: Volume 7, British and Irish Fiction Since 1940* eds. Peter Boxall and Bryan Cheyette (Oxford: Oxford University Press, 2011), pp. 494–511, p. 495. See also Douglas Gifford, 'Breaking Boundaries: From Modern to Contemporary in Scottish Fiction' in *The Edinburgh History of Scottish Literature, Vol. III*, ed. Ian Brown (Edinburgh University Press, 2006), pp. 237–52, 237.
8. Christopher Whyte, 'Masculinities in Contemporary Scottish Fiction', *Forum for Modern Language Studies* 34.3 (1998), pp. 274–85, p. 284.
9. Cairns Craig, 'Devolving the Scottish Novel in *A Concise Companion to Contemporary British Fiction*, ed. James F. English (Oxford: Blackwell, 2006), p. 135.
10. Mary McGlynn, *Narratives of Class in New Irish and Scottish Literature: From Joyce to Kelman, Doyle, Galloway, and McNamee* (Basingstoke: Palgrave Macmillan, 2008), p. 75.
11. See Brian McHale, *Postmodernist Fiction* (London: Routledge, 2001), p. 120.
12. Roel Daamen, 'A Confluence of Narratives: Cultural Perspectives in Postmodernist Scottish Fiction' in *Cultural Identity and Postmodern Writing*, eds. Theo D'haen and Peiter Vermueken (Amsterdam: Rodopi, 2006), pp. 119–45, p. 126.
13. For a detailed discussion of the postmodern play in Kuppner's novel, see Daamen, 'A Confluence of Narratives' and Platt, 'Celtic Postmodernism'.
14. James Wood, 'Hysterical Realism', *Prospect Magazine*, 20 November 2000: www.prospectmagazine.co.uk/culture/56397/hysterical-realism.
15. Fredric Jameson, *Postmodernism, or, The Cultural Logic of Late Capitalism* (London: Verso, 1991), p. 10.
16. Peter Boxall, *Twenty-First-Century Fiction: A Critical Introduction* (Cambridge: Cambridge University Press, 2013), p. 60.
17. John Berger, from 'A Man with Tousled Hair' (2002), cited as epigraph in Ali Smith, *The Accidental* (London: Penguin Books, 2005).
18. See Jameson (n 15).
19. Aijaz Ahmad, *In Theory: Classes, Nations, Literatures* (London: Verso, 1992), p. 36.
20. Andrew O'Hagan, *Caledonian Road* (London: Faber and Faber, 2024) p. 417; p. 265
21. Brian McHale, 'What Was Postmodernism?' ('Fictions Present' thread of *Electronic Book Review*, 20/12/2007) [unpaginated]: https://electronicbookreview.com/essay/what-was-postmodernism/.

22. O'Hagan, *Caledonian Road*, p. 426.
23. Ibid., p. 427, p. 265.
24. Fredric Jameson, *The Political Unconscious: Narrative as a Socially Symbolic Act* (London: Routledge, 2002), p. 88.
25. Alasdair Gray, *A History Maker* (London: Penguin, 1995), pp. 202–3.
26. Aaron Kelly, 'Farewell to the Single-End? Alasdair Gray, Scotland and Postmodernism', *Études Ecossaises* 9 (2003–4): pp. 431–46, p. 422.
27. Cairns Craig, 'Going Down to Hell is Easy: *Lanark*, Realism and the Limits of Imagination' in *The Arts of Alasdair Gray*, eds. Robert Crawford and Tom Nairn (Edinburgh University Press, 1991), p. 98.
28. Alasdair Gray, *Lanark. A Life in 4 Books* (London: Picador, 1981), p. 485.
29. Spark, *The Comforters* (Harmondsworth: Penguin, 1963), p. 63.
30. Gray, *Lanark*, p. 485.
31. Ibid., p. 499.
32. Ibid., p. 560.
33. Randall Stevenson, 'Alasdair Gray and the Postmodern' in *The Arts of Alasdair Gray*, eds. Robert Crawford and Tom Nairn (Edinburgh University Press, 1991), pp. 48–63, p. 56, p. 60.
34. Martin McQuillan, 'James Kelman', *British Council: Literature*, 2003. Retrieved from https://literature.britishcouncil.org/writer/james-kelman. Accessed 9 July 2024.
35. Tom Toremans, 'An Interview with Alasdair Gray and James Kelman', *Contemporary Literature* 44.4 (Winter 2003), pp. 564–86, p. 573.
36. Cited in Alan Chadwick, 'Colourful Language', *The Sunday Times Scotland*, 23 July 1995.
37. Jean-François Lyotard, *The Postmodern Condition: A Report on Knowledge*, trans. Geoff Bennington and Brian Massumi (Manchester University Press, 1984), p. xxiv.
38. Cairns Craig, 'Resisting Arrest: James Kelman' in *The Scottish Novel since the Seventies: New Visions, Old Dreams*, eds. Gavin Wallace and Randall Stevenson (Edinburgh: Edinburgh University Press, 1993), pp. 99–114.
39. James Kelman, *How Late It Was, How Late* (London: Vintage, 1998), p. 1.
40. McHale, *Postmodernist Fiction*, p. 120.
41. See Peter Boxall, 'Kelman's Later Novels' in *The Edinburgh Companion to James Kelman*, ed. Scott Hames (Edinburgh University Press, 2010), pp. 31–41, pp. 36–7.
42. James Kelman, *You Have to be Careful in the Land of the Free* (London: Hamish Hamilton, 2004), p. 364.
43. Rather than suggesting a 'joyful play in difference' as Simon Kövesi suggests, Jeremiah's defamiliarising transcription of his own national categories, where Scotland becomes 'Skallin' and Scottish 'Skarrish' – evoking the words 'scaling', 'scalding' and the latter, specifically, 'scar' – intimates a more profound and painful rupture with his homeland. Simon Kövesi, *James Kelman* (Manchester University Press, 2007), p. 180. For a more detailed discussion of this, see Stefanie Lehner, *Subaltern Ethics in Contemporary*

Scottish and Irish Literature: Tracing Counter-Histories (Basingstoke: Palgrave Macmillan, 2011).
44. James Kelman, *Translated Accounts* (London: Vintage, 2001), p. 202, ix.
45. Daamen, 'A Confluence of Narratives', p. 134.
46. See also Aaron Kelly, 'James Kelman and the Deterritorialisation of Power' in *The Edinburgh Companion to Scottish Literature*, ed. Berthold Schoene (Edinburgh University Press, 2007), pp. 175–83, p. 181.
47. Kelman, *Translated Accounts*, p. 268.
48. Kelman, *How Late It Was*, p. 241.
49. Boxall, 'Kelman's Later Novels', p. 41.
50. Glenda Norquay, 'Janice Galloway's Novels: Fraudulent Mooching' in *Contemporary Scottish Women Writers*, eds. Aileen Christianson and Alison Lumsden (Edinburgh University Press, 2000), pp. 131–43, p. 135.
51. Carole Jones, *Disappearing Men: Gender Disorientation in Scottish Fiction 1979–1999* (Amsterdam: Rodopi, 2009), p. 66.
52. Ibid., p. 66.
53. Norquay, 'Janice Galloway's Novels', p. 136.
54. Janice Galloway, *The Trick is to Keep Breathing* (London: Vintage, 1999), p. 14.
55. Mary McGlynn, '"I Didn't Need to Eat": Janice Galloway's Anorexic Text and the National Body', *Critique: Studies in Contemporary Fiction* 49.2 (2008), pp. 221–40, p. 230.
56. See Marshall Lewis Johnson, 'The Invaded Narrator in Eimear McBride's A Girl Is a Half-formed Thing', *Irish Studies Review*, 28:4 (2020), pp. 429–44.
57. Galloway, *The Trick is to Keep Breathing*, p. 43.
58. Ibid., pp. 51–2.
59. See ibid., pp. 201–02 and pp. 174–6.
60. Ibid., p. 235.
61. John Hodge, cited in Aaron Kelly, *Irvine Welsh* (Manchester University Press, 2005), p. 14.
62. Aaron Kelly, *Irvine Welsh* (Manchester University Press, 2005), pp. 42–3.
63. Irvine Welsh, *Trainspotting* (London: Minerva, 1994), p. 188.
64. Ibid., p. 309.
65. Kelly, *Irvine Welsh*, p. 48.
66. Angus Calder, 'Reviews: Saadi's all the rag', *The Sunday Herald*, 25 April 2004.
67. Joseph H. Jackson, *Writing Black Scotland: Race, Nation and the Devolution of Black Britain* (Edinburgh University Press, 2020), p. 162.
68. Ibid., p. 152.
69. Ibid., p. 159.
70. Suhayl Saadi, *Psychoraag* (Edinburgh: Chroma, 2005), p. 1.
71. Ibid., p. 37.
72. Ibid., p. 405.
73. Jackson, *Writing Black Scotland*, p. 168.

CHAPTER 7

Outside Postmodernism
B. S. Johnson Before, During, and After

Glyn White

As a writer B. S. Johnson (1933–73) was known for two reasons: experimentation with form – a feature of all his novels – and trenchant opposition to conventional fiction, usually summarised by reference to the statement that 'telling stories is telling lies'.[1] These two things positioned Johnson outside the British literary mainstream as an 'experimental' novelist, despite his protestations about the way he believed critics used this term as 'a synonym for unsuccessful' and the consequent marginalising effects of being so labelled.[2] Though Johnson was never quite the outsider he portrays himself to be in the 'Introduction' to his last prose collection *Aren't You Rather Young to be Writing Your Memoirs?* (e.g., his first and third novels won awards), the general situation was crystallised in similar terms by Rubin Rabinovitz in a book published in 1967: 'The critical mood in England has produced a climate in which traditional novels can flourish and anything out of the ordinary is given the denigrating label "experimental" and neglected.'[3]

This chapter looks at the work and critical reception of B. S. Johnson from 1960 to 2015, paying particular attention to the influence that the development of the critical term postmodernism has had on his reputation. Structurally, the chapter will first briefly introduce Johnson's career then discuss his critical reception in relation to postmodernism by dividing it into three stages of roughly two decades each: before postmodernism (1960–80), during postmodernism (1980–2000), and after postmodernism (2000 to present).

On the strength of Johnson's experimental reputation and antagonism to the 1960s literary status quo, he was evaluated by critics in the 1980s and 1990s as a potential entrant to the postmodern canon. However, critics made little headway in reconciling Johnson's practice and preachments with postmodern theory and, thus, his legacy became increasingly marginalised. By the time of the millennium the need to have reached 'post-postmodernism' began to grow and gradually critical criteria have again shifted so that, in the wake of postmodernism, Johnson has fully come into his own as a significant writer. During each stage outlined Johnson remained, for better or worse, at least partly outside postmodernism and thus provides an excellent case study to show how contemporary concerns shape the critical landscape.

In the sections that follow I attempt to illustrate with evidence from the writer's work the reasons for Johnson's ambivalent position in relation to postmodernism. He has not been entirely invisible to critics in these years and several have identified him as a postmodernist writer. Brian McHale, for example, describes Johnson as 'the most fully postmodern writer of the 1960s'.[4] The key term here, however, is 'most fully' which implies Johnson is still not entirely postmodern in the sense it would be used in the 1980s. Johnson's apparent position in relation to postmodernism alters significantly depending on which of his works, and elements of those works, we focus on, and therefore a concise survey is in order.

Career in Brief

B. S. Johnson produced seven novels, two collections of shorter writing, two collections of poetry, several plays, made several short films, and worked on radio and television programmes. His work was noted for its high degree of self-reflexivity, especially its use of the visual and physical form. A selection of his novels makes clear how innovative and unwilling to accept the conventions of prose fiction Johnson's writing was in its time. We will come to the others in later sections.

Johnson's first novel, *Travelling People* (1963), is told in chapters which each use different forms, including internal monologue, epistolary, and film script, with numerous authorial interludes and intrusions to explain the story of student Henry Henry working during his vacation at a private club in Wales. Henry becomes increasingly alienated by the class pretensions of the manager but, after an epiphanic evening in a working class Welsh pub, the author's surrogate goes on to a scene of Lawrentian lovemaking, the content liberated by the outcome of the *Lady Chatterley's Lover* trial.[5] By the latter stages of his career Johnson was repudiating this novel ('it now embarrasses me and I will not allow it to be reprinted'), because it used a central character clearly based on the author without exposing this (standard) conceit, a decision that the Johnson estate continues to honour.[6]

The most infamous of Johnson's works, *The Unfortunates* (1969), is presented as twenty-seven sections of a novel, unbound in a box, with 'first' and 'last' among them showing how the author, in pursuing his employment as a football reporter, visits a city (Nottingham) he knows from his acquaintance with the academic Tony Tillinghast. The normal progress of his journalistic role is interspersed, randomly, with memories of Tony and his death from cancer. This novel-in-a-box was Johnson's most radical formal experiment, but was largely dismissed by contemporary critics, apparently because of a perceived mismatch between the radical form and less radical (although effective) authorial internal monologue which represents his writer-for-hire day job, and memories of loss and death.[7]

The last novel published while Johnson was alive, *Christie Malry's Own Double-Entry* (1973), is a blackly comic narrative, self-reflexively described as 'Funny, Brutalist, and Short'.[8] The narrative is studded with five pages in double-entry book-keeping format as the protagonist becomes an urban terrorist in London recording credits and debits in his antagonistic relationship with society.

See the Old Lady Decently (1975) is the posthumously published first part of Johnson's incomplete Matrix trilogy (the unwritten novels in the trilogy would have been *Buried Although* and *Amongst Those Left Are You*, the titles of all three making up a poetic sentence in itself). Highly fragmented, it fictionalises his mother's early life but supplements it with family documents, concrete poetry, found (and filleted) texts about Britain and its empire in decline and extracts from Erich Neumann's *The Great Mother* (1963), ending in Johnson's birth. In its use of ready-made material and its consideration of the past this novel begins to adopt new techniques for Johnson that might be readily identified as postmodern, but it is unfortunately not in print.

In addition to the novels there is one further key text to consider, a provocatively polemical 'Introduction' to the collection of short pieces *Aren't you Rather Young to be Writing Your Memoirs* (1973) that has been Johnson's most quoted work, as it asserts his hostility to contemporary practice in the novel:

> Literary forms do become exhausted, clapped out ... That is what seems to have happened to the nineteenth century narrative novel ... by the outbreak of the First World War. No matter how good the writers who now attempt it, it cannot be made to work for our time, and the writing of it is anachronistic, invalid, irrelevant, and perverse.[9]

Having dismissed most of his contemporaries, Johnson then goes on to recount the salient innovations in his own novels. As Patrick Parrinder correctly noted in an influential 1977 essay, '[w]hat complicates Johnson's case is his determination to bear public witness to his own artistic development'.[10] Too often the 'Introduction' is treated as a considered manifesto, rather than a summary to date, and dealing with the author's theories is allowed to short-circuit engagement with the texts themselves. As Jonathan Coe insists, the 'self-certainty [Johnson] affects in' the 'Introduction' is 'the enemy of art' but conceals 'a layer of insecurity which gives [Johnson's novels] an astonishing rawness, a self-questioning urgency that keeps them thrillingly alive'.[11]

Before Postmodernism

During his life as a writer Johnson made no claim on the term postmodern and all links between his work and postmodernism have occurred posthumously. He was, however, a writer who was clearly aware that change was coming to literature and his insistence on its necessity put him at odds with a majority of his British contemporaries. The question here is whether the response Johnson advocated must lead the way into postmodernity or not.

The postwar British literary scene could be largely characterised as antimodernist: a very different response to the times than what would come to be called postmodernism. The paradigm for most British novelists of the period was a form of social realism that claimed links to the Victorian novel and opposed itself to modernist fiction. The Leavises' *The Great Tradition* had allowed less formally radical versions of modernism (Henry James, Joseph Conrad, D. H. Lawrence) to enter the canon and, through them, British fiction had quietly absorbed a number of elements from modernism such as increased focus on the psychology of characters and a convention of removing the author from the scene.[12] While some of Johnson's writing is assimilable to this paradigm – for example, a social realist intent – it is the background against which, in the words of David James, 'Johnson carried forward, militantly, the ethos of renewal upon which modernism was premised'[13] and his experimental forms and expressed hostility to conventional writing meant reconciliation between these aspects was ultimately impossible.

As Joseph Darlington argues, '[t]he primary obstacle facing any academic reading of B.S. Johnson is his works' combination of two approaches – social realism and experimental typography – which for the traditional literature scholar are perceived as incompatible, if not contradictory'.¹⁴ This obstacle remains today as evidenced by David Leon Higdon's claims in an essay published in 2014 that social realism began to be displaced in the early 1960s by the 'postmodernism' of novels such as Johnson's *Albert* (1964) and Anthony Burgess's *A Clockwork Orange* (1962) and that '[n]o reader ... would mistake these ... works for socially conscious, socially committed works'.¹⁵ Given that Burgess's novel is essentially a treatise on free will in society and Johnson's novel explicitly queries the state school system's engagement with working class pupils, this assertion appears odd. It would seem that the social consciousness of these two texts disappears from view when they do striking and original things with language and form which standard social realism does not. In contrast to the British context, the Francophile tradition welcomes experimentation (as in the *nouveau roman*) adding the perceived association of radical political views to any radical stylistic change. Confined to the British literary context, Johnson was placed in a double-bind, as Kaye Mitchell has noted: 'Johnson's formal experimentation is seen ... to add value to his work – not only interest value but also a kind of nominal political value – or, conversely, to detract from its value as literature, being mere gimmickry.'¹⁶ To many contemporary reviewers Johnson appeared simultaneously both too gimmicky and too political.

For example, let us take the explosive end of the conventional narration of *Albert Angelo*. The novel focuses on Albert Albert, an architect working as a supply teacher, but uses a number of innovative devices which include holes cut in pages, reproduced fortune-teller's cards, and the poorly written essays of schoolchildren in criticism of their teacher. Late-on, in a section called 'Disintegration', a belligerent author-figure emerges to reject Albert as a fictionalised surrogate and explain what he was imperfectly trying to do through the foregoing fiction before he realised that 'telling stories is telling lies'. It is an intervention which has been called 'dizzy with contradictions'.¹⁷ Disintegration begins as follows:

> ——fuck all this lying look what im really trying to write about is writing not all this stuff about architecture trying to say something about writing about my writing im my hero though what a useless appellation my first character then im trying to say something about me through him albert an architect when whats the point in covering up covering up covering over pretending pretending I can say anything through him that is anything I would be interested in saying.¹⁸

Contemporary critical reactions to this intervention are almost comic in their priggish shock. Bernard Bergonzi shrewdly observes that the break 'may point to a dissatisfaction with the impersonality of the novel form' but goes on to argue that the fact that 'Johnson nevertheless remains imprisoned in his typographical dimension is evident from the obtrusiveness of his lack of punctuation'.[19] Alan Kennedy is similarly unable to see why the abandonment of conventional punctuation is required to rip through convention and concludes that 'it represents the writer's abdication of responsibility and a surrender to cliché and inexactitude'.[20] What we are seeing here is 'a violent collision between [the representation of] proletarian experience and the literary ideology of the bourgeoisie'.[21] Johnson wishes to convey his anger and annoyance and he does so in *Albert Angelo* in the poorly punctuated idiom of the working class children his character has been trying to teach. His contemporaries appear to think this anger should be mediated and fail to appreciate the affiliation with non-standard communication which is amply evidenced through the preceding bulk of the novel.[22] The class-based discourse of taste and the artificial barrier built upon it between the supposedly popular taste of the masses and the literary tastes of the elite would be a postmodernist target. However, while Johnson's rejection of taste appears to be 'on-message' with emerging postmodernism his markedly proletarian stance (declaring for one side of the argument) militates against his co-option within bourgeois realist, elitist modernist, or even postmodernist forms.

It is tempting to see Johnson as an embattled loner at odds with the world, not unlike his character Christie Malry though, while Malry plants a bomb in a tax office, the 'terrorism' Johnson engages in is of a purely literary nature. The character Christie actually takes his creator to task in one self-reflexive exchange: 'you shouldn't be bloody writing novels about it, you should be out there bloody doing something about it'.[23] In no way is this statement incompatible with the fundamental realist claim for the relevance of fiction being its relation to the real world. Yet it clearly is at odds with the conventional and comfortable literary convention that the division between the two will not be discussed. Johnson's work constantly returns to the collision between fiction and reality, and the fragile but persistent metaphoricity of their interaction. The paradox Johnson invokes here is essentially unanswerable from within the critical paradigm of realism, dominant in British literature in the 1960s and 1970s, but while Johnson insistently and repeatedly made the point that the orthodoxy needed to be questioned he wanted there to be an answer and a way forward. The problem for his critical reputation would be that under the critical paradigm of postmodernity in the 1980s and 1990s the response was that it really was impossible to connect reality and fiction, as we will discuss in the next section.

During Postmodernism

In the period 1980–2000, when postmodernism as a critical term had entered general use, Johnson's work could be viewed retrospectively as a whole and its self-reflexive devices could be more easily taken on board. Morton Levitt first strongly linked Johnson to postmodernism in his 1985 entry for the *Dictionary of Literary Biography*, calling him 'the single most forceful exponent in this postmodernist age of the most characteristic technique of the age, self-reflexive art', but, unfortunately, Levitt named as Johnson's masterpiece the out of print *See the Old Lady Decently*.[24] A 1985 edition of the *Review of Contemporary Fiction* shows there was a brief flare of critical interest, but the two novels republished in Britain in 1984 didn't arrest the drift towards obscurity. Johnson was remembered only as token representative of the 'experimentalist' position through the anthologising of the 'Introduction' to *Aren't You Rather Young* ... and while his experiments with form continued to be catalogued in surveys of the preceding decades, his aggressive stance against fiction jarred at a time when the impossibility of linking fiction to reality in realist terms was increasingly recognised in postmodern theory.

In his influential survey, *Postmodernist Fiction* (1987), Brian McHale centres his argument on the 'shift of dominant' from that of modernist epistemology (how we know things) to postmodernist ontology (focusing on different realities). From this perspective McHale picks up on three examples from Johnson's work as examples of postmodern practice: the multiple possible endings offered by 'Broad Thoughts from a Home', the blank pages within the internal monologues of *House Mother Normal* (1971), and the format of *The Unfortunates* in which the various sections have to be handled and arranged by the reader. McHale's view that '[s]uch manipulations certainly serve to keep the materiality of the book [an ontological issue] in the forefront of the reader's consciousness',[25] is indisputable but severely limiting at the same time. Though the reader might be reminded of each text's materiality by the devices and therefore the difference between the real world and the fictional world, the primary motivation for these devices is very different.

'Broad Thoughts from a Home' (a chapter excised from *Travelling People*, Jonathan Coe tells us)[26] draws heavily on Flann O'Brien's *At Swim-Two-Birds* (first published in 1939), not least in its Dublin setting, with an interrogative format ultimately cribbed from Joyce's *Ulysses* but taken to comic excess. This short story is clearly an example of early postmodernism as an extension of modernism, but McHale's other two examples, while appearing more fully postmodernist through their disruption of standard prose text layout, can equally be read as opposed to postmodernism in that they are ultimately mimetic devices.

Johnson's *House Mother Normal* (1971) reveals one hour during one evening at an old person's 'home' through nine twenty-one-page internal monologues rigorously mapped onto one another through page numbering and parallel lineation, and brought to a satisfying and shocking conclusion with the House Mother's slightly longer account. Empathy with the elderly characters is expressed through entering into their minds 'simultaneously' in a radically experimental form. The blank pages that McHale highlights in *House Mother Normal* occur in the monologues of the oldest and most senile of the inmates: George Hedbury, who knows very little about what is going on around him, and Rosetta Stanton, whose dementia means there are very few scattered thoughts, mostly in Welsh, and who is dead for the last five blank pages of her monologue. The blank pages are, thus, primarily representational, and though they may make us think about the way in which thought is represented on the page this is not an exclusively postmodern concern.

As we have seen earlier, *The Unfortunates* makes capital out of its materiality as a 'tangible metaphor' for the scattering of thoughts and in the way that it gives responsibility for structuring the bulk of the text to the reader.[27] However, McHale himself has subsequently noted that the 'notoriously randomised novel-in-a-box … in fact proves to contain a rather tame internal monologue' and that here Johnson is not in 'postmodernist mode'.[28] Ontology is not the point of the device.

The materiality of Johnson's texts is certainly the grounding or jumping off point for many of his innovations and, as McHale accurately identifies, the reader's consciousness is the target that Johnson wishes to reach with these devices. Recently McHale has acknowledged that experimental devices on the page can point in two directions, towards the author's reality or the reader's, but he still foregrounds the idea that 'the virtual reality of fiction is eclipsed by the material reality of the book' rather than travelling the 'strange loop' that he identifies in the opposite direction, that is to say, to consider how authors co-opt the real world as support for the reality of their fictional worlds.[29] Johnson simply does not want to be sidetracked into the virtual and, ultimately, the postmodern self-reflexive and experimental devices of his work are insufficient for the author to posthumously become a 'full postmodernist' since, under close inspection, so much of his experimentation can be seen to be undertaken in service of the mimetic goal of representing reality better using words and pages.[30]

This 'reality' may be fictional, as in *House Mother Normal*, or biographical as in *The Unfortunates*.

B. S. Johnson's occasionally ranting pronouncements against realism and conventional literary practice, made in the period before postmodernism, were returned to by critics during postmodernism (1980–2000), but not productively. Judith Mackrell points out the key contradiction for criticism being 'Johnson's alternating commitment to a painstaking form of mimesis and a radical denial of the mimetic' and in the same 1985 journal Paul D'Eath identifies the 'implicit paradox of . . . postmodernist realism' in Johnson's work.[31] Patricia Waugh's verdict is that Johnson: 'developed innovative metafictional techniques but ever in the service of an absolutely oppositional concept of truth and fiction already regarded as retrograde by the progressive intellectual forces around him'.[32] While Johnson undermines and exposes the conventions of realist fiction and experiments with form quite radically it would be very hard to assimilate his novels entirely to the postmodern literary tropes of metafiction, historiographic metafiction, magical realism or avant-pop. Simply put, his focus is out of tune with his times.[33]

Jonathan Coe recognised that: 'What unites all his work, in whatever form, is its burning commitment to personal experience and to truth: a commitment which may have restricted Johnson in scope, but which nonetheless provoked him to ever more energetic feats of formal innovation.'[34] Julia Jordan further explains that Johnson's 'place at an angle to postmodernism, can . . . be understood through his singular commitment to this notion of truth'.[35] It is this commitment that won't allow him to be fitted neatly into the existing categories. Johnson's authorial search for 'truth' was so essentially incomprehensible during the dominance of postmodernity this period's critics argued he had followed a dead end. In fact, Johnson had simply gone his own way.

Johnson's experimental devices are not just markers of postmodernist anti-realism. They are grounded by print, materiality and experience, easily understood and assimilated to traditional representational intent. Philip Tew argues that: 'Being intensely focused on lived experience, Johnson uses formal devices to open out that experience.' or, as Lynn Wells succinctly puts it: 'his innovation sought authenticity'.[36] Seen broadly, Johnson's work attempts to do the impossible under postmodernism: to offer the experience of the author as a transcendental signifier. In the attempt to insert the author into the text, not as a fiction within the fiction, but as a guarantor of 'truth' (even if that truth is 'chaos') Johnson is at his most radical.

Ultimately criticism from within postmodernism served Johnson poorly, since, despite the seeming postmodern self-reflexivity of his work, its fragmentation and rejection of conventional forms, the work as a whole simply will not compute through its critical paradigms. Johnson remained outside postmodernism, and therefore outside the canon, until after the millennium. An answer to the various conundrums and contradictions in his work demands not that we bow to authorial intention but that we look more closely at the way in which this author figure is perceived to be present in his texts.

After Postmodernism

As John Lanchester pointed out in his preface to the 2001 reprint of *Christie Malry's Own Double-Entry*: 'With good writers it can take some time for us to become their contemporaries.'[37] Johnson, our narrator in *The Unfortunates* (republished in 1999), wishes he could have told his late critical friend Tony the following definition of academicism: 'Yesterday's answers to today's problems!'[38] Any retrospective survey such as this one might run the risk of providing today's answers to yesterday's problems, yet nonetheless, criticism seems to be in a much better place to understand and account for Johnson now than it was when he was writing or when it was impossible to set aside postmodern theory. One reason is that the term 'experimental' 'has enjoyed a rehabilitation',[39] and it is clear that the formal experiments in Johnson's work are no longer seen as alienating to readers in a world where computer-driven word-processing and desk-top publishing give everyone with access to them considerable control over the visual aspects of their texts. Another factor is the detailed critical work on Johnson from many hands and, absolutely key amongst them, the arrival of Coe's biography *Like a Fiery Elephant* in 2004.

In 1986 Andrew Hassam had noted that '[t]he critic of Johnson is ... caught in a dilemma' as any approach taken to the texts 'will be haunted by the spectre of an unsubstantiated biographical raw material to which the works appear to refer'.[40] This referential layer of raw material is, of course, there when we read any novel (there is an author, the book does have a history) but the difference is the way that Johnson foregrounds it within his work. *Trawl* (1966), for example, blurs the line between novel and autobiography as it recounts an ultimately therapeutic trip on a trawler into the Barents Sea during which the author autobiographically self-interrogates in what David James has called 'an immaculate simulation of retrospection'.[41] Though it might seem like autobiography on the face of it, Hassam has convincingly argued that Johnson subverts autobiographical form, and the conceit that the material is thought rather than written (remembered rather than reported) is maintained throughout, justifying Johnson's claim that it is a novel.[42]

This is, of course, a fine distinction and one Johnson could not sustain beyond *The Unfortunates*, yet the authorial focus built into his work is apparent in different ways throughout his novels, from the surrogate protagonists in *Travelling People* and *Albert Angelo*, through the autobiographical narrator of *Trawl* and *The Unfortunates*, to the authorial figure claiming responsibility for the fictional elements of *Christie Malry's own Double-Entry* and *See the Old Lady Decently*. Twice in the novels an authorial figure steps out from behind the wings late on. We have already seen this in the Disintegration section of *Albert Angelo*. It also features in *House Mother Normal* where the final monologue, that of the House Mother herself, extends one page longer than those of all the other characters and states: 'I too am a puppet or concoction of a writer (you always knew there was a writer behind it all? Ah, there's no fooling you readers!).'[43] The latter instance almost performs a revision of the former's revelation and certainly inaugurates a different policy: no longer will the narration risk being thought autobiography: it will be fiction that draws attention to its fictionality by featuring the writer at the point of writing. For example, the number of deaths from Christie Malry's reservoir poisoning is 'roughly the number of words of which the novel consists so far'[44] while, in *See the Old Lady Decently*, the invention of the early twentieth century kitchen Johnson's mother worked in is interrupted thus:

> Where were we? I did actually break off at a full stop above, at Emily's knowledge of swearwords, by the way, though it must look like a contrivance. And so must this, since that little girl with something of my mother in her face has just brought me a roll baked by her mother, bread that could not be fresher, with butter melting through it, brown and yellow-golden, interrupted me where I write in isolation at the top of the house, such sweet interposition!
>
> I shall eat now, the manuscript stained on purpose with the melting butter.
>
> What a pity it is not possible for you all to read the ms!
> Where was I again?[45]

This intervention also relates to the 'Disintegration' section of *Albert Angelo* in its cutting through the fiction to report on the author's circumstances, though in this case the interruption is temporary. The reference to the manuscript in *See the Old Lady Decently* expresses frustration at the laborious process through which a book takes (or took) shape as lamented in Disintegration: 'who knows what else will have shifted by galleyproof stage, or pageproof stage, or by publication day, or by the time you are reading this?'[46] Johnson's self-reflexive entry into the process of publication uses the materiality of the text to transport him from his study to the site of our present reading. Rod Mengham suggests this exceptional trick is performed by addressing readers 'as though they were interlocutors coming together [with the author] in the same textual moment' and thus: 'suspending the author in a limbo of preparation for the moment, for the many different moments, all in the future, when the reader encounters the authorial message issued from the past. It is that "antepostdating" dynamic which meshes together formal innovation and political radicalism.'[47] Of course, all authors from the past reach us through the uncanny medium of the book, it just seems exceptionally vivid in Johnson's case. To a degree, readers of Johnson's fiction experience a relationship with the author like that described by Jonathan Coe in his biography, where 'biographers enter into a strange relationship with their subjects: at once very intimate, and very distant'.[48] This relationship that 'thrives on prickliness and tension' is, in a nutshell, the one that Johnson's texts establish with their readers.[49]

Johnson's conspicuousness in his texts allows him to check that we, as readers, are giving a good account of ourselves when facing the challenges set for us. Jordan suggests that 'to read Johnson is to find oneself in an active struggle for control over the text, negotiating with a confrontational author, who seems at times to be let down, disappointed by our readerly shortcomings'.[50] This combative and attritional relationship between author and reader in Johnson's work is keyed at a number of registers. A nonchalant example might be the end of the 'Introduction' to *Aren't You Rather Young*, where Johnson prepares the reader for the short pieces that fill out the volume with the instruction to 'make of them what you will'.[51] Another version, and one that seems intolerably controlling (or unreasonably ambitious), can be illustrated by the most quoted extract of Johnson's 'Introduction':

> I want my ideas to be expressed so precisely that the very minimum of room for interpretation is left. Indeed I would go further and say that to the extent that a reader can impose his [*sic.*] own imagination on my words, then that piece of writing is a failure. I want him to see my (vision) not something conjured out of his own imagination.[52]

Conclusion: Post-Postmodernism

In the post-postmodern period it seems as if criticism is beginning to catch up on the implications of Johnson's brand of metafiction. For example, R. M. Berry argues that in the metafictional novel 'the reader must see what the author sees: the significance of *this* [specific] arrangement' though noting that 'no reader can be forced'.[53] For Johnson, this is a problem: might that reader not be cajoled into inhabiting the author's predicament of having to dealing with their unpredictable nature? This is what Johnson's infamous quotation goes on to do:

> How is he [*sic*.] [the reader] supposed to grow unless he will admit others' ideas? If he wants to impose his own imagination, let him write his own books. That may be thought to be anti-reader; but think a little further, and what I am really doing is challenging the reader to prove his own existence as palpably as I am proving mine by the act of writing.[54]

Johnson's experiments are almost always about establishing a connection with his readers and delivering a specific but often complex and multifaceted experience to them.

The ultimate trajectory for Johnson's use of formal experiment is to show readers his notes and get them to construct the novels: *Trawl* adopts the page shape of the parish notebooks it was drafted on; *See the Old Lady Decently* is made as fragmentary as the sources assembled to make it. The logic of the collage is also apparent in the stylistic changes in *Travelling People*, in the various found inclusions in *Albert Angelo* (such as the spiritualist's card and children's writing), the fractured and free format of *The Unfortunates*, or the assemblage of fragments of conversation across the separate monologues in *House Mother Normal*. The excess of fragmentation extends modernism to show that everything falls apart, but Johnson still resists this postmodern logic, trying – and failing – to keep track of it all with, for example, the attempt to list the lies that have replaced facts after the Disintegration of *Albert Angelo*, or the five accounting pages of *Christie Malry's Own Double-Entry* which try to balance the books but can never come out right and the account must be given up or written off. In sharing his novel-building enterprises Johnson demands we engage in the process. We don't have to like it, but we do have to react.

My first essay on Johnson, published in 1999, highlighted how marginal Johnson had become in British-based criticism.[55] Today, Johnson is no longer forgotten; his five central novels are in print, *Aren't You Rather Young to be Writing Your Memoirs* has been collected alongside a number of his scripts and journalism in *Well Done God!* (2013), and the BFI have released almost all Johnson's film and television work on DVD: *You're Human Like the Rest of Them: The Films of B.S. Johnson* (2013). New critical writing continues to appear and the B. S. Johnson Society's publication *BSJ* has reached its third edition. Despite never finding a home within postmodernity Johnson is now a recognised co-ordinate of the contemporary literary field.

It helps that literary study today is no longer saddled with a prevailing 'Great Tradition' and that local histories, specialisms and eccentric choices are allowed. In this way B. S. Johnson is a beneficiary of postmodernism's incredulity towards grand narratives, even though postmodernism's own theoretical dominance needed to be dislodged or set aside for Johnson's texts to get a full hearing. Johnson's anxieties are postmodern anxieties but while parts of his literary response might appear to be postmodern, the novels are shot through with social realist intent to look at class, education, the forces of conformity, death, decay and old age, and at how to resist them. The double-codedness of his work is what gives it life despite – rather than because of – postmodernism.[56] And Johnson is surely not the only 1960s writer whose merits may have been similarly obscured.[57]

Notes

1. B. S. Johnson, *Albert Angelo*, (London: Constable, 1964), p. 167.
2. B. S. Johnson, *Aren't You Rather Young to be Writing Your Memoirs?* (London: Hutchinson, 1973), p. 19.
3. Rubin Rabinovitz, *The Reaction against Experiment* (New York: Columbia University Press, 1967), p. 168.
4. Brian McHale, *The Cambridge Introduction to Postmodernism* (Cambridge University Press, 2015), p. 64.
5. See Nick Hubble, 'Sex, Lies and Autobiografaction: *Travelling People* and the Persistence of Modernism' in *B.S. Johnson and Post-War Literature: Possibilities of the Avant Garde*, ed. Julia Jordan and Martin Ryle (Houndmills: Palgrave Macmillan, 2014), pp. 167–82, p. 170.
6. Johnson, *Memoirs?*, p. 22.
7. See Glyn White, *Reading the Graphic Surface: The Presence of the Book in Prose Fiction* (Manchester: Manchester University Press, 2005), pp. 116–18.
8. B. S. Johnson, *Christie Malry's Own Double-Entry* (London: King Penguin, 1984), p. 165.
9. Johnson, *Memoirs?*, pp. 13–14.
10. Patrick Parrinder, 'Pilgrim's Progress: The Novels of B. S. Johnson (1933–73)', *Critical Quarterly* 19:2 (1977), pp. 45–59, p. 50.
11. Jonathan Coe, *Like a Fiery Elephant: The Story of B.S. Johnson* (London: Picador, 2004), p. 452.

12. F. R. Leavis, *The Great Tradition* (Harmondsworth: Peregrine, 1967); Martin Ryle, '"Educated and Intelligent, If Down at Heel": John Wain's *Hurry on Down* and B. S. Johnson's *Albert Angelo*', in Jordan and Ryle, *Johnson and Post-war Literature*, pp. 103–17, p. 113.
13. David James, 'B. S. Johnson Within the Ambit of Modernism', *Critical Engagements: A Journal of Criticism and Theory* 4:1/4:2 (2011), pp. 37–53, p. 44.
14. Joseph Darlington, '"A Sort of Waterfall": Class Anxiety and Authenticity in B.S. Johnson' *BSJ: The B.S. Johnson Journal* 1 (2014), pp. 69–109, p. 70.
15. David Leon Higdon, 'B.S. Johnson's *Albert Angelo* as Postmodern Counterbook', *BSJ: The B.S. Johnson Journal* 1 (2014), pp. 5–45, p. 23.
16. Kaye Mitchell, '*The Unfortunates*: Hypertext, Linearity and the Act of Reading' in *Re-reading B. S. Johnson*, ed. Philip Tew and Glyn White (Houndmills: Palgrave, 2007), pp. 51–64, p. 58.
17. Nicholas Tredell, 'The Truths of Lying: *Albert Angelo*', *Review of Contemporary Fiction* 5:2 (1985), pp. 64–70, p. 66.
18. Johnson, *Albert Angelo*, p. 167.
19. Bernard Bergonzi, 'Thoughts on the Personality Explosion' in *Innovations: Essays on Art and Ideas*, ed. Bernard Bergonzi (London: Macmillan, 1968), p. 199.
20. Alan Kennedy, *The Protean Self: Dramatic Action in Contemporary Fiction* (New York: Columbia University Press, 1974), p. 159.
21. Darlington, 'Class Anxiety', p. 76.
22. See White, *Reading the Graphic Surface*, pp. 93–114.
23. Johnson, *Christie Malry*, p. 180.
24. Morton Levitt, 'B.S. Johnson' in *Dictionary of Literary Biography: British Novelists Since 1960* (Detroit: Bruccoli Clark, 1985), p. 14, pp. 438–44, p. 439.
25. Brian McHale, *Postmodernist Fiction* (London: Routledge, 1987), p. 110, p. 183, p. 193.
26. Coe, *Fiery Elephant*, p. 88; Johnson, *Memoirs?*, pp. 91–110; but also appears in Johnson's first collection, co-authored with Zulfikar Ghose, *Statement Against Corpses* (London: Constable, 1964).
27. Johnson, *Memoirs?*, p. 25.
28. McHale, *Introduction to Postmodernism*, p. 33.
29. Brian McHale, 'Postmodernism and Experiment' in *The Routledge Companion to Experimental Literature*, ed. Joe Bray, Alison Gibbons and Brian McHale (Abingdon: Routledge, 2012), pp. 141–53, pp. 147–8.
30. See White, *Graphic Surface*, pp. 84–117.
31. Judith Mackrell, 'B. S. Johnson and the British Experimental Tradition: An Introduction', *Review of Contemporary Fiction* 5:2 (1985), pp. 42–64, p. 58; Paul M. D'Eath, 'B. S. Johnson and the Consolation of Literature', *Review of Contemporary Fiction* 5:2 (1985), pp. 77–81, p. 80.
32. Patricia Waugh, *Harvest of the Sixties: English Literature and its Background 1960–1990* (Oxford University Press, 1995), p. 132.
33. Musically, for example, Johnson expresses enthusiasm for traditional jazz rather than anything more contemporary. See B. S. Johnson, *Trawl* (London: Panther, 1968), pp. 180–6.

34. Jonathan Coe, 'Oh Fuck All This Lying! Some Notes on the Poems of B. S. Johnson', *Spleen, Sunk Island Review* 10 (1995), pp. 97–104, p. 104.
35. Julia Jordan, 'Evacuating Samuel Beckett and B.S. Johnson' in Jordan and Ryle, *Johnson and Post-War Literature*, pp. 136–152, p.148.
36. Philip Tew, 'Engagement and truth: B.S. Johnson and Post-War Experimental Aesthetics', *Critical Engagements: A Journal of Criticism and Theory* 4.1/4.2 (2011), pp. 81–108, p. 104; Lynn Wells, 'What's New, Again? B.S. Johnson's Experimentalism', *Critical Engagements: A Journal of Criticism and Theory* 4:1/4:2 (2011), pp. 27–36, p. 35.
37. John Lanchester, 'Foreword', in *Christie Malry's Own Double-Entry* (London: Picador, 2001), p. 6.
38. B. S. Johnson, *The Unfortunates* (London: Picador, 1999), section beginning 'Again the house', p. 3.
39. Jordan, 'Beckett and Johnson', p. 4. See also Bray, Gibbons, and McHale, *Experimental Literature*.
40. Andrew Hassam, 'True Novel or Autobiography? The Case of B.S. Johnson's *Trawl*', *Prose Studies* 9:1 (1986), pp. 62–72, p. 63.
41. James, 'Ambit of Modernism', p. 51.
42. Hassam, 'True Novel or Autobiography?', p. 70.
43. B. S. Johnson, *House Mother Normal: A Geriatric Comedy* (London: Collins, 1971), p. 204.
44. Johnson, *Christie Malry*, p. 147.
45. B. S. Johnson, *See the Old Lady Decently* (New York: Viking, 1975), pp. 27–8.
46. Johnson, *Albert Angelo*, p. 172.
47. Rod Mengham, 'Antepostdated Johnson', in Jordan and Ryle, *Johnson and Post-War Literature* (2014), pp. 121–35, p. 134.
48. Coe, *Fiery Elephant*, p. 451.
49. Ibid., p. 452.
50. Julia Jordan, 'Foreword' to Jonathan Coe, Philip Tew and Julia Jordan (eds.), *Well Done God!* (London: Picador, 2013), p. xvii.
51. Johnson, *Memoirs?*, p. 30.
52. Ibid., p. 28; this statement needn't be taken entirely seriously since it entirely depends on the reader's consent. See Glyn White, 'The Sadism of the Author or the Masochism of the Reader?' in Jordan and Ryle, *Johnson and Post-War Literature*, pp. 153–66, p. 164.
53. R. M. Berry, 'Metafiction' in Bray, Gibbons, and McHale, *Experimental Literature*, pp. 128–40, p. 139, emphasis in original.
54. Johnson, *Memoirs?*, p. 28.
55. Glyn White, 'Recalling the Facts: Taking Action in the Matter of B. S. Johnson's *Albert Angelo*', *Hungarian Journal of English and American Studies* 5:2 (1999), pp. 143–62.
56. 'I shall make myself so bloody awkward!' says Haakon in the concluding line of B. S. Johnson's play version of *You're Human Like the Rest of Them*: in Coe, Tew and Jordan (eds.), *Well Done God!*, p. 254.
57. See, for some examples, Kaye Mitchell and Nonia Williams (eds.), *British Avant-Garde Fiction of the 1960s* (Edinburgh: Edinburgh University Press, 2019).

CHAPTER 8

The Recovery of Genre in Contemporary British Fiction
Return of the Romance
Suzanne Keen

Once upon a time (certainly by the 1890s), serious literary fiction came into its kingdom of prestige and canonicity by overthrowing its old-fashioned older siblings, the descendants of Romance. Demoting Adventure to boys' adventure stories, relegating Fairy Tales to folklorists, handing off Romance Epic to narrative historians and filmmakers, bequeathing serial fiction to detectives, humourists, and soap operas, and giving its very family name away to erotic fiction written for and by women, Fiction became Literary. Realism, character-centred exploration of consciousness, and rigorous experimentation with formal devices preoccupied much of the celebrated literary fiction of the twentieth century prior to postmodernism. Plot itself, a staple of popular modes of storytelling, became a marker of unseriousness; modernist novelist E. M. Forster sighed about the 'low atavistic form' at the heart of all novels, 'Yes – oh, dear, yes – the novel tells a story.'[1]

Literary Fiction's Suppression of Romance

As a status-elevating strategy, distancing the novel from the popular genres descended from Romance worked very nicely indeed. In the second half of the nineteenth century, English became a subject that you could study at university, not only by learning Anglo-Saxon or reading poetry.[2] By the early decades of the twentieth century, critics facetiously segregated readers by the height of their brows.[3] Writers of novels and short stories who aspired to be considered highbrow and yearned for appreciation by an elite audience eschewed the topics, tropes, and modes popular with lowbrows or the consumers of mass-market fiction. Worse than that, though, highbrows disdained the 'betwixt and between' character of middlebrow writing,[4] with its appeal to women readers and its unseemly ambition to make money by selling a picture of 'real humanity' that, according to Virginia Woolf, was a 'mixture of geniality and sentiment stuck together with a sticky slime of calf's-foot jelly'.[5] This image of distasteful representation suggests that Woolf was really only half joking when she threatened to take her pen and stab to death anybody who called her 'middlebrow'.[6]

As for aspirant serious writers, they learned from the literary establishment (i.e., from book reviews and, in the influential American context, from the ethos of writing programmes) that credibility depended upon rejection of 'the shoddy inauthenticity of genre fiction of all kinds.'[7] As literary historian Mark McGurl describes the ideologies of 'write what you know' and 'show, don't tell' that dominated twentieth-century aesthetics of fiction, the creative writing programmes' most influential mentors insisted on the validating imprimatur of personal experience over indulgence in the imagination: 'By contrast to popular genre fiction – telling of outlaws, detectives, vampires, moon men, and other things the writer has probably never seen – autobiographical self-expressivity would remain an essential element' of late modernist fiction.[8]

Popular Genres Bounce Back

Nearly a century on from Woolf's anxious desire to avoid the 'middlebrow', the tables have turned, and genre fiction has in the late twentieth and early twenty-first centuries reoccupied the territory of literature worthy of notice. Fantasies such as Susanna Clarke's *Jonathan Strange and Mr. Norrell* (2004) and *Piranesi* (2020); mysteries by P. D. James and John Banville (*nom de plume*, Benjamin Black); dystopias such as Margaret Atwood's *Oryx and Crake* (2003); Hilary Mantel's, Rose Tremain's, and Sarah Waters' historical fiction; Jeanette Winterson's and Michael Faber's erotica; and westerns by Peter Carey, Patrick deWitt, and Michael Ondaatje: these works in genre now receive attention in highbrow journals and the weekly and bi-weekly book reviews. Genre fiction has been short-listed or even won the major literary prizes. Historical novels have been especially successful, winning the Man Booker Prize nine times since 2000, with a fantasy adventure, Yann Martel's *Life of Pi* (2001), and two dystopian novels, Margaret Atwood's *The Testaments* (2019) and Paul Lynch's *Prophet Son* (2023), extending the twentieth-century success of genre fiction into the twenty-first. Genre fiction has been adapted into celebrated, critically acclaimed films and television: beyond the lucrative *Harry Potter* and *Lord of the Rings* franchises, excellent adaptations of dystopias by Atwood, Kazuo Ishiguro and P. D. James, of historical fiction by Mantel, of fantasies by Neil Gaiman, and of countless fictional detective stories have commanded large film and television audiences. Even as genre fictions and their film adaptations have enjoyed crossover success (as in P. D. James's *The Children of Men* [1992] adapted to film in 2006 by Alfonso Cuarón), genre fiction has been folded into the generically hybrid fiction written by 'serious' authors such as Kazuo Ishiguro, Ian McEwan, David Mitchell, Will Self, and Salman Rushdie. Some contemporary British novelists elude categorisation: Nicola Barker, Emma Donoghue, Natasha Pulley, Posy Simmonds, and Scarlett Thomas write in new blends that emulsify genre and literary qualities, reaching diversified readerships as a result.

Hybrid Vigour of Contemporary British Fiction

Sticky mixtures and unseemly in-between-ness have much improved reputations, as the cachet of heteroglossia, hybridity, and liminality has improved the credibility of fiction that blends with the dominant mode of literature the devices and tropes of what Rosalie Colie long ago described as 'the resources of kind'. Writing about genre-theory in Renaissance literature, Colie endorsed with enthusiasm the literary gain to be realised in embracing the affordances of genres and in 'refusing to allow generic categories to dictate or predestine the size, scope, content, and manner in any particular literary work'.[9] Colie wrote about the potential of genres, which she called 'kinds' in the manner of the Renaissance, approvingly:

> The kinds can easily be seen as tiny subcultures with their own habits, habitats, and structures of ideas as well as their own forms. But as subcultures continually melt into or are absorbed by a neighboring culture, so did the kinds in our period melt into one another – often to enrich the possibilities of literature taken as system.[10]

From the vantage point of 2024, the contemporary novel in English appears to have been diversified and augmented by the subcultures of genre fiction.

To adopt Colie's metaphor of neighbourhoods and cultures, it is as if the London of Joseph Conrad's *The Secret Agent* (1907), E. M. Forster's *Howard's End* (1910), and Woolf's *Mrs. Dalloway* (1925) became not only the socially contiguous London of Penelope Fitzgerald's *Offshore* (1979), Margaret Drabble's *The Radiant Way* (1987), Alan Hollinghurst's *The Line of Beauty* (2004), John Lanchester's *Capital* (2012), and Ian

McEwan's *Saturday* (2005), but also the geographically more diverse Londons of Hanif Kurieshi's stories, novels, and films, Monica Ali's *Brick Lane* (2003) and Zadie Smith's *NW* (2012) and the generically revised Londons of Peter Ackroyd's *Chatterton* (1987) and *Dan Leno and the Limehouse Golem* (1994), Neil Gaiman's *Neverwhere* (1996), J. K. Rowling's Diagon Alley (1997), Ben Aaronovitch's *Rivers of London* (2011), and, in graphic narrative form, Alan Moore and Eddie Campbell's *From Hell* (1989), to name just a few. Even non-fiction narrative lays claim on the reimagined capital city, with Iain Sinclair's hybrid travel narratives/biographies/psycho-geographies, *Lights Out for the Territory* (1998), *London Orbital* (2002), and *London Overground* (2015). The 'kinds' in the contemporary period 'melt into one another', as Colie puts it, dissolving boundaries of genre and changing readers' sense of what to expect when picking up a book, when narratives are no longer necessarily fictional, written in prose, or even originally published in print. For example, Geoff Ryman's *253*, originally published as a website in 1996, was honoured with a 1998 Philip K. Dick award for science fiction, but Ryman's novel, despite its digital mode of presentation and counterfactual elements, logically extends a realistic principle of character depiction to an experimental extreme. Describing each of the 253 people on a London tube train before a fatal crash, Ryman's work depicts a microcosm of London society as a collection of selves, a traditional representational project of the novel.

Return of the Romance

This chapter asks whether (or not) the return of the romance in the generic hybrids of the past several decades of contemporary British fiction results from postmodernism's blending of high and low cultural forms. From the vantage point of academia, postmodernism seems like a good explanation for the change. Among the potentialities of postmodern literary style from the 1960s onward was openness to pastiche of subgenres, playful storytelling, metafictionality, and self-consciousness about conventions of fictional narrative. Possibly these qualities made the contemporary novel especially adaptable to the recovery of modes that had been set aside as the province of popular or low-brow fiction, at least after the 1890s. (Earlier, of course, qualities that contemporary readers regard as 'postmodern' turn up in eighteenth-century novels such as Sterne's *Tristram Shandy* [1759].) Clearly there has been a shift towards acceptance of and appetite for generic blends since the 1980s. This could be attributed to an extension of postmodern relativism's questioning of grand narratives, not excluding F. R. Leavis's influential story of the realistic novel in English, *The Great Tradition*.

But it is not the only explanation. One alternative possibility, rendering the postmodern periodicity of contemporary fiction as correlational rather than causal, concerns the fundamentally ontological worldmaking art of fiction. Novels make possible worlds, and the actions staged in imagined worlds do not have to be verisimilar or even plausible. They can have dragons and giants; historical mysteries and counterfactual histories; magicians just as well as musicians; unseen universities and underground kingdoms; detectives in disguises and otherworld portals. As developed in long prose form over many centuries, the characteristics of romance narratives do not disappear even when the novel emerges in English with an emphasis on representation of ordinary people and everyday occurrences. Though realism is the dominant mode of the novel, and the preferred baseline from which modernist experimentation departs in the twentieth century, it is not the only option, especially for writers looking for new means of innovation. Imaginative worldmaking did not remain free of a repressed romance inheritance forever. Genre fiction, with its thrilling plots, its strong affects of suspense, curiosity, and wonder, its larger-than-life protagonists and antagonists, and its uncanny flirtations with supernatural explanations or conspiracy theories, has a lot to offer the novel, and postmodern relativism may have kicked the door open to let genre in.

Yet it may also be the case that postmodern style (and poststructuralist and postcolonial theorising) came late to a party already started by writers of popular fiction, who did not require the endorsement of eggheads or graduates of writing programmes to proceed and succeed. Genre fiction attracts its own readers and viewers, and where there are audiences, writers turn up to join the fun (sometimes aspiring to make a living). Few novelists would spurn being a featured author with a book among the Richard and Judy Book Club (sponsored by bookseller WH Smith), which for two decades has consistently recommended gripping reads ranging across genres. In winter 2015 Richard and Judy had selected two gothic novels (by Kate Mosse and S. K. Tremayne), historical fiction (by Dinah Jefferies), thrillers (by Peter Swanson and Joseph Kanon), a near-future dystopia (by Catherine Chanter), a memoir (by Lucie Brownlee), and a Mann Booker-short-listed American novel (by Anne Tyler), a recipe still evident in their winter 2024 choices of two crime novels (by Andrea Mara and Jessica Knoll), suspense (by Will Dean), feminist fantasy (by Emilia Hart), a revenge comedy (by Jane Fallon), and a legal procedural (by Rob Rinder).

Enthusiastic readerships exist for a catholic variety of works in genre, cultivated by close links between book clubs and booksellers. Popular votes, sales ranks, and online opinion polls rather than university syllabi and published book reviews by the guardians of high culture rule in this world. When the previously disparaged 'subliterary' modes show up in the company of literary fiction, occupying zones of esteem, do genre fictions gain entry by wearing the gentrifying labels of postmodernism, or do they get in in their own right as works too great to be ignored? To decide among these possibilities and to entertain alternative explanations requires multiple angles of examination, including a look at the changes in status of fantasies, science fiction (including dystopias), historical fiction, and detective fiction.

The Reputation of Romance

For it cannot be overlooked that genre fiction has one great advantage in a period of dwindling audiences for the novel: genres have rafts of readers, including a younger generation of readers that grew up on Harry Potter. As Russell Lynes observed in mid-century, a publisher does have to make money by selling books:

> In order to publish slender volumes of poetry he must also publish fat volumes of historical romance, and in order to encourage the first novel of a promising young writer he must sell tens of thousands of copies of a book by an old hand who grinds out one best seller a year. He must take the measure of popular taste and cater to it at the same time that he tries to create a taste for new talent.[11]

In the intervening years, retail booksellers' requirements exerted increased influence, as Richard Todd has demonstrated in his work on commercial forces shaping the availability of new and backlisted titles and 'opening, democratizing, and in general extending the customer's imaginative and societal franchise'.[12] Even serious literary novelists, especially those hoping to live on publishers' advances and royalties, care about sales. When critically acclaimed midlist novelist A. S. Byatt won the Booker Prize for *Possession: A Romance* (1990), her sales leapt to heights previously undreamt of: she became an international bestseller. The publicity of the prize brought her to the attention of new readers, including those comprising an international audience for fiction in the vein of Umberto Eco and John Fowles, and those, mostly female, making up the lucrative market for historical romances. *Possession* combines kinds playfully, with a pastiche of letters, Victorian poetry, diaries, and fairy tales augmenting its unabashed romance story-telling, of both love story and race-and-chase adventure types. Because several of its major characters are self-aware academics, speaking the theoretical argot of 1980s theory, postmodernism and post-structuralism turn up as a matter of characterisation. The postmodernism of Byatt's novel was also immediately discussed by its critics, because it adopts many of the stylistic traits of historiographical metafictions, in Linda Hutcheon's terms. Yet the novel's revelation of a secret with a singular true answer runs counter to postmodern relativism in this romance of the archive.[13] Though its Booker Prize win played a role, not all Man Booker winners instigate such remarkable sales. It isn't at all clear whether *Possession* succeeded in spite of being a Romance and because it invoked postmodernism, or for the opposite reason, because its apparent postmodernism served a story that invited a wider range of readers, with brows of various heights, to savour the pleasures of Romance.

For at least some of those readers, the romance qualities that Byatt's novel galvanised through its evocation of genre fiction reminded them of Victorian novels such as those by the Brontë sisters or of fairytales by George MacDonald and Charles Kingsley, or even of twentieth-century children's novels by writers such as Joan Aiken, Alan Garner, Rosemarie Sutcliff, Henry Treece, Susan Cooper, or Lucy M. Boston. These writers, read with great pleasure by children, kept gothic, fantasy, quests, and uncanny varieties of historical romance alive in the cultural imagination. Some of those readers grew up to be serious novelists themselves; though they may quarrel with their childhood reading, they do not entirely forget it. C. S. Lewis's *Chronicles of Narnia* (1950–56) are not only the theological anti-matter to Philip Pullman's *His Dark Materials* (1995–2000), but they also resonate allusively in the background of works by Will Self and Lev Grossman. That Self's work would be considered 'postmodern' and Grossman's 'fantasy' merely emphasises the close family resemblance of these two forms of strongly ontological worldmaking, in the terms of Brian McHale's much-cited model of the epistemological-ontological dominant.[14]

In truth, the resurgence of genre fiction in the late twentieth and early twenty-first century is more a story about alterations of status and the relaxing of critical boundaries than of the replacement of one kind of novel with another. The situation was always more diverse and eclectic than such a narrative would suggest, and genre fiction was there all along, even at the highest levels of cultural approbation. Throughout the twentieth century, national and international prizes recognised the most accomplished literary novels and novelists, but the traces of Romance storytelling never disappeared entirely. For example, John Galsworthy, a bestselling novelist, won the Nobel Prize in 1932 and William Golding in 1983. Galsworthy had a large popular readership in his day. In a telling sign of the way the taste for modern fiction had to eschew fiction with broad appeal to assure its status, Galsworthy was disdained by many twentieth-century critics for the Victorian style of his Forsyte Chronicles (1906–33), a rambling family saga in serial instalments. Golding's *Lord of the Flies* (1954) became a set text for reading in school (a sure sign of literary stature), but it, too, owed a lot to romance, drawing on the popular tradition of boys' adventure to ground its chilling political allegory. In the same year that Golding published *Lord of the Flies*, the first volume of *The Lord of the Rings*, J. R. R. Tolkien's *The Fellowship of the Ring* (1954), began a slow transformation of taste in fiction that would contribute to the stature of genre fiction and romance. In 1957 Tolkien's epic quest fantasy was recognised with the International Fantasy Award at the 15th World Science Fiction Convention.[15] *The Lord of the Rings* now routinely ranks among the best books of the prior century in public opinion polls, no longer segregated as fantasy.[16] By 2007, the next time an English novelist won the Nobel Prize for Literature (after Golding), the committee chose a writer, Doris Lessing, whose work blends with fantasy and speculative fiction. Among her novels to engage with genre fiction are the conclusion of *The Children of Violence* sequence (1952–69), *The Four-Gated City* (1969), *The Memoirs of a Survivor* (1974), *The Fifth Child* (1988), *Mara and Dann: An Adventure* (1999), and her space fiction sequence *Canopus of Argos: Archives* (1979–83), one of which, *The Marriages Between Zones Three, Four, and Five* (1980) is an unadulterated romance novel in a legendary vein.

Lessing's Canadian contemporary, Margaret Atwood, a perennial favourite for the Nobel Prize, won the Arthur C. Clarke Award for science fiction for her novel *The Handmaid's Tale* (1985), and has explored genre in her Booker-prize-winning novel *The Blind Assassin* (2000) and in the historical novel *Alias Grace* (1996). Atwood's speculative fiction includes a near-future dystopic trilogy, *Oryx and Crake*, *The Year of the Flood* (2009), and *MaddAddam* (2013). She sometimes bristles when her work is described in terms of genres such as science fiction, preferring the labels of speculative fiction or social science fiction. Her response reminds the reader that even for a celebrated literary writer, some genre labels are less desirable than others. Among the most dignified alternatives are dystopias.

Atwood's near-future speculative fictions participate in a long and venerable literary tradition of dystopias, including such canonical works as Aldous Huxley's *Brave New World* (1932) and George Orwell's *Nineteen Eighty-Four* (1949). Both *The Handmaid's Tale* and *Oryx and Crake* have achieved the practical accomplishment of becoming canonical in an academic sense – these dystopias are frequently taught in colleges and universities, on literature, women's studies, environmental studies, and bioethics syllabi. Yet they have also succeeded in the wider market for fiction, as numerous 'reading group guides' for both works attest; Atwood receives attention from Oprah Winfrey and her vast readership. In an interview published in Oprah's magazine, *O*, Atwood responds to a question about her literary influences:

Q: Where do the scary sci-fi themes in your work come from?
MA: I was warped early by Ray Bradbury and Edgar Allan Poe. I was very fond of Franz Kafka. And I was watching all those B movies, like *Village of the Damned*.[17]

This writerly testimony may help to explain where a postmodern sensibility arises, with its playful combination of writers popular (Bradbury) and canonical (Poe and Kafka), and its openness to low-brow influences such as horror movies. In a 2009 interview Atwood lays out a commonsense description of the proper role of genre:

> Genres, anyway, are inventions of people who need to rank things on bookshelves. Genres aren't closed boxes. Stuff flows back and forth across the borders all the time. You know that part on the back of the book where it says 'Romance', for example? That's so somebody knows what shelf to put it on. It has nothing to do with anything else, really.[18]

This blithe dismissal of the legitimacy of generic categories comes from a writer who has made a career of playing with and blending those genres deftly, without any damage to her literary reputation. Indeed, her sequel to *The Handmaid's Tale*, the 2019 novel *The Testaments*, co-won the Mann Booker Prize.

Yet as Mark McGurl describes in his magisterial work of literary history, *The Program Era*, serious writing for most of the twentieth century could engage with the genres only in the self-consciously elevated manner of what he refers to as 'meta-genre', an arch attitude that involves postmodern pastiche and parody to insulate against the appearance of pandering to popular tastes.[19] McGurl writes about the US American context. The developing influence of the growing number of writing programmes in Britain, Ireland, and the postcolonial Anglophone countries may reveal a more open attitude to genre fiction. Links with publishers and connections with agents are touted on Master of Fine Arts (MFA) programme websites, and commercial success through crime fiction and popular genre writing is not an embarrassment. From the start, University of East Anglia (UEA)'s Creative Writing Course, a master's programme founded in 1970 by Malcolm Bradbury and Angus Wilson, trained writers of prose fiction with openness to genre fiction (poetry, script-writing, and creative non-fiction were added later). Distinguished graduates include Anne Enright, Emma Healey, Kazuo Ishiguro, Ian McEwan, Natasha Pulley, and Rose Tremain (BA). Among the publications of UEA's programme alums can be found detective fictions, thrillers, dystopias, time-shift fantasies, and even chick lit. Historical fiction in particular has been a strong area of performance for graduates of Britain's most prominent creative writing programme.

The Dignity of Historical Fiction

Writing historical fiction has enabled contemporary British novelists both to cash in with robust sales and to garner the laurels of critical acclaim. The fact that all the major Victorian novelists wrote historical fiction at least some of the time, and some of the modernist novelists followed suit, sets historical fiction apart from the other genres, as I have earlier argued.[20] Crossovers from serious fiction to historical fiction are so common as to be unremarkable, and do no damage to a writer's reputation. For example, Hilary Mantel's double win of the Man Booker Prize for *Wolf Hall* (2009) and *Bring Up the Bodies* (2012) followed a distinguished career of respectfully reviewed literary novels and collections of short stories. Mantel had a loyal fan base, but after she moved to historical fiction set in the Tudor period, her sales exploded, she earned an expanded international readership, and her work was adapted for stage and television. Mantel had dabbled in genre fiction with an excellent thriller *Eight Months on Ghazzah Street* (1988) and the gothic *Fludd* (1989), but she had enjoyed particular success with historical novels in *A Place of Greater Safety* (2006), a French revolution story, and a fictionalised biography, *The Giant, O'Brien* (1998). Does Mantel's move towards the historical require an explanation by way of postmodernism? Though she presents a revisionist view of Thomas Cromwell in novels that adopt his perspective, *Wolf Hall*, *Bring Up the Bodies*, and *The Mirror and the Light* (2020) do not require postmodern theorising to explain their stances or techniques. Their formal qualities owe more to the modernist restraint of an Ivy Compton Burnett or the perspectival attitude of a Ford Madox Ford than to postmodern historiographic metafictions. Serious contemporary British novelists routinely write historical fiction without the appearance of slumming.

Crossover Authors in Both Directions

Genre writers have also gained status by shifting towards the historical mode and a higher style, for the most part skirting the gender-bounded territory of historical romances. For example, Michael Moorcock, best known for his science fiction and fantasy, achieved short-list status as a literary author with his historical novel of the Blitz, *Mother London* (1988). The Joycean (or Woolfian) style in this novel about three outpatients from a mental hospital ensures that a reader wandering in from one of Moorcock's more popular multiverses will be on notice that in this fictional world, high modernist discontinuities challenge easy reading. Anthony Burgess similarly employed demanding prose styles to distinguish his most ambitiously literary works, such as *Nothing Like the Sun* (1964), *The Napoleon Symphony* (1974), or his most famous work, the dystopia *A Clockwork Orange* (1962). As an early reader and critic of James Joyce, a linguist, and a composer who claimed Stravinsky as his introduction to modernist style, Burgess's excursions into genre fiction (mysteries, comic novels, historical fiction, and family sagas) never seriously endangered his reputation as a literary novelist. If making up a language for the purposes of creating a fictional world (as in *A Clockwork Orange*) has for Burgess a genealogy that reaches back to Joyce's *Finnegans Wake* (1939), for other authors the relevant ancestor is J. R. R. Tolkien. David Mitchell, a British novelist whose work stakes claims both to high seriousness and to the resources of various sub-generic kinds, rings the changes on genre and employs high literary style and devices. When Mitchell invents a future English for the central novella of his Booker-Prize winning *Cloud Atlas* (2004), he shows the influence of both Burgess and Russell Hoban's *Riddley Walker* (1980), a science fictional dystopia. When Paul Kingsnorth creates a shadow version of Anglo Saxon for his post-Norman-Conquest novel *The Wake* (2014), it is hard not to hear echoes of Tolkien, whose glossopoeia and worldmaking go hand in hand, and whose environmental commitments make him an appropriate ancestor to Kingsnorth.

The two-way traffic on occasion admits works in genre into the ranks of serious literary fiction, as for example P. D. James' detective novels, John Le Carré's spy thrillers, Angela Carter's fairy tales, Alice Thomas

Ellis's surreal fantasies, Charles Stross's cyberpunk fictions, Jeanette Winterson's erotica, and Kingsnorth's mythopoetic historical fiction. These works are not pastiches or 'metagenre' versions of actual genre fiction. J. K. Rowling's hard-boiled detective novels, written under the *nom de plume* Robert Galbraith, are proper mysteries. After finishing the Harry Potter series, Rowling announced a break with fantasy by writing a Hardyan naturalist novel, *The Casual Vacancy* (2012), but soon returned to genre with her Cormoron Strike novels. To see Rowling's artistry praised in the pages of the *Times Literary Supplement*[21] suggests not only that she has succeeded in breaking through to the highest level of critical respect (having already conquered the book market), but also that detective fiction, like historical fiction, is a status-raiser. The story of a restored openness to the subgenres could be regarded in part as an unfinished project of feminism, for many women writers thrive as authors of detective fiction, fantasy, and historical romances. It may be that a self-conscious donning of the mantle of postmodernism is a strategy more often employed by male writers hoping to capitalise on the large market for popular fiction, while women writers who have already made careers as writers of popular genres make cross-over breakthroughs into the serious literary market without postmodern gesticulation.

The very distinction of metagenre from genre seems an unnecessary and even anxious critical gesture, designed to dignify romancing. Self-conscious reference to generic traits already exists within the genres themselves, where play with tropes and conventions provide, as they have provided Romance storytelling for centuries, fresh opportunities for invention as well as the pleasures of recognition. Detective fiction from the Golden Age of Allingham, Christie, and Sayers, has indulged in self-aware play with its own conventions, as in Christie's *The Murder of Roger Ackroyd* (1926), a modernist experiment with a surprise ending that relies on readers' assumptions about narrative reliability. John Dickson Carr, an American-born mystery novelist associated with the Golden Age of British detective fiction wrote, in the fashion of *mise-en-abyme*, a lecture on the tropes of the locked room mystery within a locked room mystery, *The Hollow Man* (1935), long antedating the metafictional detective writers. What could be more self-aware than C. S. Lewis' meditation on multiverse worldmaking and the submersive surrender of reading than the pools in 'The Wood Between the Worlds' in *The Magician's Nephew* (1955)? Terry Pratchett's fantasies possess the referential armatures of satire; his Discworld rides on the back of a giant tortoise but refers to recognisable continents, cultures, and races of Earth. Metalepsis, a frame-breaking gesture typifying postmodern metafiction, occurs throughout genre fiction, and no surprise: it is a characteristic of Romance.

The Way We Read Now

In many contemporary cases, separating the genre writer from the serious literary novelist becomes a fruitless exercise. The *oeuvre* of novelist China Miéville, whose Londons can be construed as scenes of Lovecraftian horror (*King Rat* [1998]), allegorised quest landscapes (*Un Lun Dun* [2007]), or palimpsests of urban surrealism (*Kraken*, [2010]), suggests the difficulties. Miéville writes from a Marxist perspective, cites children's novels *The Borribles* by Michael Lammentiere as an influence on his depiction of London, and sees genre as possessing both subversive and reactionary potentialities, a notion he expresses with validating poststructuralist citations. Miéville says in an interview with John Pistelli:

> I think [genre] does contain perhaps a latent bacchanal, a carnivalesque in what I suppose is a vaguely Bakhtinian way and that is I suppose perhaps latently radical but also potentially reactionary. I think you can make a case that the fantastic aesthetic has a radical core. I'm not sure I'd say the same for genre, which strikes me as more of a tool, usable for various ends of various political stamps.[22]

When an author of science fiction writes and speaks with evident awareness of a Jamesonian political unconscious, the 'deeply reactionary ideological lie of narrative', it becomes evident that the choice of genre as a vehicle expresses a great deal more than a desire for access to its lucrative markets.[23] As critic Blakey Vermeule says,[24] novelists eat theories for breakfast.

The proliferation of crossover genre fiction makes it ever harder to say whether postmodern recuperations, a general relaxation in high-culture gatekeeping, or both, should be credited with causing the change described in this chapter. Much contemporary writing proceeds with blithe unawareness of postmodernism and its philosophical underpinnings. Even works with a superficial resemblance to postmodernist narrative – due to metafictionality, pastiche, frame-breaking, playful foregrounding of conventions to lay bare the device – often disagree at root with the fundamental scepticism and relativism that motivates postmodernism. Postmodernism is best understood as a style whose adoption during the contemporary period expresses a writer's desire to be considered experimental, irreverent, up-to-date, and still 'literary' in a period when the separate distinction of literary fiction has undergone serious erosion. For practitioners of postmodernism, who make up a subset of contemporary writers, the term 'postmodern' is available as a self-adopted descriptor, as Brian McHale has argued, writing 'Postmodernism periodized itself', with attributes of historicity and a dignifying relation to modernism.[25] But that label is only one among many intersectional identities claimed by contemporary British novelists. They work now in newly diverse generic neighbourhoods, as Rosalie Colie anticipates, where the resources of kind have created new possibilities for the descendants of Romance and new pleasures for readers.

Notes

1. E. M. Forster, *Aspects of the Novel* (New York: Harcourt, Brace, and World: 1927), p. 126.
2. See Gerald Graff, *Professing Literature. An Institutional History* (Chicago, Illinois: University of Chicago Press, 1987).
3. Virginia Woolf, 'Middlebrow' in *The Death of the Moth, and Other Essays* (London: Hogarth Press, 1942), p. 177.
4. Ibid., pp. 181–2.
5. Ibid., p. 182.
6. Ibid., p. 186.
7. Mark McGurl, *The Program Era: Postwar Fiction and the Rise of Creative Writing* (Cambridge, Massachusetts: Harvard University Press, 2009), p. 103.
8. Ibid., p. 102.
9. Rosalie Littell Colie, *The Resources of Kind: Genre-theory in the Renaissance*, ed. Barbara K. Lewalski (Berkeley: University of California Press, 1973), p. 103.
10. Ibid., p. 116.
11. Russell Lynes, 'Highbrow, Lowbrow, Middlebrow' in *The Tastemakers* (New York: Harper, 1954), p. 321.
12. Richard Todd, 'Literary Fiction and the Book Trade' in *A Concise Companion to Contemporary British Fiction*, ed. James F. English (Oxford: Blackwell, 2006), p. 36.
13. Suzanne Keen, *Romances of the Archive in Contemporary British Fiction* (Toronto: University of Toronto Press, 2001), pp. 32–4.
14. Brian McHale, *Postmodernist Fiction* (New York: Methuen, 1987), p. 10, p. 59.
15. 'F.A.Q.', *The Tolkien Society*.
16. Edward James, 'Tolkien, Lewis, and the Explosion of Genre Fantasy' in *The Cambridge Companion to Fantasy Literature*, eds. Edward James and Farah Mendlesohn (Cambridge University Press, 2012), p. 62.
17. 'Margaret Atwood on her new book, *MaddAddam*', an interview in *O, the Oprah Magazine* (September 2013) www.oprah.com/entertainment/margaret-atwood-maddaddam-interview/all.

18. Jo Scott Coe, 'Margaret Atwood: an interview with Jo Scott Coe', in *NarrativeMagazine.com* (October 2009) www.narrativemagazine.com/issues/fall-2010/interviews/margaret-atwood-margaret-atwood.
19. McGurl, *Program Era*, 217.
20. Suzanne Keen, 'The Historical Turn in British Fiction' in *A Concise Companion to Contemporary British Fiction*, ed. James F. English (Oxford: Blackwell, 2006), pp. 168–9.
21. Roz Kaveney, review of Robert Galbraith's *Career of Evil*, *TLS* (13 November 2015), p. 20.
22. John Pistelli, '"A truly monstrous thing to do": The China Miéville interview, part one', in *Long Sunday*, www.long-sunday.net/long_sunday/2005/07/a_truly_monstro.html.
23. Ibid.
24. Blakey Vermeule, Discussion. 'The Narrative Conference: Society for the Study of Narrative', Berkeley, CA, 27–29 March 2003: http://narrative.georgetown.edu/conferences/conference2003/.
25. Brian McHale, 'What Was Postmodernism?' ('Fictions Present' thread of *Electronic Book Review*, 20/12/2007) [unpaginated]: https://electronicbookreview.com/essay/what-was-postmodernism/.

CHAPTER 9

Alternative Realisms
Speculation, Magic, and Miracle in British Postmodern Fiction

Andrew Tate

Literary realism is a competitive business; as a mode of writing it is defined less by a stable set of historical conventions than by rival ways of representing that most contentious of objects, the imprecise set of phenomena known as the 'real world'. For Alain Robbe-Grillet, experimental author and, from the 1950s, a defiant advocate of *le nouveau roman*, realism is not a form that unites writers under a single flag but 'the ideology which each brandishes against his [*sic*] neighbour, the quality which each believes he possesses for himself alone'. 'All writers', he dryly observes, 'think they are realists'.[1] Self-identification as such, suggests Robbe-Grillet, is a matter of ethical commitment as well as aesthetic preference and one that has perpetuated a near universal resistance to genre labels such as 'abstract, illusionistic, chimerical [and] fantastic'.[2] In the decades since Robbe-Grillet's reflections, however, attitudes have shifted. Certainly, the cultured despisers of fantasy and its avatars remain influential; and some arbiters of prestige, including the panels for lucrative literary prizes, either treat the genre with contempt or ignore it entirely. Yet the creative potential of myth, miracle, and magic has also transformed the empirical sensibilities of contemporary British novelists, particularly those whose work bears the traces of what we might now regard as a postmodern tradition. This term may seem like an oxymoron, especially if we think of the critical epithet as synonymous with hostility to any form of continuity, shared value, or investment in the idea of transhistorical connection. However, postmodernism, far from being a purely caustic, ironic, or nihilist force, has often been characterised by the recuperation of depth and mystery. Zygmunt Bauman, for example, writing in the early 1990s, argued that postmodernity could 'be seen as restoring to the world what modernity presumptuously, had taken away; as a *re-enchantment* of the world that modernity tried hard to *dis*-enchant'.[3]

Postmodernist fiction, in which the numinous collides with everyday experience, has become a literary commonplace. Andrzej Gasiorek notes that a swathe of late twentieth and early twenty-first century novelists 'have embraced the imaginative resources of literary modes that bypassed the realism/antirealism issue altogether: fantasy, gothic, fabulation, myth, carnival'.[4] Indeed, there is a long, rich, and jumbled genealogy of such writers in Britain: Doris Lessing's earliest novels were published in the 1950s; in the same decade J. G. Ballard wrote odd, vatic short stories for science fiction magazines before the first of his post-apocalyptic novels, *The Drowned World* was published in 1962; Angela Carter's enormously influential magic realist fables emerged in the late sixties as dreams of revolution were tested by escalating wars in Vietnam and racism in the UK. Salman Rushdie, who experimented with fusions of mythology and science fiction in *Grimus* (1975), won the Booker Prize for his second novel, *Midnight's Children* (1981). His fourth novel, *The Satanic Verses* (1988), a tale of colonisation, migration, and metamorphoses that includes angelic beings, miraculous salvation, and dream visions became the most controversial literary work of the postmodern era. In their separate 'flights from realism', to use Marguerite Alexander's evocative epithet, this quartet of novelists reinvigorated the possibilities of fiction in English.[5] More recently, Peter Boxall has described the diverse attempts of twenty-first-century novelists 'to grasp the texture of the contemporary real'; he cites, in particular, the theorist Paul Virilio's description of the 'otherworldly temporality' of fragmented, global post-millennial culture as a context for reading the experimental realist fictions of writers who are adapting their work 'to approach a reality that seems differently weighted, unfamiliar in both its brute thereness and in its abstraction'.[6]

Post-Millenial Fiction: Dream-Logic versus Mundane Reality

This chapter will focus on the ways in which a variety of distinctively postmodern alternative realisms have flourished in the early twenty first century, with particular reference to novels by David Mitchell, Ali Smith, and Kazuo Ishiguro. Post-millennial fiction might be characterised by heterogeneity but its diverse narratives frequently turn to ontological questions that Brian McHale famously identified as a recurrent element of postmodernism: 'What kinds of world are there[?] What happens when different kinds of world are placed in confrontation, or when boundaries between worlds are violated?'[7] More recently, McHale, writing with Len Platt, invokes the proliferation of angels in late twentieth-century postmodern narrative and describes 'the experience of "ontological shock": the shock of recognizing that there are other worlds besides this one, other orders of being beyond our own; that these other orders are at least potentially in communication with ours; that we live not in a single unitary world, but in a *plurality of worlds*.'[8]

The novels explored in this chapter are charged with a similar postmodern sense that literature might evoke a *'plurality of worlds'*, as dream-logic and mundane reality collide in comic and destabilising ways. Ghosts, angels, healers, and prophets visit recognisable suburban landscapes. The dead speak and resurrections are handled in a matter-of-fact fashion; in one story, a superannuated knight fights with a dragon whose toxic breath induces amnesia in the population; another imagines souls migrating across time and between genres. A connecting thread between the novels is that they all evoke worlds in which the boundary between the mundane and the magical is rendered porous. Each narrative, in its own idiosyncratic way, might be read as apocalyptic, a form of narrative in which veiled, hidden or buried stories are revealed. The advent of alternative realism in British fiction is a late flowering of postmodernism, one that resonates, in particular, with McHale's understanding of the 'ontological dominant' that characterises this literary moment. Literary taxonomies necessarily change for both commercial and critical reasons and one legacy of the critique offered by rival versions of postmodernist thought is a certain fragmentation of approaches to popular and experimental narrative. We may be more confident of thinking about specific genres and subgenres – the post-apocalyptic novel, or urban Gothic fiction, to name two examples – and yet these modes of writing, particularly when drawn on by experimental writers, have deep affinities with postmodern literary practice. British Postmodernism, in my view, has not been defined solely or even primarily by writers whose work rejects depth, affect or the search for meaning.

'Crossover' Fiction, Cosmopolitanism, and Creative Mischief

Twenty-first-century fiction is frequently marked by its disregard for hierarchical literary categories. Indeed, one legacy of postmodernism at its most creatively mischievous, is the freedom for writers to loot popular genres: tropes from science fiction, horror, romance, *noir*, and fantasy are almost ubiquitous in narratives that make a virtue out of trespassing across the borders of genre. M. Keith Brooker, addressing the twin careers of the late Iain Banks (as popular but serious novelist) and his alter ego, Iain M. Banks (as popular but SF-classified novelist), has noted 'the increasing difficulty of making distinctions between conventional "literary fiction" and fantasy fiction'.[9] 'Crossover' novels – often written for a teenage or Young Adult audience but which have achieved a much wider readership – have also fostered a stronger critical appreciation of fantasy. For example, Philip Pullman's *His Dark Materials* trilogy (1995–2000) moves between worlds and fuses genres including Miltonic epic, children's adventure fiction, Steampunk, and anti-theological discourse. Although *Northern Lights* and its two sequels have a strong didactic element in their representation of political despotism and critique of the conservative Christian fantasies of C. S. Lewis and J. R. R. Tolkien, the novels also thrive on many similar narrative pleasures as those quest narratives set in Narnia and Middle Earth. The commercial and critical success of Pullman's trilogy exemplifies a turn towards romance, magic, and apocalypse that is visible in the work of writers who are more commonly marketed and reviewed as 'literary' rather than as authors of genre fiction. If fiction remains popular, and marketable, it is also under pressure in an era of instant communication and fragmented news. The distinctive fictions of Ali Smith (b. 1961) and David Mitchell (b. 1969) both register the uncanny, spectral connections and divisions engendered by globalisation in its late capitalist phase. They are all, I would suggest, contributing to a distinctively British mode of postmodernism, one that fuses scepticism of authoritarianism with a sense of the sublime.

In Douglas Coupland's first novel, *Generation X: Tales for an Accelerated Culture* (1991), one of his disaffected dropouts laments that 'the world has gotten too big – way beyond our capacity to tell stories about it'.[10] This idea echoes, consciously or otherwise, Jean Francois Lyotard's famous critique of 'grand narratives' in *The Postmodern Condition* (1979; trans. 1984). The idea of '*petit récits*' – small stories – that might both replace an authoritarian, official metanarrative is fertile ground for contemporary writers. Mitchell's debut novel, *Ghostwritten* (1999), published at the end of the second Christian millennium, might be read as kind of response to the problem of narration in an era of global instability. Berthold Schoene, at once building on and challenging the limits of Benedict Anderson's *Imagined Communities*, uses Mitchell's debut as a case study to interrogate the ways in which the novel as a form might 'adapt and renew itself by imagining the world instead of the nation'.[11] *Ghostwritten*, in these terms, constitutes a 'cosmopolitan fiction', one that Schoene argues 'not so much breaks with the tradition of the English novel as it subtly deconstructs, unties, and defamiliarises it, with respect to both its treatment of the nation and its conceptualization of individuality'.[12]

Ghostwritten is haunted by multiple spectres – of terror, financial collapse, traumatic memory, chance – and, in some instances, spirits that might be holy. The novel's epigraph is from Thornton Wilder's *The Bridge of San Luis Rey* (1927), a study in the relationship between chance and tragedy: the lines reflect on two alternative visions of the universe, both theistic. From one perspective, to 'the gods we are like flies that the boys kill on a summer day'; for a more Christian outlook, 'the very sparrows do not lose a feather that has not been brushed away by the finger of God'.[13] *Ghostwritten* suggests, however, that arbitrating between these two polarities is less important than the recognition of the interdependent nature of human beings and their place in a world that is both delicate and resilient, capable of regeneration but frequently damaged by greed, arrogant behaviour and a variety of imperialisms. Theological speculation, even of a sceptical nature, prefigures Mitchell's first book and, curiously, sets the tone for his later transhistorical, cosmopolitan fictions including *Cloud Atlas* (2004) and *The Bone Clocks* (2014). In many ways, Mitchell appears to be a kind of apprentice to a variety of postmodern mentors, including Italo Calvino, Borges, and, in Britain, Rushdie: his work is playful, increasingly self-referential, and engaged with the value of storytelling itself.

Ghostwritten, a 'novel in nine parts' (a recurrent number in the work of a writer drawn to patterns and recurrence) crosses continents and multiple minds: its narrators include a murderous member of a millenarian cult, a teenage jazz musician, a corrupt lawyer unaware that he is on the verge of death, an elderly witness to the Chinese cultural revolution, a ghostwriter, a quantum physicist, and a '*noncorpum*' (a disembodied spirit that moves between host bodies). The fact of human mortality seems more of a negotiable obstacle than a final reality in Mitchell's fiction. Reincarnation, for example, is a recurrent trope from *Ghostwritten* onwards and becomes particularly important in *The Bone Clocks*. This is not, the author asserts, because he believes in the concept of rebirth as theological dogma but because it allows him to address our species-specific fear of death. Addressing questions of mortality, Mitchell indicates an understanding of the appeal of religion: 'Most sects of most of the world's religions issue passports to an afterlife in return for an unwavering faith in that sect's precepts. A part of me envies true believers, but I can't emulate them.'[14] Mitchell's 'cosmopolitan' fiction is driven by similar kinds of ethical questions to the transcendent religions that he rejects. *Ghostwritten* is

Alternative Realisms: Speculation, Magic, and Miracle

alert to mystery even as it demystifies those who make specious claims to spiritual authority or absolute truth.

The novel begins audaciously in the unsympathetic consciousness of a man who has committed mass murder: 'Quasar', a lonely and deluded individual who believes his guru is on the verge of bringing a new dawn to the world, is responsible for a nerve gas attack on the Tokyo Subway. However, religious fanaticism with its delusions and violent consequences is not the sole form of spirituality in *Ghostwritten*. Indeed, encounters with sacred occur in unexpected ways and for less than obviously saintly figures. In 'Hong Kong', for example, Neal Brose, 'bent lawyer' and lost soul, becomes an accidental pilgrim on Lantau Island. Brose is ostensibly an unlikely seeker after spiritual sanctuary: a semi-reluctant participant in a money-laundering scam, his bland acquisitiveness, reminiscent of any number of real-life financial scandals of the 1990s, is rather undercut by the fact that he is a multiply haunted man. His marriage has recently ended and, in spite of an emotionally evasive and laddish disposition, it is clear that he is a lonely person in crisis. Neal experiences a moment of epiphany: he realises too late that he is dying; in his delirium, however, he encounters truths about himself – not quite a death bed conversion or redemption but something like a spiritual revelation in the presence of a statue of the Buddha. This rather sombre chapter is followed by a narrative of the innkeeper in 'Holy Mountain': a woman who has witnessed atrocities across a century but who retains an irreverent spirituality: 'Engine-powered pilgrimages? Even Lord Buddha doesn't give a shovelful of chickenshit for engine-powered pilgrimages. How do I know? He told me himself?'[15]

In the London episode, Marco, a ghostwriter and drummer for The Music of Chance (a band named for Paul Auster's novel of this title), has a colourful spiritual career including periods of superstition, Christianity, and Marxism; he describes himself as 'not anything much these days ... A part-time Buddhist, maybe'.[16] This section thematises the novel's concerns with chance, coincidence, and contingency: Marco connects a number of the major characters – for example, he sleeps with Neal Brose's ex-wife and saves Mo Muntervary, a quantum physicist who is being pursued by the authorities, from being hit by a car. His profession is an echo of the act of writing, and one that has a particularly postmodern dimension: do writers create or simply synthesise what already exists, in a vast network of texts and lives? The novel resonates with late nineteenth- and early twentieth-century naturalist anxieties about the fact human agency is overwhelmed by determinisms less benign than the Christian God. Yet the narrative's conclusion, an uncanny tenth chapter, returns to

Quasar, this time on the Tokyo underground, before we first encountered him. This act of literary time travel also connects this desperate, murderous man via a series of transient images with other characters and locations from the novel. He attempts to flee the carriage in which he knows he has condemned other human beings to die. Mitchell does not offer a cheap redemption but, in echoing the lives of the other protagonists, emphasises the fragility and beauty of finite existence. One of the futures of religion in British fiction is surely anticipated by *Ghostwritten* – the precariously cosmopolitan form that Schoene identifies is a space in which a polyphony of voices – agnostic, atheist alongside a variety of orthodoxies – might give a stronger sense of the complex ways in which communities both coexist and fail.

Storytelling, Spirits, and Secular Resurrection

The motif of reincarnation is appropriated from Buddhist tradition but it also has aesthetic as well as spiritual resonances. Storytelling is a persistent human activity – and for some humanist thinkers it is a defining signifier of our species – but its multiple forms continually undergo cycles of death and rebirth. If life often reminds us that it is finite and that death is the only certainty, fiction, notes James Wood, 'gives us allowable resurrections, repeated secular returns'.[17] This is particularly true of contemporary alternative realism which often treats the afterlife as a good vantage point for evoking the strangeness of life on earth. Will Self's *How the Dead Live* (2000), for example, presents a version of the hereafter that resembles East London. Jenn Ashworth's *Fell* (2016) is an ostensibly realist narrative of everyday suffering and grief that resituates the myth of Baucis and Philemon, and their divine reward for hospitality, in Morecambe Bay. The twenty-first-century present timeframe is interrupted by memories of 1963 and the awakening narrative voices of a dead married couple, reincarnated, '[d]azed as newborns' and 'finding the words for things, laughing, stiff as bark' and ready to tell their story.[18] It is a narrative in which superficial divisions between, for example, the quotidian and the mystical, healing and harm and care and coercion, evaporate. These are characteristics that recur in the alternative realist strands of British postmodern fiction.

Ali Smith frequently gives a place to the figure of the revenant, spirits caught between worlds, not quite ready to leave this one. In Smith's *Artful* (2012), a dead lover, who wanders into their former home, eyeless and covered in dust, haunts the grief-struck narrator. Whether real or

Alternative Realisms: Speculation, Magic, and Miracle 151

imagined, these spectral encounters are defined neither by Gothic terror nor spiritual reassurance. Rather, the narrator is matter-of-fact about the implausible visitation – and its rational explanation as imaginative projection – but is also frustrated by an inability to understand the elliptical, idiosyncratic utterances of the revenant. The ghost is impudent and disruptive – for, example, on a trip to Brighton, it steals books from a second-hand shop. The sepulchral visitor is, amongst other things, a wayward reader. Smith's odd book – a critical-creative hybrid – embodies the erosion of the division magical and the mundane in contemporary British fiction. Germanà and Horton also identify 'a Modernist sensibility' at play in Smith's writing, 'particularly in its concern for formal consciousness and experiment'.[19] In *How to Be Both* (2014), the spirit of a Renaissance painter is intrigued by the life of a grieving twenty-first-century teenage girl. It is not clear who is haunting whom.

Hotel World (2001), unlike Mitchell's *Ghostwritten*, is geographically focused in a single (non) space – an unexceptional branch of a corporate hotel chain in the English provinces – but has a zigzagging temporal structure and a similar fascination with the depredations of globalisation. One character, a self-regarding journalist, reflects in her review, without apparent irony, that '[i]t doesn't matter where you are in the world if you're anywhere near a Global Hotel. You could be, literally, anywhere.'[20] The hotel is a threshold space, a kind of purgatory, that seems to both suspend identity in its bland assertion of sameness and to prompt its temporary dwellers, staff and guests, to confront the strangeness of being a self, even in an era that appears to have capitulated to a logic of cultural uniformity and consumer obedience.

'Past', the opening of the novel's five sections (each of which bears the name of a tense), is narrated by the increasingly amnesiac ghost of Sara Wilby, a young chambermaid in the Global Hotel. She haunts her old life, apparently powerless to move on, even as her body lies in the grave. She is, in her own faltering words, 'hanging falling breaking between this word and the next'.[21] Smith uses this frustrating breakdown in linguistic aptitude as a defamiliarising way to celebrate the everyday: Sara died when, on a whim, she clambered into a dumb waiter that plummets to the ground. Her death is represented as sudden, tragi-comic, and absurd. Her melancholy half-memories of life on earth testify to everyday pleasures, now ended ('I would give anything to taste. To taste just dust') and a longing for 'the breathtaking still-hard surface of the world'.[22] She also argues with herself, splitting body and spirit in darkly comic fashion: 'Don't you have a home to go to? Aren't you supposed to go to heaven, or hell, or somewhere?'²³ Sara's pseudo-purgatorial state also connects with the liminal lives of many of the novel's characters: a homeless woman who is secretly, and against regulations, offered a room in the Global hotel; the same kindly receptionist, in 'Future Conditional', experiences a debilitating illness which estranges her from society and restricts her movement. She, like Sara, struggles to assert a clear sense of narrative on to her experience of the world but believes that 'there was a story after all, somewhere, insistent, strung between this place and the last and the next, and she was trying to remember it'.²⁴

Hotel World resonates with the idea that magic realism might, in the words of Wendy B. Faris, 'embody liminality – the in betweenness of beings, cultures, and discourses'.²⁵ However, the string of epigraphs that preface the novel is also suggestive of its subtly metaphysical orientation: a terse aphorism from Muriel Spark's *Memento Mori* (1959) – 'Remember you must die' – that presents a stark reminder of the proximity of death to life vies, for example, with a line from William Blake's heterodox illuminated poem, *The Marriage of Heaven and Hell* (1790–3) which proclaims that 'Energy is eternal delight', and a long quotation from Edwin Muir's poem of grief and loss, 'The Child Dying', reflects on the strangeness of death and the miraculous nature of life.²⁶ The Blakean sense of energy, in particular, implies that this is a distinctively apocalyptic novel. Although this widely used term has become a synonym for the current cultural infatuation with spectacular catastrophe, the primary sense of *apokálypsis* is 'uncovering' or revelation. The last book of the Christian scriptures, The Revelation of St John, begins with this Greek term 'suggesting a disclosure or unveiling'.²⁷ Smith's intimate representation of mortality and grief in an era that intensifies the already transient nature of life recuperates this original signification of apocalypse, though it is certainly not an explicitly religious novel.

Catastrophic Futures, Myth, and Apocalpytic Amnesia

Apocalypse in its secondary and more widely recognised meaning as imminent destruction is a significant trope in alternative realist fictions. The sociologist John Urry described the turn to disaster as 'a catastrophist structure of feeling' at work in popular culture.²⁸ The commercial success of Armageddon – a phenomenon that seems infinitely repeatable on screen and page – means that apocalyptic fiction has a peculiar mobility. This fear-fascination is exemplified in the vast range of twenty-first-century narratives that imagine the imminent collapse of civilisation as a result of ecological ruin, scientific hubris, financial mismanagement, pandemic, and the end of all good things. There is an extended family of genres and subgenres that imagine a variety of forms of what Patrick Parrinder has named 'ruined future'.[29] J. G. Ballard suggested that his own excursions into the apocalyptic or speculative genres were best regarded as taking place in the 'visionary present'.[30] Such vatic fiction exceeds the boundaries of conservative iterations of representational 'reality' but frequently maintains a strong commitment to a political understanding of the everyday. David Mitchell's novels frequently return to a variety of dystopian and post-apocalyptic landscapes which are haunted by the legacies of current political and ethical problems. Two of the six stories in *Cloud Atlas* are set in the near or far future that, following a motif that runs through this short story cycle, examine the exploitation of human beings and environmental destruction. *The Bone Clocks* ends in 2043, during a post-oil era popularly known as the 'Endarkenment'. Mitchell's protagonist, Holly Sykes, who the novel has followed since adolescence, is now in her seventies and surviving in rural Ireland. She reflects on the parlous state of the world and is clear who bears the responsibility: 'My generation were diners stuffing ourselves senseless at the Restaurant of the Earth's Riches knowing – while denying – that we'd be doing a runner and leaving our grandchildren a tab that can never be paid.'[31]

The apocalyptic tradition occasionally looks backwards, rather than dreaming of the future, to explore a politics of belonging and exclusion. Kazuo Ishiguro's *The Buried Giant* (2015), for example, draws on Arthurian legend.[32] It is a novel that resonates with John Updike's claim that a myth might operate as a nation's 'bad conscience'.[33] An elderly couple, Axl and Beatrice, traverse 'the desolate, uncultivated' terrain of sixth century Britain in search of the son from whom they are estranged.[34] They embody what Michael Greaney identifies as a vulnerability that is 'creaturely ... emotional ... and cognitive', a phenomenon he reads as crucial to 'the temporalized experience of being in the world as it is imagined by Ishiguro'.[35] Their memories are fragmented and vague; the pair alternate between tender expressions of affection and moments of fractiousness, inspired by half-remembered disappointment and regrets. The quest is also made more complicated by encounters with a solitary knight, secretive monks, an enigmatic warrior, and a dragon. Courageous acts are undercut by a muted sense of the absurd as characters frequently lose their bearings and motivation. This bald description perhaps sounds more like *Game of Thrones* rewritten by Samuel Beckett than might be expected from the author of *The Remains of the Day* (1989).[36]

Yet Ishiguro's fiction has often thrived on the fuzzy distinction between fantastical phenomena and the mysteries of ordinary, waking life: *Never Let Me Go* (2005) and *Klara and the Sun* (2021), for example, deploy near-future dystopian settings to critique the ethics of post-human technologies. *The Buried Giant* by contrast, has a retrospective trajectory, travelling more than a millennium into the past, to an epoch and a land marked by the wars of the legendary King Arthur, a figure who is revered by some as a great king and resented by others as a tyrannical winner.

Ishiguro blends Christian traditions with those of alternative mythologies: characters pray to the 'God Jesus' whilst they watch a poisoned ogre drowning; Roman narratives of crossing a river to the next life vie with the hope of resurrection.[37] The writer's experiments with a popular genre are characterised by a nagging feeling that we've been here before; the logic of a recurring dream pervades this odd fable. The memory loss that vexes Axl and Beatrice is not, it transpires, merely one of the depredations of ageing but a widely shared phenomenon. Their village is one in which 'the past was rarely discussed' and even recent peril is quickly forgotten in favour of minor community squabbles. As Axl grasps at 'fragments of a remembrance' – was he really a father and if so, where are his children? – he reflects on the sinister 'mist' of forgetting that seems to have descended on the land.[38] As Cynthia F. Wong notes, Axl and Beatrice's mythic journey echoes the one undertaken by Stevens, the emotionally evasive and self-deceived protagonist of *The Remains of the Day*, a more conventionally realist novel, 'in that a personal teleology is conflated with physical movement across a terrain that keeps its own catastrophic histories intact'.[39]

Disturbed by the burgeoning awareness of collective memory loss, Axl and Beatrice slip away from their settlement, in pursuit of a prodigal son and, more pressingly, of the truth. The couple encounter Wistan, a mysterious Saxon soldier, and his charge, Edwin, an orphaned and exiled boy, with trials and tasks of their own. Their shared story does not quite follow the typical hero's journey – the two Britons have long since come of age, their own (perhaps) valiant rites of passage evaporated into the miasma of lost time. They are reminiscent of Shakespeare's Rosencrantz and Guildenstern: they know themselves to be bit players in a much bigger drama, seekers after security and meaning in a world hostile to both of those longed-for commodities. Ishiguro's title itself echoes Matthew Arnold's 'The Buried Life' (1852), an ambivalent hymn to humanity's capacity for evasion and repression: the 'nameless sadness' of life lived in flight from emotional honesty. The novel is partly about the dangers (and attraction) of willed cultural amnesia. Those things that Axl and Beatrice have failed to remember are crucial to their identity – in the supernatural sense of this fictional universe, faithful memory is regarded as a potential safeguard to a happy afterlife – but their acts of forgetting connect with a more sinister form of forgetfulness. *The Buried Giant* connects with what Yugin Teo names 'memory work', a recurrent element of Ishiguro's fiction. Teo contrasts, for example, 'the shared memories' of the exploited protagonists of *Never Let Me Go* which serves as a 'cathartic release' with the 'enforced amnesia' of Axl, Beatrice, and their peers and notes that this 'post-Arthurian tale … makes the case that it is not always possible to remember and bear witness'.[40] Axl gradually recalls fields of blood and slaughtered innocents but hopes that such 'a barbarous past' is 'gone forever'.[41] The young warrior who joins his journey laments, however, that he has 'seen dark hatred as bottomless as the sea on the faces of old women and tender children, and sometimes felt such hatred myself'.[42] The old warrior eventually slays the elderly dragon, whose breath, under an enchantment, 'polluted the air, robbing memories both happy and dark'.[43]

Although *The Buried Giant* is not an allegory in the same sense as John Bunyan's paradigmatic dream vision *The Pilgrim's Progress* (1678) the novel invites disquieting parallels between its plot and the horrors of contemporary warfare: the narrative remembers peaceable neighbours who are forced to turn against each other in times of war because of religion or ethnicity; military leaders who dispensed with humanitarian imperatives in favour of assuring power; the vulnerable sacrificed to uphold a specious ideal of purity. *The Buried Giant* may appear to be a flight into the past but it engages with timely political problems. Is it better to forget injustice in the name of peace? To whom does land belong? These questions have a strong theological charge. Wistan treats his older friends with respect but, as a Saxon raised among Britons, he is sceptical of their declared religion, one that preaches both justice and mercy but which seems quick only to excuse the private sins of the powerful. 'What kind of god is it, sir, wishes wrongs to go forgotten and unpunished?' he enquires.[44] In Robert Eaglestone's ethically oriented reading of the novel, he notes that 'both amnesia and memory have baleful consequences on individuals and on communities' but that, in relation to the undercurrent of Christian belief that is so vital for Axl and Beatrice, it is '[m]emory, not forgetting' which 'leads … to forgiveness'.[45] The catastrophe of shared amnesia is transfigured into a kind of apocalyptic remembering, in which muted, difficult truths are made legible. The search for personal peace exemplified by Axl and Beatrice is one that cannot be achieved without an awareness of the demands of a near impossible justice. *The Buried Giant* is a critique of what the theologian Walter Wink named the 'myth of redemptive violence'; the recovery of the past, it suggests, is not simply a nostalgic folly but an ethical requirement if we are to live peacefully.[46]

Ishiguro's exploration of memory and the 'buried giant' of lost history is an experiment with the limits of realism. To borrow Fredric Jameson's sequence, we might witness the historical shift (or a historical passage) from Medieval and Renaissance allegory (as equivalent) to the age of realism to modernism and, most recently, into postmodernism. Yet any solid historical boundaries between these mutating forms are another kind of fiction, one with finite usefulness. For Jameson, 'realism is opposed to romance only because it carries it within itself and must somehow dissolve it in order to become its antithesis'.[47]

The 'beautiful deformations of the real' that are at play in contemporary British fiction constitute a challenge to a standard criticism of both fantasy and postmodernist discourse as ethically vague and politically disengaged.[48] The magic and miraculous realisms of Mitchell, Smith, and Ishiguro exceed the limitations of common sense logic not in order to escape material difficulties of present politics but as a way of resisting the despairing idea that change is never possible. Whether or not these writers would own the term 'postmodernist', each of them is, I would suggest, carrying on a tradition of writing that bears the hallmarks of McHale's influential definition of the 'ontological dominant', one that retains its critical value in the twenty-first century.

Notes

1. Alain Robbe-Grillet, *For a New Novel: Essays on Fiction*, trans. by Richard Howard (Evanston: Northwestern University Press, 1989), p. 157. James Wood also cites this now very familiar aphorism in the introduction to *The Broken Estate: Essays in Literature and Belief* (London: Jonathan Cape, 1999), p. xi.
2. Robbe-Grillet, *New Novel*, p. 157.
3. Zygmunt Bauman, *Intimations of Postmodernity* (London: Routledge, 1992), p. x.
4. Andrzej Gasiorek, 'Postmodernisms of English Fiction' in *The Cambridge Companion to the Twentieth-Century English Novel*, ed. Robert L. Caserio (Cambridge University Press, 2009), pp. 192–209, p. 208.
5. Marguerite Alexander, *Flights from Realism: Themes and Strategies in Postmodernist British and American Fiction* (London: Edward Arnold, 1990).
6. Peter Boxall, *Twenty-First-Century Fiction* (Cambridge University Press, 2013) [Kindle Edition], pp. 10–11.

7. Brian McHale, *Postmodernist Fiction* (London: Routledge, 1987), p. 10.
8. Brian McHale and Len Platt, 'General Introduction' in *The Cambridge History of Postmodernism*, ed. Brian McHale and Len Platt (Cambridge University Press, 2016), pp. 1–14, p. 11.
9. M. Keith Booker, 'The Other Side of History: Fantasy, Romance, Horror, and Science Fiction' in Caserio, *Cambridge Companion to the Twentieth-Century English Novel*, pp. 251–66, p. 263.
10. Douglas Coupland, *Generation X: Tales for an Accelerated Culture* (London: Abacus, 1992), pp. 5–6.
11. Berthold Schoene, 'Tour du Monde: David Mitchell's *Ghostwritten* and the Cosmopolitan Imagination', *College Literature* 37:4 (Fall 2010), pp. 42–60, p. 43. See also Berthold Schoene, *The Cosmopolitan Novel* (Edinburgh University Press, 2009), pp. 97–124.
12. Schoene, 'Tour du Monde', p. 50.
13. David Mitchell, *Ghostwritten* (London: Hodder, 1999), n.p.
14. Paul A. Harris, 'David Mitchell in the Laboratory of Time: An Interview with the Author', *SubStance* 44:1 (2015), pp. 8–17, pp. 11–12. For a detailed exploration of spirituality in relation to Mitchell's writing see Rose Harris-Birtill, *David Mitchell's Post-Secular World: Buddhism, Belief and the Urgency of Compassion* (London: Bloomsbury, 2019).
15. Mitchell, *Ghostwritten*, p. 113.
16. Ibid., p. 271.
17. Wood, *Broken Estate*, Location 297.
18. Jenn Ashworth, *Fell* (London: Sceptre, 2016), p. 3.
19. Monica Germanà and Emily Horton, 'Introduction' in *Ali Smith: Contemporary Critical Perspectives*, ed. Monica Germanà and Emily Horton (London: Bloomsbury, 2013), pp. 14–18, p. 17.
20. Ali Smith, *Hotel World* (London: Penguin, 2002), p. 180.
21. Ibid., p. 30.
22. Ibid., p. 5, p. 4.
23. Ibid., p. 26.
24. Ibid., p. 84.
25. Wendy B. Faris, 'The Latin American boom and the invention of magic realism', in McHale and Platt, *Cambridge History of Postmodernism*, pp. 143–58, p. 143.
26. Smith, *Hotel World*, n.p.
27. Joseph L. Mangina, *Revelation* (London: SCM Press, 2010), p. 37.
28. John Urry, *What Is The Future?* (Cambridge: Polity, 2016), p. 37.
29. Patrick Parrinder, 'The Ruined Futures of British Science Fiction' in *On Modern British Fiction*, ed. Zachary Leader (Oxford: Oxford University Press, 2002), pp. 209–33.
30. J. G. Ballard, *The Complete Short Stories, Volume One* (London: Fourth Estate, 2014), viii.
31. David Mitchell, *The Bone Clocks* (London: Sceptre, 2014), pp. 533–4.

32. The following material on Ishiguro's *The Buried Giant* is developed from my review of the novel, originally published in *Third Way* magazine in 2015.
33. John Updike, 'More Love in the Western World', *The New Yorker*, 24 August 1963, pp. 90–106.
34. Kazuo Ishiguro, *The Buried Giant* (London: Faber, 2015), Kindle edition, location 28.
35. Michael Greaney, '"Some Wound or Something": Kazuo Ishiguro and the Forms of Vulnerablity' in *Contemporary Vulnerabilities*, ed. Pier Palo Piciucco (Torino: Nuovo Trauben, 2023), pp. 298–314, p. 298.
36. For Wang Yinping, however, there is an affinity between these two novels which she reads as 'New Legends of England': 'novels [that] approach the myth and legend genres with transformational presentation of the individual and collective memories of war in the contemporary world'. See Wang Yinping, 'Ethnic War and the Collective Memory in Kazuo Ishiguro's The Buried Giant', *English Studies* 102:2, pp. 227–242, p. 227.
37. Ishiguro, *Buried Giant*, location 3423.
38. Ibid., location 81.
39. Cynthia F. Wong, '"Emotional Upheaval" in *An Artist of the Floating World* and *The Buried Giant*' in *The Cambridge Companion to Kazuo Ishiguro*, ed. Andrew Bennett (Cambridge University Press, 2023), pp. 200–12, p. 202.
40. Yugin Teo, 'Memory and Understanding in Ishiguro' in Bennett, *The Cambridge Companion to Kazuo Ishiguro*, pp. 226–39, p. 226, p. 231. See also Yugin Teo, 'Monuments, Unreal Spaces and National Forgetting: Kazuo Ishiguro's *The Buried Giant* and the Abyss of Memory', *Textual Practice* 37.4 (2023), pp. 505–26.
41. Ishiguro, *Buried Giant*, location 1927.
42. Ibid., location 1925.
43. Ibid., location 4169.
44. Ibid., location 3818.
45. Robert Eaglestone, 'Ethics and Agency in Ishiguro's Novels', in Bennett, *The Cambridge Companion to Kazuo Ishiguro*, pp. 187–99, p. 195, p. 196.
46. See, for example, Walter Wink, *The Powers that Be: Theology for a New Millennium* (New York: Doubleday, 1999).
47. Fredric Jameson, *The Antinomies of Realism* (London: Verso, 2013), p. 138.
48. Wood, *Broken Estate*, xi.

CHAPTER 10

'Queer' Postmodernism? British Gay and Lesbian Fiction

Kate Haffey

In 1992, Jeanette Winterson published *Written on the Body*, a novel whose narrator never discloses their gender. Heralded by some as brilliantly innovative and ridiculed by others as overly gimmicky, the novel quickly spawned dozens of articles that sought to make sense of this omission. *Written on the Body* is perhaps the perfect example of the intersection between postmodern literary practice and queer theory, which was emerging in the years leading up to the novel's publication. In its removal of gender as a grounding characteristic for the narrator, the novel forces its readers to deconstruct their own assumptions. In classic postmodern fashion, readers become active participants in the construction of the text and are urged to consider the ways that gender norms frame their perceptions of reality.

Winterson's novel explored issues that were starting to come to the forefront of academic discussions in the early 1990s. In 1990, Teresa de Lauretis coined the term 'queer theory' and in doing so she gave a name to a particular thread of the scholarship on sexuality that had just begun to flourish. Influenced by post-structuralism's critiques of subjectivity, this emerging work challenged the understandings of identity upon which the majority of gay liberationist and lesbian feminist scholarship was founded. While much of the earlier scholarship on sexuality took for granted a stable gay or lesbian subject whose history merely needed to be uncovered and reclaimed, queer theory explored sexual identities as cultural and linguistic constructs that were the product of specific historical processes.

Queer theory's critiques of sexual identities were made possible by the work of post-structuralist philosopher Michel Foucault. Foucault's *The History of Sexuality* (1976) charts the emergence of 'the homosexual' from the psychological and medical discourses of the late nineteenth century. While individuals have always engaged in same-sex sexual activity, prior to the late nineteenth century forbidden sexual acts like sodomy were imagined as actions that any person might engage in. However, in the

1870s psychological and medical professionals began to categorise individuals by the sexual acts they participated in. The scientific discourses they produced spoke of 'the homosexual' as a particular *type* of person, a person whose sexuality was at the core of their being. As Foucault says, the homosexual's sexuality existed as a 'singular nature' that was 'everywhere present in him'.[1] Foucault's description of the emergence of 'the homosexual' demonstrated that sexual identity categories are historically specific and constructed through discourses of power.

Queer theory is also indebted to the work of feminist scholars who began in the 1980s to question the category of 'woman'. Lesbian feminists showed the ways in which the category relied upon an unquestioned presumption of heterosexuality, while feminists of colour explored how mainstream scholarship often assumed a white subject. Building on this work and on the work of Foucault, Judith Butler argues in *Gender Trouble* (1990) that feminism may undermine its own goals if it uses 'woman' as the grounding category for analysis. This is because the category of 'woman' does not represent the natural unity of 'a gendered self' but instead functions as a regulatory fiction that naturalises heterosexuality and reproduces normative gender relations. Butler's book, while framed within the feminism of its moment, would later be considered one of the founding texts of queer theory. It is in *Gender Trouble* where Butler first articulates her theory of gender performativity, a concept that has remained central to queer scholarship. According to Butler, gender needs to be understood not as a being, but as a doing. 'Gender', she claims, 'is the repeated stylization of the body, a set of repeated acts within a highly rigid regulatory frame that congeal over time to produce the appearance of substance, of a natural sort of being'.[2] In other words, the repeated enactment of gender norms, which are thought to be the mere expression of a gendered subjectivity, actually creates the fiction of a gendered essence at the centre of the subject. Butler's work thus thoroughly denaturalised gender and provided a critical framework for the deconstruction of gender, sexuality, and sexual desire.

Butler's work paved the way for others to develop a carefully theorized concept of 'queer'. Perhaps the best early description of the term comes from Eve Kosofsky Sedgwick. 'One of the things that "queer" can refer to', she states, is 'the open mesh of possibilities, gaps, overlaps, dissonances and resonances, lapses and excesses of meaning when the constituent elements of anyone's gender, of anyone's sexuality aren't made (or *can't be* made) to signify monolithically'.[3] Here Sedgwick is attuned to the ways in which identity categories posit a cohesive understanding of sexuality that does not account for its various contradictions and incoherencies. It is for this reason, perhaps, that theorists have sought to keep the term strategically capacious and somewhat ill-defined.

It is important to note that the word 'queer' sometimes causes confusion because it is used in at least two different, and at times conflicting, ways. On the one hand, 'queer' is utilised as an umbrella term for the diverse array of identities that may include, but are not limited to, lesbian, gay, bisexual, transgender, questioning, intersex, asexual, aromantic, and so on. On the other hand, 'queer' names the trend in contemporary theory described above, one that grows out of poststructuralist feminism and deconstruction and is critical of coherent, unitary, and stable models of the self. While the former deployment may sometimes be in line with the assumptions of queer theory, it might also be mobilised in ways that rely upon a more stable and cohesive model of the self. For example, calls to normalise queerness are at odds with queer theory's drive to deconstruct the binary between normal and deviant, as laid out most convincingly in Michael Warner's *The Trouble with Normal*.[4] Indeed, as David Halperin has noted, 'Queer is by definition whatever is at odds with the normal, the legitimate, the dominant. There is nothing in particular to which it necessarily refers. It is an identity without an essence.'[5]

In its focus on performativity, its perception of reality as constructed through language, and its carnivalesque celebration of indeterminacy, queer theory is very much in line with the assumptions of postmodernism. It is thus no surprise that postmodern literary techniques have often been the method through which novelists approach queer identity and desire in their texts. Even before 'queer theory' was coined in 1990, a number of British novelists (Jeanette Winterson, Alan Hollinghurst, Hanif Kureishi, Peter Ackroyd, to name a few that this chapter will address) had already written novels that explored concepts that would become central to queer theory using postmodern techniques. These authors employed postmodern narrative strategies in a variety of different ways, but most often they sought to deconstruct the traditional narrative conventions and the discourses of power that had rendered queer desire unspeakable or unthinkable for much of the twentieth century.

The emergence of this type of literature was made possible by a series of historical events that allowed queer desire to be expressed more openly as the twentieth century progressed. After years of debate, in 1967 sex acts between consenting men in private were decriminalised through the Wolfenden legislation. The late 1950s and 1960s also saw the relaxing of previous media censorship, allowing artists to explore homosexuality in film, theatre, and literature. These new freedoms resulted in the formation of political groups and in the creation of more visible gay and lesbian publications. The Gay Liberation Front, a political organisation that celebrated gay identity and advocated that gays and lesbians 'come out' publicly, met for the first time in the basement of the London School of Economics in 1970. In 1972, *The Gay News* was launched and, with a circulation of 20,000, was available at major newsstands.[6] But as the 1970s neared their close, the political climate began to change when the conservatives won the 1979 election in a landslide and named Margaret Thatcher Prime Minister. Thatcherism 'signaled an end of collective-minded progressive values that might have offered homosexual men and women full standing as citizens'.[7] The situation only worsened as the AIDS crisis came increasingly into the public eye in the 1980s. Although the epidemic produced creative new forms of activism, it also spawned fierce homophobia and set the stage for Clause 28, a portion of The Local Government Act of 1988, which stated that local authorities were prevented from promoting 'homosexuality as a pretended family relationship'. When the act was passed, it enshrined in law the perception that homosexuality was harmful to society. While few can point to instances in which the law was actually enforced, its rhetoric had far-reaching results. As the twentieth century came to a close, the law was still in effect (it was not repealed until 2003). Despite the many challenges that queer individuals faced during these years, the final decades of the millennium saw the production of a diverse set of literary texts that reimagined queer identity and countered homophobic attitudes and representations.

The Queer Bildungsroman

When novelists began to write stories that explicitly dealt with same sex desire in the late 1960s and 1970s, the coming out story emerged not only as a literary genre but also as a narrative convention that affected the ways that gays and lesbians told stories about themselves. Influenced both by the activism of gay liberation movements, which urged people to come out publicly and tell their stories, and by the consciousness-raising of the feminist movement, which emphasized the political dimension of personal experience, the coming out story was often a teleological narrative of self-discovery in which an individual came to understand their own sexuality and assumed a public identity as gay or lesbian. As such, the coming out story follows a bildungsroman-like structure in which an individual progresses through a series of stages. The protagonist struggles with their sexuality in private, recognising that their desire is at odds with the values of their culture. But instead of learning to accept dominant cultural values and ascending to their rightful place in society, as would happen in a traditional bildungsroman, the protagonist learns to reject society's normative values and develop their own queer-affirming ones. They reach maturity when they accept themselves as gay or lesbian and learn that it is the society, and not they themselves, that needs to change.

This is essentially the plot of E. M. Forster's novel *Maurice*, which was completed in 1914 but not published until 1971, a year after his death. Other coming out stories followed, and many of these relied upon a particular imagining of the self, one that was stable, monolithic, and unified, a self whose true essence could be discovered and represented. However, in the 1980s and beyond, in a literary landscape that had been altered by postmodernism, we start to see a new type of coming out story, one that queers the bildungsroman form even further by questioning the very notion of identity upon which the bildungsroman structure is built.

Perhaps the best example of this is Jeanette Winterson's 1985 novel *Oranges Are Not the Only Fruit*, which employs postmodern narrative techniques to produce a new kind of coming out story, one that doesn't rely upon the fiction of an essential self. Winterson's semi-autographical novel is the story of Jeanette, a girl adopted by Pentecostal Evangelists who is growing up in an industrial town in northern England. Following the structure of most coming out stories, Jeanette begins to question the beliefs and values of her community when she experiences 'unnatural passions' for another girl. However, interspersed with this realist narrative of Jeanette's childhood are several unconventional fairytales and fantasy stories. While the fairytales are somewhat short and contained at first, as the novel goes on, they begin to interrupt Jeanette's story with greater frequency. Each of these stories functions as an alternative way for Jeanette to narrate her life. The novel ultimately becomes a postmodern pastiche of narratives, none of which can supply the complete story of Jeanette's early life, and all of which are limited and enabled by the conventions of their genre. In Winterson's hands, the coming out story is not a quest for an individual to discover their 'true self,' but an acknowledgement that the self is constituted through acts of narration. This model of the self is clearly aligned with postmodern notions of subjectivity. The self is imagined as a story, and one that could be narrated in multiple ways, as opposed to a unified entity about which 'the truth' could be spoken.

Another example of this type of queer bildungsroman is Hanif Kureishi's 1990 novel *The Buddha of Suburbia*, which tells the story of Karim Amir, a self-described 'funny kind of Englishman', who is the son of an Indian immigrant father and a white British mother. Karim, the narrator of the story, describes himself as 'a new breed ... having emerged from two old histories'.[8] The novel follows Karim's movement from the South London suburbs to London and later to New York City as he self-consciously explores his various hybrid identities while navigating the complexity of racial tensions, class conflict, and sexual possibility in 1970s England. Throughout the story, Karim has sexual relationships with both men and women; however, he never describes himself as occupying a specific identity category – bisexual or otherwise. Instead, he discusses his sexuality by describing the sex acts in which he likes to engage:

> It was unusual, I knew, the way I wanted to sleep with boys as well as girls. I liked strong bodies and the backs of boys' necks. I liked being handled by men, their fists pulling me; and I liked objects – the ends of brushes, pens, fingers – up my arse. But I liked cunts and breasts, all of women's softness, long smooth legs, and the way women dressed. I felt it would be heartbreaking to have to choose one or the other.[9]

Karim's treatment of his own sexuality does not follow an identitarian framework in which he 'is' a particular type of person because of the sexual acts he engages in. If Foucault's scholarship points to the ways in which homosexuality emerged as a category of being, as a type of person in the late nineteenth century, then Kureishi thinks against this categorising by attending to sexuality as a set of bodily practices that make nonsense of the linguistic categories that purport to speak an essential truth about the individual.

Confronting the AIDS Epidemic

Queer postmodern writing not only seeks to counter the constructions of identity that smooth over or erase complexity and fluidity, it also challenges dominant representations of LGBT individuals that circulate in popular discourses. This is especially true of the narratives about gay men that circulated during the AIDS epidemic. As Patrick Woods claims, the coverage of AIDS confirmed two images of homosexual men that already existed in the cultural imagination: 'the self-destructive pervert whose sexual acts are so extremely and obviously "against Nature" as to call down the righteous wrath of God' and 'the diseased victim whose condition demands not blame but compassion, not punishment but prayers'.[10] As Woods acknowledges, while one of these models is fundamentalist and the other liberal, both are 'heterosexist, homophobic, anti-gay'.[11] Beyond this, the popular press often constructed gay men as a type of contaminant that threated to infect the national body. In the face of such pervasive rhetoric, AIDS activists had the difficult task of drawing attention to a health crisis that was threatening populations that had been both demonised and ignored. Operating from the postmodern assumption that reality as we know it is not something 'natural, something innocently "given"' but instead is 'always already manufactured, an ideological illusion sustained by the matrix of postindustrial capitalism and media culture',[12] AIDS activists and academics alike sought to deconstruct these manufactured narratives. As Lee Edelman claims, 'intellectual efforts to theorize the epidemic, its constructions and its representations, frequently invoke ... some notion of the postmodern'.[13] The connection between AIDS and postmodernism can be seen clearly in the art and literature that has responded to AIDS.

This is particularly true of the work of Alan Hollinghurst. Hollinghurst's first novel *The Swimming Pool Library* (1988) is narrated through the point of view of Will Beckwith, a handsome twenty-five-year-old gay aristocrat, who is set to inherit a fortune and spends his days swimming at the local gym and picking up men. The novel is set in 1983 but is narrated from a time some years later, after the AIDS epidemic has vastly changed the cultural landscape for gay men. And yet, *The Swimming Pool Library* is not a book that ever explicitly mentions AIDS. The closest it ever comes is in its opening when Will states: 'My life was in a strange way that summer, the last summer of its kind there ever was to be. I was riding high on sex and self-esteem ... but all the while with a faint flicker of calamity, like flames around a photograph, something seen out of the corner of the eye.'[14] The trauma of the AIDS epidemic haunts the text, subtly present in Will's narration of that summer as a force that affects the memories that are described. This method of narration creates a layered temporality in which multiple times are held in ironic tension. The novel adds a third layer of time when Will is asked to compose a book by Lord Nantwich, an elderly gay man whom he resuscitated at a public lavatory, and he begins to study Nantwich's diaries, which recount homosexuality during the period in which 'gross indecency' could send a man to jail in England. The presence of these three moments of gay history in the text – the period of criminalization, the years of freedom which followed the Wolfenden legislation, and the haunting of the text by the yet-to-come AIDS epidemic – creates a queer form of temporal irony that is reminiscent of the double coding of postmodernism. Double coding is a term that comes from Charles Jencks's work on postmodern architecture and describes buildings that combines new and old features, making visible the past and the present alongside one another. This rendering of time imagines history outside of a teleological framework and allows for an analysis of the ways that histories of oppression were psychically experienced by gay men.

While *The Swimming Pool Library* engages the AIDS crisis indirectly, Hollinghurst's 2004 Man Booker Prize winning novel *The Line of Beauty* takes on Thatcherism and the effects of the AIDS crisis explicitly. The novel tells the story of openly gay Nick Guest, a young middle-class man who is renting a room in the family house of an Oxford friend whose father is a conservative MP under Margaret Thatcher. The novel jumps from 1983, when Nick meets his first boyfriend Leo, to 1986, in which Nick has fully integrated himself into the London gay scene and is dating closeted Wani, and finally to 1987, at which time Wani is dying of AIDS and Nick is waiting for his latest HIV test results. Because Nick is a gay man living with the family of a Conservative MP, the novel has many opportunities to make visible and deconstruct the rhetoric of Thatcherism around issues of sexuality. One instance of this occurs when Rachel Feddens, the wife of the MP, uses the phrase 'vulgar and unsafe' to describe the behaviour of a government official who has been caught having sex with a man, causing a public scandal.[15] Nick immediately recognises this 'sudden hard formulation' as an ideological construction of his own sexuality.[16] Indeed, the phrase echoes through the text as a scrap of discourse that recurs over and over in Nick's thoughts and which he seems to understand as part of the dominant narrative of gay sexuality in Thatcher's 1980s. At one point, when considering whether he should bring his lover back to his room at the Feddens' house, he thinks, 'he just couldn't do that to Rachel and Gerald, it was vulgar and unsafe'.[17] While the novel does not set out to counter such representations by positing gay sexuality as safe and wholesome, it does make visible the ways in which the rhetoric of homophobic politicians during the 1980s had catastrophic effects for the psychological and physical health of gay men.

A similar critique of the rhetoric of conservative politicians can be seen across a series of connected novels by Paul Magrs. *Marked for Life* (1995), *Does It Show?* (1997), and *Could It Be Magic?* (1998) tell the stories a group of neighbours who live in Phoenix Court, a council estate in Aycliffe. The large cast of working-class characters who reappear across different novels includes gay, straight, bisexual, and transgender individuals. These three novels all employ a carnivalesque magical realism indebted to Angela Carter, on whom Magrs completed his doctoral thesis. This genre allows Magrs the freedom to counter the dominant narratives of queer sexuality in ways that would otherwise be impossible. This is especially true in *Could it be Magic?* which tells the story of Andy, a young gay man who becomes pregnant after a condom breaks during a one-night stand with another man. Shortly after the encounter, Andy worries that he may have become infected with HIV, a fear that becomes greater when he later begins to see spots emerging on his body. These marks, however, resemble leopard spots more than they do Kaposi Sarcoma, and after several months, Andy cuts open his calf to deliver his own hairy leopard-spotted baby boy. Through this odd turn of events, Magrs is able to interrupt the 'dominant order's association of homosexuality with death' and consider AIDS alongside the other possible effects of unprotected sex, such as pregnancy.[18] As Emma Parker claims, 'It permits us to imagine new worlds and realities that are not irrevocably constrained by the HIV/AIDS pandemic and institutionalized state homophobia.'[19]

Magrs's novel also engages with the language embedded in Clause 28, the section of law that banned the promotion of 'homosexuality as a pretended family relationship'. In the final chapter of *Could It Be Magic?* one character thinks about how the path of her life has allowed her 'to gather her invented family around her', a family that includes individuals of diverse gender and sexual identities.[20] Though the phrase 'invented family' is not a perfect match for the 'pretended family' of Clause 28, the change speaks to the novel's understanding of such families not as the imaginary delusion of an ill mind, as the law seemed to imply, but as the creative and inventive construction of queer communities made necessary by the AIDS epidemic and the historical reality of societal homophobia.

Queering History

If writing about AIDS allowed queer authors to counter the dominant discourses circulating about the epidemic, then reimagining the historical novel has enabled writers to explore queer histories that have often been absent from official accounts of the past. The authors who use this genre to explore homosexuality in the past do so with an understanding of postmodern critiques of history. Specifically, they recognise history as a constructed narrative that creates a vision of the past from a particular perspective, and they seek to prioritise those perspectives that could offer an alternative view. This queer historical turn also speaks to an affective need for LGBT-identified individuals to be able to imagine a past that has space for queer desire. Carolyn Dinshaw calls this 'a queer desire for history', and her work shows how postmodernism's playful temporalities can be mobilised to create 'the possibility of touching across time, collapsing time through affective contact between marginalized people now and then'.[21]

In the hands of those who use the historical novel to explore queer desire, the genre becomes a tool capable of reimagining the past outside of the assumptions of compulsory heterosexuality. Some novelists do this by writing historical novels with gay and lesbian characters at the centre rather than the margins, creating a past populated with unquestionably queer characters. Pat Barker, for example, creates characters based on actual historical figures who are known to have experienced same-sex attraction. Her *Regeneration* trilogy (1991–95) tells the story of several World War I shell-shocked officers, including the poets Siegfried Sassoon and Wilfred Owen, and the doctor who treated them for their condition, Dr W. H. R. Rivers. While Barker doesn't make the sexual identity of the several homosexual or bisexual soldiers the central focus of the novels, she doesn't shy away from the topic either. Instead, Barker's depiction of the societal mandate for men to suppress same-sex desires becomes one piece of the novel's subtle analysis of the cultural construction of masculinity in wartime England under the regime of military nationalism.

While Barker's novels are meticulously researched and draw on the historical documents of the figures she fictionalises, the novels of Sarah Waters respond to possible erasures of the historical record, especially where lesbians are concerned. LGBT history has tended to focus on gay male identity, partly because women's subordinate position in society has resulted in fewer opportunities to leave behind historical traces. Waters must therefore actively construct what might have been from the scraps of a scarcer historical archive. Thus, a novel like *Tipping the Velvet* (1998) set in the 1880s and 1890s, both attempts to creatively construct a queer past from available historical evidence and intermittently winks at its reader by making subtle allusions to twentieth-century lesbian literature and pop culture. Through her ironic use of such cultural references, Waters emphasises the point that we construct the past through the lens of the present. As Waters herself states, when writing the novel she was aware of the fact that 'we can't reconstruct the past or capture the past, we can only reinvent it, so [she] wanted the novel to be very self-consciously a piece of lesbian historical fantasy'.[22]

While Waters's later novels are less obviously self-conscious in their presentation of history, they often explore the gaps in the historical record regarding lesbian desire by examining the primary documents that become the basis for history. For example, one of the narrators of her 1999 novel *Affinity* destroys her diary that accounts for much of the story we've just read, an act that makes the story of her desire for another woman unavailable for future historians. Likewise, *Fingersmith* (2002) ends with one of its characters writing a pornographic book that, as she tells her lover, records 'all the words for how I want you'.[23] Of course this expression of same sex desire would be invisible to the historical record, embedded as it is in Victorian pornography, in a text that does not bear its author's name or gender, because 'ladies don't write such things'.[24] As Jodie Medd claims, Waters's fiction 'suggests that the archive of lesbian experience may exist where we least expect it'.[25]

At times Waters's novels lean toward the genre that postmodern critic Linda Hutcheon has called historiographic metafiction. This genre is one in which the 'theoretical self-awareness of history and fiction as human constructs . . . is made the grounds for its rethinking and reworking of the forms and contents of the past'.[26] This genre has been an important one for prominent British postmodern writers including Peter Ackroyd, who has written a number of novels that could be termed historiographic metafiction. Indeed, Ackroyd is also famous as a biographer, and his biographies, like his novels, tend to be ironic and self-aware in a rather postmodern fashion. As Brian Finney has claimed, Ackroyd has refused 'to distinguish between the genres of biography and fiction'.[27] Ackroyd's 1983 novel *The Last Testament of Oscar Wilde* is one that blurs the line between these two genres as it presents readers with a version of the famous author who interrogates his own position as a historical figure. The novel takes the form of a diary written by Wilde after he is released from his sentence of two years hard labour. Ackroyd's Wilde imagines himself as a linguistic construct produced through the discourse of others. In this sense, the novel's assumptions are in line with the critical work on Oscar Wilde that would later come out of queer theory, which examined how the popular media coverage of his trials actually helped to produce and define the image of 'the homosexual' in the cultural imagination.[28] As Ackroyd's Wilde states in the first few paragraphs of the novel, 'I am an "effect" merely: the meaning of my life exists in the minds of others and no longer in my own.'[29] By highlighting Wilde as a discursive construction, Ackroyd is able to produce a metafictional critique of the forces of representation.

Another writer who has made frequent use of historiographic metafiction is Jeanette Winterson. Two of her most critically acclaimed novels, *The Passion* (1987) and *Sexing the Cherry* (1989), employ the conventions of this genre to question the reliability of stories that are accepted as truth and to consider history as it is experienced by those at its margins, whose stories are rarely told. As such, Winterson's novels utilise what Linda Hucheon has termed 'ex-centric narrators', who are 'are anything but proper types: they are ... the marginalized, the peripheral figures of fictional history'.[30] Winterson's 'ex-centrics', like Villanelle in *The Passion*, often experience queer desire, but they are located in a past before terms like 'homosexual' or 'heterosexual' were part of the lexicon. Beyond exhibiting queer desire, Winterson's narrators are 'ex-centric' in a whole host of other ways. In *The Passion*, Villanelle is a cross-dressing Venetian woman with webbed feet who is forced to become a prostitute in Napoleon's army, and Henri, the novel's other narrator, is Napoleon's diminutive cook, who ends the novel in a prison asylum. Dog Woman, one of the narrators of *Sexing the Cherry*, is a giantess caring for her foundling son in seventeenth-century England. These characters' outsider positions allow them to critique the discourses of power of the societies in which they are embedded. Their stories are the 'petit récits' or 'little narratives' that Jean-François Lyotard discusses, stories that offer limited truths specific to a context rather than the unity of an overarching truth posited by grand narratives. Indeed, Winterson's texts, especially *Sexing the Cherry*, treat normative heterosexuality as one of those grand narratives that Lyotard has defined. In that novel, Winterson rewrites the marriage plot ending of Grimm Brothers' 'The Twelve Dancing Princesses' by providing a first-person narrative account of each princess's life after she married her prince. These subversive accounts, several of which highlight queer desires, not only function to critique the patriarchal mandates of the fairytale genre but they also make visible the alternative possibilities that become available when stories are told from historically marginalised perspectives.

Homonormativity in the Twenty-First Century

The twenty-first century has brought many tangible gains for LGBT-identified individuals in the UK, including marriage equality and the right to legally change one's gender. However, despite these advances LGBT people still experience institutionalised heterosexism, discrimination, and violence. This is particularly true of transgender individuals, who have suffered an increase in transphobic hate crimes in recent years and have been targeted by politicians and popular media figures.[31] There have been critiques, from both inside and outside the academy, that the political movements fighting for LGBT rights have focused primarily on those issues that are most conducive to mainstream values, that is, marriage, adoption, military service, and thus have sought to normalise LGBT-identities instead of engaging in a radical critique of the forces of normalisation. Attention is also being drawn to the ways in which queers have become consumers of an increasingly homogenised version of identity. As Alan Sears has argued, 'in the context of commodification, a person becomes visible as "queer" only through the deployment of particular market goods and services'.[32]

If during the twentieth century queer writers had the task of countering homophobic discourses that demonised and erased queer desire, then the challenge of the twenty-first century is slightly different. Alongside those queer-eradicating discourses that certainly still exist, an increasingly homonormative story is being told, one that charts a narrative of progress for certain gay and lesbian subjects. Gays and lesbians are imagined as affluent and powerful, individuals who have emerged from adversity to ascend to their rightful place in society. This narrative, however, is one that admits only certain LGBT-identified people and is often guilty of eliding racial, class, and national differences. It is a narrative that forgets the ways in which 'the discourses of sexuality are inextricable from prior and continuing histories of colonization, nationalism, racism, and migration'.[33]

But this is not to say that the British literature of the past several decades hasn't engaged with the complex issues facing an increasingly globalised, multicultural UK. This work has already been undertaken in limited ways by some of the writers discussed in this chapter – in Paul Magrs's renderings of working-class queers, in Hanif Kureishi's exploration of hybrid and intersectional identities, in Alan Hollinghurst's considerations of connections between queerness and empire. It can be seen clearly in a novel like Jackie Kay's *Trumpet* (1998), which analyses the media narratives and medical records that seek to explain and contain the life of Joss Moody, a famed black Scottish jazz musician who, upon his death, is discovered to have been assigned female at birth. The novel highlights the ways in which stories of queer lives are violently forced to fit normative narrative frames that erase the specific material realities of those occupying queer racialised bodies. Violent erasures like this are what is at stake if a single narrative of LGBT history is allowed to dominate. Though they must evolve in new directions, the tools of postmodern literary practice, with their perpetual deconstruction of totalising narratives, will remain as important as ever in countering the forces of normalisation in the twenty-first century.

Notes

1. Michel Foucault, *History of Sexuality: An Introduction*, trans. Robert Hurley (New York: Vintage, 1978), p. 43.
2. Judith Butler, *Gender Trouble: Feminism and the Subversion of Identity* (New York: Routledge, 1990), pp. 43–4.
3. Eve Kosofsky Sedgwick, *Tendencies* (Durham, North Carolina: Duke University Press, 1993), p. 8.
4. Michael Warner, *The Trouble with Normal: Sex, Politics, and the Ethics of Queer Life* (New York: Free Press, 1999), pp. 59–60.
5. David Halperin, *Saint Foucault: Toward a Gay Hagiography* (New York: Oxford University Press, 1995), p. 62.
6. Neil Miller, *Out of the Past: Gay and Lesbian History from 1869 to the Present* (New York: Alyson Books, 2006), p. 362.
7. Robert L. Caserio, 'Queer Fiction: The Ambiguous Emergence of a Genre,' in *A Concise Companion to British Fiction* ed. James F. English (Malden, Massachussetts: Blackwell, 2006), p. 210.
8. Hanif Kureishi, *Buddha of Suburbia* (New York: Penguin, 1990), p. 3.
9. Ibid., p. 55.
10. Patrick Wood, *A History of Gay Literature: The Male Tradition* (New Haven: Yale University Press, 1998), p. 370.
11. Ibid., p. 370.
12. Bran Nicol, *The Cambridge Companion to Postmodern Fiction* (Cambridge: Cambridge University Press, 2009), p. 13.
13. Lee Edelman, *Homographesis: Essays in Gay Literary and Cultural Theory* (New York: Routledge, 1994), p. 95.
14. Alan Hollinghurst, *The Swimming Pool Library* (New York: Random House, 1988), pp. 6–7.
15. Alan Hollinghurst, *The Line of Beauty* (New York: Bloomsbury, 2005), p. 23.
16. Ibid., p. 23.
17. Ibid., p. 31.
18. Emma Parker, 'Male Pregnancy and Queer Utopia in Paul Magrs's Could It Be Magic?' *Textual Practice* 28:6 (2014), p. 1036.
19. Ibid.
20. Paul Magrs, *Could it be Magic?* (London: Chatto & Windus, 1997), p. 325.
21. Carolyn Dinshaw, Lee Edelman, Roderick A. Ferguson, and Carla Freccero, 'Theorizing Queer Temporalities: A Roundtable Discussion' *GLQ* 13:2–3 (2007), p. 178.
22. Kaye Mitchell, '"I'd Love to Write an anti-Downton!": An Interview with Sara Waters' in *Sarah Waters: Contemporary Critical Perspectives* ed. Kay Mitchell (London: Bloomsbury Publishing, 2013), p. 131.
23. Sarah Waters, *Fingersmith* (New York: Riverhead Books, 2002), p. 582.
24. Ibid., p. 581.

25. Jodie Medd, 'Encountering the Past in Recent Lesbian and Gay Fiction' in *The Cambridge Companion to Gay and Lesbian Writing* ed. Hugh Stevens (Cambridge: Cambridge University Press, 2011), p. 177.
26. Linda Hutcheon, *A Poetics of Postmodernism: History, Theory, Fiction* (New York: Routledge, 1988), p. 5.
27. Brian Finney, 'Peter Ackroyd, Postmodernist Play, and *Chatterton*' *Twentieth Century Literature* 38:2 (1992), p. 246.
28. See Alan Sinfield, *The Wilde Century: Effeminacy, Oscar Wilde, and the Queer Moment* (New York: Columbia University Press, 1994) and Joseph Bristow, *Effeminate England: Homoerotic Writing after 1885* (New York: Columbia University Press, 1994).
29. Peter Ackroyd, *The Last Testament of Oscar Wilde* (New York: Harper & Row, 1983), p. 2.
30. Linda Hutcheon, *A Poetics of Postmodernism: History, Theory, Fiction* (New York: Routledge, 1988), p. 114.
31. 'Hate crimes against transgender people hit record high in England and Wales', *The Guardian*, 5 October 2023.
32. Alan Sears, 'Queer Anti-Capitalism: What's Left of Lesbian and Gay Liberation?' *Science & Society* 69:1 (2005), p. 108.
33. Gayatri Gopinath, *Impossible Desires: Queer Diasporas and South Asian Public Cultures* (Durham: Duke University Press, 2005), p. 3.

CHAPTER 11

Black British and British Asian Fiction
Postmodernism and Beyond

Kristian Shaw

From the 1950s onwards, the end of Empire brought a sense of autonomy to newly independent nation states and heralded the unprecedented post-war migration of peoples to Western Europe. The transformation of Britain into a multicultural nation led to a gradual reshaping of the literary landscape, as the work of culturally diverse authors contained a renewed concentration on ethnic and historical difference. The 1980s in particular witnessed an increase in black British and British Asian authors from a variety of backgrounds. In his survey of the modern British novel Malcolm Bradbury places an emphasis on this decade, noting that 'British fiction in the eighties ... felt less like the fiction of a communal and agreed culture than the fiction of multiplying cultures, each adding to the sea of stories'.[1] Salman Rushdie and Hanif Kureishi were the figureheads of this movement, their writing demonstrating a postmodern style traditionally associated with white British novelists such as Julian Barnes or Graham Swift. Rushdie's *Midnight's Children* (1981), with its complex intermingling of colonial histories and political interjections, signalled the emergence of a British author whose writing reflected a mediated negotiation between the structural experimentation of postmodern thought and the political idealism of postcolonialism.

Similarly, Kureishi's seminal text *The Buddha of Suburbia* (1990) registers a postmodern critique of identity politics which captured the reality of the late-twentieth-century British Asian experience. The protagonist Karim's much quoted pronouncement, 'I am an Englishman born and bred, almost', perfectly expresses the in-between state of racial dislocation, as well as the mood of second generation ethnic minority authors in general and their ambivalence towards the heterotopian potential of multicultural Britain.[2] Kureishi continued this postmodern critique in *The Black Album* (1995), resisting the categorisation of ethnic identity to emphasise the importance of individual ethical agency: 'These days everyone was insisting on their identity, coming out as a man, woman, gay, black, Jew – brandishing whichever features they could claim, as if without a tag they wouldn't be human.'[3] A generation of authors followed *The Buddha of Suburbia* in engaging with the identity politics and subject formation surrounding cross-cultural adaptation and integration, evident in Gautam Malkani's *Londonstani* (2006) and Suhayl Saadi's *Psychoraag* (2004). Further, the religious extremism integral to *The Black Album* is especially prophetic in a post 9/11 and post 7/7 environment of intense racial scrutiny, discernible in Moshin Hamid's *The Reluctant Fundamentalist* (2007) and Sunjeev Sahota's *Ours are the Streets* (2011).

Whereas once figures such as Rushdie or Kureishi occupied the margins, now they are considered pioneers of a distinctive multicultural movement – arguably the most important transformation in British literature in the late-twentieth century. One only has to consider the literary success of Zadie Smith, Monica Ali, Meera Syal, or Courttia Newland to recognise how the literary landscape has changed. Many fictions published today, from authors as diverse as Nadeem Aslam or Fred D'Aguiar (as well as those names mentioned above), would have been deemed 'postmodern' in the 1980s and 1990s. However, the ethno-political critiques of Western society inherent in Rushdie or Kureishi's fiction exposed the fact that postmodernism was not 'the primary framework within which most of the world's population carries out its daily life', revelling in abstractions and possessing no pragmatic application.[4]

These criticisms support the widespread conviction that the postmodern period is now over and that literature has transitioned into a (tentatively titled) 'post-postmodern' era. The notion of post-postmodernism has been floated for several years, despite the term's elusive linguistic nature, and calls for an emergent sincerity that rejects postmodernism's ironic stance and cynicism at the beginning of the new millennium. As Linda Hutcheon writes, 'the postmodern may well be a twentieth-century phenomenon, that is, a thing of the past', with twenty-first century literature now reflecting its 'transformation' to overlap with 'race and ethnicity theory' and account for 'the hybrid, the heterogeneous, and the local'.[5] David Rudrum and Nicholas Stavris concur, arguing that postmodernism 'was always vulnerable to the charge that it was an essentially Western phenomenon' and failed to assimilate ethnic minority voices, but acknowledge that 'offshoots of the postmodern' are now 'striking out in a multitude of directions'.[6] Certainly, postcolonial and postmodern paradigms are no longer a viable means of representing the realities of the contemporary moment following globalisation and various competing paradigms have emerged. Christian Moraru, for example, argues for an outward-looking 'cosmodernism' founded on the 'historically unrivalled intensity and extensity' of 'being-in-relation' with others and a concentration on how this theme is 'ethically explored'. In comparison, Nicolas Bourriaud forwards a related vision of 'altermodernism' that attempts to fuse postmodern aesthetics with emergent globalising connections to represent the networked nature of cultural space.[7] In British fiction specifically, one can identify what Shaw and Upstone define as the *transglossic* – a forward-looking and global-oriented paradigm (founded on a *critical* cosmopolitanism) that moves away from multicultural paradigms which attempt to reduce and restrict the identity of citizens back to their cultural origins, forces an alignment of aesthetics and ethico-political imperatives, and necessitates a post-postmodern recuperation of contingent identity and subjectivity.[8]

There are obvious difficulties in labelling, categorising, or limiting the number of British authors who fall under this banner. The inherent heterogeneity of authors' cultural backgrounds is immediately problematic and leads to generalisation, while grouping texts based on group inclusivity and exclusivity conditions the subsequent reading and interpretation of the texts themselves. Yet the growth in literary diversity forces a realignment and reconsideration of national identity to account for cross-cultural influences and contemporary changes to societal interaction and demographics. In an interview with *The Guardian* at the Hay Festival in 2004, John Updike praised this development: 'With the empire coming back to Britain, you have a lot of different kinds of voices' (leading Guardian critic John Ezard to announce that the British novel had been 'saved by ethnic minorities').[9] There is no doubt that postmodernism, with its concentration on the politics of relational identity construction and difference (as well as its preoccupation on hybridity and multiplicity), provided minority writers a voice through which to chronicle life from the margins, with their fiction reshaping the sensibilities and thematic concerns of late-twentieth-century literature.

Accordingly, this chapter will focus on the new generation of authors who have inherited the legacy of postmodern frames of thought. It will be suggested that black British and British Asian fiction could only gain its voice in the wake of postmodernism, utilising and imbuing postmodern forms with ethno-political power (traditionally associated with postcolonialism). The selected authors in this chapter reveal how the label of postmodernism possesses a reductive quality, limiting the socially transformative potential of narratives. This development could come only have come about with the death of postmodernism; postmodernism, as an ironically hegemonic metanarrative, effectively had to 'die' before ethnic minority authors could find their voice. The fiction of Hari Kunzru, Bernardine Evaristo, and Zadie Smith, among other emergent works in this period, both engages with and breaks away from the postmodern, via an interrogation of identity politics, the rewriting of black history, the persistence of racism, and a determined attempt to 'situate' ethnic minority voices within British society. My view is that the end of postmodernism as a historical moment has brought about a new ethical turn or cosmopolitan mode – characteristic of the transglossic – that avoids postmodern depthlessness and poststructuralist discourses. Rather, these authors are reappropriating the postmodern to forge empathetic responses to the cultural and socio-economic interdependencies of the post-millennial state. This turn is reflective of a heightened global consciousness in British fiction in general, sensitive to the dynamic interplay and heterogeneous nature of British society, shaped by a legacy of colonial rule, multicultural engagement, and an emergent globalised condition. A concentration on cultural interdependence is also evident in the postmodern writings of white British authors such as *Ghostwritten* (1999) by David Mitchell and *Hotel World* (2001) by Ali Smith.

First, this chapter will consider Hari Kunzru's application of postmodern aesthetics, examining the performativity of racial identities in his 2002 novel, *The Impressionist*. Kunzru preserves the late-twentieth-century trend of engaging with colonial history and the imperial enterprise, demonstrating how the issue of race continues to haunt contemporary society. The chapter will then examine the black British fiction of Bernardine Evaristo, specifically her reworking of postmodern historiographic metafiction to respond to the enduring nature of racial discrimination (often leading to a historical reengagement with institutions and structures that maintain cultural inequality). A concluding discussion of Zadie Smith's fiction will strengthen the suggestion that authors are eschewing postmodernism to capture the realities of twenty-first-century urban life and, in so doing, move beyond the postmodern period.

Becoming British

A diverse range of British Asian authors emerged in the wake of Rushdie and Kureishi whose works refer back to the postmodern 'burden of representation' evident in *Midnight's Children* and *The Black Album*. Such works include: Vikram Seth's *A Suitable Boy* (1993), Nadeem

Aslam's *Maps for Lost Lovers* (2004), and Jhumpa Lahiri's *Unaccustomed Earth* (2008). Hari Kunzru's body of fiction in particular bears the mark of Rushdie's postmodern celebration of racial deconstruction and cultural rootlessness, as symptoms of migratory dislocation. *The Impressionist* acknowledges both the preoccupations of postcolonialism and postmodernism, employing intertextuality and pastiche to critique the British colonial project and the literary narratives of the period. Rather than merely reiterating the in-between state of dislocated migrants to criticise racial purity and Western ideological structures, however, the novel utilises the colonial period (and Anglo-Indian relations more widely) to gesture towards contemporary forms of belonging and representation in an age of mass transnationalism.

The Impressionist identifies the haunting legacy of colonialism as a major influence on subsequent forms of cultural identification and critiques oppressive structures continuing to dictate racial relations in the contemporary moment. Both *Transmission* (2005) and *Gods Without Men* (2009), Kunzru's subsequent novels, continue his fascination with postmodern aesthetics and the postcolonial legacy of cultural dislocation. By concentrating on the role of individual ethical agency, Kunzru works through postmodernism to actively interrogate the complexity of the globalised condition. Kunzru's ethical stance is evident in his refusal to accept the John Llewellyn Rhys Prize for *The Impressionist* due to its connections with the Mail on Sunday, a newspaper whose editorial policy involves 'vilifying and demonising refugees and asylum-seekers'.[10] The central character of *The Impressionist*, Pran, a young Kashmiri male, undergoes a process of transformation as he attempts to overcome the racial hierarchies governing ethno-political relations at the turn of the twentieth-century. Pran is the product of an illicit sexual encounter between an English man and a Kashmiri woman, whose intermingling encapsulates the themes of hybridisation and racial mixing that will be explored later in the novel (a reversal of Kunzru's origins, who was born in London to a Kashmiri father and British mother). After his mixed, illegitimate parentage is revealed, Pran is forced from his home and becomes a social chameleon, shedding his skin to inhabit different environments, including a stint as a (seemingly female) prostitute where he is given the name Rukhsana (echoing Judith Butler's assertion that drag and gender, as with race, are postmodern social constructions). The brothel, owned by hermaphrodites, intimates the novel's larger critique on the dialogic performativity of identity, whereby the markers of ethnicity, race, and caste can be empty symbols attached or removed from an individual. Pran's evolving and unstable racial identities correspond to Paul Gilroy's scepticism that ethnic or racial grouping 'can provide a unique protection against various postmodern assaults on the coherence and integrity of the self'.[11]

What follows in the novel is a process of dislocation, mutation, and dissemination as Pran first becomes a sexual pawn in a political conspiracy that leads to his involvement in the 1919 Amritsar massacre; heads to Bombay where he lives with Christian missionaries and assumes the moniker Pretty Bobby; and steals the identity of a murdered acquaintance to sail to England and finally become Jonathan Bridgeman, graduate of Oxford University. Notably, Pran is not satisfied by assuming the role of a British male, striving for the much more exclusive and narrower category of 'Englishness'. Whiteness not only haunts Pran's bodily incarnations, but the systems and institutions to which he attaches himself. While studying in Oxford, Pran falls for Star Chapel, the English daughter of an Oxford don, who ironically rejects him in favour of a black jazz musician, claiming Pran is not exotic enough for her tastes. To win Star's hand, he embarks on an anthropological expedition to Africa, resulting in Pran's long-awaited encounter with repressed Indian identity, a re-evaluation of the 'blinding alien whiteness' that he has cultivated for himself, and a broader confrontation with the spectre of vilified blackness that he has worked so hard to escape.[12]

The concluding section of the novel, set in the fictional African desert space of Fotseland, is the scene for Pran's final transformation. After suffering a radical identity crisis in such an uninscribed landscape, free of cultural markers, he wanders the desert, hallucinating and disoriented from heatstroke, before eventually encountering the Fotse tribe. A tribal elder strips Pran of his carefully constructed 'European spirit', leaving him a nomadic subject, untethered from his various constructed selves and subject positions: 'he is an abyss . . . leaving only a nightmare, a monstrous disorder'.[13] Such cultural nomadism is illustrative of the legacy of hybridity, migrancy, and global diaspora, central to both postmodern and postcolonial paradigms. For Peter Childs and James Green, Pran's dissolution takes 'the joint postcolonial and postmodernist assault on the imperial/humanist subject to its logical conclusion'.[14] Rather than ultimately discovering an authentic version of himself in the blank space of the desert, Pran's various incarnations prove incommensurable and we witness the deconstruction of the colonial subject – a free-floating artifice cast adrift from both India and England, devoid of cultural rootedness, and deracinated from history: 'How easy it is to slough off one life and take up another! Easy when there is nothing to anchor you. [Pran] marvels at the existence of people who can know themselves by kneeling down and picking up a handful of soil . . . he is not one of them.'[15]

On the one hand, it is difficult to perceive Pran's liminal and hollow state as anything other than that of a postmodern subject – his array of unstable identities remains fundamentally disjunctive and irreconcilable (further evidence of Kunzru's preoccupation with late-postmodernism). His acts of mimicry and appropriation suggest that identity is ultimately performative, constructed, and dialogic; a mutable construction made up of signifiers and symbols that can be endlessly modified or acquired through experience. Through such (dis)identification the narrative echoes the unstable and relational aspect of postmodern identity formation and the Jamesonian diagnosis of the postmodern subject, broken down into 'randomly heterogeneous' fragments until there is simply the 'rubble of distinct and unrelated signifiers'.[16] Due to the radical deconstruction of Pran's identity throughout the course of the novel, many critics (such as Childs and Green) have identified the difficulty in naming or referring to his character. Naming the protagonist Pran, his 'original' identity, contradicts the novel's argument that no one identity should hold precedence over the others (or that an authentic ethnic identity exists). The constructed nature of his ethnic selfhood is reflected in an impressionist Pran encounters in a Parisian bar: a blatant exhibition of the postmodern/postcolonial themes of mimicry and mongrelisation hinted at throughout the text. The impressionist's act serves as a microcosmic performance of Pran's own cross-cultural journey, indicating the postmodern flattening and superficiality of his various assumed identities. Like the impressionist, Pran too 'exists only when being observed': 'One after the other, characters appear . . . In between each impression, just at the moment when one person falls away and the next has yet to take possession, the impressionist is completely blank. There is nothing there at all.'[17]

On the other hand, although *The Impressionist* arguably engages in a familiar critique of fixed subjectivities and rigid hierarchies so often associated with postcolonial and postmodern frameworks, Pran's personal dissolution and multiplicity involve purposeful acts of individual agency that resist ethnic categorisation and register more cosmopolitan forms of identification. The destabilisation of identity in the novel is more than a form of postmodern deconstruction. Rather, Kunzru is questioning the legitimacy of multicultural paradigms and the monolithic nature of dominant social institutions to emphasise the potential for individuals to escape assumed affiliations, overcome racial hierarchies, and create new formations indicative of the contemporary globalised condition.

Writing B(l)ack

Contemporary black British fiction undoubtedly remains influenced by the early work of Sam Selvon and George Lamming, who documented the inherent racism of immediate postwar Britain and the subsequent struggle to assimilate in a country that was actively pursuing anti-immigration policies. The second generation of black British authors developed the approach of these pioneers during the 1980s and 1990s by challenging the formulation of Britishness in a climate of emerging multiculturalism, positioning themselves against the right-wing ideology of the Thatcherite government and its aftermath. A rejection of the postmodern is notably apparent in the gritty urban fictions of Courttia Newland and Diran Adebayo; both *Society Within* (1999) and *Some Kind of Black* (1997) employ realist forms and rooted narratives which serve as a political response to Thatcherite social policies and spatial politics. While the alienation and marginalisation experienced by this generation is still evident in literature today, one can recognise a subtle shift towards a re-inscription of British space and the employment of postmodern strategies for ethno-political purposes.

Peter Fryer's historical overview of black Britishness, *Staying Power* (1984), accentuates how 'traces of black life have been removed from the British past to ensure that blacks are not part of the British future'.[18] The decision to write black history into the British consciousness was actively taken up by several authors in the 1980s and 1990s, including Caryl Phillips, Bernardine Evaristo, and Andrea Levy. Phillips' essay, 'The Pioneers: Fifty Years of Caribbean Migration to Britain', emphasises the impact of the Windrush generation and their descendants in forever altering the British landscape: 'it was clear to us that a British future involved not only kicking back when kicked, but continuing to kick until a few doors opened and things changed'.[19] The fiction of Phillips, who was born in St Kitts but raised in Leeds, documents the historical connections between white and black culture and their role in reshaping the cultural landscape of British life. *Dancing in the Dark* (2005) is his postmodern response to enduring issues surrounding 'blackness' and the constructed nature of racial identities. Set in America at the turn of the twentieth century, but with a definitively transatlantic angle, the self-reflexive novel follows the life of Bert Williams, a 'blackface' vaudeville performer. Bert's performances deconstruct the 'mask' of blackness or otherness as he attempts to achieve the identity of a 'Real Coon' to entertain a racially segregated America.[20] As with Kunzru's Pran, Bert suffers a radical identity crisis, his racially charged renditions eroding and disintegrating, rather than confirming and reclaiming, his sense of self. The fragmentary selfhood of the central character is mirrored by the narrative's disjointed structure – also evident in Phillip's earlier novel *Crossing the River* – exposing the instability, temporality, and inauthenticity of racial performativity.

Yet certain authors are also adapting and developing the postmodern to rewrite dominant white histories, forcing British society to account for the perspectives of ethnic diaspora. A concentration on marginalisation and representation leads to black British fiction enjoying a unique position within British literature. This 'character' of black British writing, according to Upstone, 'speaks to something different: to a form both realist and speculative . . . experimental not with the dramatic interruptive power of the postmodern'.[21] Evaristo's early fiction, from *Lara* (1997) to *Soul Tourists* (2005), reveals these postmodern revisionist tendencies, often accompanied by experimental prose that adds an Afro-Caribbean flamboyance to British writing (Evaristo was born in London to a Nigerian father and English mother). *Lara*, a semi-autobiographical remapping of familial and racial relations through free verse, traverses global space and temporal zones to interrogate racial identity politics, positioning Britain as an 'island, the "Great" Tippexed out of it/Tiny amid massive floating continents, the African one', which haunts her cultural identity: as she becomes 'an embryo within'.[22] *Soul Tourists* involves a similar remapping of British space to account for marginalised minority figures erased from historical memory. The personal trajectory of the central character, Jessie O'Donnell, who identifies as 'a Yorkshire woman, and reet proud of it' hints at the locatedness (rather than rootlessness) of black Britons within national space.[23]

But it is *Blonde Roots* (2008), Evaristo's first novel of prose (rather than experimental verse), that most clearly evinces a deconstructive postmodern sensibility, providing a satirical and reflexive epistolary slave narrative which functions as a social commentary on contemporary race relations and legacies of cultural inequality. The narrative employs AVE as standard speech to chart the fate of Doris Scagglethorpe, a 'whyte' girl, or 'wigga', abducted from her English cabbage farm to become Omorenomwara, a slave in Great Ambossa.[24] *Blonde Roots* parodies experiences of colonial rule to emphasise the absurdity of deracination, in this case inverting the transatlantic slave trade to position Africa as the site of cultural hegemony and Europe as the home of slaves. Andrea Levy has also come to echo Evaristo's historical revisionism, marking a break from the brutal realism of her earlier fiction. Like *Blonde Roots*, Levy's *The Long Song* (2010) provides a detailed account of the lives of eighteenth-century slaves, mimicking narrative histories of this period.

In the style of Alasdair Gray's *Poor Things* (1992), the novel reproduces fictional historical documents and adopts various textual forms to emphasise the constructedness of narrative memory. However, the novel is more than a playful exercise in postmodern formal innovation intended to destabilise historical veracity or 'truth'. The brutal portrayal (or, more accurately, reimagining) of the slave experience prevents the narrative from operating at the level of postmodern irony and satire alone. The tension between the speculative and the factual, the past and the present, and reliable and unreliable narrators, serves to disrupt established perspectives on black history and signals a renewal of postmodern techniques by black British authors to offer subversive political undertones. Evaristo's appropriation of historiographic metafiction to account for marginalisation and cultural domination allows the novel to escape Hutcheon's criticism of postmodern texts, which she argues hold the potential to further 'totalising strategies of domination' (in this sense facilitating a postcolonial critique by deconstructing grand narratives).[25]

The alternative, fictionalised history of *Blonde Roots* even retains a legitimate historical validity that implores readers to actively respond to its ethical message. Counter-hegemonic voices in the novel draw attention to the dangers of assuming one discursive position (a modality founded on dominant European discourses), and a progressive counter-discourse emerges that speaks to the racial tensions of contemporary society, imagines potential futures for a culturally diverse Britain, and attempts to provide answers to the inheritance of the historical wound. As Gilroy argues, 'posing the world as it is against the world as the racially subordinated would like it to be' indicates a desire to work towards a 'politics of fulfilment: the notion that a future society will be able to realize the social and political promise that present society has left unaccomplished'.[26] While Hutcheon's notion of historiographic metafiction has been a staple of postmodern fiction for several years, these selected black British and British Asian authors adapt and 'own' the form to speak directly to their marginalised communities and histories, thus correcting Frederic Jameson's claim that postmodernism involves a flattening of historical process.[27] By inverting the racial and cultural positions of Europe and Africa, *Blonde Roots* gestures towards Gilroy's notion of 'planetary humanism', which calls for the abolition of race, a renegotiation of cultural categorisation that moves beyond postcolonial paradigms, and the need for a credible and pragmatic cosmopolitan solidarity.[28] In doing so, the novel gives voice to black British history and reveals the developing ties between postmodernism and racial identities, thus redirecting postmodernism to her own ends.

Beyond the Postmodern

Ever since the publication of *White Teeth* (2000) at the turn of the new millennium, Zadie Smith has been positioned as the face of British multicultural writing, her writing garnering immediate critical attention and shaping the direction of twenty-first century fiction. Smith is not only the literary poster girl for multiculturalism, but is often considered the heir to a postmodern/postcolonial moment. Despite such labelling, characters across Smith's body of fiction resist multicultural categorisation as a marker of identity. In *White Teeth*, Millat's ties to a radical Islamic group conceals his love of African-American rap music and Western cinema, whereas his brother Magid is sent to Bangladesh to reconnect with his 'roots' but ultimately becomes a 'pukka Englishman'.[29] The central protagonist of *The Autograph Man* (2002), Alex, a half-Chinese, half Jewish Londoner: 'detest[ed] groupings of all kinds – social, racial, national or political – he had never joined so much as a swimming club'.[30] Similarly, the struggles of Levi, another mixed race character in *On Beauty* (2005), echoes the quest of many ethnic minority individuals to forge an authentic identity – this time attempting to pass for 'black'. Smith has previously called attention to postmodernism's concentration on identity politics at the expense of other factors. Her characters

> don't struggle to find an identity because they're mixed race, they struggle because they are ... the product of a twentieth century that invented and patented this piece of claptrap called 'finding an identity', and it drives everybody nuts, mixed race or no. The search for an identity is one of the most wholesale phony ideas we've ever been sold.[31]

White Teeth celebrates the thriving cultural heterogeneity within post-millennial London, exposing the fallacy of essentialised identities, interrogating the construction of national belonging, and exploring the effects of migration on subsequent generations. Smith's celebrated debut novel, however, both draws upon and parodies postmodern irony and excess, leading notable literary critic James Wood to define *White Teeth* as 'hysterical realism' – fiction that ruminates on the falsity and the fury of endlessly proliferating plots while failing to conceal the hollowness at the heart of much of contemporary society.³² Despite the evident irony in Smith's tone and playful commentary on multicultural paradigms throughout the narrative, the overtly optimistic vision of a post-millennial Britain, a utopian 'greenandpleasantlibertarianlandofthefree' where 'roots won't matter anymore' contains a pre-9/11 optimism that fails to account for the racially charged conflict and discord of urban space.³³

In 'Two Directions for the Novel', taken from her 2009 essay collection *Changing My Mind*, Smith cites postmodern fiction as a 'fascinating failure, intellectual brinkmanship that lacked heart' and declares a desire to 'shake the novel out of its present complacency', which can be read as an apathetic stance to decades of self-referentiality.³⁴ According to David James, Smith 'has spent a number of years ... pondering the challenge of retooling the ethical efficacy of fiction in an age after postmodernism'.³⁵ Her fourth novel, *NW* (2012), purposefully assumes a critical cosmopolitan approach that attends to the dissonances and tensions of urban life in London, directly engages with the bleak realities of class and socio-economic inequality, and charts the network of cross-cultural interdependencies that govern the contemporary moment. The novel thus moves beyond *White Teeth*'s undeniable focus on the multicultural politics of the twentieth-century – the 'century of strangers, brown, yellow and white ... the great immigrant experiment' – following the Windrush.³⁶

As Iain Chambers noted, '[t]he migrant's sense of being rootless, of living between worlds, between a lost past and a non-integrated present, is perhaps the most fitting metaphor of this (post) modern condition'.³⁷ *NW* moves beyond this rootlessness to situate the novel firmly in the twenty-first century, retaining a distinctly narrow and parochial focus on the interconnected lives and struggles of a handful of London's multi-ethnic residents. The title of *NW* itself betrays a rootedness and concentration on the specifics of localised space, rather than the migratory flows of postcolonial writing. More importantly, the novel contradicts *White Teeth*'s more harmonious millennial sentiments, while also escaping the postmodern implications of hysterical realism by attempting to 'map out more local, more empowering connections to mine the present for those rare, fragile moments of contact'.³⁸ It is the novel's meticulous study of Natalie De Angelis which captures both Smith's own resistance to multicultural categorisation and the experiential reality of urban life. Natalie, of Jamaican heritage, struggles to extricate herself from Willesden and break ties with her cultural background, seeking the isolation afforded by a lack of communal ties. Through a complex examination of Natalie's evolving identity, Smith signals a shift towards a recalibration of ethics and belonging in urban localities, thus enabling the novel to operate 'post-hysterics' (and resulting in Wood's reassessment of Smith as a 'great urban realist').[39]

Sabine Nunius writes that Smith's fiction acts 'in contrast to "postmodern" literature', by moving beyond the notion of a 'general void or lack of meaning in contemporary society' and instead promoting a 'feeling of coherency and communality'.[40] While this assessment admittedly neglects the fragile social ties and lingering racial tensions within Smith's body of work, Nunius recognises her emphasis on empathetic identification with cultural otherness. That is not to say the novel signals a distinct break from experimental form or aesthetics – both modernist and postmodernist stylistic techniques are apparent throughout the narrative, evident in Leah's rhythmic stream of consciousness giving way to Natalie's fragmented vignettes. Rather, the novel engages with the postmodern to move beyond its self-absorbed parameters and represent the evolving racial and socio-economic circumstances of cultural inequality and marginalisation. In this sense, *NW* reflects a larger trend in post-millennial fiction towards an emergent ethical sensibility and cosmopolitan orientation that differs significantly from the playful constructions of late-twentieth-century postmodernism and the historical trauma of postcolonialism.

Smith continues her fascination with the localised ethics of cultural engagement in *The Embassy of Cambodia* (2013). The short story (published as a single volume) follows Fatou, a domestic servant from the Ivory Coast, in her day-to-day duties for an affluent London family. To escape the drudgery of her restricted domesticity, Fatou regularly visits a swimming pool and becomes intrigued by the embassy of Cambodia she passes on her route. The embassy represents the reflexive and interconnected relationship between local and global spheres within London, once again emphasising how the prosaic and pedestrian often operate in tension with sweeping globalism and transnational fragility in Smith's fiction. By employing the first-person plural 'we' throughout the narrative – 'We are from Willesden. Our minds tend toward the prosaic' – the story emphasises Smith's continued efforts to impose a cosmopolitan empathy upon the capital and its residents (as well as an ironic nod to those critics who positioned her as the multicultural figurehead of British literature).[41] Despite the postmodern experimentation and comic satire evident in her early fiction, Smith's non-fiction and criticism has since revealed her desire to engage with the ethics and realities of contemporary globalised society: 'the ethical realm exists nowhere if not here ... Narrative itself is the performance of that very procedure'.[42] Such engagement can be positioned as post-postmodernist in its attempts to interrogate the actually existing realities of post-millennial life and the novel's value in reaching that end, as opposed to an ironic take on late-twentieth-century social relations. Yet it is perhaps more accurate to suggest that Smith's later fiction exhibits a progressive and future-oriented *critical* cosmopolitanism conscious of the need to transcend postmodern forms of relationality and sensitive to the practice of localised cosmopolitan ethics.

As Peter Morey has recently noted, 'the exploration of non-white histories – and the way identity is always constructed in the gaze of a curious and sometimes hostile Other – is likely to preoccupy black British and Asian novelists for some years to come'.[43] Colonial or imperial discourse undoubtedly remains a prevalent feature of British fiction, yet there is also an active revisionist attempt to reinscribe the past with the concerns and anxieties of the present. The rewriting and reimagining of historical struggle and racial hierarchies by contemporary Black British and Asian authors, such as Evaristo, Kunzru, and Smith, is an overtly political act – an intervention involving an appropriation of both postmodern and postcolonial preoccupations that in fact modifies these existing literary frameworks to highlight the persistence of socio-economic inequality, overcome culturally performative expectations and give voice to contemporary racial concerns. Writing from a marginalised position continues to serve as an emancipatory and empowering strategy, especially in the wake of the postmodern period.

While the postmodern remains a useful paradigm, challenging established narratives, deconstructing hierarchies, and offering counter-discourses for race and ethnicity, certain authors strive to escape the deconstructive pessimism of postmodern identity politics, create new formations of cultural interdependence, and capture an emergent cosmopolitan mode that moves beyond postmodern representation to establish an ethical humanism characteristic of the transglossic. The relationship of black British and British Asian fiction and postmodernism, then, is not a case of 'either/or' but rather 'both/and', concerning an adaptation of postmodern styles. Smith's fiction in particular sets itself the task of breaking away from postmodernism to interrogate the tensions, instabilities, and conflicts inherent in British society, pointing towards the need for new modes of ethno-political understanding, sincerity, and authorial responsibility. Postmodern aesthetics and narrative strategies are not employed for the sole purpose of playful experimentation, but rather synthesise and juxtapose differing perspectives to demonstrate the limitations in constructing networks of solidarity amidst intense and enduring racial division. Although contemporary black British and British Asian fiction demonstrates both a concentration on provincial engagement and rooted belonging on the one hand, and a fascination with wider transnational networked systems on the other, this complex mobilisation between the local and global is reflective of both a cultural environment coming to terms with the complexity and diversity of post-millennial life, and a literature moving beyond the postmodern condition.

Notes

1. Malcolm Bradbury, *The Modern British Novel: 1878–2001*, 2nd ed. (Harmondsworth: Penguin, 2001), p. 462.
2. Hanif Kureishi, *The Buddha of Suburbia* (London: Faber and Faber, 2000), p. 3.
3. Hanif Kureishi, *The Black Album* (London: Faber and Faber, 1995), p. 92.
4. Bill Ashcroft, Gareth Griffiths, and Helen Tiffin, eds. *The Post-Colonial Studies Reader* (London: Routledge, 1995), p. 11.
5. Linda Hutcheon, 'Epilogue: The Postmodern ... In Retrospect: "What was Postmodernism?"', in *Supplanting the Postmodern*, eds. David Rudrum and Nicholas Stavris (London: Bloomsbury, 2015), p. 5.
6. David Rudrum and Nicholas Stavris, 'Introduction', in Rudrum and Nicholas Stavris, *Supplanting the Postmodern*, p. xxv; p. xiii.
7. Christian Moraru, *Cosmodernism: American Narrative, Late Globalization, and the New Cultural Imaginary* (Ann Arbor: University of Michigan Press, 2011), p. 2; p. 313; Nicolas Bourriand, 'Altermodern', in Rudrum and Nicholas Stavris, *Supplanting the Postmodern*, pp. 255–69.
8. Kristian Shaw and Sara Upstone, 'The Transglossic: Contemporary Fiction and the Limitations of the Modern', *English Studies*, 102:5 (June 2021), pp. 573–600.
9. John Ezard. 'UK novel saved by ethnic minorities', *The Guardian*, 31 May 2004. Retrieved from: www.theguardian.com/uk/2004/may/31/highereducation.artsandhumanities.
10. Hari Kunzru, 'Society: Making Friends with the Mail', 18 December 2008. Retrieved from: www.harikunzru.com/making-friends-with-mail-2003.
11. Paul Gilroy, *After Empire: Melancholia or Convivial Culture?* (Abingdon: Routledge, 2004), p. 6.
12. Hari Kunzru, *The Impressionist* (London: Penguin, 2003), p. 64.
13. Ibid., p. 477.
14. Peter Childs and James Green, *Ethics and Aesthetics in Twenty-First Century British Novels* (London: Bloomsbury, 2013), p. 73.
15. *The Impressionist*, p. 285.
16. Frederic Jameson, *Postmodernism, or, The Cultural Logic of Late Capitalism* (Durham, North Carolina: Duke University Press, 1991), p. 33.
17. *The Impressionist*, p. 347; p. 419.
18. Peter Fryer. *Staying Power* (London: Pluto Press, 1984), p. 399.

19. Caryl Phillips, 'The Pioneers: Fifty Years of Caribbean Migration to Britain', in *A New World Order* ed. Caryl Phillips (London: Vintage, 2002), p. 276.
20. Caryl Phillips, *Dancing in the Dark* (London: Vintage, 2006), p. 41.
21. Sara Upstone, 'Postcolonial and Diasporic Voices – Bringing Black to the Union Jack: Ethnic Fictions and the Politics of Possibility' in *The 1990s: A Decade of Contemporary British Fiction*, ed. Nick Hubble, Philip Tew and Leigh Wilson (London: Bloomsbury, 2015), pp. 125–6.
22. Bernardine Evaristo, *Lara* (Tunbridge Wells: Angela Roy Publishing, 1997), p. 140.
23. Bernardine Evaristo, *Soul Tourists* (London: Hamish Hamilton, 2005), p. 198.
24. Bernardine Evaristo, *Blonde Roots* (London: Penguin, 2009), p. 5.
25. Linda Hutcheon, *The Politics of Postmodernism* (London: Routledge, 1989), p. 36.
26. Paul Gilroy, *The Black Atlantic* (London: Verso, 1993), p. 37.
27. Frederic Jameson, *Postmodernism, or, The Cultural Logic of Late Capitalism* (Durham, North Carolina: Duke University Press, 1991), p. 60.
28. Paul Gilroy, *Against Race: Imagining Political Culture Beyond the Color Line* (Cambridge, Massachussetts: Harvard University Press, 2000), p. 17.
29. Zadie Smith, *White Teeth* (London: Penguin, 2001), p. 407.
30. Zadie Smith, *The Autograph Man* (London: Hamish Hamilton, 2002), p. 167.
31. Zadie Smith, 'A Conversation with Zadie Smith'. Reading Guides: *On Beauty*. Retrieved from: www.bookbrowse.com/author_interviews/full/index.cfm/author_number/344/zadie-smith.
32. James Wood, 'Books of the Year', *New Yorker* (17 December 2012).
33. *White Teeth*, p. 465; p. 527.
34. Zadie Smith, *Changing My Mind: Occasional Essays* (London: Hamish Hamilton, 2009), p. 73; p. 93.
35. David James, 'Worlded Localisms: Cosmopolitics Writ Small' in *Postmodern Literature and Race*, ed. Len Platt and Sara Upstone (Cambridge University Press, 2015), p. 55.
36. Smith, *White Teeth*, p. 326.
37. Iain Chambers, *Migration, Culture, Identity* (London: Routledge, 1994), p. 27.
38. David Marcus, 'Post-Hysterics: Zadie Smith and the Fiction of Austerity', *Dissent* (Spring 2013): www.dissentmagazine.org/article/post-hysterics-zadie-smith-and-the-fiction-of-austerity.
39. Ibid.; James Wood, 'Human, All Too Inhuman', *New Republic*, 24 July 2000: https://newrepublic.com/article/61361/human-all-too-inhuman.
40. Sabine Nunius, '"Sameness" in Contemporary British Fiction: (Metaphorical) Families in Zadie Smith's *On Beauty* (2005)' in *Multi-Ethnic Britain 2000+: New Perspectives in Literature, Film and the Arts*, ed. Lars Eckstein, Barbara Forte, Eva Ulrike Parker, and Christoph Reinfandt (Amsterdam: Rodopi, 2008), p. 110.
41. Zadie Smith, *The Embassy of Cambodia* (London: Hamish Hamilton, 2013), p. 6.

42. Zadie Smith, 'Love, Actually', *The Guardian*, 1 November 2003: www.theguardian.com/books/2003/nov/01/classics.zadiesmith.
43. Peter Morey, 'Black British and British Asian Fiction' in *The Oxford History of the Novel in English: British and Irish Fiction Since 1940. Volume 7*, ed. Peter Boxall and Bryan Cheyette (Oxford: Oxford University Press, 2016), p. 478.

CHAPTER 12

History and the British Novel After Postmodernism
Alison Lee

In Graham Swift's *Waterland* (1983), history teacher Tom Crick is faced with a classroom full of students who see no relevance to his subject because the world is in crisis from terrorism and the build-up of nuclear arms and seems about to end. What matters, says his student, Price, is the 'here and now. Not the past. The here and now – and the future.'[1] Despite Crick's revealing his own personal history intertwined with public historical events – 'those grand Narrative[s]' like the French Revolution – the past, at least to his students, is a very foreign country.[2] Even Crick cannot marshal the events of the past to provide an explanation for the present. Wendy Wheeler points out that, for Crick, the present is 'a reality of such immediacy as to be [. . .] intolerable – and a thing which, unless tamed by narratives, drives people mad'.[3] As a postmodern novel, *Waterland* focuses on the textual and discursive means by which historical events are communicated to the present through storytelling. Tom Crick hopes that revisiting the past might help to explain why his wife stole a baby from a supermarket and why his headmaster is 'cutting back on history', but the problem, as he recognises, is that history is not a settled body of facts with a clear narrative line, and so the answer to 'why' is multifaceted.[4] History takes detours and, despite his desire for answers, Crick knows that history is 'the attempt to give an account with incomplete knowledge of actions themselves undertaken with incomplete knowledge'.[5] This last comment is axiomatic of postmodern fiction's concerns and marks, perhaps, one of the crucial differences between postmodern and post-millennial fiction. Whereas postmodern fiction focussed on questioning the reliability of the written historical record, that scepticism, as Victoria Stewart suggests, seems now to be taken as read: 'the extreme self-referentiality and metafictionality of postmodern fiction is refigured as an acceptance of the gaps in, and unreliability of the historical record'.[6] Much of post-millennial fiction, instead, takes up a version of Price's plea to contemplate the 'here and now' although to do so is almost impossible. As

Thomas Docherty argues, 'a presentation of the present must always involve a re-presenting, which has the effect of marking the present moment with the passage of time'.[7] Post-millennial fiction seeks to create a sense of the present while recognising that the present is always historical.

Whether inspired by the verifiable past (*The Tudors*, *The Borgias*, *Mary and George*), an entirely fictional yet somehow historical past (*Game of Thrones*, *Bridgerton*), and even if accessed through the conventions of science fiction (*Outlander*), history, in the entertainment industry, is ubiquitous. History of the *Downton Abbey* variety, to take as an example the successful TV series which ran from 2010 to 2015 (and spawned a film version in 2022), portrays historical events and attitudes that are Google-able, but constructs those events in particular ways for entertainment and profit, to create nostalgia for an imagined time of shared national identity, and as an escape from a present that looks, for the majority, nothing like the well-heeled world of the Granthams. Viewers, of course, are hardly looking to costume drama for accuracy; indeed, Zadie Smith's description of the 1989 fall of the Berlin Wall in *White Teeth* (2000) makes it clear that real historical events, even when mediated by television, can be crushingly dull. With the idea of witnessing history-in-action, the Iqbals and Joneses convene for an evening to watch the fall of the Berlin Wall on television, although

> [n]o one really knew quite who had put it up or who was tearing it down or whether this was good, bad or something else; no one knew how tall it was, how long it was, or why people had died trying to cross it or whether they would stop dying in future, but it was educational all the same.[8]

No one is as interested in the event as they are in performing their own irritation at being forced to watch something that is supposed to be educational when *Last of the Summer Wine* is just a press of the remote button away. Irie quotes media clichés about 'the dark cloud of Eastern communism' and 'the light of Western democracy';[9] Millat is bored because the TV coverage shows the 'Same. Same. Same. Dancing on the wall, smashing it with a hammer.'[10] Archie and Samad, though they were soldiers in World War II, get the history wrong. 'Me and Samad, *we were there*', says Archie; 'you *weren't*', counters Irie: 'You and Dad left in 1945. They didn't do the wall until 1961.'[11] For Alsana and Clara, this moment is one of the 'where were you when . . . ?'[12] variety, whereas Archie and Samad use it to make a point about the 'gulf between books and experience'.[13] *White Teeth* is not, strictly speaking, a postmodern novel (it lacks self-referentiality), though its point as to how 'raw' events are narrativised in order to make them meaningful is one that echoes postmodern techniques. Like other post-millennial novels, *White Teeth* considers the historical past as well as how characters read the past through the present.

The novels I will examine below also take the present as the condition for the past and the future. Each of them animates how 'the time that was continues to tick inside the time that is',[14] but each also has as a theme the paradox of re-presenting the present. Ali Smith's *How to Be Both* (2014) and Colum McCann's *TransAtlantic* (2013) invoke past and present through an illusion of narrative simultaneity. Jeanette Winterson's *The Gap of Time* (2015), a 'cover story' of Shakespeare's *The Winter's Tale*, and Hilary Mantel's *Wolf Hall* (2009) both investigate how the powerful can write and rewrite the present and the past and in doing so can disrupt perceptions of temporality. In David Mitchell's *The Bone Clocks* (2015), humans embody finite time but are pitted against supernatural figures called Atemporals who can manipulate the present. The labour to which history is put in post-millennial novels is varied, and it is as yet unclear as to whether there is a 'next big thing' after postmodernism or, indeed, whether next-big-thingism is a fruitful way of thinking. Instead, by revisiting postmodernism, it is possible to historically position post-millennial fiction's moment.

Postmodernism and History

Charles Jencks once characterised postmodernism as 'the continuation of modernity and its transcendence'.[15] This is an interesting comment through which to contemplate post-millennial fiction because, while postmodernism as an epoch may be dead, its spectre persists, and an afterimage endures. It is perhaps too soon to know whether transcendence is a term we can apply to contemporary fiction, but when Patrick O'Donnell makes the point that contemporary writers 'regard postmodern experimentation as something of a toolbox; their writing is hybrid, by turns engaging in renovated forms of realism and linguistic playfulness, at once honoring generic traditions and mangling them in the mash-up or the parodic overture', he seems to suggest lines of both difference and continuity.[16] Certainly, contemporary writing has taken new directions, especially with regard to the archaeological and didactic aspects of 'historiographic metafiction'. Postmodernism's self-conscious focus on the 'graphic' part – that is, to do with writing history – of historiographic metafiction seems to have been replaced, in a number of texts, by an overt concern with politics, specifically with cultures of violence and crisis, brought about not just by armed conflict, but by post-industrialism, unemployment, austerity, and climate change. As Lauren Berlant has argued, neoliberal economic policies mobilize instability, and that instability is evident in contemporary fiction's representations of history, genre, and identity.[17]

The historical novel is a remarkably malleable genre; as Jerome de Groot argues, it is both flexible and intergeneric,[18] and explores 'the gaps between known factual history and that which is lived to a variety of purposes'.[19] Anne Rigney adds that historical novels 'link up with the ongoing collective attempts to represent the past and invite comparisons with what is already known about the historical world from other sources'.[20] When Mantel describes her representation of Cromwell in *Wolf Hall* (2009), she agrees that the historical novel draws from sources both historical and fictional:

> My Cromwell shakes hands with the Cromwell of the *Book of Martyrs*, and with the trickster Cromwell of the truly awful but funny Elizabethan play about him. I am conscious of all his later, if fugitive, incarnations in fiction and drama. I am conscious on every page of hard choices to be made, and I make sure I never believe my own story.[21]

Sarah Waters, whose novels are set in the nineteenth and early twentieth centuries, comments that 'it's precisely the difference of the past that makes it exciting for me. I think we always need to be reminded that the moment that we live in is very temporary. Historical fiction at its best can remind us of that.'[22] The multiplicity of narratives of and about historical novels make it clear that there is no one determining feature that characterises contemporary historical fiction.

Like historians themselves, postmodern writers asked questions about how we come to know the past, much like those Michel Foucault asks in *The Archaeology of Knowledge*:

> What link should be made between disparate events? How can a causal succession be established between them? What continuity or overall significance do they possess? Is it possible to define a totality, or must one be content with reconstituting connexions?[23]

Indeed, one of the arguments made by postmodern theorists was that historians and fiction writers have the same creative processes at their disposal. They both consider the facts of the past, but fill in the gaps by answering some of the questions above. What most of us know about the past, we 'know' through books, movies, or television shows of indeterminate accuracy, and in each of these, events of the past are configured so as to make a particular point, often a comment on the present. As de Groot argues, the historical novel has always been a complex genre that works in the 'gaps between known factual history and that which is lived to a variety of purposes'.[24] Recognising how the past is put to work, in the media, in fiction, or in political discourse, is part of the reader's critical stance.

Such a scepticism is one of the legacies of postmodern fiction, which aims to re-visit historical moments with a critical, ironic eye, while focusing always on the ways in which we come to know history from written traces. For this reason, Linda Hutcheon coined the term 'historiographic metafiction' to describe novels that combined a self-consciousness about their own processes as fiction, while also foregrounding the question of how we come to know about historical events. History and fiction are presented in these novels (e.g., John Fowles, *The French Lieutenant's Woman* [1969]; Salman Rushdie, *Midnight's Children* [1981]; Angela Carter, *Nights at the* Circus [1984]; Jeanette Winterson, *Sexing the Cherry* [1989]; Alasdair Gray, *Poor Things* [1992]) as discourses 'that both constitute systems of signification by which we make sense of the past. In other words, the meaning and shape are not *in the events*, but *in the systems* which make those past "events" into historical "facts".'[25] The politics of postmodern fiction was in its textual self-consciousness, its impulse to question systems of power and authority, and its overt encouragement of sceptical reading. Most importantly, postmodern fiction explored the gaps in the historical record that often omitted the participation of those on the margins of traditional history and in so doing omitted discussions of gender, race, and sexuality, what Hutcheon calls the 'ex-centric' parts of historical narrative.[26] In other words, postmodernism trades on uncertainty as a fruitful condition for thought with its unreliable narrators, gaps in the text, and foregrounding of language's construction of reality. Postmodern novels are like puzzles, and they require the reader to engage in their playfulness *and* their politics. They are bigger on the inside.

British Historical Fiction after Postmodernism

Like its postmodern predecessors, contemporary fiction does not provide answers so much as ask significant questions. For example: what does it mean to be *now*, to recognise that the past and the present exist simultaneously, and how does this translate into an understanding of temporality? Calling attention to temporality is often overtly political because it responds both to the technological participation in 'the alleged debilitation of memory or contraction of attention-span in the contemporary world', but also to the ongoing crisis and precarity of the neoliberal present.[27] As Berlant comments, '[w]e understand nothing about impasses of the political without having an account of the production of the present'.[28] Focus on the present, she continues, 'isn't invariably shallow presentism, or "the narcissism of the now" ... but even when it is, it involves anxiety about how to assess various knowledges and intuitions about what's happening and how to eke out a sense of what follows from those assessments'.[29] Postmodern fiction pointed to the contingency of historiography, the idea that what readers know of an historical event depends on where that information comes from, and how it is narrated. What has changed since postmodern fiction's peak in the 1980s is that technology now provides us with conflicting and competing histories, 24/7. What was considered a radical notion for postmodern fiction is perhaps considered now as nothing more than a boring truism. Memory is something phones have, catastrophes flicker and disappear from the screen, and the news cycle ensures that the Western world lives in a perpetual present often represented as a lurch from one crisis to the next. Fiction is always in and of the world, and post-millennial fiction responds to the 'presentness' of historical understanding as a way of assessing the 'various knowledges and intuitions about what's happening' now. Recognising that history is always with us goes some way towards understanding that what is present quickly becomes the past, but not without consequences. In the examples of contemporary British fiction below, the past and the present are co-creative: history is created by the present and authors explore this concept by reimagining ideas of temporality and simultaneity.

Smith's *How to Be Both* explores the temporal layering of past and present, putting the reader in the position of being in both at once. As Smith puts it: 'whereas in life all sorts of things can happen at the same moment, on the page one event must precede another'.[30] For the linguistically sophisticated young George, her mother's death has meant a clash of past and present as she remembers her mother at the same time as she remembers that her mother is dead, forcing her to adjust her grammatical tenses: 'Her mother doesn't say. Her mother said.'[31] The concurrence of past and present is confounding to George '[b]ecause if things really did happen simultaneously it'd be like reading a book but one in which all the lines of the text have been overprinted, like each page is actually two pages but with one superimposed on the other to make it unreadable'.[32] The novel proceeds to make simultaneity legible. Complicating matters, *How to Be Both* has two Part Ones; half of the novels printed begin with the story of George, and half begin with the narrative of fifteenth-century artist,

Francescho del Cossa. Francesco del Cossa is an historical figure; Smith's *Francescho* del Cossa is part fact, part fiction, and is presented as biologically female, having had to pass as male in order to secure an education and respect as an artist. If George's story comes first (as in my copy) the reader won't know until the second Part One that Francescho is looking over George's shoulder in the first Part One, but this new information will change the first Part One retrospectively. The past reads the present and the present reads the past: *both*. The many examples of temporal layering include 'subverts', pop-up images created by George's mother, Carol, whose aim is 'to subvert political things with art things, and to subvert art things with political things'.[33] Technology allows for simultaneity in a way unavailable to narrative, and so not only do subverts appear randomly on top of other websites, but George can watch the beginning of a programme about the Flying Scotsman on her laptop while she watches the end of the programme on TV.[34] Smith's experimentation with simultaneity is a contemporary version of the frescos, painted by del Cossa, that George and her mother visit in Italy, and which create a conundrum about whether the underdrawing of the fresco precedes the surface, since what the viewer sees first is the surface.[35] One of Carol's most retweeted subverts – 'Art makes nothing happen in a way that makes something happen'[36] – is itself a reference to W. H. Auden's 'In Memory of W.B. Yeats' (1939) that enacts precisely this question: which version of 'Art makes nothing happen' comes first?[37] Readers do not so much revisit the past as they watch the past visit the present. Francescho appears to have been yanked somehow through layers of bones and rocks to follow George as she memorialises her mother by sitting in the National Gallery looking at Francesco's painting of St Vincent Ferrar.

The simultaneity of the past, present, and future is why Smith introduces DNA as a structuring principle in the novel. DNA's twisted double helix, a model of which George sees from the train on her way from London to Cambridge, is repeated in the text as a dance, a plot turn, and the typographical representation of Francescho's emergence from the ground. Francescho and George's narratives intertwine like twin strands of the helix. The past and the present, fiction and history, are intertwined. George has to negotiate the effects of the past and the present on each other in order to have a sense of the future. If the past and the present are happening at the same time, the present will become the past momentarily, and the two are revealed to share an intimate relationship. The reader is in many ways the focus of this novel because its structure performs the simultaneity of past and present that the reader has to negotiate. *How to*

Be Both is a novel that plumbs the postmodern toolbox in its inclusion of a non-linear structure, focus on identity and history, and construction of the reader as a co-creator.

The simultaneity of McCann's *TransAtlantic* is less formally experimental but, as in *How to Be Both*, public and private histories are layered, and retrospective reading puts the reader in the position of occupying past and present at the same time. *TransAtlantic* is a novel about migration between Ireland and North America. Book One tells the story of four men who made the trip across the Atlantic: John (Jack) Alcock and Arthur (Teddy) Witten Brown who flew the first transatlantic flight in 1919; Frederick Douglass who fled the US to engage the Irish in his fight for abolition in 1845; and Senator George Mitchell who was the US Special Envoy for Northern Ireland, and one of the chief negotiators for the 1998 Good Friday Agreement. Interwoven through this story of historically verifiable men are the stories of three generations of fictional women, the first of whom, Lily Duggan, is a maid in the Dublin household that hosts Frederick Douglass.

'We prefigure our futures by imagining our pasts', thinks George Mitchell, and the novel suggests how difficult it is to negotiate the present when you're in the middle of it.[38] For Brown and Alcock as they fly across the Atlantic, the present is terror as the weather worsens and an engine dies. Douglass is unable to cope with the shocking and disturbing congruence between American slavery and Irish famine.[39] Even though these men are part of official history, the narrative concentrates on their day-to-day presents. Brown and Alcock savour sandwiches as they fly, Douglass is at the mercy of his Irish publisher, and feels awkward among the well-heeled who will contribute to his cause, Senator Mitchell has holes in his socks and rejoices in finding the only shower in the tower block where the negotiations take place. This perspective on history may be Lily's great-granddaughter Hannah's as she puts pen to paper 'precisely because I have nobody left to whom I can tell the story'.[40] One reviewer of the novel wrote that the shift to first person in Hannah's section is perplexing, and one of the novel's weakest sections.[41] However, if Hannah is writing the novel, this appeal to historiography underlines precisely that the past and the present write one another.

The device that binds the stories together is a letter written by Lily's daughter Emily which Lily's granddaughter, Lottie, asks Alcock and Brown to take with them to Ireland in their mailbags. The letter is never delivered to its addressee but is returned to Emily many years later by Teddy Brown, whom she is interviewing for a newspaper story.

A seemingly insignificant detail, that the 'one dollar overprint for the transatlantic post' has sold out, has devastating consequences many years later for Lottie's daughter Hannah whose poverty might have been ameliorated had the letter, a family heirloom that has never been opened, had a proper postmark that affirmed it had been carried across the Atlantic by Alcock and Brown.[42] The letter would have been even more valuable had its contents pertained to Douglass. When it is finally opened, it reveals a polite thank you from Emily to the Jennings family in Cork, who had done a kindness for her mother. The seeming inconsequence of the letter's contents leaves the reader to consider what makes an historic moment. In trying to ascertain a value for the letter, Hannah meets David Manyaki whose family may buy the cottage that Hannah's bank has put up for auction. The present has unexpected consequences and 'the smallest moments: they return, dwell, endure'.[43] These women's lives run parallel to the famous men's and are affected by them in unforeseen ways.

TransAtlantic is about parallel histories. Some are considered important, some pedestrian or insignificant to official history. Others are not seen as related until placed into confrontation with one another. The epigraph to Book Two puts the novel in conversation with Smith's: 'But this is not the story of a life. It is the story of lives, knit together, overlapping in succession, rising again from grave after grave.'[44] The women in Book Two offer the past as the present – an ordinary or smaller experience of the world, a position defined by their gender and their roles as supporting characters in official history. The significance of the letter is lessened when it has been revealed to tell us nothing new about Douglass. However, its value to the historian is based on a reading of official history; in the parallel story of Lily and her family, the letter changes the present by making an unforeseen connection that may allow the present to continue into the future.

How to Be Both and *TransAtlantic* use non-linear narratives to communicate temporal dislocation. In both cases, the reader is put into the position of having to negotiate the simultaneity of past and present. Both combine historical and fictional characters, but rather than taking readers to a distant, historical past they demonstrate history's presentness. Of all of the novels I discuss here, *Wolf Hall* is the one most apt to be called realist in its detail and narrative linearity, though its narrative technique – third person, yet focalised through Thomas Cromwell – brings readers' attention to story as opposed to history. Leigh Wilson points out that Mantel breaks 'the rule of English grammar that says that a pronoun refers to the last named noun', and that in *Wolf Hall*, Cromwell is referred to with an 'unprecursed pronoun'.[45] This technique focuses readers' attention on the constructedness of the narrative and undermines the apparent immersiveness of realism. Sarah Knox argues that *Wolf Hall*'s attention to 'what-is-knowable but also to who-knows-what leads us to narrative authority and to techniques of narration, but also brings into view the historiographical nature of historical fiction'.[46] While *Wolf Hall* is not, I would argue, a postmodern novel because it is not specifically self-reflexive about the *writing* of history, any work of historical fiction, especially about such a well-known story, may be necessarily historiographic if readers recognise that it is one of many iterations.

The life of Henry VIII, as Mantel points out above, has been well documented, but also well fictionalised in novels and media representations, and any fictional (and perhaps even any historical) work will always be in conversation with these other texts, at least for those who read them. Certainly the novel thematises both history and storytelling, but its emphasis seems to be what happens to both history and story in the hands of a powerful tyrant who can change the past. In order to secure the future, the past has to be changed, and because Henry is King, he can demand that his servants and councillors work with him in rewriting history: 'But there is no doubt of what Henry wants now. An annulment. A declaration that his marriage never existed. "For eighteen years", the cardinal says, "he has been under a mistake".'[47] For Henry, the inconvenient past lies in his marriage to Katherine, the annulment of which has the aim of securing an heir to the future with Anne Boleyn.

This tyranny over the past is as contemporary as Leo's rewriting the story of his past in order to deny his paternity in *The Gap of Time*. Winterson's novel rewrites *The Winter's Tale* as the story of Leo, a hedge fund manager, who is suspicious that his friend Xeno is having an affair with his wife Mimi. His rage is such that he tries to kill Xeno, he rapes pregnant Mimi, and then has his baby daughter abducted and sent to New Bohemia. Despite his wealth, in the aftermath of these events, Leo is powerless over how others see the past. Leo feels 'the backward pull of time' because he can't face the consequences of his actions and wishes to reverse them.[48] Mimi, however, finds that 'the past is right in front of her and every day she walks slam into it like a door that locks the future on the other side'.[49] Mimi's grief over the loss of her daughter, death of her son, and end of her marriage has locked her in a perpetual present. The same is true of Leo, but what compels him to be locked in the present is capital. Leo goes to a charity function wearing a t-shirt that proclaims, 'I AM THE ONE PER CENT',[50] and much of what happens in the novel is intimately linked to the privilege that comes from that statement. Leo reads the present through his wealth. He can pay to alter the past as he does when, though seemingly redeemed, he attempts to tear down the Roundhouse to erase the memory of Mimi's last concert there. The 'affordable' homes he plans to build in its place are hidden from the 'prestige' homes by a designer forest and wall of water. He has bribed his way to planning permission, and fails to understand why the 99 per cent is protesting against his attempt to rewrite the past.

Rewriting a previous text is another way to create simultaneity between past and present: *The Gap of Time* reads *The Winter's Tale* and vice versa, but these are not the only layers. Winterson's novel must be read through interpretations of the play, as well as through the narrator-Winterson's eyes who cites her own beginnings as a 'foundling' as part of her inspiration.[51] The narrative 'I' sits at the back of the theatre watching Mimi and Leo at the end of the novel, and Leo calls up Mimi's Wikipedia page on which it is revealed that her acting debut took place in 'Deborah Warner's adaptation of *The PowerBook* – a novel by the British writer Jeannette Winterson'.[52] In postmodern fiction, this combination of real and fictional characters implied that they occupied the same ontological level, and here the suggestion is that Mimi is as real as Jeannette Winterson, while also that Winterson, the narrator, is a fictionalised self, too. Winterson layers *The Gap of Time*, not only with Shakespeare's play (and all the stories upon which Shakespeare drew), but also with her other works.

Mitchell's *The Bone Clocks* is part of what the author calls his 'uber book' in that it 'recursively loops through Mitchell's previous books and ultimately interlaces all his books into an intricate, sprawling intertext'.[53] As in *The Gap of Time*, *The Bone Clocks* achieves narrative simultaneity with characters who exist in the past and in the present of his other works. Like Smith, Mitchell explores how 'the things we watch happening right in front of us and still can't really see' have an effect on the future.[54] The novel follows Holly Sykes through six interconnected chapters from 1984 to 2043, particularly her experiences with near-immortals called Atemporals or Horologists who protect humans from the carnivorous immortals called Anchorites. These supernatural figures can manipulate characters' perceptions of time and erase their memories, while themselves travelling across times and Mitchell's other fictions, but they also make clear that human 'bone clocks' are simultaneously present and past through memory. Of all the characters, Ed Brubeck, Iraq war reporter, is the one who sees a special urgency in reading the present, and insists on continuing his coverage of the war under increasingly dire conditions. His desire to make 'a tiny dent in the world's memory' makes him an 'archivist for the future'.[55] For other characters, however, reading the present is less crucial, and by the end of the novel, corporatisation and wilful ignorance of climate change has led to chaos. Throughout the novel are almost throwaway clues to the pending crisis, often overheard in the background, that oil is running out or that airplanes cause pollution. One of the sponsors of writer Crispin Hershey's reading at the Hay festival is the FutureNow Bank whose name suggests that the future is already mortgaged by the corporate world.[56] By the end of the novel, the inevitability of entropy is visible and critical. Food and medicines are scarce, electronic communication has broken down and a nuclear reactor is close to meltdown. Government sponsored militiamen steal whatever they can carry with the explanation that the world as it is has been ruined by the world that was: 'The bill's due', says a militiaman as he steals solar panels at gunpoint, 'Today, you start to pay'.[57] In the midst of this chaos, Holly thinks: 'For most of my life, the world shrank and technology progressed; this was the natural order of things. Few of us clocked on that "the natural order of things" is entirely man-made.'[58]

Conclusion

Postmodernism focussed on what is provisional and indeterminate in historical narrative. It may be that, current political situations being what they are, too much around us is provisional and indeterminate for us to want to see it reflected in fiction. Perhaps the fate of all 'radical' movements is to be absorbed by the mainstream and lose their edge. Fredric Jameson complained in 1991 that the 'most offensive' features of postmodernism 'no longer scandalize anyone and are not only received with the greatest complacency but have themselves become institutionalized and are at one with the official or public culture of Western society'.[59] In 2000, Hardt and Negri seem to agree that postmodernist 'strategies that appear to be liberatory would not challenge but in fact coincide with and even unwittingly reinforce the new strategies of rule!'[60] None of these authors is dealing directly with British fiction, but the question remains as to whether postmodern techniques have indeed become part of the mainstream.

It is hard to imagine that, after postmodernism, it is possible to approach any narrative that purports unproblematically to represent the world 'as it is' without a critical eye. Above all, postmodernism wanted to produce a critical reader, as a co-creator; a reader who was conscious of the constructedness of 'common sense' and who approached anything presented as an absolute Truth with suspicion. British postmodern fiction, both formally and textually, asked readers to be self-reflexive, to be aware of who is speaking, what language they are using, and to what end. This is arguably just good reading practice, no matter what the text, but postmodernism made this kind of reading overt and political. Post-millennial fiction, while resistant to any 'ism', has continued to use postmodern techniques, but has shifted the focus and complicated British literature's relationship to the past. That relationship, while no longer 'postmodern', is the result of historical postmodernism. The difference seems to be defined by postmodernism's interest in the reader's relationship to the past through the *documents* of history, and a post-millennial attempt to understand history's presence in the *lived experience* of the here and now.

Notes

1. Graham Swift, *Waterland* (New York: Vintage, 1992), p. 6.
2. Ibid., p. 53.
3. Wendy Wheeler, 'Melancholic Modernity and Contemporary Grief: The Novels of Graham Swift' in *Literature and the Contemporary: Fictions and Theories of the Present*, ed. Roger Luckhurst and Peter Marks (Harlow: Longman, 1999), p. 69.
4. Swift, *Waterland*, p. 5.
5. Ibid., p. 108.
6. Victoria Stewart, *The Second World War in Contemporary British Fiction* (Edinburgh: Edinburgh University Press, 2011), p. 14.
7. Thomas Docherty, 'Now, Here, This' in *Literature and the Contemporary: Fictions and Theories of the Present* ed. Roger Luckhurst and Peter Marks (Harlow: Longman, 1999), p. 50.
8. Zadie Smith, *White Teeth* (London: Penguin, 2000), p. 237.
9. Ibid., p. 239.
10. Ibid., p. 238.
11. Ibid., p. 239, p. 240.
12. Ibid., p. 238.
13. Ibid., p. 240.
14. Eduardo Galeano, see epigraph to book two of Colum McCann's *TransAtlantic* (Toronto: Random House, 2013), p. 153.
15. Charles Jencks, *What is Postmodernism?* 4th ed. (London: Academy Editions, 1996), p. 30.
16. Patrick O'Donnell, 'New British Fiction', *Modern Fiction Studies* 58:3 (2012), pp. 429–35, p. 431.
17. Lauren Berlant, *Cruel Optimism* (Durham: Duke University Press, 2011), p. 192.
18. Jerome de Groot, *The Historical Novel* (London: Routledge, 2010), p. 2.
19. Ibid., p. 3.

20. Ann Rigney, *Imperfect Histories: The Elusive Past and the Legacy of Romantic Historicism* (Ithaca: Cornell University Press, 2000), p. 19.
21. Qtd. in Susan Bordo, 'When Fictionalized Facts matter: From "Anne of a Thousand Days" to Hilary Mantel's New *Bring Up the Bodies*' *Chronicle of Higher Education*, 6 May 2012.
22. Qtd. in Lisa Allardice, 'Uncharted Waters' *Guardian*, 1 June 2006.
23. Michel Foucault, *The Archeology of Knowledge*, trans. A. M. Sheridan Smith (New York: Pantheon Books, 1972), p. 3.
24. de Groot, *The Historical Novel*, p. 3.
25. Linda Hutcheon, *A Poetics of Postmodernism: History, Theory, Fiction* (New York: Routledge, 1988), p. 89.
26. Ibid., p. 12.
27. Steven Connor, 'The Impossibility of the Present: or, From the Contemporary to the Contemporal' in *Literature and the Contemporary: Fictions and Theories of the Present* ed. Roger Luckhurst and Peter Marks (Harlow: Pearson Education Ltd., 1999), p. 21.
28. Berlant, *Cruel Optimism*, p. 4.
29. Ibid.
30. 'There are two ways to read this novel, but you're stuck with it – you'll end up reading one of them': Alex Clark interview with Ali Smith, *The Guardian* (6 September 2014).
31. Smith, *How to Be Both*, p. 10.
32. Ibid.
33. Ibid., p. 69.
34. Ibid., p. 40.
35. Ibid., p. 102–3.
36. Ibid., p. 46.
37. W. H. Auden, 'In Memory of W. B. Yeats' in *The Norton Anthology of English Literature: The Twentieth Century and After*, Vol. F. 9th ed. Ed. Jahan Ramazani and Jon Stallworthy (New York: Norton, 2012), pp. 2685–7.
38. McCann, *TransAtlantic*, p. 145.
39. Ibid., p. 59.
40. Ibid., p. 261.
41. Erica Wagner, 'Cross Over "TransAtlantic", by Colum McCann' *The New York Times*, 20 June 2013.
42. McCann, *TransAtlantic*, p. 18.
43. Ibid., p. 188.
44. Wendell Berry, 'Rising'. From Colum McCann's *TransAtlantic* (Toronto: Harper Collins), p. 153.
45. Leigh Wilson, 'Historical Representations. Reality Effects: The Historical Novel and the Crisis of Fictionality in the First Decade of the Twenty-first Century' in *The 2000s: A Decade of Contemporary British Fiction*, ed. Nick Bentley, Nick Hubble, and Leigh Wilson (London: Bloomsbury, 2000), p. 156.

46. Sara Knox, 'Hilary Mantel and the Historical Novel' in *Twenty-First-Century British Fiction*, ed. Bianca Leggett and Tony Venezia (Canterbury: Gylphi, 2015), p. 137.
47. Hilary Mantel, *Wolf Hall* (Toronto: HarperCollins, 2009), p. 26.
48. Jeanette Winterson, *The Gap of Time: The Winter's Tale Retold* (Toronto: Alfred A Knopf, 2015), p. 232.
49. Ibid., p. 219.
50. Ibid., p. 73.
51. Ibid., p. 268.
52. Ibid., p. 49.
53. Paul A. Harris, 'David Mitchell's Fractal Imagination: *The Bone Clocks*', *Substance: A Review of Theory and Literary Criticism* 44:1 (2015) pp. 148–53, p. 148.
54. Smith, *How to Be Both*, p. 104.
55. David Mitchell, *The Bone Clocks* (Toronto: Knopf Canada, 2014), p. 210, p. 211.
56. Ibid., p. 295.
57. Ibid., p. 599.
58. Ibid., p. 595.
59. Frederic Jameson, *Postmodernism: or, the Cultural Logic of Late Capitalism* (Durham, North Carolina: Duke University Press, 1991), p. 4.
60. Michael Hardt and Antonio Negri, *Empire* (Cambridge, Massachusetts: Harvard University Press, 2000), p. 138.

CHAPTER 13

Neo-Victorian Fiction
Patricia Pulham

The historical novel has a long, established history. Reputedly invented by Sir Walter Scott in the early nineteenth century, it endures in the present both in its traditional form and in significant sub-genres such as the neo-Victorian novel. While it was not until the early twenty-first century that neo-Victorian fiction was named as such, its genesis is discernible in 1960s novels such as Jean Rhys's *Wide Sargasso Sea* (1966) and John Fowles' *French Lieutenant's Woman* (1969), co-opted into the genre retrospectively. This was followed by a dramatic rise in its popularity and public acclaim in the last two decades of the Twentieth Century fostered through the emergence of prominent literary successes including A. S. Byatt's *Possession: A Romance* (1990); Sarah Waters's *Tipping the Velvet* (1998), *Affinity* (1999), and *Fingersmith* (2002); and Michel Faber's *The Crimson Petal and the White* (2002). Neo-Victorian fiction remains an important marketplace winner and is a regular fixture in twenty-first-century fiction lists. Influenced by debates that questioned historians' ability to represent the 'truth' of the historical past, and highlighting the fine line between history and fiction, the neo-Victorian novel is a genre that sits on the boundaries between realist and experimental fiction; high and low-brow literature; accuracy and authenticity. This chapter examines how the neo-Victorian novel is informed by Anglo-American and European postmodernist theories that challenged the division between history and literature. It demonstrates how neo-Victorianism has intersected with British political discourse; and how authors' investment in Britain's history and Victorian literary culture problematises the neo-Victorian novel's position in the academy and the quality of its perceived prestige.

Postmodernism, History, and Fiction

Following postmodern theorists' challenge to the knowability of 'truth', in the late twentieth century the unassailability of historical documentation came under increasing scrutiny. In *The Postmodern Condition* (1979), François Lyotard encouraged the rejection of 'grand' or 'master' narratives, conceiving these as ideological narratives that aim to make sense of history, portraying it as sets of interconnected events leading to development and progress. For Lyotard, postmodernism destabilises and fragments grand narratives that are seen as repressive and posits that all forms of knowledge are narratives and thus open to interpretation. In works such as 'The Burden of History' (1966), *Metahistory: The Historical Imagination in Nineteenth-Century Europe* (1973), and *Tropics of Discourse* (1978), Hayden White recognised the storytelling implicit in historical documents, arguing that when viewed 'simply as verbal artifacts histories and novels are indistinguishable from one another'.[1]

In *The Reality of the Historical Past* (1984), Paul Ricoeur challenges Hayden White's view of history as narrative and contends that it is the 'recourse to documents' which 'marks a dividing line between history and fiction'.[2] Unlike the novel, he notes that 'the constructions of the historian are intended to be reconstructions of the past. Through documents . . . the historian is constrained by *what once was*' (original emphasis).[3] Despite these varying perspectives, such debates destabilised the notion of objectivity previously attached to historical documentation and, in literature, opened the door to neo-Victorian fiction which often challenges the 'grand narratives' of existing Victorian novels, reclaiming voices and topics silenced in their representations.

Towards the end of the twentieth century fictional reconstructions of historical periods had already been subjected to criticism in Fredric Jameson's 1984 essay, 'Postmodernism and the Cultural Logic of late Capitalism', where he contends that postmodernity's permeation of contemporary culture has affected our sense of history. For Jameson, cultural reproductions of historical eras – whether literary or filmic – lack depth, relying instead on empty mimicry, a form of pastiche: 'the imitation of dead styles, speech through all the masks and voices stored up in the imaginary museum of a now global culture'.[4] Countering Jameson, in *A Poetics of Postmodernism* (1988) Linda Hutcheon points out that postmodernism 'does not so much erode our "sense of history" and reference . . . as erode our old sure sense of what both history and reference meant. It asks us to rethink and critique our notions of both'.[5]

The creative momentum of neo-Victorian fiction in the 1980s and 1990s, was informed by such postmodern debates about history and fiction, and is especially illustrative of the kind of critique Hutcheon advocates. Coining the term 'Neo-Victorian' in her influential 1997 article, 'The Redemptive

Past in the Neo-Victorian Novel', Dana Shiller reflects on Jameson's concerns and builds on Hutcheon's concept of historiographic metafiction to define neo-Victorian literature as 'at once characteristic of postmodernism and imbued with a historicity reminiscent of the nineteenth-century novel'.[6] Neo-Victorian fiction combines the self-reflexivity of historiographic metafiction and its knowing challenges to prejudices of the past with historicity's specificity, often engaging with historical events or personages alongside fictive inventions. As such it is a sub-genre of both historiographic metafiction and the historical novel. According to Shiller, neo-Victorian fiction counters Jameson's reservations by offering 'a historicity that is indeed concerned with recuperating the substance of bygone eras, and not merely their styles'.[7] She argues that its 'revisionist approach to the past' borrows from postmodern historiography 'to explore how present circumstances shape historical narrative' but also intersects with traditional cultural views of history.[8]

Political Neo-Victorianism

The sub-genre's development in the late twentieth century, alongside the rise of Thatcherism in Britain, illustrates this duality. While the neo-Victorian novel is clearly a postmodern phenomenon, it is also bound up with a political investment in traditional perceptions of Victorian culture that were highlighted in the 1980s under the leadership of the then UK Prime Minister, Margaret Thatcher. They are still prominent in twenty-first-century Britain where references to the Victorians and their cultural legacy remain ubiquitous. In 2001, they were the subject of the BBC documentary series, *What the Victorians Did for Us*; in 2002 they were subjected to A. N. Wilson's scrutiny in *The Victorians*; and in 2009 they received Jeremy Paxman's attention in a further four-part BBC TV series accompanied by a book of the same name published in 2010.[9]

More recently, on the 23 May 2019, the day of what were, for the foreseeable future at least, the last European Parliament elections in the UK, a book entitled *The Victorians: Twelve Titans who Forged Britain* by then Conservative MP Jacob Rees-Mogg appeared in bookshops and was ready for purchase online. While acknowledging the importance of Lytton Strachey's *Eminent Victorians* (1918) and its impact on his own work, in his introduction Rees-Mogg laments Strachey's irreverent comments on iconic nineteenth-century figures such as the nursing reformer, Florence Nightingale; the Archbishop of Westminster, Cardinal Henry Edward Manning; the historian Thomas Arnold; and the military commander,

General Charles Gordon. He asks his readers to 'look again at some of these eminent Victorians', to 'reassess their effect upon and contribution to their world and our own' and to consider what they offer the United Kingdom as it remakes its own image and leaves the European Union.[10]

This 'backwards glance' at Britain's own nineteenth-century past in the early years of a new millennium, is one that Simon Joyce identifies as embedded in nostalgic attempts to embrace Victorian successes and traditions, in recognising the similarities and the differences between Victorian and contemporary Britons, and designed to appropriate those that suit social, cultural, and political agendas.[11] The initial return to the Victorian era during this period is to some extent due to Thatcher's prominent invocation of 'Victorian values', associated with a nostalgic impulse to recuperate Britain's steady decline from imperial power. Whereas Queen Victoria had ruled over an ever-expanding empire, in Thatcher's time Britain had become 'an increasingly obscure island off the shore of north-west Europe'; then, as now, Britain needed to remodel its image.[12] Additionally, Thatcher's investment in the Victorians eschewed historical specificities in favour of stereotypical inventions that served her own vision. In his own solicitation of the Victorians Rees-Mogg, like Thatcher, focuses on conventional notions of Victorian society as a blueprint for a 'new' Britain, albeit one that rejects her pro-European vision of its future.

Neo-Victorian Fiction in the Academy

This obsession with all things Victorian is one that Cora Kaplan calls 'Victoriana'.[13] For Kaplan, it stems from a 'British postwar vogue which shows no sign of exhaustion', manifesting not only in material collectibles, and in politics, but embracing a 'miscellany of evocations and recyclings of the nineteenth century' which have become 'markers for particular moments of contemporary style and culture'.[14] Her broad definition of the term includes neo-Victorian fiction, and its 'self-conscious rewriting of historical narratives to highlight suppressed histories of gender and sexuality, race and empire, as well as challenges to the conventional understandings of the historical itself'.[15] However, she acknowledges that, as a phenomenon, it is difficult to pin down, suggesting that the 'variety and appeal of Victoriana over the years' is the product of 'the historical imagination on the move ... permanently restless and unsettled'.[16]

This 'restlessness' additionally informs its fluctuating status as the offspring of Victorian and postmodern literature that awards it an anomalous position in contemporary literary studies, underpinned by an intellectual symbiosis between creative writing, critical theory, and literary criticism, that problematises its position within the academy. Following the establishment and popularisation of the term 'neo-Victorian' over others such as 'retro' or 'faux' Victorian, existing postmodern novels set in the nineteenth century were relabelled. As neo-Victorian fiction became the object of academic study, an ever-expanding canon was formed. The neo-Victorian novel has become firmly implanted in literary culture, and this is reflected in publishers' interest in academic monographs on the topic and the launch in 2008 of the online *Journal of Neo-Victorian Studies*.[17]

Wide Sargasso Sea, Rhys's 'prequel' to Charlotte Brontë's *Jane Eyre* (1847), and *The French Lieutenant's Woman*, Fowles's playful engagement with Victorian tropes, were immediately adopted into this canon.[18] Other prominent examples include Charles Palliser's *The Quincunx* (1989), which has drawn comparisons with Dickensian heavyweights such as *Bleak House* (1852–53), and *Oscar and Lucinda* (1988), Peter Carey's tale of a Plymouth Brethren minister and an Australian heiress set in the nineteenth century. Marketplace successes such as Byatt's *Possession*, featuring a twin storyline that doubles avatars of Victorian poets, Robert Browning and Christina Rossetti, with academic researchers in the 1990s, and Carey's *Jack Maggs* (1997), which fabricates a meeting between barely disguised versions of Dickens (Tobias Oates) and Magwitch (Maggs) from *Great Expectations* (1860), have also become canonical, along with Waters's Victorian trilogy, that revisits topics such as Victorian decadence, spiritualism, and class through revisionist lenses.

The appropriation of contemporary novels that are set in the Victorian period and their rapid canonisation is continually in process. Recently, following Yorgos Lanthimos's 2023 cinematic interpretation of Alisdair Gray's *Poor Things* (1992), with its focus on Bella Baxter's sexual and intellectual awakening amid exaggerated Victorian costuming and steampunk mise-en-scène, this novel has been incorporated into the neo-Victorian canon. Similarly, revisiting the notorious 1874 case of the Tichborne Claimant, and bringing to the fore peripheral characters to critique Victorian attitudes to race and gender, Zadie Smith's 2023 novel, *The Fraud*, was immediately primed for neo-Victorian critical attention and canonical status.[19] What canonical neo-Victorian novels have in common, regardless of authors' nationalities, is an investment in the legacies of British nineteenth-century fiction, its writers, and the impacts of imperialism and cultural exclusion, all of which are subjected to challenge and/or reclamation.

Periodisation and Prestige

Popular with readers, neo-Victorian fiction is often nominated for literary prizes: *Possession* and Eleanor Catton's *The Luminaries* won the Man Booker prize in 1990 and 2013 respectively; *Fingersmith* was shortlisted for the Booker and Orange prizes. It has also become the progenitor of many film adaptations, including *The French Lieutenant's Woman* (dir. Karel Reisz, 1981), *Wide Sargasso Sea* (dir. John Duigan, 1993), and *Possession* (dir. Neil LaBute, 2002), as well as several TV series including *Fingersmith* (BBC, 2005), Michel Faber's *The Crimson Petal and the White* (BBC, 2011), *The Luminaries* (TVNZ, 2020) and, most recently, Apple TV's 2022 adaptation of Sarah Perry's 2016 novel, *The Essex Serpent*.

Despite the accolades and its commercial success, however, the neo-Victorian novel continues to occupy a contested position in postmodern culture. Deemed variously conservative, derivative, and insufficiently experimental, it sits precariously on its literary perch; promoted by publishers, enjoyed by readers, yet often reviled and dismissed by critics of Victorian and contemporary fiction alike. In *Nostalgic Postmodernism* (2001) Christian Gutleben, drawing on Jameson, considers the neo-Victorian novel a form of pastiche, mere mimicry of Victorian works that lack the prestige of the original.[20] Writing in 2004, J. Hillis Miller asked, 'Upwards of fifty thousand Victorian novels already exist ... Why do we need another one, and a fake simulacrum at that?'[21] These early critiques signal neo-Victorian fiction's anomalous position in literary culture. For Gutleben, neo-Victorian fiction's celebration of the Victorian tradition means it cannot be deemed subversive and that, 'because radical subversiveness is a characteristic often associated with postmodernism', the connection between neo-Victorian fiction and postmodernism is inevitably problematic.[22] Likewise, Samantha Carroll acknowledges that 'neo-Victorian fiction serves not one but two masters: the "neo" as well as the "Victorian"'.[23] Furthermore, she concedes that while it engages with the 'new' in its use of 'postmodern revisionary critique', its postmodernity is often complicated by its predominant adherence to realist narratives.[24]

Yet Carroll counters Gutleben's critiques, suggesting that his concerns are misplaced, that the need to define the neo-Victorian novel in relation to the Victorian novel 'as fake to genuine, replica to original' is based on 'the binary logic that must valorise the Victorian at the expense of the neo-Victorian novel'.[25] She reminds us that the neo-Victorian novel is in fact 'a *contemporary* genre' (original emphasis).[26] While the neo-Victorian novel's apparent longevity might indicate that such critiques have subsided, questions of 'value' and 'authenticity', intrinsic to the postmodern context of its origins, still dog the sub-genre, not least because, falling between two fields of literary studies – the Victorian and the contemporary – it complicates and contests academic investment in questions of periodisation.

The prestige attached to periodisation is the subject of Ted Underwood's 2013 book *Why Literary Periods Mattered: Historical Contrast and the Prestige of English Studies*. Underwood notes that 'Periodization has endured in a discipline where almost nothing else does, and has endured not just in broad outline but in detail.'[27] English departments still divide teaching into historical periods, following a model instigated in the 1840s. Despite the endurance of this model, Underwood's title is 'Why Literary Periods Mattered' not why they currently matter – and this repositioning is worth considering when reviewing the neo-Victorian novel's value and its complex relationship to postmodern fiction, negotiating, as it does, two historical periods.

Underwood identifies this organisation of literary studies as a commitment to 'historical contrast' rather than 'periodisation' because of the difficulties inherent in defining temporal boundaries. For example, while the Victorian period may be demarcated by Queen Victoria's dates of birth and death, issues that span the long nineteenth century – usually covering the period 1789–1914 – are frequently discussed in the context of Victorian studies.[28] What is crucial, he argues, is that '[t]he prestige of the discipline has long depended on the ruptures that separate periods and movements'.[29] He suggests that what is feared is the loss of 'our ability to believe in cultural history as a form of collective immortality' and to exemplify his point examines examples of historiographic metafiction that would be commonly labelled 'neo-Victorian' (though he does not use this term).[30] Byatt's *Possession*, set in a parallel past and present, seems, he contends, invested in a desire to bridge the gap between historical continuity and discontinuity, while functioning as a threat to both. For Underwood, the negative responses such works have, at times, elicited from the academy centre on critical perceptions of 'the waning prestige of historical contrast' because for literary scholars, 'the value of historical contrast is still a fundamental intellectual premise, as well as a primary mode of disciplinary organization'.[31]

In some senses, as in Byatt's *Possession*, as a field of academic study neo-Victorian studies tries to have it both ways: the neo-Victorian novel can be 'a different way into the Victorians', one that is not 'a substitute for the nineteenth century' but 'a mediator into the experience of reading the "real" thing'.[32] Yet it shares with Victorian studies – as taught in universities and engaged in by academic researchers – the motive of 'understanding the impact of the nineteenth century and its enduring legacy into the present'.[33] Yet, paradoxically, given the neo-Victorian novel's postmodern origins, in both cases the prestigious point of critical entry is Victorian literature. This means that, as Carroll puts it, 'the nineteenth-century "parent"' is frequently venerated 'at the expense of the estrangement and/or occlusion of the postmodern one'.[34]

In part, this may be due to the fact that though the neo-Victorian novel often displays characteristics of its postmodern parent, such as embedded narratives, mash-ups, and the use of literary bricolage, the academic structures of contemporary studies in literature and theory have – to an extent – disowned it, some deeming the neo-Victorian novel 'anti-intellectual'.[35] Additionally, contributing to the marginalisation of the neo-Victorian novel's postmodernity, neo-Victorian authors – many of whom are themselves literary critics – rely on historical and theoretical criticism as the basis for their work, but often ignore or fail to acknowledge the critical fields, including feminist, postcolonial, and queer theories, that emerged from postmodernist thought, on which their novels depend. What most often gets lost in such debates is neo-Victorian literature's contemporaneity and its postmodernity. As Carroll puts it:

> To state the obvious, neo-Victorian fiction and its writers are not native to the nineteenth century, but to the twentieth and twenty-first centuries. Certainly, neo-Victorian novels that locate or restore eclipsed narratives of the Victorian past might complicate our understanding of the nineteenth century. However, neo-Victorian fiction's representation of the Victorian past is also the lens through which a variety of *present* concerns are examined. (original emphasis)[36]

What Carroll identifies here is a continuity of past concerns in the present as opposed to a discontinuity that validates the Victorians and elevates them to the model against which we judge our own period, as Thatcher and Rees-Mogg sought to do. Among these present concerns she lists 'advances in cultural theory'; 'developments in postmodern criticism'; and 'the imaginative restoration of voices lost or constrained in the past, with repercussions for the present'.[37] Such reclaimed voices allow for the articulation of marginalised identities and social injustices existing in the hinterlands of Victorian novels: othered races and classes on whose labour Victorian imperialism and economic power relied; othered sexualities whose existence was denied, medicalised or criminalised; disabilities which were othered and displayed in the Victorian freak show.

Albeit complicated by temporal disjunctions, *Wide Sargasso Sea* reclaims the silenced voice of Brontë's Creole heiress, Bertha, released from the attic and provided with a back story that resonates with, yet challenges, the narrative promoted by *Jane Eyre*. In doing so, it illustrates Gayatri Spivak's contention that Brontë's construction of Bertha as a monstrous, inchoate creature, aligns her not with her fellow woman, but with the dominant culture that disregards and dehumanises those at the periphery.[38] *Wide Sargasso Sea* is one of a number of novels – including later works such as *Jack Maggs, The Luminaries*, and Margaret Atwood's *Alias Grace* (1996) – that provide 'a highly visible, highly aestheticized code for confronting empire again and anew'; neo-Victorian fiction offers a literary space 'within which the memory of empire and its surrounding discourses and strategies of representation can be replayed and played out'.[39] As Elizabeth Ho observes, to offer means of 'recovery from that Imperial past, neo-Victorianism offers those situated in various postcolonial moments and specific locations a powerful conceptual and aesthetic vocabulary for exploring the past'; this in turn, 'offers ways of coping with the temporal palimpsests of the present'.[40]

Likewise, exploring the impact of Victorian attitudes to non-normative bodies, alongside discourses of race, neo-Victorian texts such as Barbara Chase-Riboud's *Hottentot Venus* (2003) and Darin Strauss's *Chang and Eng* (2000) explore nineteenth-century freak shows and press us towards ethical considerations of the politics of such exposures. However, while humanising their subjects and reclaiming their bodies from the unsavoury carnival setting, such novels find it difficult to escape the problems inherent in a sub-genre that replicates Victorian representations for the purposes of popular entertainment.[41]

Nevertheless, these revisionist approaches to characters and tropes familiar to readers and consumers of Victorian culture function as a form of 'recognitive justice' that is familiar from postmodern culture's investment in identity politics.[42] Deploying the critical framework of historiographic metafiction posited by Hutcheon, Sarah Waters's novel *Affinity*, for example, 'works *within* conventions in order to subvert them' (original emphasis), positioning the hidden worlds of spiritualism and female homosexuality centre stage, reclaiming sexual identities that existed but often remained wilfully unacknowledged in all but bohemian circles, and legally ignored in the nineteenth century.[43] Similarly, Waters's *Affinity* can be said to work both within and against the invisible history of lesbianism proposed in Terry Castle's *The Apparitional Lesbian: Female Homosexuality and Modern Culture* (1993), employing its theoretical approach in a creative context.[44]

This brief discussion of Waters's work demonstrates the elision of the boundary between literary critic and creative writer that is common in neo-Victorian fiction. Waters's work is clearly influenced not only by Hutcheon's theory, developed in *A Poetics of Postmodernism*, but also by queer studies more generally. Other examples include Patricia Duncker's *James Miranda Barry* (1999) and Wesley Stace's *Misfortune* (2005), written in the wake of Judith Butler's influential theoretical meditations on gender and performativity including *Gender Trouble: Feminism and the Subversion of Identity* (1990), and *Bodies that Matter: On the Discursive Limits of 'Sex'* (1993). Both novels are currently experiencing a revival of interest in the context of transgender studies.[45]

While commonly known in academic circles, there is less general awareness in popular culture of the theoretical and critical work that underpins these novels. The influence of such work on neo-Victorian writing has been discussed at length by Alan Robinson. In his study of historiography and the contemporary novel, Robinson notes how what he calls the 'present past' in Byatt's *Possession* 'appears influenced by Lillian Faderman's *Surpassing the Love of Men: Romantic Friendship and Love between Woman from the Renaissance to the Present* (1981), Jan Marsh's *Pre-Raphaelite Sisterhood* (1985), Pamela Gerrish Nunn's *Victorian Women Artists* (1987), and Martha Vicinus', *Independent Women: Work and Community for Single Women, 1850–1920* (1985)'.[46] Furthermore, he observes that while 'Waters's *Affinity* revises the marginal topic of "romantic friendship" in Byatt's *Possession*, in keeping with the intervening developments in gender history', both *Affinity* and *Tipping the Velvet* (1998) are 'shaped by' and allude to 'critical, theoretical and historiographical models which Waters knew from her doctoral research on "lesbian and gay historical fictions, 1870 to the present"'.[47]

While in Byatt's *Possession* academics are at the forefront of the novel, albeit as competitive and rather unlikable characters, and feminist criticism is often mentioned in abstract terms, general readers are nonetheless left to decipher the academic studies that underpin her text. These underpinning sources remain similarly obscure in Waters's *Affinity*. Melissa Pritchard's *Palmerino* (2014), a novel whose main protagonist is a fictional historical novelist, Sylvia, who resurrects Vernon Lee, a late-Victorian British writer of supernatural fiction, highlights criticism within her text only to revile it. Possessed by Lee's revenant, Sylvia channels her ghostly denigrations of contemporary critical approaches to her life and work. Ironically, Sylvia's own fictionalisation of Lee relies on materials, biographies, and a collection of scanned photos amassed from her excursions to real-life archives, suggesting that Pritchard herself, like Sylvia, must have engaged in considerable academic research to write the novel. Yet the novel undermines research and criticism, especially queer studies of Lee's life and writings, though it employs the ghost of Lee to do so, dismissing scholars who write 'tiresome books' and deliver 'dull papers' that they present at Vernon Lee conferences in Paris, Rome or Budapest, asking 'who reads, who listens?'[48]

Borrowed Celebrity

On the one hand, Pritchard's novel may be read as a meditation on postmodern historiography and scholars' inability to truly know what a subject's life may have been, no matter how meticulous their research. On the other hand, she makes a claim for the primacy of creative writing and the imagination in depicting the 'truth' of the subject's life. The anti-intellectual sentiments expressed in her novel perhaps reflect the anxieties of the neo-Victorian author, given that the sub-genre has itself been referred to as 'anti-intellectual'.[49] It is worth remembering that Byatt and Waters taught English Literature at university level (Byatt at UCL; Waters at Queen Mary, University of London), and Pritchard is currently Professor Emerita at Arizona State University. At the time of writing, all would therefore have been only too aware of the scholarly work underpinning their fiction.

The silencing and/or devaluation of critical work in neo-Victorian fiction is arguably bound up with the neo-Victorian novel's popular prestige. To acknowledge the academic work that underlies such writings could be problematic and alienate one's public. Yet to become popular – with some exceptions – may mean the acquisition of success and celebrity at the expense of prestige and cultural capital. For Pierre Bourdieu, two forms of capital are especially significant in the field of cultural production: '*Symbolic capital*', the idea of 'accumulated prestige, celebrity, consecration or honour' that is 'founded on a dialectic of knowledge ... and recognition', and '*Cultural capital*' which is concerned with 'forms of cultural knowledge, competences or dispositions' (original emphases).[50] Bourdieu 'defines cultural capital as a form of knowledge, an internalized code or a cognitive acquisition which equips the social agent with empathy towards, appreciation for, or competence in deciphering cultural relations and cultural artefacts'.[51] In this formulation, 'a work of art has meaning and interest only for someone who possesses the cultural competence, that is, the code, into which it is encoded'.[52] The ability to read this code depends on the nature of familial, social, and institutional education.

To some extent both the neo-Victorian novel and its readership inhabit awkward positions in the literary marketplace. Many successful neo-Victorian writers have had considerable popular and economic success but, as Bourdieu's analyses of the field of cultural production suggest, 'economic success (in literary terms . . .) may well signal a barrier to specific consecration and symbolic power'.[53] In other words, writing a best seller doesn't guarantee cultural prestige. Despite its popularity and the reservations of the academy, in neo-Victorian fiction 'prestige' is often necessarily borrowed from the Victorian texts and authors with which such novels interact and intersect. *Possession* benefits from its allusions to Browning and Christina Rossetti and *Fingersmith* draws on the work of Dickens, Wilkie Collins, and Mary Elizabeth Braddon.[54] Such novels can and are of course enjoyed by those readers who only know Dickens from TV and film adaptations, or those who enjoy historical novels but may not recognise the Victorian texts or writers to which the neo-Victorian novel may allude. By contrast, Pritchard cannot acquire this kind of instant and borrowed celebrity, as that would depend on either canonicity or popularity, neither of which can be claimed for Vernon Lee. Instead, Pritchard knows that her ready readership is most likely composed of academics who know of Lee's works, and who might like to see what she has done with her biography and writings; essentially to write about Lee is in some ways to invite recognition of the codes of her cultural capital.

Inevitably, there is a particular enjoyment for those 'in the know', who can spot the allusions, know the references, and recognise the theories and texts that underpin neo-Victorian fiction. In terms of its readership, then, the neo-Victorian novel inhabits the space in-between, straddling the boundaries of literary and popular fiction, general and academic readerships, choosing to make spectral the critical theories and histories that inform it which are then materialised by the literary critics who write about it. In doing so, it epitomises postmodernism's acceleration of the collapse between high and popular culture.

Accuracy and Authenticity

In her critique of *Nostalgic Postmodernism*, Samantha Carroll challenges Gutleben's lament that many British neo-Victorian novels fail to exhibit the postmodern playfulness of John Fowles's *The French Lieutenant's Woman* and are grounded in the stylistic experimentation of late-modernism rather than postmodernism. She also counters the idea that the mainstream success of neo-Victorian fiction's anomalous position in contemporary culture has contributed to postmodernism's 'demise'.[55] Instead, she argues that despite critical concerns that postmodernism's impact has dwindled, 'it still garners vocal opposition from its right-wing detractors'.[56] Reading her article in the third decade of the twenty-first century, it is worth noting that, far from opposing postmodernism, the 'right-wing detractors' to whom Carroll refers have now embraced its destabilisation of objective 'truth' and that our cultural milieu more generally has welcomed the opportunities for creative misinformation that deep fake simulacra offer.

In the context of critical approaches to historical fiction, film, and TV, these cultural shifts have led to discussions that highlight distinctions between accuracy and authenticity. Writing in 2020 of the complexities surrounding historical fiction, Laura Saxton argues that neither accuracy nor authenticity can result in the 'translation of absolute truth onto the page'.[57] However, by separating the terms and seeing them as 'as distinct but interrelated categories', we can explore how literary techniques and historical research can each contribute to 'painting a plausible representation'.[58] The term 'authenticity' acknowledges the interstitial spaces between historical fact and fiction in which the neo-Victorian novel operates. As Saxton notes, historical fiction relies on novelistic inventions that fill the 'gaps' in historical knowledge.[59] This is especially the case when recreating an historical figure whose intimate thoughts, speech, and daily lives can only be imagined. Therefore, historical accuracy cannot be guaranteed; we can only expect credible authenticity.

Adopting realism as its predominant mode of narrative, the neo-Victorian novel has always been in the business of 'painting a plausible representation' of the nineteenth century, and this is perhaps to be expected given that realism is always already a representation that can never be entirely accurate, only plausibly authentic. Furthermore, neo-Victorian novels are not simply – and sometimes not solely – set in the past but actively challenge or question that past. While it is true to say that 'verisimilitude is a conventional technique of the historical novel', in neo-Victorian fiction, and in neo-historical novels more generally, 'verisimilitude only ever aims at conveying a surface image of the real'.[60] The mode of realism deployed by neo-Victorian fiction therefore simultaneously offers, yet rejects an accurate representation of the past.[61]

For George Lettisier, neo-Victorian fiction's commitment to plausible authenticity has an ethical basis, one that resonates with Carroll's understanding of its investment in 'recognitive justice'. This is especially notable in the emphasis on diversity in recent film and TV adaptations. Examples include the 'colour blind casting' in Lanthimos's recent adaptation of Gray's *Poor Things*, in which an African American actor was cast as Harry Astley, the Caucasian 'Malthusiast' in Gray's novel, and the casting of British Indian, Dev Patel, as the eponymous character in Armando Iannucci's 2019 film *David Copperfield*, which might be deemed 'neo-Victorian' in style.[62] Such casting choices have drawn particular attention in Shonda Rhimes's adaptation of Julia Quinn's Georgian romances in the *Bridgerton* series (Netflix, 2020–24).[63] These examples are not committed to accuracy, but instead to an authenticity that acknowledges the racial diversity commonly occluded in historical drama.

Bridgerton is Jane Austen's nineteenth-century world reconstructed and adapted for the twenty-first-century viewer. Dialogue merges contemporary and more archaic forms of address, and the soundtrack often employs rearrangements of contemporary music in baroque style, performed by string quartets. While it promises Austenian authenticity by placing marriage plots, class, and money at its centre, it highlights issues relating to gender, sexualities, and race. Most prominent has been the series' recasting of some of Quinn's white characters as black, a decision which, while well-intentioned, has received its own share of criticism. In her article, '"Bridgerton" sees race through a colourist lens', published in *The Observer*, 1 January 2021, Carolyn Hinds challenges the 'progressive' nature of Bridgerton's racial diversity. While she acknowledges the value of featuring Black characters, she notes that 'race is practically ignored for almost the entire show, except for a few vague references in their dialogue'.[64] If race truly didn't matter, she argues, 'there would be an equal number of Black, Asian, Middle Eastern, Latinx etc. *and* white people represented in the show. But there aren't' (original emphasis).[65] Especially problematic is the fact that the faux-Regency world these characters inhabit, including grand country estates and houses in London and Bath, owes its provenance to racism and slavery.[66]

Conclusion

Bridgerton exemplifies how the distinction between 'authenticity' and 'accuracy' has become increasingly problematised by contemporary neo-Victorian experiments in film and TV culture. Playing with Austenian tropes, but eschewing the subtleties of Austen's narratives in favour of accessible dialogue and increasingly extravagant fashions based loosely on those of the period, *Bridgerton* illustrates that 'flattening' of history that concerned Frederic Jameson and, subsequently, in the specific context of neo-Victorian fiction, Christian Gutleben. Yet, arguably, such examples as *Bridgerton* and *Poor Things* are indicative of what we might now recognise as symptomatic of a cultural 'post-authenticity'.[67] In this context, authenticity no longer depends entirely on an original source, but is instead continually '(re)negotiated, updated, recycled', and, as a result, 'hybridised'.[68]

Destabilised, and detached from any guaranteed historical referent, authenticity is always in flux and becomes performative.[69] This 'performed authenticity' is, of course, a form of inauthenticity, one which contemporary readers and viewers of neo-Victorian productions accept in an unspoken pact as Baudrillardian simulacra.[70] In centring on 'recognitive justice' they work instead in terms of affective response. Using contemporary dialogue makes emotion – whether laughter or sorrow – more relatable, and the 'flattening' of historical specificity elides the boundary not only between past and present, but also between geographical spaces and lived experiences. In an article published in 2015 Gutleben asks 'Whither Postmodernism?' and offers 'Four Tentative Neo-Victorian Answers'. Here, in contrast to his arguments in *Nostalgic Postmodernism*, he contends that 'neo-Victorianism broadens the scope of postmodernism' by offering its consumers a universalising aesthetic that imagines 'alternative forms of fictional historiography, by challenging forms of orthodoxy and by questioning the limits of the human'.[71] Still, if we consider that theorists suggest we have moved beyond postmodernism and live in a post-postmodern world, then current examples of neo-Victorianism suggest an acknowledgement of this shift, encompassing temporal and geospatial fluidities. Emerging from the contested space between Victorian and contemporary literary studies and embracing and celebrating its own artificiality, neo-Victorianism is a fitting symptom of decadent postmodernity.

Notes

1. Hayden White, *Tropics of Discourse: Essays in Cultural Criticism* (Baltimore: John Hopkins University Press, 1978), p. 122.
2. Paul Ricoeur, *The Reality of the Historical Past* (Milwaukee: Marquette University Press, 1984), p. 1.
3. Ibid., p. 2.
4. Fredric Jameson, *Postmodernism, or, The Cultural Logic of Late Capitalism* (Durham, North Carolina: Duke University Press, 1991), p. 18.
5. Linda Hutcheon, *A Poetics of Postmodernism: History, Theory, Fiction* (London: Routledge, 1988), p. 46.

6. Dana Shiller, 'The Redemptive Past in the Neo-Victorian Novel', *Studies in the Novel* 29:4, No. 4 (Winter 1997), pp. 538–60, p. 538.
7. Ibid., pp. 539–40.
8. Ibid., p. 538.
9. *What the Victorians Did for Us* ran from the 8 September–23 October 2001; Paxman's *The Victorians* ran from 15 February–28 March 2009.
10. Jacob Rees-Mogg, *The Victorians: Twelve Titans who Forged Britain* (London: W.H. Allen, 2019), p. xi.
11. Simon Joyce, *Victorians in the Rear-View Mirror* (Athens, Ohio: Ohio University Press, 2007).
12. Louisa Hadley, *Neo-Victorian Fiction and Historical Narrative: The Victorians and Us* (Basingstoke: Palgrave Macmillan, 2010), p. 3.
13. See Cora Kaplan, *Victoriana: Histories, Fictions, Criticism* (New York: Columbia University Press, 2007).
14. Ibid., p. 3.
15. Ibid., p. 3.
16. Ibid., p. 3.
17. See: www.neovictorianstudies.com/.
18. While *Wide Sargasso Sea* is often referred to as a 'prequel' to *Jane Eyre*, the timelines across the two novels do not match exactly, allowing Rhys's characterisation of Antoinette/Bertha to be representative rather than specific.
19. See Sharon Bickle, 'Slavery, illusion and dead white men: Zadie Smith's *The Fraud* explodes the historical novel', in *The Conversation*, 20 September, 2023: https://theconversation.com/slavery-illusion-and-dead-white-men-zadie-smiths-the-fraud-explodes-the-historical-novel-212863.
20. Christian Gutleben, *Nostalgic Postmodernism: The Victorian Tradition and the Contemporary British Novel* (Amsterdam: Rodopi, 2001).
21. J. Hillis Miller. 'Parody as Revisionary Critique: Charles Palliser's *The Quincunx*', in *Refracting the Canon in Contemporary British Literature and Film*, ed. Susana Onega Jaén and Christian Gutleben (Amsterdam: Rodopi, 2004), pp. 129–48, p. 134.
22. Gutleben, *Nostalgic Postmodernism*, pp. 218–19.
23. Samantha J. Carroll, 'Putting the "Neo" back into Neo-Victorian: The Neo-Victorian Novel as Postmodernist Revisionist Fiction', *Neo-Victorian Studies* 3:2 (2010), pp. 172–205, p. 173.
24. Ibid., p. 173.
25. Ibid., p. 179.
26. Ibid., p. 179.
27. Ted Underwood, *Why Literary Periods Mattered: Historical Contrast and the Prestige of English Studies* (Stanford: Stanford University Press, 2013), p. 2.
28. Ibid., p. 3.
29. Ibid., p. 14.
30. Ibid., p. 14, p. 2.
31. Ibid., pp. 14–15.

32. Mark Llewellyn, 'What Is Neo-Victorian Studies', *Neo-Victorian Studies* 1:1 (2008), pp. 164–85, p. 168.
33. Ibid., p. 169.
34. Carroll, 'Putting the "Neo" back into Neo-Victorian', p. 181.
35. Ibid., p. 176.
36. Ibid., p. 180.
37. Ibid., p. 180.
38. See Gayatri Chakravorty Spivak, 'Three Women's Texts and a Critique of Imperialism', *Critical Inquiry* 12:1, '"Race," Writing, and Difference' (Autumn 1985), pp. 243–61.
39. Elizabeth Ho, *Neo-Victorianism and the Memory of Empire* (London: Bloomsbury, 2012), p. 5.
40. Ibid., p. 6.
41. See Helen Davies, *Neo-Victorian Freakery: The Cultural Afterlife of the Victorian Freak Show* (Basingstoke: Palgrave Macmillan, 2015).
42. Carroll, 'Putting the "Neo" back into Neo-Victorian', p. 195.
43. Hutcheon, *A Poetics of Postmodernism*, p. 5.
44. See Terry Castle, *The Apparitional Lesbian: Female Sexuality and Modern Culture* (New York: Columbia University Press, 1999).
45. See Claire O'Callaghan, '"Pronouns are Problematic": The Trans* Body and Gender Theory; Or, Revisiting the Neo-Victorian Wo/Man', *Neo-Victorian Studies* 13:1 (2020), pp. 75–99.
46. Alan Robinson, *Narrating the Past: Historiography, Memory and the Contemporary Novel* (Basingstoke: Palgrave Macmillan, 2011), pp. 127–8.
47. Ibid., p. 140.
48. Melissa Pritchard, *Palmerino* (New York: Bellevue Literary Press, 2014), p. 128.
49. Carroll, 'Putting the "Neo" back into Neo-Victorian', p. 176.
50. Randall Johnson, 'Editor's Introduction: Pierre Bourdieu of Art, Literature and Culture', in Pierre Bourdieu, *The Field of Cultural Production: Essays on Art and Literature*, ed. and trans. Randall Johnson (New York: Columbia University Press, 1993), pp. 1–25, p. 7.
51. Ibid., p. 7.
52. Pierre Bourdieu, *Distinction: A Social Critique of the Judgement of Taste*, trans. Richard Nice (Cambridge, Massachussetts: Harvard University Press, 1984), p. 2.
53. Johnson, 'Editor's Introduction', p. 8.
54. *Fingersmith* contains recognisable allusions to Charles Dickens's *Oliver Twist* (1838), Wilkie Collins's *The Woman in White* (1860), and Mary Elizabeth Braddon's *Lady Audley's Secret* (1862).
55. Carroll, 'Putting the "Neo" back into Neo-Victorian', p. 190.
56. Ibid., p. 190.
57. Laura Saxton, 'A True Story: Defining Accuracy and Authenticity in Historical Fiction', *Rethinking History* 24:2, pp. 127–44, p. 141.
58. Ibid., p. 141.

59. Ibid., p. 129.
60. Elodie Rousellot, 'Introduction', in *Exoticizing the Past in Contemporary Neo-Historical Fiction*, ed. Elodie Rousselot (Basingstoke: Palgrave Macmillan, 2014), pp. 1–18, p. 4.
61. Ibid., p. 4.
62. Georges Letissier, 'Neo-Victorianism and the Victorian Heritage: Authenticity, Post-Authenticity and Presentism', in *Authenticité et héritages, HAL Open Science (open archive)*, ed. Rose Borel, Jeanne Barangé, Maxime Blanchard (Bordeaux, France: Mar, 2024), pp. 1–14, p. 6: https://nantes-universite.hal.science/hal-04504161/document.
63. Ibid., p. 6.
64. Carolyn Hinds, '"Bridgerton" sees race through a colourist lens', published in *The Observer*, 1 January 2021 accessed 1 August 2024: https://observer.com/2021/01/bridgerton-sees-race-through-a-colorist-lens/.
65. Ibid., n.p.
66. Ibid., n.p.
67. Letissier, 'Neo-Victorianism and the Victorian Heritage', p. 12.
68. Ibid., p. 2.
69. Ibid., p. 2.
70. Ibid., p. 9.
71. Christian Gutleben, 'Whither Postmodernism? Four Tentative Neo-Victorian Answers' *Études Anglaises* 68:2 (2015), pp. 224–36, p. 224.

CHAPTER 14

The End of Postmodernism?

Bran Nicol

'Let's just say: it's over', wrote Linda Hutcheon in the 2002 edition of her book, *The Politics of Postmodernism*.[1] Other major voices in the postmodern debate expressed similar sentiments throughout the first decade of the twenty-first century. Ihab Hassan published an essay entitled 'Beyond Postmodernism' in 2003.[2] Brian McHale's 'What Was Postmodernism?' appeared in 2007.[3] In the same year, Pelagia Goulimari's collection *Postmodernism. What Moment?*[4] – its title both promising a retrospective summary and asking a sceptical rhetorical question – featured contributions by a stellar cast of theorists known for their work on postmodernism, from Robert Venturi to Fredric Jameson. Their conviction that postmodernism was now over was matched, throughout that first decade, by themes of journal special issues and numerous studies of contemporary fiction.[5]

Why was there this broad consensus that postmodernism has ended? One obvious explanation is that any theory which explicitly styled itself as a way of understanding the contemporary, as postmodernism once did,[6] can last only as long as the conditions it defines as contemporary. The parameters of the contemporary are moving all the time. If we assume it is still a way of understanding contemporary culture and aesthetics it is therefore hard to find the kind of stable, historically distanced, position to analyse postmodernism retrospectively which is available (though not without a degree of contention in some cases) to scholars of other literary periods. Another reason is simply that critical fashion was changing. A feature of early twenty-first-century literary criticism has been a widespread reluctance to deploy 'totalising' paradigms, or to draw on those theories which explain everything that happens at a particular moment in literary or cultural history. A related development has been a suspicion about periodization itself, despite or because of the centrality historical periods have always had in literary study. (Note the provocative past tense of the title of Ted Underwood's book, *Why Literary Periods Mattered*.)[7] Twenty-first-century approaches to studying literature have tended to examine a literary period – or a moment within one – in less of a totalising or periodising way than is typical of postmodernist or Marxist perspectives, preferring to conceive of it as multi-dimensional and multiplicitous.[8] More generally, there has been a move away from theoretically-driven readings altogether, rejecting what Rita Felski has termed 'critique' and in favour of a more personal 'affect-based' or empirical method of reading which avoids depicting fiction as if it is really theory in disguise.[9]

In a way, postmodernism saw this coming. It was distinguished from other literary periods, such as modernism or the Early Modern or Victorian eras, by what McHale refers to as its 'self-conscious[ness] about its identity *as* a period'.[10] Postmodern writers and artists considered themselves *as* postmodernists in a way which, say, modernists did not. Since 'Postmodernism periodized itself', McHale reasoned, it did not require anyone to do it retrospectively. 'And since it conceived itself as coming after something, it also imagined itself being superseded by something yet to come.'[11]

Succeeding Postmodernism

Its built-in self-consciousness about periodisation explains why the death knell for postmodernism was in fact first sounded long before the early twenty-first century, and in fact at the very same moment it had apparently reached its loftiest position in literary study: the 1990s. Linda Hutcheon and Brian McHale, the two most influential theorists of postmodernism from a literary-studies perspective, each published their two most important contributions in the late 1980s and early 1990s.[12] Given postmodernism's existential self-awareness it was a logical step for those interested in it to conclude that this pinnacle was also the beginning of the end. In 1990 John Frow published his essay 'What Was Postmodernism?', its title – as well as being one McHale would deliberately borrow seventeen years later – signalling his view that postmodernism had by that point 'changed tense', that is, moved from a contemporary phenomenon to one now in the past.[13] In the following year, 1991, a high-profile symposium entitled 'The End of Postmodernism: New Directions' was held in Stuttgart, at which prominent postmodern novelists, such as Malcolm Bradbury, Raymond Federman, and John Barth, were in attendance. In 1993 the American writer David Foster Wallace, who would become one of the definitive 'post-postmodern' writers over the next decade, published his essay 'E Unibus Pluram: Television and U.S. Fiction' which argued that the postmodern devices used in the writing of radical American metafictionist forebears such as Barth and Thomas Pynchon had become such ubiquitous staples in mainstream television shows that they had lost their critical power.[14]

The end of postmodernism was also heralded in the early 1990s in British fiction and literary criticism. Malcolm Bradbury's 1992 campus novel *Doctor Criminale* includes almost thirty references to postmodernism, many of which convey the assumption that it is over. The book ends with a conference held in – where else? – Stuttgart, entitled 'The Death of Postmodernism: New Beginnings' which features '[s]everal of the great American postmodern writers, like John Barth and William Gass, Raymond Federman and Ihab Hassan' and at which the eponymous figure, Doctor Criminale, gives a lecture entitled 'The Postmodern Condition'.[15] The novel clearly sprang from the same source as the paper Bradbury himself (a prominent literary critic as well as a novelist) had delivered at the real Stuttgart conference in 1991, and underscored his fictional Doctor's flippancy with a serious and persuasive argument that postmodernism was losing its value as a discourse because it 'coexisted with nearly all the things a postwar cultural life could exist with: existentialism and post-existentialism, structuralism and post-structuralism, deconstruction and post-deconstruction, feminism and post-feminism, the new historicism and the post-new historicism'.[16]

A compatible but more powerful argument had been developed in 1992 by the British theorist of postmodernism, Patricia Waugh, in her book *Practising Postmodernism, Reading Modernism*, where she proposed that the initially marginal, antagonistic discourse of postmodernism had by that point over-reached itself. It had become something of a 'grand narrative' in itself, capable of colouring any field of enquiry with scepticism and relativism.[17] As Ihab Hassan – one of the initial 'pioneering' 1970s American theorists of postmodernism – put it, by the late 1990s postmodernism had become so successful as a 'hermeneutic device' that 'we now see the world through postmodern-tinted glasses'.[18]

The perspective of these critical arguments is neatly captured in the doubleness of the title of Mary K. Holland's 2013 book, *Succeeding Postmodernism*.[19] Examining American fiction of the twenty-first century – that is, late work by Don DeLillo, and fiction by a new generation of American writers including Wallace, Mark Z. Danielewski, and Jonathan Safran Foer, whose writing preserves postmodernist play with language and structure but resists the irony, metafiction, and introspection of 'classic' postmodernism – Holland argues that postmodernism has been surpassed precisely because it has 'succeeded' in enabling us better to understand our world. The paradigm helped clarify the effects of the kinds of fundamental 'contemporary' social and cultural phenomena it was preoccupied with: late capitalism, consumer culture, technology and information, the loss of historicity, the crisis of representation, and the very nature of being human. As a result, postmodernism figured as a kind of 'foundational' level of education, clearing the way for the advent of 'the newly humanist twenty-first century literature'.[20]

If it is foundational, postmodernism must logically give way to something different, something which built upon what has been learned. But what the succeeding phase is exactly or what it should be called, is still – a quarter-century into the new millennium – not yet clear. While some literary critics and theorists have championed a specific terminological successor to postmodernism, such as digimodernism, post-postmodernism, metamodernism, or epimodernism,[21] most choose to assess twenty-first-century literature without referencing a prevailing overall paradigm (though the category they tend to use, 'contemporary fiction', is arguably close to functioning as one). As for the endurance of postmodernism itself, some of the most influential critics in the heyday of the debate, its 'peak' period (see my Introduction to this *Companion*), such as McHale and Jameson, assume – despite the literary-critical shift away from totalising and periodising paradigms – that it still continues, albeit in a modified form. Jameson's position, articulated in an interview in 2014, is to remind people of the link between postmodernity, the underlying social and economic conditions, and postmodernism, the various means of cultural and aesthetic expression:

> You can say that postmodernism is over, if you understand postmodernism in a narrow way, because art has certainly changed in many respects since the '80s. But I don't think that you can say that the whole historical period – the third stage of capitalism, I would like to call it – has come to an end, unless you are able to specify what has followed it.[22]

One of the enduring effects of postmodernity that is still apparent, Jameson argues, is what he calls 'the end of temporality', a condition brought on by the ceaseless late-capitalist process of commodifying all areas of life.[23] This produces a 'historical deafness', a cultural inability to grasp 'historical depth'[24] (or the temporal gulf between historical periods), which was one of the dominant features of postmodernism in its peak period, and means we live – still – fixed in a 'perpetual present'.[25]

This 'presentist' experience of temporality is at the core of an influential Jamesonian critique of contemporary culture developed by the late British Marxist critic, Mark Fisher. In his 2013 essay 'The Slow Cancellation of the Future', he builds on Jameson's ideas about the 'nostalgia mode' of postmodernism – in Fisher's words, 'a *formal* attachment to the techniques and formulas of the past, a consequence of a retreat from the modernist challenge of innovating cultural forms adequate to contemporary experience'[26] – and explains that it persists because the dramatic decline of communism in the early 1990s led to a widespread acceptance that there is simply no alternative to capitalism. According to Fisher, contemporary culture continually gives those who consume it an experience of 'broken time', of being 'unable today to focus our own present, as though we had become incapable of achieving aesthetic representations of our own current experience'.[27] One obvious cultural symptom of this malaise is uncertainty about when a particular cultural production originated. Fisher thinks this is most apparent in popular music, in examples such as the Arctic Monkeys's 2005 song 'I Bet You Look Good on the Dancefloor', or Mark Ronson's 2007 version of 'Valerie', featuring Amy Winehouse. Such songs 'perform anachronism'[28] and are undatable without knowing the details about their release.

A similar out-of-time quality has been identified as typical of our age by the Canadian novelist Douglas Coupland. In a 2012 review of the British post-postmodern writer Hari Kunzru's book *Gods Without Men* (2011) he argued that during the first decade of the twenty-first century 'we appear to have entered an aura-free universe in which all eras coexist at once – a state of possibly permanent atemporality given to us courtesy of the Internet'.[29] Ours is a world, he contends, with no dominant 'era' because of the advent of the internet, the smartphone, and facilities such as Wikipedia, Google, YouTube, Twitter (or X), TikTok and so on – which collapse both temporal and geographical distance. Kunzru's novel, he speculates, like other examples such as David Mitchell's *Cloud Atlas* (2005), might be representative of a new genre called 'translit'. This kind of fiction reflects and embodies 'our new world of flattened time and space' by knitting together overarching narratives composed of multiple substories, and jumps from place to place and from time to time rapidly. Coupland lists the substories in *Gods Without Men* which revolve around 'the Pinnacles', a rock formation in the Mojave desert, and are set in 1775, 1871, 1920, 1942, 1947, 1958, 2008, and 2008–09, but not presented in chronological order.[30] The experience of reading translit, he suggests, resembles 'watching a TV show that's simultaneously happening on multiple channels, a story filmed in different eras using differing technologies, but which taken together tell the same single story, echoing and reinfecting itself'.[31]

Out of Time: Readings of Ali Smith's *The Accidental* and David Mitchell's *Cloud Atlas*

The effect of being 'out of time', or of all time being present all at once so we are unable to distinguish our present moments from previous ones, is indeed observable in examples of British 'post-postmodern' fiction produced in the mid-2000s – coincidentally or otherwise around the same time postmodernism was being declared over by literary critics and theorists. This is the moment that postmodernism, as a theory and an aesthetic practice, settles into a curious 'out of time' state itself, one simultaneously over and still relevant – a status it still has. Some theorists naturally chose to portray this state as uncanny: postmodernism as a spectral or zombie-like phenomenon that remains among the living despite being once thought safely despatched years ago.[32]

The fiction I shall explore in the rest of this chapter – Ali Smith's *The Accidental* (2005) and David Mitchell's *Cloud Atlas* (2004) (as analysed in relatively recent work by Peter Boxall and Fredric Jameson respectively), and Kazuo Ishiguro's *Never Let Me Go* (2005), a novel I will eventually concentrate on – all convey in their narratives, in different ways, an uncanny 'out-of-timeness', but do so using techniques which means each novel is both recognisably postmodern (or at least an interpretation of it can be accommodated in an expanded understanding of postmodern aesthetics) and signals a move beyond the postmodern at the same time.

Boxall suggests that Smith is aware of writing in 'the aftermath of a cultural event or period which is defined by its cancellation of historical progression, its collapsing of past, present and future into the same narrative moment'.[33] This is clear, he suggests, if we compare her 2005 novel *The Accidental* (2005) to Salman Rushdie's canonical work of postmodern fiction, *Midnight's Children* (1981). *Midnight's Children* tells the exactly contemporaneous stories of its narrator, Saleem Sinai, and modern India itself. Both are born at the stroke of midnight on 15 August 1947. The 'real', historical, national story, is, however, filtered through Saleem's self-reflexive, unreliable narration, and the consequence is a chaotic temporality which complicates and challenges official history. In this way Rushdie persuades readers that dissolving historical difference opens up other methods of writing history than those favoured by the colonising power: *Midnight's Children* creates an alternative temporality, a zone Boxall terms 'postcolonial time'. The problem, though, is that while this conclusion has an undoubted value for postcolonial politics, when considered from the perspective of a twenty-first-century moment when our experience of the past is now even more intensely mediatised and spectacular than it was at the beginning of the 1980s when Rushdie's novel appeared, there is a danger, Boxall thinks, in being 'casual about the question of accuracy'.[34] The process of decolonisation requires maintaining a clear distinction between the past itself and the representation or recreation of that past. Rushdie's novel, in other words, generates a temporal confusion which looks uncomfortably close to everyday reality over three decades later, when the media universe causes temporal distance to collapse and is, moreover, able to generate confusion about what is real and what is fake.

This media landscape, Boxall contends, is the backdrop for Smith's *The Accidental*. Her novel, unlike Rushdie's, carefully separates the sense of the real past from the narration of the past. One of the ways it does this is by repeating Rushdie's trick of featuring a character who is representative of the year she was born. Smith's character Amber was born in 1968 and her history, like Saleem's, overlaps with an official version of the past. In her case, though, it is a patently illusory, media-constructed, version of the 1960s rather than anything more accurately 'historiographic'. Amber's statements, 'My father was Alfie, my mother was Isadora' and 'My father was Terence and my mother was Julie' reference 60s movie stars and is clearly not intended to be accurate.[35] Where *Midnight's Children* is happy for its contrasting histories to suggest the possibility for official history and its writers to be challenged by a 'subaltern' history, *The Accidental* points to an uncomfortable gap in our understanding of the past. Her 'out-of-timeness' remains as a knotty problem for the novel's understanding of time and history, what Boxall calls a 'dead zone' in the narration of history, a gap or space which equates to an unpresentable 'latent historicity'.[36] We cannot make sense of Amber nor the version of the past she represents. In contrast, for all the unreliability of Saleem's narration, we fully acknowledge the political value of what he – and Rushdie – are doing.

Post-postmodern fiction in this guise does not return to straightforward, linear narrative, as if postmodernism never happened, but nor does it suggest, in the manner of Hutcheon's category of historiographic metafiction, that history is always already narrated, and is essentially a malleable aesthetic form. Instead it points to the existence of a historical actuality outside narration and media representation. Following the temporal confusion about the very notion of historical 'periods' which results from the condition of being simultaneously postmodern and post-postmodern, a novel such as *The Accidental* makes us ponder what history itself *is* at a broader, more conceptual, less schematic level, rather than examining specific historiographical examples.

The End of Postmodernism?

This is also the value of another British post-postmodern novel, according to Fredric Jameson. David Mitchell's *Cloud Atlas* (2004) is a rare example of a contemporary text fêted by Jameson for escaping the postmodernist cultural bind and countering the diminished historicity of the present day. *Cloud Atlas* is not science fiction, but Jameson thinks it cleverly appropriates the time-honoured science fiction 'portals into other worlds' trope in order to present a visual, spatial representation of time which is different both from the linear history favoured by the conventional historical novel and the typical historiographic-metafictional device of setting of one period against another (as in, for example, *Midnight's Children*, John Fowles's *The French Lieutenant's Woman* (1969), or Julian Barnes's *Flaubert's Parrot* (1981)). Jameson contends that the combination of different narrative worlds in *Cloud Atlas* resembles the elevator in the 2010 science fiction movie, *Inception*, by which characters are able to travel at will to points in the past, present, or future.[37] Each of the six stories in *Cloud Atlas* figures as a 'floor' in the novel's elevator-like progress 'on its way to the far future'.[38]

The novel is organised into a more complex 'nesting' structure: the six narratives are offered first in chronological order, each one breaking off for the next to begin. They are picked up again in reverse chronological order, resuming from the very sentence which had been broken off in the first part, so that the middle story – 'Sloosha's Crossin' an' Ev'rythin' After' – is told intact, from start to finish. We then read the others in descending order. This effect, Jameson argues, like scaling and descending a mountain, combines time and space into one. Besides sustaining mystery during the 'ascent' of the stories before providing resolution on the way 'down', the pattern means we follow a specific temporal journey: starting at the furthest point in history, in 1850 in the first narrative, then progressing through the early twentieth century to the present day and then to two stories which take place in the future. The 'elevator' of *Cloud Atlas* thus moves from the past to the future, and then back again through our own time, returning to the past.

One of the enduring principles in Jameson's literary criticism is that 'the most valuable works are those that make their points by way of form rather than content'.[39] The great advantage of Mitchell's structure in *Cloud Atlas* is that rather than focusing on just a specific period or moment of history and its relation to the present day, as postmodern historiographic metafiction requires us to, we can contemplate history objectively, spatially, as a *total* phenomenon. Reading *Cloud Atlas* is a process of passing from a world of dystopia, regression, savagery, and barbarism, as we reach those future stories encased in the middle of the book, to worlds back in the past, where we begin and end, and from where we re-examine our present and imagine our future. Jameson concludes that the passage through apocalyptic regression implores readers to consider how they might 'be able again to think politically and productively, to envisage a condition of genuine revolutionary difference, to begin once again to think Utopia'.[40]

Kazuo Ishiguro's *Never Let Me Go*

Ideas of utopia and dystopia are explored in a stylistically and structurally very different British post-postmodern novel from 2005: Ishiguro's *Never Let Me Go*. Jameson's and Boxall's readings of *Cloud Atlas* and *The Accidental* present these texts as alternatives to classic postmodern 'historiographic metafiction' yet emphasise how they guide readers to read history (and politics in Jameson's case) as History, as an overall, conceptual entity rather than specific lived experience at different periods in the past. *Never Let Me Go* creates a counterpart to the 'out-of-time' atmosphere which Fisher and Coupland have identified. But unlike Smith's and Mitchell's novels, at least in Boxall's and Jameson's readings, it presents readers not with a 'reasoned position' about history but causes us to feel the out-of-time sensation ourselves.

Never Let Me Go draws on the tradition of dystopian science fiction and is about an imagined late 1990s England in which people's lives are prolonged by a government-sanctioned programme of human cloning which involves the clones being raised in special establishments which resemble private schools. The 'students' are largely kept in the dark about their fate, until, as young adults, they start donating their vital organs until they are 'complete' (or dead). The novel contains most of the definitive features of the classic modern dystopia genre, as can be found in Aldous Huxley's *Brave New World* (1932), George Orwell's *1984* (1949), or Margaret Atwood's *The Handmaid's Tale* (1985). It portrays a world which has changed dramatically following some cataclysmic event which is not described in detail; is ruled by a totalitarian or authoritarian state which fixes people into hierarchical social groups; is shaped by technological advances which exceed the capability of the time it was published (2005); and in which a protagonist or group of people begin to question this state of affairs. Like other modern dystopias *Never Let Me Go* introduces a new vocabulary ('donors', 'carers', 'completion', etc.) which reflects its world and provides a lexical key to enable readers to understand it.

But what distinguishes Ishiguro's novel from a 'classic' modern dystopia is that these generic features are either implicit or relevant only in an 'off-stage' part of its fictional world, and not dwelled upon extensively. There is no detailed information about the methods or ideology of the presiding government, for example. Perhaps the novel's most significant departure from the modern dystopian tradition is to do with its historical moment. Where *Brave New World* or *The Handmaid's Tale* is set far in the future, Ishiguro's novel opens with the paratextual designation, 'England, late 1990s'. It is therefore a novel about the 'recent past' rather than the future. I think this is a symptom of the prevailing twenty-first-century sensation I have been discussing above of existing in an 'absolute' or 'extreme' present. A few years ago the celebrated contemporary American science fiction author, William Gibson, acknowledged that around the turn of the twenty-first century he stopped writing novels set in the far future and turned to writing fiction 'of the recent past' because of his conviction that the present is already 'science-fictional'.[41] In *Never Let Me Go* Ishiguro does something compatible with this view, but different. Its world is marked not by rapid technological change but by an eerie out-of-time-ness. The public school environment and language it depicts is more redolent of the 1950s or 1960s than the 1990s. Its opening historical peritext, 'England, late 1990s', has the effect of derailing readers' generic expectations, wrong-footing them before they even start the process of making sense of the fictional world in the standard 'accumulated knowledge' fashion required by dystopia (e.g., by deducing what unfamiliar terms mean as they recur and thereby constructing a picture of its world).

Its recent-past setting, and its 'backgrounding' of the litany of typical dystopian features does not mean, as some critics have concluded,[42] that *Never Let Me Go* cannot be a dystopia. The novel is better understood as a *perspective* on a dystopia, a dystopian world viewed through a different lens. Its 1990s setting means that rather than some environmental or political catastrophe in the world currently inhabited by the reader having led to the breakdown of social conditions, the triggering factors have occurred in what we know to be our own recent past, that is, the late decades of the twentieth century. But this past has been altered, eerily changed. *Never Let Me Go* thereby brings into the foreground one dimension of dystopia which usually remains in the background in classic modern versions (and gives examples of the genre their own peculiar out-of-time quality): contemporary critique. To cite some British examples, it is a commonplace that Orwell's *1984* (1949) is really about the troubling rise of authoritarian regimes following the Second World War, John Wyndham's *The Chrysalids* (1955) is about Cold War fears of nuclear apocalypse, and L. P. Hartley's *Facial Justice* (1960) is as much a critique of the 1950s Welfare State as a prediction of the future. In the case of *Never Let Me Go* readers are invited to treat the novel as allegory and to ask questions about what it might be, in our own recent past in the 1990s, which would make public opinion or scientific research shift to the point that a cloning programme was actually implemented and sustained, and whether this would have required an authoritarian regime.

One of the novel's most troubling departures from modern dystopian tradition is that, although the donors continually wonder about their predicament, they do not rebel nor even challenge it. Is this also a comment on the political apathy of Britain in the late-twentieth and early-twenty-first centuries? Because the characters do not question their situation, the responsibility to do so would seem to fall onto the shoulders of its readers. In an echo of the value placed on textual reconstruction and testimony in modern dystopian works (e.g., through the genre's fondness for retrospective narratives or found texts), Kathy H.'s narrative, her memoir as she moves towards the end of her short life, is addressed to a community of readers who seem most obviously to be people she imagines as fellow donors, but which is also *us*, those inhabitants of the near future. It feels like a message to the future from a hidden fold within our own past.

Never Let Me Go's uncanny out-of-time effect was drawn attention to by one of the marketing gimmicks deployed by the publisher, Faber and Faber, to publicise the book. A promotional USB stick was sent to reviewers inside a cassette case (a 'retro', 1990s touch) of *Songs After Dark*, an album apparently released by the fictional singer in the novel, Judy Bridgewater, and which included a recording of her song 'Never Let Me Go', which animates one of Kathy H.'s key recurring memories in the novel. The real origin of the recording is unattributed, and is as difficult to place historically as the pop songs Mark Fisher regards as so representative of our atemporal age.

It is significant that the period covered by Ishiguro's novel – from the 1970s of Kathy H.'s childhood to the late 1990s – happens to coincide closely with the emergent and peak periods of postmodernism. Ishiguro is not speculating that postmodernism or postmodernity is somehow to blame, for in fact the novel is uninterested in postmodernism and not even a text we could comfortably classify as 'postmodern'. Nor is Ishiguro a didactic novelist of ideas. He has always been something of a post-postmodernist writer, in that typical postmodern preoccupations or techniques are not easy to identify in his writing. His fictions are more like non-parodic reanimations of modernist forms, especially the reconstructive-retrospective personal narrative. Yet

Never Let Me Go does lead us, in its understated way, to consider whether some social and political attitudes of the late twentieth century led us into a temporal no-man's-land, that the world of the novel's shadowy hidden history from the 1970s to the 1990s is a symbolic interpretation of the drifting, historical and geographical uncertainty which characterised the late twentieth century and was highlighted in the postmodern theory of Jameson or Hutcheon and has shaped our current temporal dislocation.

But this is as far as the novel takes us. It does not provide a commentary on social or political or historical change, but makes readers feel the kind of temporal and historical dislocation and disorientation experienced by its clone protagonists. The donors suffer from a lack of individual and family history. They do not know who their parents were and are given to speculating about 'possibles', that is, the original people from whom they are cloned. Kathy spends much of the narrative engaged in the modernist enterprise (as in Marcel Proust's *A la recherche du temps perdu* or Ford Madox Ford's *The Good Soldier*) of rebuilding the past through narrative, especially 'reconstructing' Hailsham, the institution in which she and her fellow 'students' were held. But is never clear exactly where Hailsham is – even to Kathy, who is never able to revisit the place.

Just as *Never Let Me Go* subtly provides a perspective on postmodernity as a disorienting experience of out-of-timeness, so the novel's treatment of time and history provides an alternative to the didactic theory-as-practice methods of classic postmodernism – exemplified by Hutcheon's definition of historiographic metafiction, and more general defences of postmodern fiction as 'critically productive'[43] – which have passed out of critical fashion. It impels readers to consider the value of historical certainty and memory in a way that differs from historiographic metafiction, and although it is similar to the effect Boxall and Jameson explore in *The Accidental* and *Cloud Atlas*, it is even less 'theoretical'. It does not invite readers to engage with an underlying argument glimpsed through its narrative but causes us to experience temporal uncertainty. In this respect *Never Let Me Go* resembles Coupland's description of 'translit', that is, a kind of writing that crosses genres, places, and times, but which does so in order to suggestively replicate in fiction the experience of twenty-first century life rather than dazzle readers with 'some sort of postmodern party trick'.[44] *Never Let Me Go*'s rather traditionally 'retrospective' modern form also avoids 'tricks' and means that it is not easy to conclude it is really 'about' literature in the way one could about earlier works of postmodern fiction. It does not place a specific genre in the spotlight. It is neither a parody nor a pastiche of dystopia, but a disorienting temporal distortion of the genre.

Conclusion: Late Postmodernism

My argument in this chapter has been that the willingness on the part of theorists, novelists, and critics to declare postmodernism at an end is itself part of the crisis in temporality which defines the cultural production both of the last decades of the twentieth century and the first decades of the twenty-first. The perception of postmodernism's end is a feature of postmodern thinking itself, and the perception of having moved somehow beyond this end-point changes how we experience time and history and the way some novelists have chosen to write about these things. Twenty-first-century ways of thinking about the contemporary as a concept, like the experience of contemporaneity itself, is characterised by a self-consciousness about time and the inability to be certain when one period begins and ends which was so much a feature of postmodern theory in its 'living' years.

Yet where in earlier or peak postmodernism, in the 'parallel lives' structure of historiographic metafiction in particular, there was both a confidence that different historical periods could shine a light on each other and also, paradoxically, an understanding that it did not really matter whether they did or not, what is distinctively post-postmodern is the *anxiety* about this temporal indistinction. This is why I think *Never Let Me Go* might be regarded as the exemplary 'post-postmodern' work because instead of a systematic analytic impulse behind it there is a desire to invite readers to pause and think. Yet it still works on an ahistorical-atemporal terrain which was traversed by earlier, postmodern, writers. Neither this novel, nor any of the readings of early twenty-first-century British fiction by Jameson, Coupland, or Boxall convince me that there is something going on here that is worthy of a new paradigm, beyond postmodernism – not yet, at least.

Postmodernism's own current 'out-of-time-ness', its status as simultaneously over and continuing, surely begs for a more cautious, tactical term to designate where we are now, after peak postmodernism, one such as Jeremy Green's 'late postmodernism',[45] perhaps (even though this is problematic given that the designation 'late' presupposes knowledge of an end), rather than a fully blown new periodising label. What is highlighted by readings like Jameson's and Boxall's of *Cloud Atlas* and *The Accidental*, and, I hope, my own analysis of *Never Let Me Go* in this chapter, is how recent British fiction has responded to an intensification or modification of the conditions of postmodernism – a crisis in temporality, an anxiety about the status of narrative, the attempt to understand and inhabit one's own individuality – by using variations of the same technique. They replicate the cultural condition of 'out-of-time-ness' and depict how narrative and communications technology contribute to or point to ways of overcoming this condition. The post-postmodernism or late postmodernism of the first quarter of the twenty-first century remains troubled by a collapse in the distinction between historical periods and indeed a lack of confidence in understanding historical distinction itself. When will this uncertainty actually end? Perhaps time will tell.

Notes

1. Linda Hutcheon, *The Politics of Postmodernism*, 2nd ed. (London: Routledge, 2002).
2. Hassan Ihab, 'Beyond Postmodernism: Towards an Aesthetic of Trust', *Angelaki: Journal of the Theoretical Humanities*, 8:1 (2003), pp. 3–11.
3. Brian McHale, 'What Was Postmodernism?' ('Fictions Present' thread of Electronic Book Review, 20 December 2007) [unpaginated]: https://electronicbookreview.com/essay/what-was-postmodernism/.
4. Pelagia Goulimari, *Postmodernism. What Moment?* (Manchester University Press, 2007).
5. Andrew Hoberek, 'After Postmodernism: Form and History in Contemporary American Fiction', *Twentieth-Century Literature* 53:3 (2007), pp. 233–247; Robert Hicks Rebein, *Tribes, and Dirty Realists: American Fiction after Postmodernism* (Lexington: University Press of Kentucky, 2001); Gavin Keulks, *Martin Amis: Postmodernism and Beyond* (London: Palgrave, 2006); Josh Toth, *The Passing of Postmodernism: A Spectroanalysis of the Contemporary* (New York: SUNY Press, 2010); Stephen J. Burn, *Jonathan Franzen at the End of Postmodernism* (London: Continuum, 2011); Graham Matthews, *Ethics and Desire in the Wake of Postmodernism: Contemporary Satire* (London: Continuum, 2012).
6. Charles Altieri, *Postmodernisms Now: Essays on the Contemporary: Essays on Contemporaneity in the Arts* (Pennsylvania State University Press, 1998); Steven Connor, *Postmodernist Culture: An Introduction to Theories of the Contemporary* (Oxford: Blackwell, 1989).
7. Ted Underwood, *Why Literary Periods Mattered: Historical Contrast and the Prestige of English Studies* (Stanford University Press, 2013).
8. Susan Stanford Friedman, 'Alternatives to Periodization: Literary History, Modernism, and the "New" Temporalities', *Modern Language Quarterly* 80:4 (2019), pp. 379–402.
9. Rita Felski, *The Limits of Critique* (London: University of Chicago Press, 2015). See also Valentine Cunningham, *Reading After Theory* (Oxford: Blackwell, 2002) and Jean-Michel Rabaté, *The Future of Theory* (Oxford: Blackwell, 2002).
10. McHale, 'What Was Postmodernism?'
11. Ibid.
12. Hutcheon, *The Politics of Postmodernism*; Linda Hutcheon, *The Poetics of Postmodernism* (London: Routledge, 1988); Brian McHale, *Postmodernist Fiction* (London: Methuen, 1987); Brian McHale, *Constructing Postmodernism* (London: Routledge, 1992).

13. John Frow, 'What Was Postmodernism?', in *Past the Last Post: Theorizing Post-Colonialism and Post-Modernism*, ed. Ian Adam and Helen Tiffin (Calgary: University of Calgary Press, 1990), pp. 139–59.
14. David Foster Wallace, 'E Unibus Pluram: Television and U.S. Fiction', *Review of Contemporary Fiction* 13:2 (1993), pp. 151–94.
15. Malcolm Bradbury, *Doctor Criminale* (London: Picador, 1992), p. 314.
16. Malcolm Bradbury, 'What Was Postmodernism? The Arts in and After the Cold War', *International Affairs (Royal Institute of International Affairs 1944–)* (October 1995), pp. 763–74, p.771.
17. Patricia Waugh, *Practising Postmodernism, Reading Modernism* (London: Edward Arnold, 1992).
18. Hassan, 'Beyond Postmodernism', p. 3.
19. Mary K. Holland, *Succeeding Postmodernism: Language and Humanism in Contemporary American Literature* (London: Bloomsbury, 2013).
20. Ibid., p. 16.
21. Alan Kirby, *Digimodernism: How New Technologies Dismantle the Postmodern and Reconfigure Our Culture* (London: Continuum, 2009); Jeffrey Nealon, *Post-Postmodernism: or, The Cultural Logic of Just-in-Time Capitalism* (Stanford University Press, 2012); Nick Bentley, 'Trailing Postmodernism: David Mitchell's Cloud Atlas, Zadie Smith's NW, and the Metamodern', *English Studies* 99:7 (2019), pp. 723–43; Emmanuel Bouju, *Epimodernism: Six Memos for Literature Today* (London: Palgrave Macmillan, 2023).
22. Nico Baumbach, Damon R. Young, and Genevieve Yue, 'Revisiting Postmodernism: An Interview with Fredric Jameson', *Social Text* 34:2 (June 2016), pp. 143–60, p. 144.
23. Fredric Jameson, 'The End of Temporality', *Critical Inquiry* 29:4 (2003), pp. 695–718.
24. Fredric Jameson, *Postmodernism, or the Logic of Late Capitalism* (London: Verso, 1991), p. xi.
25. Fredric Jameson, *The Antinomies of Realism* (London: Verso, 2013), p. 28.
26. Mark Fisher, 'The Slow Cancellation of the Future', in *Ghosts of My Life: Writings on Depression, Hauntology and Lost Futures* (Winchester: Zero Books, 2014), pp. 2–29, pp. 11–12. See also Mark Fisher, *Capitalist Realism* (Winchester: Zero Books, 2009).
27. Fisher, 'Slow Cancellation', p. 12.
28. Ibid., p. 11.
29. Douglas Coupland, 'Convergences: Gods Without Men by Hari Kunzru', in *Shopping in Jail: Ideas, Essays, and Stories for the Increasingly Real Twenty-First Century*, by Douglas Coupland (Berlin: Sternberg Press, 2013), pp. 24–28, p. 24.
30. For further analysis of this novel see Bran Nicol, 'The Fiction of Every-Era /No-Era: *Gods Without Men* as "Translit"', in *Hari Kunzru*, ed. Kristian Shaw and Sara Upstone (Manchester University Press, 2023), pp. 103–24.
31. Coupland, 'Convergences', p. 25.
32. Hassan, 'Beyond Postmodernism'; Toth, *The Passing of Postmodernism*.

33. Peter Boxall, *Twenty-First Century Fiction: A Critical Introduction* (Cambridge University Press, 2013), p. 58.
34. Ibid., p.57.
35. Ali Smith, *The Accidental* (London: Penguin, 2012), p. 104, p. 105.
36. Boxall, *Twenty-First Century Fiction*, p. 64.
37. *Inception*, dir. Christopher Nolan [motion picture], 2010.
38. Jameson, *Antinomies*, p. 303.
39. Ibid., p. 311.
40. Ibid., pp. 308–9.
41. Joshua Rothman, 'How William Gibson Keeps His Science Fiction Real', *The New Yorker Magazine* (9 December 2019): www.newyorker.com/magazine/2019/12/16/how-william-gibson-keeps-his-science-fiction-real.
42. John Mullan, 'On First Reading Never Let Me Go', in *Kazuo Ishiguro: Contemporary Critical Perspectives*, ed. Sean Matthews and Sebastian Groes (London: Continuum, 2009), pp. 104–13.
43. John Duvall, ed., *Productive Postmodernism: Consuming Histories and Cultural Studies* (New York: SUNY Press, 2001).
44. Coupland, 'Convergences', p. 27.
45. Jeremy Green, *Late Postmodernism: American Fiction at the Millennium* (Basingstoke: Palgrave Macmillan, 2005).

CHAPTER 15

British Fiction Beyond Postmodernism
Nick Bentley

As we continue to experience a set of social conditions that include the march of globalisation, a prevailing late capitalism, the preponderance of media-saturated cultures, the demise of grand narratives, the end of ideology, a philosophical and ethical relativism, post-truth politics, post-human fears about new computer technologies, and a continued disruption and pluralisation of discrete identities related to the cultural politics of class, gender, ethnicity, nation, age, sexualities, and dis/ability it could be argued that we are still very much immersed in the era of postmodernity. From the perspective of the arts and humanities, however, postmodernism is thought to have reached its peak in the last decades of the twentieth century and writers, creative practitioners, and literary and cultural critics of the new millennium have been keen to move beyond its debilitating relativism and ethical ambivalence. There is now a palpable sense amongst novelists that postmodernism has had its day and that the search for something beyond its parameters and limitations should be embraced. *Post*-postmodernism is a term that has been suggested, and which adds an unfortunate prefix to an already cumbersome formulation. This is not the place to go into the paradoxes and tautologies of such a concept, but suffice it to say that a number of terms and approaches have arisen in the early decades of the twenty-first century that promote a strategic distancing from postmodernism. These terms, categories and loose movements include altermodernism (Bourriard), remodernism (Childish and Thompson), metamodernism (Vermeulen and van den Akker), digimodernism (Kirby), the new puritans (Blincoe and Thorne), the new sincerity (Foster Wallace; Kelly), Dogme 95 (Lars von Trier), and epimodernism (Bouju) amongst others.[1]

In this chapter I will discuss a number of British writers who have entered into a critical dialogue with postmodernism in their work. Many of them continue to use some of the techniques and literary strategies established in the postmodern period in Britain, but adapt them in ways to reflect changed socio-cultural circumstances and new outlooks. The novelists I discuss fall into three main categories, within which there will inevitably be overlaps and cross-reference. First, I will argue that there is a recognisable shift in the work produced by some writers whose careers were established in the last quarter of the twentieth century and who had often been associated with postmodern techniques (namely Martin Amis, Julian Barnes, A. S. Byatt, Kazuo Ishiguro, Ian McEwan, Salman Rushdie, Will Self, and Jeanette Winterson). There appears to be what might be called an ethical turn in the work of some of these writers, who begin to distance themselves from the ambivalence and fluidity of the postmodern ethics of their twentieth-century fiction. In particular, I will compare Martin Amis's *London Fields* (1989) with *Yellow Dog* (2003), Julian Barnes's *A History of the World in 10½ Chapters* (1989) with *The Sense of an Ending* (2011), Jeanette Winterson's *Oranges Are Not the Only Fruit* (1985) with *Why Be Happy When You Can Be Normal?* (2012), Ian McEwan's *The Cement Garden* (1978) with *Saturday* (2005), and A. S. Byatt's *A Possession: A Romance* (1989) with *The Children's Book* (2009). Second, I will examine British writers who emerged after 9/11, and who, although they adopt several techniques associated with postmodernism, incorporate a new, tentative idealism and elements of realism in both the sense of literary form and philosophical belief. The works discussed in this section will include David Mitchell's *number9dream* (2001), Nicola Barker's *Behindlings* (2002), and Ali Smith's *How to be Both* (2014). It is in this context that we might identify something akin to nostalgia for the postmodern, a desire to look back to a period (especially the 1990s) when moral and ethical decisions could be delayed or circumvented due to postmodernism's scepticism towards all totalising narratives. In these novels, postmodernism seems to provide a freedom from responsibility that is initially attractive, although ultimately it is seen to be untenable. The third way in which 9/11 can be seen as a watershed moment is in the way that discourses of postcolonialism and multiculturalism impact with postmodernism. In the final section of the chapter I will compare pre-9/11 fiction by Salman Rushdie with what appears to be a return to realism (and/or modernism) in the work of Zadie Smith (*White Teeth* [2001] and *NW* [2012]), with reference to other texts such as Monica Ali's *Brick Lane* (2003), and Andrea Levy's *Small Island* (2004).

Distancing Postmodernism

The first category of writers rose to prominence during the period when postmodernism was at its height, and indeed were often instrumental in the attempt to define the characteristics of a postmodern literary practice in a British context. It can be argued that the attacks on the World Trade Center and the Pentagon on 11 September 2001 had a crucial influence on some British writers; indeed, 9/11 represented a moment when many commentators on both sides of the Atlantic talked about the end of the end of history and a new set of global arrangements that threatened to challenge the unassailable power of Western capitalism.[2] One of the key figures in this context is Martin Amis, who in a series of novels in the 1970s and 1980s established a style of writing that was self-aware of its relations with postmodernism as an aesthetic practice. His metafictive, ironic approach to contemporary late-capitalist economics and his parodic attitude to the literature and culture of previous generations brought him to the forefront of the literary field. In his best-known novel, *Money: A Suicide Note* (1984), he presents John Self, the epitome of the excesses and moral turpitude of 1980s individualist culture. In his next novel, *London Fields* (1989), Amis produces a parody of a hard-boiled detective/film noir narrative that finds the main character, Samson Young, an American author living in London, ostensibly creating a novel from the encounters he has with a triptych of characters ironically rendered vis-a-vis their types in the standard hard-boiled novel. As Samson explains on the first page of the novel:

> This is the story of a murder. It hasn't happened yet. But it will. (It had better.) I know the murderer, I know the murderee. I know the time, I know the place. I know the motive (her motive) and I know the means. I know who will be the foil, the fool, the poor foal, also utterly destroyed.[3]

The metafictional complexity of the novel results in a work in which it is difficult to determine any solid ground from which to judge the motivations and actions of the characters. The performative aspect of the central *femme fatale*, Nicola Six, is particularly strong in this context, which generated at the time of the novel's publication a heated debate on whether it was sexist and misogynist or whether its intention was to foreground and interrogate the sexism and misogyny embedded in the society that was the real target for its satire. Two members of the Booker Prize judging panel, Maggie Gee and Helen McNeil, famously persuaded the other judges to keep *London Fields* off the shortlist in 1989 because they objected to what they saw as the novel's sexism.[4]

In his 1980s novels, and into the next decade, Amis's fiction presents the reader with characters and plots whose moral and ethical relativism are a source for consternation. They represent a form of postmodern satire in which both the reader and the satirical target are so far immersed in the culture that it is difficult to identify a position outside or above the satirised subject that could be perceived as a normalised or advocated set of beliefs. In Amis's 1995 novel, *The Information*, for example, the main protagonist, novelist Richard Tull, offers a convincing critique of a debased and consumer-fuelled contemporary cultural climate for literary fiction, while himself being a 'marooned modernist' producing novels that are 'unreadable'.[5] In such works, it is difficult to know who or what is being satirised – the moral and ethical relativism lends itself to an ironic attitude towards all systems of thought and action, where all grand narratives and subject positions are put under pressure.

It is significant, then, that Amis's *Yellow Dog*, his first novel after 9/11, is noticeably different in its advocacy of a clearer set of moral positions. The novel certainly includes satirical attacks on a culture saturated in pornographic images and a misogynist tabloid press, and was criticised for its unpalatable representations of incest and paedophilia, but its conclusions point towards a more specific set of solid ethical positions that were lacking in Amis's previous work. Several critics have read the novel as a response to the 9/11 attacks[6] and its concerns with the effects of masculine, sexualised violence and the victims of such violence have been read as a veiled commentary on the escalation of posturing and aggression following the attacks on the World Trade Center and the Pentagon.

Ian McEwans's novel *Saturday* (2005) has also been read as a response to 9/11 and covers a similar terrain of examining violent masculinity and its threat to a privileged liberal humanism. The novel describes the encounter between the main character, Henry Perowne, a neurosurgeon, and Baxter, a London gangland thug. When they confront each other after their cars collide on a back street, Perowne diagnoses Baxter as suffering from Huntington's disease, the anticipated violence of this initial encounter being thwarted by the neurosurgeon's quick diagnosis. Later, however, Baxter returns to invade Perowne's comfortable Fitzrovian home and threaten his family. After Perowne and his son overpower the intruder and throw him down the stairs, the neurosurgeon's third meeting with Baxter occurs when Perowne is asked to perform an operation on him due to the head injuries he sustained in the fall. This establishes one of the main ethical dilemmas the book presents: how far should Perowne use his position of power when protecting his family and how far is the urge for personal revenge to be tempered by a professional need to protect life in the abstract – a concern concretised in this final encounter between surgeon and patient in the operating theatre. Perowne's views and ideologies are not identical to McEwan's (as he has stated in interview); however, the novel as a whole presents a position that tends to corroborate the surgeon's rational humanism in the face of the threat posed by violent thugishness, and by analogy the threat to Western ideologies represented by the September 11 attacks.[7] In this sense, the ethical positions of the novel are more straightforward than in the fiction McEwan was producing in the 1980s and 1990s, which often presented a moral relativism. *The Cement Garden*, for example, is far less clear on judging the incestuous relationship that develops between siblings Jack (aged fifteen) and Julie (seventeen) after their parents have died, as while the relationship is described in detail, the reader is not guided towards a judgement of the protagonists' actions. As with Amis, McEwan's post-9/11 fiction is far less likely to leave the reader floundering in ethical dilemmas and seems to gesture towards an advocated ethical framework of condoned behaviours.

Other writers whose careers span the turn of the millennium can also be seen to have made significant shifts in their approach to using narrative techniques associated with postmodernism. One example is A. S. Byatt, whose 1991 Booker Prize winning novel *Possession: A Romance* is a clear example of Linda Hutcheon's concept of historiographic metafiction in its presentation of a dual narrative: one set in the present, the other in the Victorian period.[8] The oscillation and thematic conversation between the two narratives serves to collapse the historical distance to the extent that it seems to corroborate Fredric Jameson's famous criticism that postmodernism promotes a lack of historicity.[9] *Possession* also includes parodic references to genre fiction (romance) and blurs the boundaries between fiction and fact in ways that problematize a reliance on historical veracity. Compare this with *The Children's Book* (2009), Byatt's later historical novel, which also weaves together a set of fictional and historical characters and events but in which the historical detail is researched to such a degree that the reader is no longer directed towards postmodern questions of the unreliability of all narratives. A similar comparison with respect to neo-historical fiction can be made between Julian Barnes's 1980s texts *Flaubert's Parrot* (1984) and *A History of the World in 10½ Chapters* (1989), and his twenty-first century novels *Arthur and George* (2005) and *The Sense of an Ending* (2011). I have always thought of Barnes as a reluctant postmodernist, but there is a marked shift from the radical dismantling of historical narrativisation and authorial intention in the earlier novels to the much more sensitive way in which the fictional stories and characters are embedded within historical contexts and events in *Arthur and George* and *The Sense of an Ending*. These texts might be described as post-postmodern, in the sense that they are aware of the ultimate fragility of any authorial truth claims, but having accepted this position make an attempt to reclaim a meaningful relationship with the past for each of the characters involved. *The Sense of an Ending*, for example, interrogates the work of memory and subjective time and their relationship to verifiable events, but steps back from an irresponsible relativism. As the main character Tony Webster concludes after reflecting on his past life: 'There is accumulation. There is responsibility.'[10]

Another interesting comparison is between Jeanette Winterson's *Oranges Are Not the Only Fruit* (1985) and *Why Be Happy When You Can Be Normal?* (2012), both of which lay claim to the contested terrain between truth and fiction, *Bildungsroman* and autobiography. In an introduction to *Oranges* in 1991, Winterson asks, in typical postmodern fashion 'Is Oranges an autobiographical novel? No not at all and yes of course.'[11] This antic outmanoeuvring of any attempt to fix the writing in one particular mode gives it extra piquancy in its representation of the character Jeanette's experiences. Later in the novel she interrogates the possibility of history being able to achieve an absolutely accurate account of the past: 'Some people say there are true things to be found, some people say all kinds of things can be proved. I don't believe them . . . It's an all purpose rainy-day pursuit, this reducing of stories called history' (p. 91). In *Why Be Happy*, however, a work that covers a similar historical period in Winterson's life, there is less concern with questioning the potential for the narrative to reveal truths about the past or the historical veracity of the presented narrative. In the Coda, Winterson notes: 'When I began this book I had no idea how it would turn out. I was writing in real time. I was writing about the past and discovering the future.'[12] There is a hesitancy towards the final implications of the writing here, but gone are the concerns between the distinctions of fiction and fact. *Why Be Happy*, of course, is presented as autobiography in a more clear way than *Oranges*, but for a writer who had previously embraced the scepticism of postmodern forms in capturing the past, this new confidence in the relationship of writing to the historical is striking. Winterson's account of her childhood might be challenged by others' accounts but the text presents its discourse as an accurate portrayal of the past as experienced by its writer.

All the cases referred to above are of writers who emerged at the height of postmodernism and who used its techniques in intriguing ways, but who have since stepped back from the implications of its philosophical dismantling of rational and ethical discourses. It may be that age is a factor in this difference; perhaps there is something attractive to the younger writer in presenting a world in which the demarcation between fact and fiction is an interesting and stimulating paradox to explore, while the more mature writer seeks to have some solid ground to hold on to. I think, however, that this is more a case of overfamiliarity and frustration with a postmodern relativism that represents British fiction responding to a broader cultural shift. It might be that the shift was already in place before 9/11, but it is significant that this moment represents a mediatised world event that had a profound effect and it would seem inevitable that something of this collective anxiety would seep into the fiction produced in the years following the attacks.

Repurposing Postmodernism

Alongside the range of established writers who have gradually distanced themselves from their postmodernist pasts, a group of writers have emerged in the twenty-first century who have grown up with postmodernism, and for whom the literary mode represents a dominant which they have felt it necessary either to distance their work from or to enter into a productive dialogue with. Adam Kelly has discussed this generational context with respect to a number of American writers, but a similar trend can also be identified in the British novel.[13] In the American context, the years around the millennium saw the development of a 'new sincerity' that interrogates the enervating relativism of a philosophical postmodernism. However, it might also be possible in the British context to identify a number of writers who have continued to be attracted to postmodernism's mischievous narrative techniques. Indeed, Richard Bradford has highlighted a group of British novelists coming to prominence in the 1990s and the early years of the twenty-first century who he dubs the 'new postmodernists'. In particular he cites Nicola Barker, Jonathan Coe, Toby Litt, David Mitchell, Will Self, and Ali Smith as writers who were going through university at a time when postmodernism and poststructuralism were the dominant critical paradigms that enjoyed a 'mutually supportive symbiotic relationship'.[14] According to Bradford, this allowed them to embed a certain amount of literary experimentation in texts that were also able to attain popular and commercial success. In this context, it might be possible to discern a certain amount of nostalgia for the postmodern in some of the writers who have emerged in its wake, a longing for a period, especially the 1990s, when moral and ethical decisions could be delayed or circumvented due to postmodernism's scepticism towards all totalising narratives. My view is that the 1990s represents the period of 'popular postmodernism' in which postmodern techniques become part of the mainstream of Western cultural production and lose any potential claim to a radical avant-garde such approaches may have claimed in the 1960s, 1970s, and 1980s.[15] In some of these novels a return to the postmodern seems to provide a freedom from ethical responsibility and commitment that is attractive, although ultimately untenable.

Post-postmodernism, then, can be seen to have (at least) two competing drives: first, a look backwards to the experimental freedoms and ironic insouciance of the postmodern, and second, a drive to distance one's practice from an outmoded dominant form of the previous generation. David Mitchell, in particular, seems to have been able to negotiate this new attitude towards the postmodern in a series of novels produced around the turn of the millennium. His first three novels, *Ghostwritten* (1999), *number9dream* (2001), and *Cloud Atlas* (2004), establish a style of writing that is expansive in terms of location and historical setting and uses complex divisions of narrative, but which does so in a style that is accessible and engaging and more life-affirming than the nonchalant sceptical irony of much postmodern writing of its classical period (1970–90). *number9dream*, for example, is initially set in what one might consider to be an appropriate postmodern environment, contemporary Tokyo, and is related from the perspective of Eiji, a Japanese teenager who has arrived in the city from rural Japan in order to seek his lost father. Eiji filters his understanding of the world he encounters through a series of mediated discourses, including those related to Japanese gangster movies, cyberpunk, and gaming narratives, all of which offer an oblique relation to any sense of the truth behind the various facades. There is much, then, that is typically postmodern in the framing of this teenager's narratives, however Eiji's quest for meaning beyond the complexities of the late-capitalist surfaces of a media-saturated pop culture is treated with respect. The novel is divided into nine chapters with the final chapter being left blank, suggesting that the quest is to be frustrated, or that it can only point towards an understanding of meaning that lies beyond the power of language to articulate. Yet, the novel remains faithful to the search itself; it insists that there is something of value worth pursuing behind the shifting ideologies and ethics of late capitalism. Eiji's quest may be fruitless, but his faith in it is not a source for irony.

Another writer in Bradford's list is Nicola Barker, who has also produced a number of novels that use impish narrative techniques and situations in a broadly realist setting. This is exemplified by her 2002 novel *Behindlings* in which the eponymous group is a collection of disparate individuals who, for a variety of reasons, are 'following' a character in the novel named Wesley.[16] The original impetus of this desire to follow the enigmatic quasi-leader is related to a competition called 'The Loiter' instigated by a confectionary manufacturer, which involves working out a series of clues associated with Wesley. However, the emotional investment each of the characters has with the pursuit far exceeds the original desire to crack the puzzle. The novel develops the backstory and motivations of several of the 'behindlings' and it becomes apparent that many of the psychological and emotional hang-ups they have are displaced onto the act of following Wesley, either as a means of solving their own puzzling conditions, or in order to provide a meaning to their lives that in some way diverts them from inclusion in mainstream society. Wesley himself recognises his function in the emotional lives of those following him: '"I'm a vessel," he said, falling backwards, reeling away from her, "they inhabit me. They find a home in me. I give them breath. I give them meaning".'[17]

It is in this sense that the novel explores the desire to locate a fixed meaning and direction to one's life in the face of postmodernism's interrogation of all legitimising systems of thought and behaviour. Wesley is impossible to pin down; nevertheless, he acts as a material (and secular) icon for the human desire to place faith in something or someone – he remains a cipher, a locus point that is not a destination in itself despite the desires of the followers. This can be seen in a conversation he has with Josephine Bean towards the end of the novel, when she does in fact catch up with him:

> 'I like you,' he said, drawing a deep breath, 'and it's incredibly sweet, this need you have, to tidy everything up. It's very ... ' he struggled, 'very *quaint*. ... But as a *philosophy*, as a way of *life*,' he stared at her, incredulously, 'it's just ... it's fucking *tripe*. It's *shit*. Because things don't automatically fall into place, Bean. Things don't automatically make sense or add up ... '.[18]

This passage emphasises the distinction between Wesley and Jo Bean as representing two differing philosophical outlooks in the novel. Jo's need for closure, for complete knowledge, represents the Enlightenment desire for epistemological finality – the drive to know everything about a certain situation. Wesley, in contrast, represents the postmodern trait of the impossibility of full knowledge.

In the end, Wesley effectively continues to walk out of the novel, ensuring it extends beyond the liminal space of the narrative, while Jo's decision to stop following him represents her frustrated desire to bring the experience to a close:

> She waited for an end to it –
> She waited for a conclusion –
> She waited for a rounding off – a flattening out – a consummation –
> She waited for a termination – an ultimation – a comeuppance (*Oh God, yes, please, anything*) – a noun – a verb – a full ... a full ... a full ... a full ... *Stop*[19]

Barker's novel is distinctive in its use of typography, where italicised sections are most often used to represent the inner monologues of characters. This ending thus offers hesitancy, a kind of negative capability, which both suggests and frustrates closure simultaneously. The repetition of 'full' leads the reader on to the final word and consequently to end the narrative. However, the final '*Stop*' is significantly supplied not by the third-person narrator, but by Jo's consciousness, as indicated by the italics. The suggestion is that full explanation is denied and that the mystery of why so many are compelled to pursue the unattainable and mysterious Wesley continues interminably. This ending is reminiscent of Samuel Beckett's closing sentence in his existential novel *The Unnameable*: 'perhaps they have carried me to the threshold of my story, before the door opens on my own story ... I don't know, I'll never know, in the silence you don't know, you must not know, you must go on, I can't go on, I'll go on.'[20]

Beckett's ending reflects on the necessity to carry on in the face of the absurdity of life and the inevitability of death and something of this sentiment is achieved at the end of Barker's novel. Barker, however, seems to register more of the comic than Beckett, in a celebration of the multifarious nature of the human condition, containing outsiders and misfits, but which suggests a potential human connection in their very similarity as marginalised. *Behindlings* represents a narrative in which postmodern undecidability is placed in opposition to a humanist desire for storytelling with its emphasis on direction, arrival and closure. That the novel refuses to come down on either side tells us something of its scepticism towards postmodernism itself.

Ali Smith's fiction also combines serious, politically engaged subject matter with playful narrative techniques. Her 2014 novel *How to Be Both*, for example, was published in two formats, one of which reversed the order of the novel's two parts. Reminiscent of the interweaving of past and present narratives in postmodern novels like A. S. Byatt's *A Possession*, Jeanette Winterson's *Sexing the Cherry*, and Peter Ackroyd's *The House of Doctor Dee*, Smith's novel juxtaposes one narrative describing a fifteen-year-old girl's relationship with her mother told largely in flashback after the mother's death, with the fictionalised, day-to-day reflections of the real-life fifteenth-century Italian artist Francesco del Cossa as he appears as a revenant observer of the contemporary moment. Connections are made between the narratives through artistic reference and thematic parallels. This is clearly a work of postmodern historiographic metafiction, but the focus on the power of art to communicate across centuries and to establish meaningful human relationships with those that have gone before articulates sentiments that are closer to modernism's faith in aesthetic practice as the most valuable inheritor of an authentic spirituality in a post-God world.

It might be argued that this mingling of modernist seriousness of theme with a playfulness of form represents a combination that extends beyond the postmodern by looking not forwards but backwards and indeed a number of contemporary British writers and their works have come to signal a renewed conversation with modernist aesthetics. Will Self's novels *Umbrella* (2012) and *Shark* (2014) unashamedly announce their allegiance to a modernist stream-of-consciousness style, while Alan Hollinghurst evokes the spirit of Henry James in his Booker Prize winning novel *The Line of Beauty*. David Lodge's *Author, Author* and Colm Toibin's *The Master* also re-address the formal and thematic legacies of James and Zadie Smith's *On Beauty* offers a loose re-writing of E. M. Forster's *Howards End*. This penchant for intertextual re-engagement with writers and works of the past is nothing new to postmodernism, but the tone is different in these novels. Where postmodernism's dominant relationship to past texts was through parody and pastiche, these novels feel more like homage or the re-invigoration of a form that is wholly appropriate in conveying the lived and authentic experiences of contemporary British life.

Diversifying Postmodernism

Zadie Smith's fiction also represents another important aspect of British fiction beyond the postmodern, and in particular the complicated relationship between postmodernism and postcolonialism. Postmodernism's dismantling of grand narratives proved a useful technique for some in exploring the decline of British imperial power in the postwar period. The towering figure in this context is Salman Rushdie whose ludic and effervescent narratives destabilised the relationships between fact and fiction, history and myth, and artifice and authentic object. For Rushdie, postmodern whimsicality and irreverence towards any narratives that claimed authority over others made it the ideal form for an interrogation of colonial and postcolonial politics in both the newly decolonised states and the old colonial centres. Postmodernism, however, has not always been championed as the ideal aesthetic expression of postcolonial ideas and a cultural politics of race, ethnicity, and nation. For example, bell hooks, in her influential essay 'Postmodern Blackness' interrogates a critical body of theory that promised to challenge essentialist master narratives on an abstract level but that made little reference to the everyday concerns of marginalised groups in Western societies in terms of race, gender, and class, and asks: 'Should we not be suspicious of postmodern critiques of the "subject" when they surface at a historical moment when many subjugated people feel themselves coming to voice for the first time.'[21] The identity politics of the late twentieth century thus had to navigate between the identification of discrete identities around which a cultural politics could be developed and postmodernism's scepticism towards all essentialist notions of identity. Stuart Hall was one critic who offered a way through this opposition with his call for a recognition of 'new ethnicities', accepting the ways in which identities are developing in contemporary multi-ethnic societies but drawing back from the anything-goes approach of postmodernism's deconstruction of identity as a concept. Hall writes '"black" is essentially a politically and culturally *constructed* category ... The immense diversity and differentiation of the historical and cultural experience of black subjects ... inevitably entails a weakening or fading of the notion [of] "race"'.[22]

This new understanding of the politics of identity, race, and ethnicity forms rich ground for several novelists who emerged in the first decade of the twenty-first century who engaged with issues of multiculturalism, and black and Asian British identities and histories. Many of these novelists use narrative techniques that could be described as experimental, but the tendency is also to ground their fictional worlds in realistic settings. Despite some disruption of linear narrative, for example, in Monica Ali's *Brick Lane*, Andrea Levy's *Small Island*, and Caryl Phillips's *A Distant Shore* (2002), the prevailing mode is a politically engaged realism, as it is in the subcultural novels of Courttia Newland, Gautam Malkani, and Alex Wheatle, which also engage with Britain's sense of itself as a multicultural nation.[23] Formally, this trend could be described as a new articulation of realism, one that accommodates and incorporates some of the playful techniques associated with postmodernism; indeed James Wood provocatively suggested (with particular reference to Zadie Smith) that a kind of 'hysterical realism' was emerging at the end of the twentieth century. Wood described this new mode as 'not to be faulted because it lacks reality – the usual charge against botched realism – but because it seems evasive of reality while borrowing from realism itself'.[24] It could be argued, of course, that a culture that recognises postmodern attitudes as a powerful influence on its own zeitgeist (as it could be claimed of British culture in the 1990s) should incorporate postmodern elements in the name of a realistic portrayal of contemporary life. Smith herself has entered this debate on appropriate literary forms: in an echo of David Lodge's claim in his 1969 essay 'The Novelist at the Crossroads' that the novel could head in two directions – broadly speaking towards a continued tradition of (English) realism or towards further experimentation – she has commented on a similar dichotomy of direction for twenty-first-century fiction. For Smith, the experimental novel is represented by Tom McCarthy's *Remainder*, which 'Meticulously ... works through the things we expect of a novel, gleefully taking them apart, brick by brick'.[25]

Something of this authentic re-engagement with experimental narrative form is exemplified by Smith's 2012 novel *NW* which combines an exploration of new ethnicities in contemporary London with a narrative style that marries realism and experimentalism. Several critics have suggested that the direction for this novel is actually not forward to a post-postmodernism but a re-visiting of modernist styles and techniques. David James and Urmila Seshagiri, for example, have identified her as one of a number of writers who have formally returned to modernism in recent years.[26] Smith certainly adopts a mode of writing in the novel that has resonances with the modernists, especially in the sections that are focalised through the character Leah Hanwell. The novel's opening section, in particular, offers an impressionistic account of location, mood, and moment:

> The fat sun stalls by the phone masts. Anti-climb paint turns sulphurous on school gates and lamp posts. In Willesden people go barefoot, the streets turn European, there is a mania for eating outside. She keeps to the shade. Redheaded. On the radio: I am the sole author of the dictionary that defines me. A good line – write it out on the back of a magazine. In a hammock, in the garden of a basement flat. Fenced in, on all sides.[27]

This is recognisably modernist writing in its rhythms, references to popular culture and snippets of public language reconfigured to mean something different in the perceiving mind of the focalising consciousness. However, the use of a neo-modernistic mode in this section of the novel is only one aspect of a formally complex text that also includes passages of conventional realism, as well as recognised postmodern techniques. The third section of the novel, for example, focalises primarily through the character

Keisha/Natalie Blake, presented in numbered passages that detail significant experiences in her life. Although the ordering is linear, the sections vary in length, tone, and significance and the chapter as a whole delivers a fragmented narrative of a character whose identity is drawn in several directions. This use of multiple narrative techniques reflects something of the multicultural context of the characters' experiences and histories. For Smith, the fracturing and complexity of identity suggested by multiple forms reflects the plurality of contemporary identities, ethnicities, classes, and genders. Far from being past forms for a writer like Smith, modernism and postmodernism can still be seen to provide important and appropriate techniques to convey Britain's postcolonial legacies.

Many British novelists, then, have continued to be intrigued, influenced, and often frustrated by the attitudes, techniques, and ethical ambiguities of postmodernism. In this chapter I have identified three ways in which that conversation has developed in the twenty-first century. What is apparent, however, is that postmodernism's place within the literary history of British fiction is secure, and several writers and critics continue to write within, against, and beyond its parameters.

Notes

1. Nicholas Bourriaud, *Altermodern* (London: Tate Publishing, 2009); Timotheus Vermeulen and Robin van den Akker, 'Notes on Metamodernism', *Journal of Aesthetics & Culture* 2 (2010), pp. 1–14; Billy Childish and Charles Thompson, 'Remodernism', stuckism.com, 1 March 2000, www.stuckism.com/remod.html; Alan Kirby, *Digimodernism: How New Technologies Dismantle the Postmodern and Reconfigure Our Culture* (London: Continuum, 2011); Nicholas Blincoe and Matt Thorne (eds.), *All Hail the New Puritans* (London: Fourth Estate, 2001); Adam Kelly, 'David Foster Wallace and the New Sincerity in American Fiction', in *Consider David Foster Wallace: Critical Essays*, ed. David Hering (Los Angeles: Sideshow Media Group Press, 2010), pp. 131–46; Emmanuel Bouju, *Epimodernism: Six Memos for Literature Today* (London: Palgrave, 2023).
2. See, for example, George F. Will, 'The End of Our Holiday from History' in *The Washington Post*, 12 September 2001; and Charles Krauthammer, 'Holiday from History' in *The Washington Post*, 14 February 2003.
3. Martin Amis, *London Fields* (London: Jonathan Cape, 1989), p. 1.
4. https://thebookerprizes.com/the-booker-library/prize-years/1989.
5. Martin Amis, *The Information* (London: Flamingo, 1995), p. 170, p. 77.
6. See James Diedrick, *Understanding Martin Amis* (Columbia, South Carolina: University of South Carolina Press, 2004), pp. 226–44 and Dominic Head, *The State of the Novel: Britain and Beyond* (Oxford: Blackwell, 2008), p. 141.

7. Ian McEwan, 'Novels Are Not All About You, Natasha', *The Guardian*, 7 April 2007, www.guardian.co.uk/politics/2007/apr/07/bookscomment.books.
8. Linda Hutcheon, *A Poetics of Postmodernism: History, Theory, Fiction* (New York: Routledge, 1988).
9. Fredric Jameson, *Postmodernism, or, The Cultural Logic of Late Capitalism* (London: Verso, 1991).
10. Julian Barnes, *The Sense of an Ending* (London: Jonathan Cape, 2011), p. 150.
11. Jeanette Winterson, *Oranges Are Not the Only Fruit* (London: Vintage [1985] 1991), p. xiv.
12. Jeanette Winterson, *Why Be Happy When You Can Be Normal?* (London: Vintage, 2012), p. 226.
13. Adam Kelly, 'Beginning With Postmodernism', *Twentieth-Century Literature* 57:3 & 4 (2011), pp. 391–422.
14. Richard Bradford, *The Novel Now: Contemporary British Fiction* (Malden: Blackwell, 2007), p. 64.
15. See 'Introduction: Mapping the Millennium: Themes and Trends in Contemporary British Fiction' in *British Fiction of the 1990s*, ed. Nick Bentley (London and New York: Routledge, 2005), pp. 1–18.
16. The following section on Nicola Barker's *Behindlings* is reproduced (and adapted) from a short section in my monograph, Nick Bentley, *Youth Subcultures in Postwar and Contemporary Fiction* (London: Palgrave Macmillan, 2025), pp. 267–269.
17. Nicola Barker, *Behindlings* (London: Flamingo, 2002), p. 533.
18. Ibid., p. 530.
19. Ibid., p. 534.
20. Samuel Beckett, *The Beckett Trilogy: Molloy, Malone Dies, The Unnamable* (London: Picador, 1979), p. 381.
21. bell hooks, 'Postmodern Blackness', *Postmodern Culture*, 1:1 (1990), n.p. [Online Journal].
22. Stuart Hall, 'New Ethnicities', in *ICA Documents 7: Black Film, British Cinema*, ed. Kobena Mercer (London: Institute of Contemporary Arts, 1989), pp. 27–30.
23. See, for example, Courttia Newland, *Society Within* (London: Abacus, 1999); Alex Wheatle, *Brixton Rock* (London: Black Amber Books, 1999); *The Dirty South* (London: Serpent's Tail, 2008); and Gautam Malkani, *Londonstani* (London: Fourth Estate, 2006).
24. James Wood, 'Human, All Too Inhuman', *The New Republic*. 30 August 2001. www.newrepublic.com/article/61361/human-all-too-inhuman.
25. Zadie Smith, 'Two Directions for the Novel', in *Changing My Mind: Occasional Essays* (London: Penguin, 2009), pp. 71–96, p. 84.
26. David James and Urmila Seshagiri, 'Metamodernism: Narratives of Continuity and Revolution', *PMLA* 129:1 (2014), pp. 87–100.
27. Zadie Smith, *NW* (London: Harmondsworth, 2012), p. 3.

CHAPTER 16

Postmodern British Fiction
Then and Now

Hans Bertens

British postmodern fiction came late and much of it was not very postmodern, while some of it did not seem postmodern at all, at least not by the usual criteria. It did, however, have remarkable staying power and is still alive and well. As Martin Paul Eve said fairly recently, 'postmodern stylistics and themes never faded'.[1] So what are those usual criteria? Postmodern fiction is ironic, often playful, and always aware of its artificiality, a status which it does not try to hide from its readers. On the contrary, it employs an array of strategies that disrupt the illusion that in reading a postmodern novel we are dealing with the real world. It may rewrite history, resurrect familiar literary characters in new and unfamiliar settings, introduce authors as characters in their own fiction, present the most outlandish or even supernatural events with the straightest face, address the reader in unsettling asides, and so on. Virtually anything that transgresses the boundaries of realist fiction will do. But all of this takes place against a background that we recognize: the world as we know it. Postmodern fiction, then, implicitly invites us to adopt two incompatible sets of reading instructions. We have textual elements that suggest that they refer to the real world and that seem to offer the depth and meaning that call for traditional interpretation. Other elements, however, deliberately frustrate such interpretation because they quite blatantly do not refer us to the world or make it in other ways impossible to arrive at a coherent reading. As a result we are always left with questions rather than answers – questions concerning the (constructed) nature of reality, the possibility of (historical) knowledge, and even, indirectly, the status (and coherence) of the self, of individual identity.

Let us first look at that relatively late emergence. If you go through overviews of postwar or even more recent British fiction you will find the same authors again and again associated with postmodernism. Some are represented by only one or two novels, others by their whole oeuvre: John Fowles, B. S. Johnson, Iain Sinclair, Graham Swift, Christine Brooke-Rose,

Martin Amis, Julian Barnes, A. S. Byatt, Peter Ackroyd, Jeanette Winterson, D. M. Thomas, Angela Carter, Salman Rushdie, Alasdair Gray (to mention only those who feature in virtually all overviews). Of these writers, Brooke-Rose, Johnson, and Fowles published fiction that is seen as postmodern in the 1960s, but the postmodern fiction of the others dates from the early 1980s and after. However, the inclusion of Brooke-Rose and Johnson in the postmodern canon is not uncontroversial. There are good reasons to see their work as experimental rather than postmodern,[2] even if Brooke-Rose was very much aware of postmodern theorising. But leaving out the verb 'to be' (in her 1968 novel *Between*), or having twenty-six narrators whose names invariably begin with a different letter of the alphabet (*Next*, 1998), suggest more affinity with the experimental French Oulipo writers than with postmodernism. Her own qualification of *Thru* (1975) – 'It is the most postmodern'[3] – would indeed seem to suggest a distance between her fiction and postmodernism.

There can be no doubt, however, about the postmodern status of John Fowles's *The French Lieutenant's Woman*, with its violation of the boundary between narrative levels and its two endings. With Fowles, metafiction – succinctly defined by Amy J. Elias as 'fiction that calls attention to its representational techniques and knowledge claims'[4] – enters mainstream British fiction. But Fowles's novel dates from 1969. Elsewhere, in for instance France and the US the postmodern canon includes fiction published in the late 1950s and very early 1960s. In Alain Robbe-Grillet's *Dans le labyrinthe* of 1959 we find a narrator engaged in a sophisticated duel with the reader, presenting a story that again and again backtracks a bit and then resumes its now slightly different course, an exercise that remains thoroughly confusing until the disoriented reader sees through Robbe-Grillet's larger strategy – and in so doing is perhaps again deceived. In the US, John Barth's *The Sot-Weed Factor* (1960) offered a sprawling, labyrinthine pseudo-historical narrative that very openly played fast and loose with historical reality, much like Thomas Pynchon's *V.* (1963), although *V.*'s historical scenes also introduce gruesome events that are all too real, such as the genocide on the Herero people in early twentieth-century Namibia. Like all his later work, Pynchon's novel gleefully announces its departure from the realist tradition through the often bizarre names it bestows on its characters, its often outlandish scenes, and the apparently spontaneous songs that every now and then interrupt the narrative.

By the late 1960s American postmodernism had with Barth's *Lost in the Funhouse* (1968) and Robert Coover's *Pricksongs & Descants* (1969) become as metafictional and self-reflexive as it would ever be. It would not be an exaggeration to say that when British postmodern fiction really hit its stride in the early 1980s (Salman Rushdie, *Midnight's Children*, 1981; Alasdair Gray, *Lanark*, 1981; D. M. Thomas, *The White Hotel*, 1981; Angela Carter, *Nights at the Circus*, 1984; Peter Ackroyd, *Hawksmoor*, 1985, and so on) postmodernism elsewhere was already past its prime. By the later 1970s Thomas Pynchon had published *Gravity's Rainbow* (1973), generally seen as the absolute high-water mark of postmodernism, and Carlos Fuentes (*Terra Nostra*, 1975), Robert Coover (*The Public Burning*, 1977), and Günter Grass (*Der Butt*, 1977) had, like Pynchon, produced enormously ambitious novels that, again like Pynchon, recognised few bounds in their presentation of fantastical characters and occurrences and that freely rewrote history (with Fuentes marrying off England's Virgin Queen, Elizabeth I, to Spain's Philip II, and Coover having Ethel and Julius Rosenberg, convicted of spying for the Soviet Union, publicly executed on New York City's Times Square). And in France Georges Perec had published his *La Vie mode d'emploi* (1978), another encyclopaedic and complex novel in which an overarching story involving the amateur painter Bartlebooth (a combination of Herman Melville's Bartleby and Valery Larbaud's pseudonym Barnabooth) frames embedded tales devoted to every single inhabitant of a Parisian apartment block. We see, with hindsight, that even William Gaddis's *The Recognitions* of 1955 and Grass's *Der Blechtrommel* of 1959 are already more postmodern than either modernist or realist. There are good reasons, then, to claim that British postmodern fiction came late, and not just in comparison with other leading national literatures. In for instance *Turkenvespers* (*Turkish Evensong*, 1977) by the Dutch writer Louis Ferron, the Turkish armies under Suleiman Pasha lay siege to Vienna, a historically well-documented fact that, however, happened more than two hundred years before the fin-de-siècle period in which the novel is situated.

In comparison with the great canonical postmodern novels, much British postmodern fiction is, as I have said above, not very postmodern. It is, in any case, almost never radical and it is always compassionate and humane. If postmodernism is the cultural logic of late capitalism, as Fredric Jameson claimed in 1983, and countless followers have claimed since then, British late capitalism is a much more humane affair than most of us (me included) would have thought possible. If, as Brian McHale has argued, postmodernism distinguishes itself from realism and modernism through its privileging of an ontological rather than an epistemological perspective, a concern with a given fictional world as it is rather than how we can know that world,[5] then British postmodern fiction has an extraordinarily prominent epistemological dimension. If, on the other hand, and as Linda Hutcheon has equally persuasively put forward, and as I have suggested above, postmodern fiction both refers to the real world and presents itself as wholly autonomous and therefore self-reflexive,[6] then British postmodern fiction as often as not is more concerned with referentiality than with maintaining its textual autonomy. No matter how postmodern its narrative strategies and the liberties it takes with the real world (and its history), it generally comes down on the side of reference. Both McHale's privileging of the ontological over the epistemological and Hutcheon's balance between referentiality and autonomy are seen by postmodern critics as radically undermining the established order. For those critics, postmodern fiction exposes whatever view of reality we have as a linguistic construction, as the product of ideology and not, as we tend to assume, the result of an understanding of the world based on reason and experience. Simultaneously, postmodern fiction is seen as illustrating the failure of language to represent reality so that all attempts at faithful representation are bound to fail. From this perspective, postmodern fiction is radically subversive since it questions everything we think we know about our world and its history.

British Postmodern Fiction and the Principle of Minimal Departure

So how does British postmodern fiction fail to live up to the demanding standards of postmodern theory? Let us have a look at two novels that have an undisputed status in the British postmodern canon, Graham Swift's *Waterland* (1983) and Julian Barnes's *Flaubert's Parrot* (1984). *Waterland*'s Tom Crick, a history teacher, tells his students that after forty years of thinking about history he has come to the conclusion 'that history is a yarn',[7] that 'history is that impossible thing: the attempt to give an account, with incomplete knowledge, of actions themselves undertaken with incomplete knowledge'.[8] But he also tells them that 'above all, what history teaches us is to avoid illusion and make-believe, to lay aside dreams, moonshine, cure-alls, wonder-workings, pie-in-the-sky – to be realistic'.[9] If history is a yarn, it is a yarn that still enables us to recognise falsehoods. In other words, there is no sign of the radical relativism usually attributed to postmodernism. On the contrary, some yarns are more truthful than others. What is more, Crick's own yarn is remarkably complete. By the end of the novel, we have a pretty clear idea of the reasons for the suicide of Crick's older brother, no matter how long ago, and of the bond of guilt between Crick and his wife. Crick makes much of his failure to find what he calls 'an Explanation',[10] but if such a metaphysical Explanation remains out of reach, we have enough lower-case explanations to understand the Cricks' tragedy. Crick's real grievance is that he does not find meaning – 'Events elude meaning, but we look for meanings'.[11] However, the failure to find meaning is not particularly postmodern. Nor is the realisation that history will not necessarily reveal all its secrets.

For Julian Barnes's amateur Flaubert historian Geoffrey Braithwaite, too, such a realization would seem to come as an unpleasant surprise. Trying to recover the past 'is like trawling the ocean with a net filled with large holes: just as much escapes as is recovered'.[12] And so 'every so often' he is tempted 'to declare that history is just another literary genre'.[13] Ever since Barnes's novel appeared critics have argued[14] that the elusiveness of history, here illustrated by Braithwaite's failure to identify the stuffed parrot that he is looking for – and that apparently was one of Flaubert's sources of inspiration when writing 'Un Coeur simple' – places the novel within a postmodern framework, as do Braithwaite's musings on the art of fiction. But those musings are wholly in character given his interest in and knowledge of Flaubert's life and work, and his equation of history with a literary genre is no more than a temporary fit of despondence. If *Flaubert's Parrot* tells us anything it is that we have an impressive knowledge of Flaubert's life and oeuvre. Like Crick's history, that knowledge is textually mediated, but there is nothing in these novels that would warrant the radical distrust of language associated with postmodern theory. Novels such as *Waterland* and *Flaubert's Parrot* may seem postmodern next to a nineteenth-century novel that exudes belief in an objectively available reality, but it makes more sense to see them in terms of a late twentieth-century realism that, while rejecting the claims of nineteenth-century realism, still strives for authenticity and accuracy in representation and assumes that such authenticity and accuracy are not completely impossible and can be partially realised.

We find a similar, even if at first sight more postmodern, attitude in another canonical postmodern novel, Martin Amis's *Money: A Suicide Note* (1984). Interestingly, the critical response has it two ways. For Gavin Keulks, the novel is a 'decidedly classical postmodern work' while for Patricia Waugh it was 'one of the most coruscating literary critiques of monetarism', a critique that shows us 'the spiritual void at the heart of secularized liberal culture'.[15] So let's have a closer look. *Money's* claim to postmodern fame rests on intertextual (literary) references – the Dimmesdale Room, the 'Bartleby', 'The Ashbery', and so on – and a number of mostly cameo appearances of a character called Martin Amis in a novel otherwise devoted to the exploits of a vulgar, overbearing, hard-drinking, pornographic-minded advertising tycoon, repulsive in the best self-made tradition. But in the single real conversation that this unsavoury but linguistically remarkable gifted character has with the Martin Amis character nothing much happens. The author's appearances in his own text are mildly amusing, but the novel would not have been any different if the Amis character would not have appeared at all. His only notable statement – 'I sometimes think that, as a controlling force in human affairs, motivation is pretty well shagged out by now'[16] – which suggests a downplaying of the importance of individual agency that is widely seen as a feature of postmodern theory, is in fact belied by the novel's characters (even if their motivation does not bear much moral scrutiny). More in line with the novel's spirit is a remarkable salutation by the now more or less reformed protagonist at the end of the novel: 'Humans, I honour you.'[17]

The classification of *Money* as postmodern is all the more remarkable since much of the British reading public cannot have been unfamiliar with such violations of ontological boundaries. Short-circuiting leaps from the world of the telling to the world of the told (or vice versa) were fairly common in the later stages of the so-called Golden Age of British detective fiction. In John Dickson Carr's brilliant mystery *The Hollow Man* (1935), his massive detective Dr Fell is asked why he wants to discuss detective fiction.

> 'Because', said the doctor, frankly, 'we're in a detective story, and we don't fool the reader by pretending we're not. Let's not invent elaborate excuses to drag in a discussion of detective stories. Let's candidly glory in the noblest pursuits possible to characters in a book'.[18]

In Edmund Crispin's *The Moving Toyshop* (1946) one of the novel's characters suggests a left turn at a fork in the road because of its publisher's political leanings ('After all, Gollancz is publishing this book').[19] Crispin's *Swan Song* (1947) and Margery Allingham's *The China Governess* (1962) again use other strategies to call attention to their characters' fictional status. Assuming that the reader enjoys the game aspect of the classic mystery, writers do not hesitate to add ontological impossibilities to their repertoire. True enough, these examples of metalepsis – defined by Gérard Genette as 'an existential crossing of the boundaries between the extradiegetic and diegetic levels of a narrative or the (intra)diegetic and metadiegetic levels'[20] – do not necessarily suggest to us that we, too, are fictional, the result of writing taking place at a higher level of which we are unaware – which is for Genette metalepsis's most disturbing aspect. Metalepsis here 'functions as a figure of the creative imagination',[21] or, in Marie-Laure Ryan's terms, as a rhetorical metalepsis which 'opens a small window that allows a quick glance across levels, but ... closes after a few sentences', with 'the operation end[ing] up reasserting the existence of boundaries'.[22] But that is how *Money*'s form of metalepsis functions. It is qualitatively different from that of *The French Lieutenant's Woman* where a far more decisive authorial intrusion – 'ontological metalepsis', in Ryan's terms, 'opens a passage between levels that results in their interpenetration, or mutual contamination'.[23]

It is only fair to say that this was at least partly recognised by some contemporary critics. Although Alison Lee's *Realism and Power: Postmodern Fiction* of 1990 places *Waterland*, *Flaubert's Parrot*, and *Money* firmly within the emerging canon of British postmodernism, it is very much aware that 'British postmodern fiction seems to be more closely and more interestingly tied to the Realist tradition. Surfiction such as that of William Gass, Raymond Federman, Ronald Sukenick, or Donald Barthelme plays with the conventions of Realism in a much more overt way.'[24]

Still, Lee also finds in these and other British postmodern novels a decentring of 'the humanist notion of "individuality", of a coherent essence of self which exists outside ideology'.[25] It is hard to see how the individuality of the supposedly postmodern characters of Swift, Barnes, or Amis is more decentred than those of naturalist or modernist fiction but Lee is in good company in placing these authors in the postmodern camp, with some critics sharing her sensitivity to the realist dimension of this postmodernism. Amy L. Elias, introducing the term 'postmodern Realism' in her discussion of, again, *Waterland*, *Money*, and *Flaubert's Parrot* suggests that these novels 'may be examples of this, new postmodern Realism',[26] which 'records the multiple worlds/texts within contemporary culture and recognizes the *inability* to evaluate society's conflicting values'.[27] It seems to me (and to Waugh, in the case of *Money*) that these novels have no problem evaluating society's values and that Elias reads too much postmodern theory into her postmodern Realism. In any case, if we must call this postmodernism it is a postmodernism that obeys the 'principle of minimal departure', as Marie-Laure Ryan has called it, and that leaves a realistic, mimetic world model virtually intact.[28] If it is a 'metafictionalized realism', as Patricia Waugh has termed it,[29] then the metafiction is far outweighed by the late twentieth-century realist mode that I have sketched above.

More Substantial, But Never Maximal Departures

There is of course British postmodern fiction that departs a good deal more than minimally from a contemporary realist norm. Those extraordinarily fruitful 1980s also saw the publication of Salman Rushdie's *Midnight's Children* (1981), Alasdair Gray's *Lanark* (1981), D. M. Thomas's highly controversial *The White Hotel* (1981), Angela Carter's *Nights at the Circus* (1984), Peter Ackroyd's *Hawksmoor* (1985), Jeanette Winterson's *Sexing the Cherry* (1989), and other novels that freely and with great gusto made use of fantastical elements, hinted at dimensions beyond the rational, rewrote history, openly paraded their intertextuality, or in other ways matched the postmodern fiction of the American 1970s. We find tantalising and unexplained near-parallels between two narratives (most explicitly in *Hawksmoor*), rewritings of Freud (*The White Hotel*) and classic fairy tales (Carter's *The Bloody Chamber*, Winterson's *Sexing the Cherry*), exuberant metafictional gameplaying (*Lanark*), seemingly supernatural phenomena and supernatural zones (*The White Hotel*), and fantastic creatures or events (in most of the above and in *Nights at the Circus* represented by a pig with a keen business sense, literate and ambitious chimpanzees, teleportation, tigers that disappear into mirrors). In some of these and other novels we find fragments that remind us of postmodern theorising. In Jeanette Winterson's *Sexing the Cherry*, for instance, we hear that '[l]anguage always betrays us' and that 'our inward life tells us that we are multiple not single, and that our existence is really countless existences holding hands like those cut-out paper dolls'.[30] But in spite of their obvious theoretical interests, their sudden narrative swerves (including confidential asides to the reader), their intertextual playfulness, their use of the fantastic and the marvellous, novels such as *Sexing the Cherry* and *Nights at the Circus* – which presents its own Foucauldian panopticon for female murderers and slyly refers to 'magic realism'[31] – have a strongly articulated feminist agenda that connects them firmly to 1980s actuality.

Alison Lee's 1990 study had drawn attention to the indebtedness of, for instance, *Midnight's Children* to the realist tradition.[32] But for the most part the realisation that even this exuberant strand of British postmodern fiction also has less affinity with postmodern theory than many critics had originally argued, came later. In 2000 we find Steven Earnshaw arguing that because of its focus on 'manners and mores within a liberal humanist framework' British postwar fiction 'steer[s] a middle course in reaction to modernist and postmodernist dominance'.[33] Five years later Patricia Waugh found that 'In the British context ... even overtly experimental novelists have usually conducted their textual playfulness in tension with an underlying if conflicted attachment to an attenuated realism.'[34] In an assessment that also took in her 'metafictionalized realism' she argued that 'the metafictional turn usually remained the ethical tool of an epistemological interrogation rather than an indiscriminate ontological pluralization and relativization of worlds'.[35] The next year, now discussing postwar woman writers, she argued that 'social constructionisms and postmodern textualisms have been cautiously assimilated into an indigenous fictional tradition where ethical commitment has often allied itself with a broad empiricism skeptical of the claims and preoccupations of academic high theory'.[36] For Waugh, postmodern female writers had created 'a postmodernism which is more an elaboration and exaggeration of already available codes then an apocalyptic break with aesthetic tradition'.[37]

Philip Tew discusses novels by A. S. Byatt, John Fowles, Salman Rushdie, and Jeannette Winterson 'to demonstrate how texts that have been taken as representing the dissolution of meaning and universals can be read as more concerned with a social integration and concretion that expresses at least implicitly some weariness about relativistic readings and the threats of the loss of meaning'.[38]

Bran Nicol's *The Cambridge Introduction to Postmodern Fiction* (2009) even rehabilitated postmodernism *tout court*, claiming that postmodern fiction 'has a strong desire to analyse contemporary reality'.[39] One can readily agree with Nicol's claim, and with Pieter Vermeulen's argument that in Britain 'a postmodern emphasis on disorientation, uncertainty and the proliferation of images was more often than not framed by a realist commitment'.[40] However, in British postmodern fiction such social analysis is more immediately tied up with moral judgment than in its American counterpart. As Steven Earnshaw remarks, 'there does appear in the British novel a clear connection between a particular type of world we inhabit, one that is taken to be empirically verifiable, and the evaluation of moral behaviour'.[41] In British postmodernism, a certain, often substantial, measure of realism would seem to be a prerequisite for the moral evaluation that is expected, an evaluation that is as characteristic of British fiction as it is of British criticism.

In spite of its social engagement, British postmodern fiction often remained the target of a virulent criticism based on what would seem to continental Europeans largely incomprehensible moralistic demands.[42] The tone of that criticism was set by the American Marxist critic Fredric Jameson's intervention of 1983 and the expanded version that he published the following year.[43] Jameson dismissed postmodern literature as depthless, as lacking authentic emotion and a sense of history, and as the servile accomplice of an exploitative capitalism. As Adam Kelly observed in 2011 with reference to postmodern fiction, 'grappling with postmodernism inevitably means grappling with Jameson's now canonical formulations – the death of affect, the loss of history, the fragmentation of the subject, the subsumption of the natural into the cultural, and so on'.[44] Let me just cite one of the countless echoes of Jameson's dismissal: 'The standard features of cultural Postmodernism', Julian Murphet tells us in *The Cambridge History of Twentieth-Century English Literature*, are 'a two-dimensional, denaturalized world; a hollowed-out subjectivity and affectless voice; a prosthetic, technological object world; and an imaginative prostration before the culture industry'.[45] What interests me here is that such out-of-hand dismissals are now used to set up a misleading comparison between a humane and compassionate new fictional practice and an outdated and nihilistic postmodernism. In their *Twenty-First Century Fiction* of 2013 Siân Adiseshiah and Rupert Hildyard tell us that '[t]he postmodern project itself certainly seems to be discredited. A growing consensus is critical of its paralyzing self-reflexivity, knavish use of irony and the ludic, and relativistic approach to historiography.'[46] They then argue that 'the most significant' twenty-first-century fiction rebels against this overwhelming negativity. And in her introduction to a collection of essays on the fiction of David Mitchell, Sarah Dillon creates a similar distance between Mitchell, whose use of 'postmodern literary techniques' she readily acknowledges, and postmodernism, contending that 'he does not adhere to the political and antisocial nihilism of postmodernity'.[47] However, Mitchell and some of the writers covered in Adiseshiah and Hildyard's *Twenty-First Century Fiction* are at least as postmodern as most postmodern fiction of the early 1980s, as I will try to show below. For many critics writing on contemporary fiction postmodernism stands for a cynical nihilism that a new generation of writers has fortunately overcome and left behind. This is indeed what prominent American writers such as David Foster Wallace and Jonathan Franzen have rather loudly proclaimed, but it is, certainly in the case of British postmodern fiction, an academic legend, one of the many surrounding postmodernism.

Post-postmodernism All Along?

Pointing out that in Thomas Pynchon's *Gravity's Rainbow* '[c]ontacts with emissaries from other worlds – angels, apparitions, spirits of the dead – recur throughout the novel',[48] Brian McHale argues that one of postmodernism's strategies 'involves juxtaposing a recognizable real world with an adjacent fantastic world, or mingling naturalistic and supernatural elements in the same world'.[49] Not surprisingly, there has been consistent critical interest in the postmodern fantastic. Some time ago Martin Horstkotte even saw the fantastic 'in its postmodern form' as the mode that was dominant in contemporary British fiction.[50] In 2014, Irmtraud Huber called our attention to the recurrence of fantastic and/or supernatural or marvellous elements in a number of recent novels.[51] In a move similar to those made by Adiseshiah and Hildyard and Dillon, she did not want to classify these features as postmodern in spite of 'the fantastical machines of postmodernism' that are at work in them. For Huber these novels – which include Mitchell's *number9dream* – go beyond postmodernism because in their mingling of fantastic and recognisably realistic elements and in their metafictional transgressions they paradoxically transcend postmodern self-negation: 'the authenticity and sincerity of the narrative voice is asserted in the act of exposing its construction'.[52] But if that is the case, why wouldn't the same be true of, say, *The French Lieutenant's Woman*, of A. S. Byatt's *Possession* or Julian Barnes's *England, England*?

Let us look briefly at contemporary fiction that is easily as postmodern as that of the 1980s. I will start with Nicola Barker's *Darkmans* (2007) and *In the Approaches* (2014) and then present more of an overview of the postmodern dimension of the work of David Mitchell. A sprawling novel, *Darkmans* is stuffed with Pynchonesque overinformation. Its narrative style resembles that of the conversational habits of one of its characters – 'conversational stock-car racing – the dramatic zoom past, the sudden handbrake turn, the skid, the spin'[53] – and frequently involves interruptions in which one of the novel's characters would seem to be directly addressed by the unnamed (and extradiegetic) narrator in what is a classic violation of narrative levels:

> 'Now hang on –
>   Just . . . just back up a second –
>   What are you saying here, exactly?'[54]

However, far more intrusive are the increasing signs that an impious and cruel spirit from the past, a fifteenth-century court jester, is playing havoc with the lives of some of *Darkmans*'s characters – planting memories, directing their thoughts, even inhabiting them at will and forcing them to do damage to themselves and others. But things never really add up. We are offered various ways of reading the novel, just as we are offered possible philosophies: 'The truth', Peta smiled, 'is that there is not truth. . . . The truth is simply an idea, a structure which we employ – in very small doses – to render life bearable'.[55] But the speaker is an untrustworthy professional forger, whose name, Peta Borough, itself smacks of fraud.

Like *Darkmans*, *In the Approaches* tells a deeply serious story, described by one reviewer, who calls the novel's characterisation 'rich and powerful', as a 'meditation on faith, suffering, guilt and the relativity of truth'.[56] That characterisation is indeed powerful, except in the case of the parrot Teobaldo, whose mental processes are so elementary that his chapters are the only ones told by an extradiegetic narrator (who resorts to toddler language to make sure we do not get the wrong impression). And then we have the chapters told by Mr Clifford Bickerton who is very much aware that, apart from being himself, he is also a character in a novel and who worries a good deal about the author's intentions: 'Perhaps I'll be involved in an accident at work at an especially critical moment in the plot . . . . Yes, I quite fancy that idea. Rusty Bickerton: Mr Brave but Mr Dispensable. A tragic afterthought dreamt up by a mean cow of an Author to add that tiny bit of extra depth.'[57]

He is also, mysteriously, aware of Teobaldo's contributions ('a little light relief'),[58] of Barker's *oeuvre* ('I'm thinking these thoughts in October 1984 and she only started writing seriously in 1987 . . . . I just *can't* be having these thoughts right now, about her other books'),[59] and other things only the 'cow Author' can know, while he also manages to be critical of what she is doing: 'there's enough mystical mumbo-jumbo in this book already'.[60] When the author finally lets him go, another character sees to her astonishment line after line of properly punctuated black typescript flooding out of his nose. No wonder he feels drained afterwards.

Towards the end of the novel another character is also aware that he lives inside a novel, telling us that 'the last chapter – 50 – was sheer torture for me' and directly addressing the reader in another ontological transgression: 'Fill this in the best you can.'[61] But we can't, any more than he can, because the way Barker has set up her novel leaves us with questions we cannot answer. Yet all of this 'mumbo-jumbo' – far more transgressive than anything in *Waterland*, *Flaubert's Parrot*, *Money*, or *Possession* – does not undermine the moral seriousness of *In the Approaches*.

Like those of Barker, the novels of David Mitchell have their author's telltale fingerprints all over them. We have countless, often tongue-in-cheek literary allusions, ranging from Borges ('Paths forked off and forked off some more')[62] via Malcolm Lowry and Nabokov (in *number9dream* – its title itself taken from a John Lennon song – its narrator sees posters of films titled *Dark as the Grave Wherein My Friend is Laid* and *The Life and Times of John Shade*) to Paul Auster (in *Ghostwritten* we have a band called The Music of Chance, the title of an Auster novel). Then we have sneaky mise en abymes. In for instance *Cloud Atlas* the young composer Robert Frobisher's last composition is 'Cloud Atlas', a 'sextet for overlapping soloists ... In the first set, each solo is interrupted by its successor: in the second each interruption is recontinued, in order.' This is of course the structure of *Cloud Atlas* itself and Mitchell obviously enjoys the joke, having Frobisher wonder: 'Revolutionary or gimmick? Shan't know until it's finished.'[63] In the same novel we also have a less obvious but fundamentally more disruptive 'tricksy device' (in another self-mocking gesture Mitchell has one of his characters speak disparagingly of 'tricksy devices' which 'belong in the 1980s with M.A.'s [*sic*] in postmodernism and chaos theory').[64] It turns out that Luisa Rey, the protagonists of one of the six only marginally related stories that together make up *Cloud Atlas*, does not exist on the same narrative level as the other protagonists, but is the main character of a story submitted to the narrator of the previous story, a publisher. That second-order fictionality creates an intractable problem. Since Rey reads the letters – and meets a former lover – of Frobisher, his story, too, must belong to this fiction-within-fiction and the same must be true of Adam Ewing, the protagonist of the novel's first section, because it is his diary that Frobisher finds and that we read. Rey's second-order fictionality causes dominoes to fall both backwards and forwards (when the interrupted stories told by Ewing and Frobisher are continued). To complicate matters further, Rey had a small part in one of the sections of the earlier *Ghostwritten*. And in that novel, a minor female character had a comet-like birthmark, just like all the protagonists of *Cloud Atlas*, which ranges in time from the nineteenth century to a distant post-apocalyptic future. However, nothing is explained. Mitchell leaves all of this up the reader, as is also the case in the last chapter of *number9dream*, which is merely a blank page.

'Describing our world's unknowability in terms of labyrinths and mirrors no longer cuts the metaphysical mustard', Mitchell has said,[65] and so he creates only marginally and coincidentally overlapping worlds (nine of them in *Ghostwritten*, six of them in *Cloud Atlas*). But even in *number9dream*, which features only one protagonist, we encounter a variety of worlds and have 'the kind of spatial (dis)order – eclecticism realized at the level of the world itself'[66] – that Brian McHale sees as a classic postmodern strategy. Mitchell does not only place worlds alongside each other, he also stacks them vertically (by embedding them), creating heterotopias that escape overall interpretations. Most baffling from the point of interpretation may be the appearance, in *Ghostwritten*, of a non-corporeal sentient intelligence who migrates from human host to host (and claims to know others like him/her). In *The Bone Clocks* of 2014 Mitchell returns to the theme of a parallel supernatural world, introducing the Horologists, who would seem to be virtually immortal and also move from host to host. These Horologists are engaged in an all-out war with similarly gifted evil antagonists in scenes that remind us of Jedi Knights and the Dark Side, fortunately minus ankle-length cloaks and lightsabers. Just as in *Darkmans*, the effect is an ontological hesitation that we recognise as quintessentially postmodern.

But just like Barker Mitchell succeeds in making us care about his characters and about the world. Some years ago, Nick Bentley found that '[i]n many ways both David Mitchell's *Cloud Atlas* (2004) and Zadie Smith's *NW* (2012)' – another novel that I might have discussed here – 'are typical postmodern novels in their use of fragmented form, multiple narratives, and complex models of identity and characterisation'. But he goes on to argue that these novels are 'also interested in the possibility of exceeding or moving beyond postmodern scepticism and identifying the potential for reconstructive (rather than postmodern deconstructive) possibilities'.[67] In a 2004 article, Robert McLaughlin had already discussed writers whose focus 'is less on self-conscious wordplay and the violation of narrative conventions and more on representing the world we all share'. Yet these writers also 'show that it's a world that we know through language and layers of representation; language, narrative, and the processes of representation are the only means we have to experience and know the world, ourselves, and our possibilities for being human'.[68] McLaughlin had in mind a number of younger American authors, tentatively called post-postmodernists. Barker and Mitchell perfectly fit the bill. But so does practically all British postmodern fiction. It has never lost sight of the native empirical tradition or of its moral dimension. Without saying so explicitly it has rejected the more radical postmodern propositions – such as language being incapable of reaching the world or the subject being just a temporary meeting-point for a variety of discourses. It has acknowledged the merits of such propositions – especially through its emphasis on the mediating role of language and the importance of representation – but it has never, *pace* its critics, abandoned moral responsibility.

Notes

1. Martin Paul Eve, 'Late Modernism, Postmodernism and After', in *The Cambridge Companion to British Fiction: 1980–2018*, ed. Peter Boxall (Cambridge University Press, 2019), pp. 137–49, p. 146.
2. See Brian McHale, 'Postmodernism and Experiment', *The Routledge Companion to Experimental Literature*, ed. Joe Bray, Alison Gibbons, and Brian McHale (Abingdon: Routledge, 2012), pp. 141–52.

3. Christine Brooke-Rose and Maria del Sapio Garbero, 'A Conversation with Christine Brooke-Rose', in *British Postmodern Fiction*, ed. Theo D'haen and Hans Bertens (Atlanta, Georgia: Rodopi, 1993), pp. 101–20, p. 105.
4. Amy Elias, 'Postmodern Metafiction', in *The Cambridge Companion to American Fiction After 1945*, ed. John N. Duvall (Cambridge University Press, 2011), pp. 13–29, p. 15.
5. Brian McHale, *Postmodernist Fiction* (London: Routledge, 1987).
6. Linda Hutcheon, *A Poetics of Postmodernism* (London: Routledge, 1988).
7. Graham Swift, *Waterland* (London: Vintage, 1992), p. 47.
8. Ibid., p. 94.
9. Ibid., p. 81.
10. Ibid., p. 47.
11. Ibid., p. 122.
12. Julian Barnes, *Flaubert's Parrot* (London: Picador, 1985), p. 38.
13. Ibid., p. 90.
14. Alison Lee, *Realism and Power: Postmodern British Fiction* (London: Routledge, 1990).
15. Gavin Keulks, *Martin Amis: Postmodernism and Beyond* (London: Palgrave, 2006), p. 161; Patricia Waugh, *Harvest of the Sixties: English Literature and Its Background, 1960–90* (Oxford University Press, 1995), pp. 30–1.
16. Martin Amis, *Money: A Suicide Note* (Harmondsworth: Penguin, 1984), p. 331.
17. Ibid., p. 394.
18. John Dickson Carr, *The Hollow Man* (London: Orion, 2013), pp. 186–7.
19. Edmund Crispin, *The Moving Toyshop* (London: Collins, 2015), p. 68.
20. Gérard Genette, *Narrative Discourse Revisited*, trans. Jane E. Lewin (Ithaca, New York: Cornell University Press, 1988), pp. 234–5.
21. Ibid., p.88.
22. Marie-Laure Ryan, *Avatars of Story* (Minneapolis: University of Minnesota Press, 2006), p. 207.
23. Ibid., p. 207.
24. Lee, *Realism and Power*, p. xii.
25. Ibid., p. xi.
26. Amy Elias, 'Meta-mimesis? The Problem of British Postmodern Realism', in D'haen and Bertens, *British Postmodern Fiction*, pp. 9–31, p. 14.
27. Ibid., p. 12.
28. Marie-Laure Ryan, 'Fiction, Non-Factuals, and the Principle of Minimal Departure', *Poetics* 9:4 (August 1988), pp. 403–22, p. 403.
29. Patricia Waugh, 'The Woman Writer and the Continuities of Feminism', in *A Concise Companion to Contemporary British Fiction*, ed. James F. English (Oxford: Blackwell, 2006), pp. 118–208, p. 192.
30. Jeanette Winterson, *Sexing the Cherry* (London: Bloomsbury, 1989), p. 88.
31. Angela Carter, *Nights at the Circus* (London: Picador, 1985), p. 260.
32. Lee, *Realism and Power*, p. 48.
33. Steven Earnshaw, 'Novel Voices', in *Literature and Culture in Modern Britain, vol. 3: 1956–1990*, ed. Clive Bloom and Gary Day (Harlow: Longman, 2000), p. 65.

34. Patricia Waugh, 'Postmodern Fiction and the Rise of Critical Theory', in *A Companion to the British and Irish Novel 1945–2000*, ed. Brian W. Shaffer (Oxford: Blackwell, 2005), pp. 65–82, p. 69.
35. Ibid., p. 74.
36. Waugh, 'The Woman Writer', p. 193.
37. Ibid., p. 205.
38. Philip Tew, *The Contemporary British Novel*, 2nd ed. (London: Continuum, 2007), p. 224.
39. Bran Nicol, *The Cambridge Introduction to Postmodern Fiction* (Cambridge University Press, 2009), p. 30.
40. Pieter Vermeulen, 'The 1990s', in *The Cambridge Companion to British Fiction: 1980–2018*, ed. Peter Boxall (Cambridge University Press, 2019), pp. 32–46, p. 39.
41. Earnshaw, 'Novel Voices', p. 65.
42. See Hans Bertens, 'Critical and Literary Theory', in *Europe in British Literature and Culture*, ed. Petra Rau and William Rossiter (Cambridge University Press, 2024), pp. 303–21.
43. Fredric Jameson, 'Postmodernism, or the Cultural Logic of Late Capitalism', *New Left Review* 146 (1984), pp. 53–92.
44. Adam Kelly, 'Beginning With Postmodernism', *Twentieth-Century Literature* 57:3 & 4 (2011), pp. 391–422, p. 398.
45. Julian Murphet, 'Fiction and Postmodernity', in *The Cambridge History of Twentieth-Century English Literature*, ed. Laura Marcus and Peter Nicholls (Cambridge University Press, 2005), p. 731.
46. Siân Adiseshiah and Rupert Hildyard (eds.), *Twenty-First Century Fiction: What Happens Now* (Basingstoke: Palgrave Macmillan, 2013), p. 4.
47. Sarah Dillon, 'Introducing David Mitchell's Universe', in *David Mitchell: Critical Essays*, ed. Sarah Dillon (Canterbury: Gylphi, 2011), pp. 3–24, p. 18.
48. Brian McHale, *The Cambridge Introduction to Postmodernism* (Cambridge University Press, 2015), p. 148.
49. Ibid., p. 146.
50. Martin Horstkotte, *The Postmodern Fantastic in Contemporary Fiction* (Trier: Wissenschaftlicher Verlag, 2000), p. 59.
51. Irmtraud Huber, *Literature after Postmodernism: Reconstructive Fantasies* (London: Palgrave Macmillan, 2014), p. 48.
52. Ibid., p. 27.
53. Nicola Barker, *Darkmans* (London: Harper Perennial, 2011), p. 98.
54. Ibid., p. 10.
55. Ibid., p. 824.
56. Edward Docx, 'In the Approaches review – Nicola Barker spawns wild chaos', *The Guardian*, 15 June 2014: www.theguardian.com/books/2014/jun/15/in-the-approaches-review-nicola-barker-wild-chaos.
57. Nicola Barker, *In the Approaches* (London: Fourth Estate, 2014), p. 85.
58. Ibid., p. 85.
59. Ibid., p. 90.

60. Ibid., p. 214.
61. Ibid., p. 491, p. 497.
62. David Mitchell, *Ghostwritten* (London: Sceptre, 1999), p. 81.
63. David Mitchell, *Cloud Atlas* (London: Sceptre, 2005), p. 445.
64. Ibid., p. 150.
65. David Mitchell, 'Enter the Maze – review of Calvino's *If On A Winter's Night A Traveller*', *The Guardian*, 22 May 2004: www.theguardian.com/books/2004/may/22/fiction.italocalvino.
66. McHale, 'Postmodernism and Experiment', p. 144.
67. Nick Bentley, 'Trailing Postmodernism: David Mitchell's *Cloud Atlas*, Zadie Smith's *NW*, and the Metamodern', *English Studies* 99:7 (2018), pp. 723–43, p. 723.
68. Robert L. McLaughlin, 'Post-Postmodern Discontent: Contemporary Fiction and the Social World', *symploke* 12:1–2 (2004), pp. 53–69, p. 66.

Further Reading

Individual Authors

For single-author studies about the work of the individual writers covered in this volume, see book series such as: Routledge's *Contemporary Writers: Critical Essays* (from 2011–22, published by Gylphi), Bloomsbury Academic's *Contemporary Critical Perspectives*, and Manchester University Press's *Twenty-First Century Perspectives*.

Postmodern Theory

Adam, Ian and Tiffin, Helen, eds., *Past the Last Post: Theorizing Post-Colonialism and Post-Modernism* (University of Calgary Press, 1990).

Altieri, Charles, *Postmodernisms Now: Essays on Contemporaneity in the Arts* (Pennsylvania State University Press, 1998).

Baudrillard, Jean, *Simulations*, trans. Paul Foss Paul Patton and Philip Beitchman (New York: Semiotext(e), 1983).

Baudrillard, Jean, *Selected Writings*, ed. Mark Poster, trans. Jacques Mourrain, 2nd ed. (Stanford University Press, 2001).

Bauman, Zygmunt, *Intimations of Postmodernity* (London: Routledge, 1992).

Best, Steven and Kellner, Douglas, *The Postmodern Turn* (New York: Guilford Press, 1998).

Butler, Judith, *Gender Trouble: Feminism and the Subversion of Identity* (New York: Routledge, 1990).

Callinicos, Alex, *Against Postmodernism: A Marxist Critique* (Cambridge: Polity, 1990).

Connor, Steven, *Postmodernist Culture: An Introduction to Theories of the Contemporary* (Oxford: Blackwell, 1989).

Eagleton, Terry, *The Illusions of Postmodernism* (Oxford: Blackwell, 1992).

Fisher, Mark, *Capitalist Realism: Is There No Alternative?* (Winchester: Zero Books, 2009).

Harvey, David, *The Condition of Postmodernity: An Enquiry into the Origins of Cultural Change* (Hoboken: Wiley, 1992).

Huyssen, Andreas, *After the Great Divide: Modernism, Mass Culture, Postmodernism*, (Bloomington: Indiana University Press, 1986).

Jameson, Fredric, *Postmodernism, or the Cultural Logic of Late Capitalism* (London: Verso, 1991).
Jameson, Fredric, *The Cultural Turn: Selected Writings on the Postmodern, 1983–1998* (London: Verso, 1998).
Jencks, Charles, *The Language of Post-Modern Architecture* (London: Academy Editions, 1984).
Jencks, Charles, *What is Post-Modernism?* (London: Academy Editions, 1996).
Kroker, Arthur and Cook, David, *The Postmodern Scene: Excremental Culture and Hyper-Aesthetics* (Basingstoke: Macmillan, 1988).
Lyotard, Jean-François, *The Postmodern Condition: A Report on Knowledge*, trans. Geoff Bennington and Brian Massumi (Minneapolis: University of Minnesota Press, 1984).
Sardar, Ziauddin, *Postmodernism and The Other: New Imperialism of Western Culture* (London: Pluto Press, 1998).
Soja, Edward W., *Postmodern Geographies: The Reassertion of Space in Critical Social Theory* (London: Verso, 1989).
Spivak, Gayatri, *In Other Worlds: Essays on Cultural Politics* (London: Routledge, 1988).
White, Hayden, *Tropics of Discourse: Essays in Cultural Criticism* (Baltimore: John Hopkins University Press, 1978).
Zima, Peter V., *Modern/Postmodern* (London: Continuum, 2012).

Studies of Postmodern Fiction or Relevant to Postmodernism

Adair, Gilbert, *The Postmodernist Always Rings Twice: Reflections on Culture in the 90s* (London: Fourth Estate, 1992).
Baker, Stephen, *The Fiction of Postmodernity* (Edinburgh University Press, 2000).
Bertens, Hans and Fokkema, Douwe, eds., *International Postmodernism: Theory and Literary Practice* (Amsterdam: John Benjamins, 1997).
Currie, Mark, *Postmodern Narrative Theory* (Basingstoke: Palgrave, 2010).
Currie, Mark, ed., *Metafiction* (London: Routledge, 2014).
D'haen, Theo and Bertens, Hans, eds., *British Postmodern Fiction* (Amsterdam: Ropodi, 1993).
Dix, Hywel, *Postmodern Fiction and the Break-Up of Britain* (London: Continuum, 2010).
Duvall, John, ed., *Productive Postmodernism: Consuming Histories and Cultural Studies* (New York: SUNY Press, 2001).
Elias, Amy, *Sublime Desire: History and Post-1960s Fiction* (Baltimore: Johns Hopkins University Press, 2001).
Felski, Rita, *The Limits of Critique* (London: University of Chicago Press, 2015).
Goulimari, Pelagia, *Postmodernism. What Moment?* (Manchester University Press, 2007).
Green, Jeremy, *Late Postmodernism: American Fiction at the Millennium* (Basingstoke: Palgrave, 2005).

Hutcheon, Linda, *Narcissistic Narrative: the Metafictional Paradox* (Toronto: Wilfred Laurier University Press, 1980).
Hutcheon, Linda, *A Poetics of Postmodernism: History, Theory, Fiction* (London: Routledge, 1988).
Hutcheon, Linda, *The Politics of Postmodernism*, 2nd ed. (London: Routledge, 2002).
Jameson, Fredric, *The Antinomies of Realism* (London: Verso, 2013).
Lee, Alison, *Realism and Power: Postmodern British Fiction* (London: Routledge, 1990).
Lee, Jae-Seong, *Postmodern Ethics, Emptiness, and Literature: Encounters between East and West* (Lanham: Lexington, 2015).
McCaffrey, Larry, ed. *Storming the Reality Studio: A Casebook of Cyberpunk and Postmodern Science Fiction* (Durham: Duke University Press, 1991).
McHale, Brian, *Postmodernist Fiction* (London: Methuen, 1987).
McHale, Brian, *Constructing Postmodernism* (London: Routledge, 1992).
McHale, Brian, *The Cambridge Introduction to Postmodernism* (Cambridge University Press, 2015).
McHale, Brian and Platt, Len, eds., *The Cambridge History of Postmodern Literature* (Cambridge University Press, 2016).
Nicol, Bran, *The Cambridge Introduction to Postmodern Fiction* (Cambridge University Press, 2009).
Platt, Len and Upstone, Sara, eds., *Postmodern Literature and Race* (Cambridge University Press, 2015).
Reed, T. V., *The Bloomsbury Introduction to Postmodern Realist Fiction: Resisting Master Narratives* (London: Bloomsbury Academic, 2021).
Waugh, Patricia, *Metafiction: The Theory and Practice of Self-Conscious Fiction* (London: Routledge, 1984).
Waugh, Patricia, *Practising Postmodernism, Reading Modernism* (London: Edward Arnold, 1992).

After Postmodernism and Post-Postmodernism

Bouju, Emmanuel, *Epimodernism: Six Memos for Literature Today* (London: Palgrave Macmillan, 2023).
Bourriaud, Nicholas, *Altermodern* (London: Tate Publishing, 2009).
Evans, Joel, *Conceptualising the Global in the Wake of the Postmodern: Literature, Culture, Theory* (Cambridge University Press, 2019).
Haines, Tasha, *Redemptive Hybridism in Post-Postmodern Writing* (London: Bloomsbury Academic, 2023).
Holland, Mary K., *Succeeding Postmodernism: Language and Humanism in Contemporary American Literature* (London: Bloomsbury, 2013).
Huber, Irmtraud, *Literature after Postmodernism: Reconstructive Fantasies* (London: Palgrave Macmillan, 2014).
Kirby, Alan, *Digimodernism: How New Technologies Dismantle the Postmodern and Reconfigure Our Culture* (London: Continuum, 2009).

Moraru, Christian, *Cosmodernism: American Narrative, Late Globalization, and the New Cultural Imaginary* (Ann Arbor: University of Michigan Press, 2011).
Nealon, Jeffrey, *Post-Postmodernism: or, The Cultural Logic of Just-in-Time Capitalism* (Stanford University Press, 2012).
Ning, Wang, *After Postmodernism* (London: Routledge, 2024).
Rudrum, David and Stavris, Nicholas, eds., *Supplanting the Postmodern* (London: Bloomsbury, 2015).
Toth, Josh, *The Passing of Postmodernism: A Spectroanalysis of the Contemporary* (New York: SUNY Press, 2010).

Contemporary British Fiction

Adiseshiah, Siân and Hildyard, Rupert, eds., *Twenty-First Century Fiction: What Happens Now* (Basingstoke: Palgrave, 2013).
Alexander, Neal, *Late Modernism and the Poetics of Place* (Edinburgh University Press, 2022).
Arias, Rosario and Pulham, Patricia, eds., *Haunting and Spectrality in Neo-Victorian Fiction: Possessing the Past* (Basingstoke: Palgrave, 2009).
Bentley, Nick, ed., *British Fiction of the 1990s* (London: Routledge, 2005).
Bentley, Nick, *Contemporary British Fiction* (Edinburgh University Press, 2008).
Boxall, Peter, *Twenty-First-Century Fiction: A Critical Introduction* (Cambridge University Press, 2015).
Boxall, Peter, ed., *The Cambridge Companion to British Fiction: 1950–2018* (Cambridge University Press, 2019).
Boxall, Peter and Cheyette, Bryan, eds., *The Oxford History of the Novel in English: Volume 7, British and Irish Fiction Since 1940* (Oxford University Press, 2016).
Bradbury, Malcolm, *The Modern British Novel: 1878–2001*, 2nd ed. (Harmondsworth: Penguin, 2001).
Bradford, Richard, *The Novel Now: Contemporary British Fiction* (Malden, Massachusetts: Blackwell, 2007).
Bray, Joe, Gibbons, Alison, and McHale, Brian (eds.), *The Routledge Companion to Experimental Literature* (Abingdon: Routledge, 2012).
Brooker, Joseph, *Literature of the 1980s: After the Watershed* (Edinburgh University Press, 2010).
Carruthers, Gerard, David Golde and Alistair Renfrew, eds., *Beyond Scotland: New Contexts for Twentieth Century Scottish Literature* (Amsterdam: Rodopi, 2004).
Caserio, Robert, ed., *The Cambridge Companion to the Twentieth-Century English Novel* (Cambridge University Press, 2009).
Childs, Peter, and Green, James, *Ethics and Aesthetics in Twenty-First Century British Novels* (London: Bloomsbury, 2013).
Connor, Stephen, *The English Novel in History: 1950–1995* (London: Routledge, 2006).
Currie, Mark, *About Time: Narrative, Fiction and the Philosophy of Time* (Edinburgh University Press, 2010).

Davies, Alastair, and Sinfield, Alan, *British Culture of the Post-War: An Introduction to Literature and Society, 1945–1999* (London: Routledge, 2000).
D'haen, Theo and Vermuelen, Pieter, eds., *Cultural Identity and Postmodern Writing* (Amsterdam: Rodopi, 2006).
Eckstein, Lars, Korte, Barbara, Pirker, Eva Ulrike and Reinfandt, Christoph, eds., *Multi-Ethnic Britain 2000+: New Perspectives in Literature, Film and the Arts* (Amsterdam: Rodopi, 2008).
Edwards, Caroline, *Utopia and the Contemporary British Novel* (Cambridge University Press, 2019).
English, James F., *A Concise Companion to Contemporary British Fiction* (Oxford: Blackwell, 2006).
Gasiorek, Andrejz, *Post-War British Fiction: Realism and After* (London: Edward Arnold, 1995).
Greaney, Michael, *Contemporary Fiction and the Uses of Theory: The Novel from Structuralism to Postmodernism* (Basingstoke: Palgrave, 2006).
Haffey, Kate, *Literary Modernism, Queer Temporality: Eddies in Time* (London: Palgrave Macmillan, 2019).
Hammond, Andrew, *British Fiction and the Cold War* (London: Palgrave, 2013).
Head, Dominic, *The Cambridge Introduction to Modern British Fiction: 1950–2000* (Cambridge University Press, 2002).
Heilmann, Ann, and Llewelyn, Mark, *Neo-Victorianism: The Victorians in the Twenty-First Century, 1999–2009* (Basingstoke: Palgrave, 2010).
James, David, *Contemporary British Fiction and the Artistry of Space: Style, Landscape, Perception* (London: Continuum, 2008).
James, David, *The Legacies of Modernism: Historicising Postwar and Contemporary Fiction* (Cambridge University Press, 2011).
James, David, *Modernist Futures: Innovation and Inheritance in the Contemporary Novel* (Cambridge University Press, 2012).
James, David, ed., *The Cambridge Companion to British Fiction Since 1945* (Cambridge University Press, 2015).
Jay, Paul, *Global Matters: The Transnational Turn in Literary Studies* (Ithaca, New York: Cornell University Press, 2010).
Keen, Suzanne, *Romances of the Archive in Contemporary British Fiction* (Toronto: University of Toronto Press, 2001).
Kirsch, Adam, *The Global Novel: Writing the World in the 21st Century* (New York: Columbia University Press, 2017).
Leader, Zachary, ed., *On Modern British Fiction* (Oxford University Press, 2002).
Leggett, Bianca, and Venezia, Tony, *Twenty-First-Century British Fiction* (Canterbury: Gylphi, 2015).
Lehner, Stefanie, *Subaltern Ethics in Contemporary Scottish and Irish Literature: Tracing Counter-Histories* (Basingstoke: Palgrave, 2011).
Luckhurst, Roger and Marks, Peter, eds., *Literature and the Contemporary: Fictions and Theories of the Present* (Harlow: Longman, 1999).
MacPhee, Graham, *Postwar British Literature and Postcolonial Studies* (Edinburgh University Press, 2011).

Marcus, Laura and Nicholls, Peter, eds., *The Cambridge History of Twentieth-Century English Literature* (Cambridge University Press, 2005).
Marks, Peter, *Literature of the 1990s: Endings and Beginnings* (Edinburgh University Press, 2018).
Matthews, Graham, *Ethics and Desire in the Wake of Postmodernism: Contemporary Satire* (London: Continuum, 2012).
McGurl, Mark, *The Program Era: Postwar Fiction and the Rise of Creative Writing* (Cambridge, Massachusetts: Harvard University Press, 2009).
McNally, Lisa, *Reading Theories in Contemporary Fiction* (London: Bloomsbury Academic, 2013).
Osborne, Deirdre, ed., *The Cambridge Companion to British Black and Asian Literature: 1945–2010* (Cambridge University Press, 2016).
Shaffer, Brian W., ed., *A Companion to the British and Irish Novel 1045–2000* (Oxford: Blackwell, 2005).
Shaw, Kristian, *Cosmopolitanism in Twenty-First Century Fiction* (London: Palgrave Macmillan, 2017).
Shaw, Kristian, *Brexlit: British Literature and the European Project* (London: Bloomsbury Academic, 2021).
Sinfield, Alan, *Literature, Politics and Culture in Postwar Britain* (London: Continuum, 1997).
Stein, Mark, *Black British Literature: Novels of Transformation* (Columbus, Ohio: Ohio State University Press, 2004).
Stewart, Victoria, *The Second World War in Contemporary British Fiction* (Edinburgh: Edinburgh University Press, 2011).
Tate, Andrew, *Apocalyptic Fiction* (London: Bloomsbury Academic, 2017).
Underwood, Ted. *Why Literary Periods Mattered: Historical Contrast and the Prestige of English Studies* (Stanford, California: Stanford University Press, 2013).
Upstone, Sara, *British Asian Fiction: Twenty-First-Century Voices* (Manchester University Press, 2010).
Upstone, Sara, *Rethinking Race and Identity in Contemporary British Fiction* (London: Routledge, 2016).
Vermeulen, Pieter, *Contemporary Literature and the End of the Novel* (London: Palgrave Macmillan, 2015).
Walkowitz, Rebecca L., *Born Translated The Contemporary Novel in an Age of World Literature* (New York: Columbia University Press, 2017).

Index

2008 financial crash, 28, 29
9/11, 242, 243

Aaronovitch, Ben
   Rivers of London, 132
Acker, Kathy, 4
Ackroyd, Peter, 10, 11, 161, 169, 256
   Chatterton, 9, 132
   Dan Leno and the Limehouse Golem, 132
   Hawksmoor, 9, 71–2, 262
   The House of Doctor Dee, 249
   The Last Testament of Oscar Wilde, 169
Adair, Gilbert, 2
Adebayo, Diran, 8
   Some Kind of Black, 181
Adiseshiah, Siân and Rupert Hillyard
   Twenty-First Century Fiction, 264
Ahmad, Aijaz, 100
AIDS epidemic, 13, 162, 164–7
Alexander, Marguerite, 145
Ali, Monica, 5, 15, 175
   Brick Lane, 132, 251
Allingham, Marjorie
   The China Governess, 260
altermodernism (Nicolas Bourriaud), 176
Amis, Martin, 5, 9, 10, 15, 29, 92, 95, 241, 242–3, 256
   London Fields, 242
   Money: A Suicide Note, 9, 12, 16, 23, 85–90, 94, 242, 259–61, 266
   Night Train, 93
   The Information, 243
   Time's Arrow, 90, 93
   Yellow Dog, 243
Anderson, Benedict, 147
anticolonial resistance. *See* postcolonialism
apocalypse, 152–6
Appiah, Kwame Anthony, 56, 62
Arendt, Hannah, 60, 62
Ashworth, Jen
   Fell, 150

Aslam, Nadeem, 175
   Maps for Lost Lovers, 178
Atwood, Margaret, 136
   Alias Grace, 136, 214
   Oryx and Crake, 130, 137
   The Blind Assassin, 136
   The Handmaid's Tale, 136, 137, 232
   The Testaments, 130, 137
Augé, Marc, 74
Austen, Jane, 87
Auster, Paul, 149

B. S. Johnson Society, The, 126
Ballard, J. G., 7, 9, 11, 75–6, 153
   Concrete Island, 75
   Crash, 75
   HIgh-Rise, 21
   The Atrocity Exhibition, 75
   The Drowned World, 145
Ballard, J. G., 11
Banks, Iain, 98, 147
   The Bridge, 99
Banville, John, 130
Barker, Nicola, 5, 15, 16, 131, 246, 268
   Behindlings, 247–9
   Darkmans, 265, 268
   In the Approaches, 266
Barker, Pat
   Regeneration Trilogy, 168
Barnes, Julian, 5, 9, 10, 11, 15, 29, 35, 174, 241, 256
   A History of the World in 10½ Chapters, 9, 244
   Arthur and George, 244
   England, England, 25–6, 44–6, 265
   Flaubert's Parrot, 9, 16, 231, 244, 258, 259, 261, 266
   Metroland, 76
   The Sense of an Ending, 244
Barth, John, 2, 4, 83, 225, 226
   Lost in the Funhouse, 256
   The Sot-Weed Factor, 256
Barthelme, Donald, 4

Index

Baudrillard, Jean
  hyperreality, 70
  simulation, 25, 70, 220
Bauman, Zygmunt, 145
Beckett, Samuel, 7
  The Unnameable, 249
Begley, Jon, 86
Bell, Eleanor, 98
Berger, John, 100
Berlant, Lauren, 194, 196
Bhabha, Homi, 49
Bildungsroman
  'queer' Bildungsroman, 162–4
Bildungsroman, the, 245
Black British and British Asian Fiction, 7, 174–88
Black British writing, 14
Black history, 177, 181
Booker Prize, 8, 82, 103, 130, 134, 138, 211, 242, 244
Borges, Jorge Luis, 19, 148
Bourdieu, Pierre
  'cultural capital', 216, 217
Bourriaud, Nicolas, 176
Boxall, Peter, 145, 229–30, 232, 235, 236
  'postcolonial time', 229
Bradbury, Malcolm, 2, 9, 138, 174, 225
  Dangerous Pilgrimages, 82
  Doctor Criminale, 226
Bradbury, Ray
  Fahrenheit 451, 19
Bradford, Richard
  'the new postmodernists', 246
break-up of Britain, 26
Brexit, 29, 44, 45, 209
bricolage, 213
Bridgerton (TV series), 192, 219–20
British Asian fiction, 14, 108–9
British Empire, 174, 176
British imperialism, 250
British media, 27
Brooker, Joseph, 86, 90
Brooke-Rose, Christine, 7, 11, 255–6
  Between, 74, 256
  Next, 256
  Thru, 256
Brophy, Brigid, 7, 11
  In Transit, 75
Burgess, Anthony, 7, 139
  A Clockwork Orange, 117, 139
Burns, Alan, 7
Burroughs, William, 4
  Naked Lunch, 19
Butler, Judith, 178
  Bodies that Matter, 215
  gender performativity, 160, 215
  Gender Trouble: Feminism and the Subversion of Identity, 160, 215
Byatt, A. S., 5, 9, 15, 216, 241, 256
  Possession: A Romance, 9, 13, 14, 134, 206, 210, 211, 212–13, 215, 217, 244, 249, 265, 266
  The Biographer's Tale, 9
  The Children's Book, 244

Calvino, Italo, 19, 68, 148
Carey, Peter, 130
  Jack Maggs, 210, 214
  Oscar and Lucinda, 210
Carr, John Dickson, 140
  The Hollow Man, 140
Carroll, Samantha, 212, 213, 217
Carter, Angela, 5, 9, 11, 22, 40–1, 70, 83, 139, 256
  Nights at the Circus, 195, 257, 262
  The Bloody Chamber, 262
  The Infernal Desire Machines of Doctor Hoffman, 70
  Wise Children, 26
Catton, Eleanor
  The Luminaries, 211, 214
Chambers, Iain, 185
Chase-Riboud, Barbara
  Hottentot Venus, 214
Chatwin, Bruce
  Utz, 9
Christie, Agatha
  The Murder of Roger Ackroyd, 140
Cixous', Hélène
  écriture féminine, 105
Clarke, Susanna
  Jonathan Strange and Mr. Norrell, 130
  Piranesi, 130
Clause 28 (Section 28 of the Local Government Act 1988), 162, 167
Coe, Jonathan, 5, 116, 121, 124, 246
  Like a Fiery Elephant, 122
Cold War, 19
Colie, Rosalie, 131, 142
colonialism, 49, 50
condition of England novel, 28
Connor, Steven, 35
Conrad, Joseph, 116, 131
consumer society, 108
Coover, Robert, 4, 83
  Pricksongs and Descants, 256
  The Public Burning, 257
cosmopolitanism, 147, 148, 150, 176, 184, 187
Coupland, Douglas, 228, 232, 236
  'translit', 228, 235
Coupland', Douglas
  Generation X: Tales for an Accelerated Culture, 147

Crace, Jim, 29
  Arcadia, 24
  The Gift of Stones, 9
Craig, Amanda
  Hearts and Minds, 27
Craig, Cairns, 98, 102, 103
creative writing programmes, 138, 216
Crispin, Edmund
  Swan Song, 260
  The Moving Toyshop, 260
Crumey, Andrew
  D'Alembert's Principle, 82
cyberpunk, 247

D'Aguiar, Fred, 175
Daamen, Roel, 99
Danielewski, Mark Z., 226
David Copperfield (movie), 219
David Foster Wallace
  Infinite Jest, 82
de Groot, Jerome, 194, 195
de Lauretis, Teresa, 159
decadence, 220
declinism, 11, 33–46
decolonisation, 230
deconstruction, 161
DeLillo, Don, 4, 226
  Mao II, 94
  Underworld, 82
  White Noise, 93
devolution (Scotland), 98, 109
deWitt, Patrick, 130
digi-modernism, 31
digital technology, 15
Dinshaw, Carolyn, 167
Docherty, Thomas, 192
Donoghue, Emma, 131
double-coding, 12, 126, 165
Dover Beach (Matthew Arnold), 51, 52
Drabble, Margaret
  The Radiant Way, 131
Duffy, Maureen, 11
  Capital, 72
Duncker, Patricia
  James Miranda Barry, 215
dystopia, 69, 102, 232–4

Earnshaw, Steven, 262, 263
Eco, Umberto, 134
Edelman, Lee, 165
Egan, Jennifer, 84
Eggers, Dave, 4, 93
Elias, Amy J., 256
  'new postmodern realism', 261
Ellis, Alice Thomas, 140

Emecheta, Buchi, 7
Enright, Anne, 138
entertainment industry, the, 192
European Union (EU), 44, 45
Evaristo, Bernardine, 5, 14, 177, 181, 182–4, 187
  Blonde Roots, 182–4
  Lara, 182
  Soul Tourists, 182
Exchange Rate Mechanism, 25
experimental fiction, 120, 121, 145, 251, 252, 256

Faber, Michael, 130
  The Crimson Petal and the White, 206
fabulation, 13
Fagan, Jenni, 99
fantastic, the, 265
Faris, Wendy B., 152
Farrell, J. G.
  The Siege of Krishnapur, 20, 23
Faulks, Sebastian
  A Week in December, 28
Federman, Raymond, 2, 225
Felski, Rita, 225
feminism, 22, 160, 161, 213, 262
Ferron, Louis
  Turkenvespers, 257
Fisher, Mark, 3, 227, 232, 234
Fitzgerald, Penelope
  Offshore, 131
Foer, Jonathan Safran, 226
Ford, Ford Madox, 235
Forster, E. M., 92, 129, 131
  Howard's End, 250
  Maurice, 163
Foucault, Michel, 164
  The Archeology of Knowledge, 194
  The History of Sexuality, 159
Fowles, John, 5, 11, 35, 36, 134, 255
  The French Lieutenant's Woman, 1, 7, 14, 20, 195, 206, 210, 217, 231, 256, 261, 265
  The Magus, 20, 27, 35, 38
Frankenstein (Mary Shelley), 85
Franzen, Jonathan, 84, 264
  The Corrections, 94
From Hell (Alan Moore and Eddie Campbell), 132
Fryer, Peter, 181
Fuentes, Carlos
  Terra Nostra, 257
Fukuyama, Francis, 101

Gaddis, William, 4
  The Recognitions, 257
Gaiman, Neil
  Neverwhere, 132

Galloway, Janice, 98, 99, 109
  The Trick is to Keep Breathing, 99, 101, 105
Galsworthy, John, 136
Gasiorek, Andrzej, 145
Gass, William, 2
gay and lesbian fiction, 13–14, 159–71
Gay Liberation Front, The, 162
Gee, Maggie, 5, 242
Genette, Gérard, 260
genre, 131
genre fiction, 244
genre-blending, 13
geography, 11
Gilroy, Paul, 179, 183
globalisation, 240
Golding, William, 136
  Lord of the Flies, 136
grand narratives, 126, 147, 170, 183, 207, 226, 240, 250
Grass, Günter, 257
Gray, Alasdair, 11, 12, 98, 99, 109, 256
  Lanark, 9, 69, 82, 99, 101–3, 108, 257, 262
  Poor Things, 183, 195, 210, 219
Green, Jeremy
  'late postmodernism', 236
Grossman, Lev, 135
Gutleben, Christian, 220
  Nostalgic Postmodernism, 211, 217, 220

Hall, Steven
  The Raw Shark Texts, 82
Hall, Stuart
  'new ethnicities', 251
Halperin, David, 161
Hames, Scott, 98
Hamid, Moshin
  The Reluctant Fundamentalist, 175
Hardt, Michael and Antonio Negri, 202
Harris, Wilson, 7
Harvey, David, 66, 87
Hassan, Ihab, 224
  The Dismemberment of Orpheus, 35
Hawksmoor, Nicholas, 71
Healey, Emma, 138
Heart of Darkness (Joseph Conrad), 85
Heath, Edward, 21
Heller, Joseph, 86
Higdon, David Leon, 117
historical novel, the, 14, 130, 138, 167–70, 194–5
historiographic metafiction, 9, 14, 20, 36, 72, 98, 169, 177, 183, 193, 231, 232, 236, 250
Hoban, Russell, 139
Holland, Mary K.
  Succeeding Postmodernism, 226
Hollinghurst, Alan, 5, 13, 161, 171

The Line of Beauty, 131, 166, 250
The Swimming Pool Library, 165–6
homonormativity, 13, 170–1
homosexuality, 161–2, 164, 167
hooks, bell
  'Postmodern Blackness', 251
Horstkotte, Martin, 265
House, Richard
  The Kills, 89
Huber, Irmtraub, 265
Hutcheon, Linda, 44, 98, 170, 175, 195, 207, 224, 225, 235, 258
  historiographic metafiction, 9, 36, 39–40, 169, 183, 195, 208, 214, 235
  Narcissistic Narrative, 36
Huxley, Aldous
  Brave New World, 137, 232
hyperspace, 67

identity politics, 175, 177, 187
imperialism, 55–8, 177, 187
Inception (movie), 231
internet, 88
intertextuality, 262
Invasion of Iraq by US and UK, 50
Invisible Cities (Italo Calvino), 68
irony, 54
Ishiguro, Kazuo, 10, 11, 13, 15, 43–4, 130, 138, 153–6, 241
  Klara and the Sun, 154
  Never Let Me Go, 15, 154, 229, 232–5, 236–7
  The Buried Giant, 153–6
  The Remains of the Day, 36, 153, 154

James, David, 116, 122
James, Henry, 116, 250
James, P. D., 130, 139
  The Children of Men, 131
Jameson, Fredric, 3, 22, 28, 67, 100, 141, 156, 180, 202, 208, 211, 219, 224, 227, 229, 232, 235, 236, 244, 263
  'cognitive mapping', 103
  'perpetual present', 196
  Postmodernism, or, the Cultural Logic of Late Capitalism, 10, 18, 67, 100, 207, 257
  'waning of affect', 100
Jencks, Charles, 21, 165, 193
Johnson, B. S., 7, 12, 35, 36, 113–26, 255
  Albert Angelo, 35, 36–7, 38, 117–18, 123, 125
  Aren't You Rather Young to be Writing Your Memoirs?, 113, 115, 124, 125
  'Broad Thoughts from a Home', 119
  Christie Malry's Own Double-Entry, 9, 115, 118, 122, 123, 125
  House Mother Normal, 120, 123, 125

Johnson, B. S (cont.)
  See the Old Lady Decently, 115, 123, 124, 125
  The Unfortunates, 115, 120, 122, 123, 125
  Travelling People, 114, 119, 123, 125
  Trawl, 122, 123, 125
  You're Human Like the Rest of Them
  The Films of B.S. Johnson, 126
Jones, Carole, 105
Journal of Neo-Victorian Studies, 210
Joyce, James, 139
  Finnegan's Wake, 139
  Ulysses, 119
Joyce, Simon, 209

Kaplan, Cora
  'Victoriana', 210
Kay, Jackie
  Trumpet, 171
Kearney, Richard, 98
Keen, Suzanne
  postmodern 'historical turn', 35, 42
Kelly, Adam, 246, 264
Kelman, James, 98, 99, 103–5, 108, 109
  A Disaffection, 103
  How Late it Was, How Late, 103, 104
  Mo Said She Was Quirky, 31
  The Busconductor Hines, 103
  Translated Accounts, 104–5
  You Have to be Careful in the Land of the Free, 103
Kennedy, A. L., 9, 12, 98
  The Blue Book, 99
Kennedy, Alan, 118
Kenyan Emergency (1952–60), 53
Kingsnorth, Paul, 139
Kneale, Matthew
  English Passengers, 9
Koestler, Arthur, 38
Künstlerroman, 69, 101
Kunzru, Hari, 5, 12, 14, 95, 177, 187
  Gods Without Men, 178, 228
  The Impressionist, 177, 178–80, 181
  Transmission, 93–4, 178
Kuppner, Frank, 98
  A Concussed History of Scotland, 99
Kureishi, Hanif, 5, 7, 9, 11, 13, 14, 132, 161, 171, 174, 175
  The Black Album, 174, 177
  The Buddha of Suburbia, 9, 77, 163–4, 174

Lady Chatterley Trial, The, 114
Lady Chatterley's Lover (D. H. Lawrence), 114
Lahiri, Jumpa
  Unaccustomed Earth, 178
Lanchester, John, 122

Capital, 28, 131
Lanthimos, Yorgos
  Poor Things (movie), 210, 219
late capitalism, 3, 8, 11, 19, 107, 240, 247, 257
late modernism, 130
late postmodernism, 10, 180, 236–7
Lawrence, D. H., 116
Le Carré, John, 39, 139
  A Perfect Spy, 42
Leavis, F. R.
  The Great Tradition, 116, 133
Lee, Alison, 2
  Realism and Power: British Postmodern Fiction, 261, 262
Lee, Vernon, 215, 217
Lessing, Doris, 7, 9, 11, 35, 40, 136, 145
  The Fifth Child, 40
  The Golden Notebook, 6, 9
Levy, Andrea, 5, 15, 181
  Small Island, 251
  The Long Song, 182
Lewis, C. S., 135, 140, 147
Lewycka, Marina
  Various Pets Alive and Dead, 30–1
literary marketplace, 15, 217
Litt, Toby, 5, 246
Lively, Penelope, 11, 39
  Moon TIger, 42
Lodge, David, 9
  Author, Author, 250
  'The Novelist at the Crossroads', 252
logocentrism, 49
Lott, Tim
  The Seymour Tapes, 27
Luckhurst, Roger, 72
Lynch, Paul
  Prophet Son, 130
Lyotard, Jean-François
  metanarratives, 3, 49, 51, 54, 61, 147
  '*petits récits*', 4, 50, 51, 54, 61, 147, 170
  The Postmodern Condition, 49, 147, 207

MacDiarmid, Hugh, 98
Mackay, Shena
  Heligoland, 30
magic realism, 152
Magrs, Paul, 14, 171
  Could It Be Magic?, 166–7
  Does It Show?, 166
  Marked for Life, 166
Malkani, Gautam, 251
  Londonstani, 175
Mantel, Hilary, 13, 130, 138
  Wolf Hall, 14, 193, 194, 199–200
Martel, Yann

Life of Pi, 130
Marxism, 49
McBride, Elmear
  A Girl is a Half-formed Thing, 106
McCann, Colum
  TransAtlantic, 193, 198–200
McCarthy, Tom, 5, 12, 91–2, 94, 95
  C, 92
  Men in Space, 91
  Remainder, 92, 252
  Satin Island, 91
McEwan, Ian, 8, 11, 15, 23–4, 29, 131, 138, 241, 243–4
  Saturday, 50–2, 63, 132, 243–4
  The Cement Garden, 244
McGlynn, Mary, 99, 106
McGurl, Mark, 130
  The Program Era, 137
McHale, Brian, 2, 34–5, 84, 99, 100, 114, 142, 224, 225, 227, 258, 265, 267
  history of postmodernism, 5–6
  'ontological dominant', 119–21, 135, 145, 156, 258
McLaughlin, Robert, 268
metafiction, 1, 4, 9, 24, 36–7, 38, 42, 68, 78, 83, 85, 90, 103, 105, 124, 125, 141, 191, 208, 226, 242, 256, 263, 264
metalepsis, 260
Miéville, China, 5, 13, 22, 141
migration into Britain, 7, 174
Miller, J. Hillis, 212
Mitchell, David, 5, 12, 13, 15, 16, 94, 95, 131, 139, 147, 156, 246, 247, 264, 266–8
  Cloud Atlas, 15, 153, 228, 229, 231–2, 235, 236, 247, 266–7, 268
  Ghostwritten, 93, 147–50, 151, 177, 247, 267
  number9dream, 247, 265, 267
  The Bone Clocks, 14, 28–9, 148, 153, 193, 201–2, 267
Mitchell, Kaye, 117
modernism, 22, 34, 35, 116, 118, 130, 133, 139, 151, 235, 250, 252, 257, 261
Moorcock, Michael, 11, 139
  Mother London, 72
Moraru, Christian
  cosmodernism, 176
Moretti, Franco, 84
Morey, Peter, 187
Morrison, Toni, 4
multiculturalism, 12, 109, 171, 174, 175, 176, 184, 241, 251, 253
Murdoch, Iris, 83, 84
Murphet, Julian, 264

Nabokov, Vladimir, 4, 86
Naipaul, V. S., 7

neo-historical fiction, 218, 244
neoliberalism, 50
neo-modernism, 31
neo-Victorian fiction, 14, 207–20
network society, 88–95, 188
Newland, Courttia, 8, 175, 251
  Society Within, 181
'new sincerity' in fiction, the, 246
Nicol, Bran, 83
  The Cambridge Introduction to Postmodernism, 263
Nixon, Richard, 21
Norfolk, Lawrence
  Lemprière's Dictionary, 9, 82
Norquay, Glenda, 105
nouveau roman, the French, 117

O'Hagan, Andrew
  Caledonian Road, 97, 99–101
O'Brien, Flann
  At-Swim Two Birds, 119
O'Donnell, Patrick, 193
Ondaatje, Michael, 130
Orwell, George
  Nineteen Eighty-Four, 137, 232
Ossian (James MacPherson), 98
Oulipo (France), 256
'out-of-time-ness', 15, 229–30, 232, 236

Palliser, Charles
  The Quincunx, 210
parody, 28
Parrinder, Patrick, 116, 153
pastiche, 28, 42, 163
Peace, David, 22
Perec, Georges, 19
  La Vie: mode d'emploi, 257
performativity, 13, 161, 182
periodisation, 212–13, 224
'perpetual present'. *See* Jameson, Fredric
Perry, Sarah
  The Essex Serpent, 211
Phillips, Caryl, 181
  A Distant Shore, 251
  Crossing the River, 182
  Dancing in the Dark, 181–2
Poor Things (movie), 220
postcolonialism, 11, 22, 49–63, 174, 175, 178–80, 183, 186, 213, 241, 250–1
post-humanism, 31
post-imperialism, 73
post-millennial fiction, 10, 14, 15, 145, 186, 191, 193, 196, 203
postmodern ethics, 15, 241, 243, 246, 268

post-postmodernism, 10, 15, 16, 103, 125, 175, 230–1, 234, 236–7, 240, 244, 247
  alternative terms for, 227, 240
poststructuralism, 161
Pratchett, Terry, 140
'precariat', the, 30
Pritchard, Melissa
  Palmerino, 215, 217
Proust, Marcel, 235
Pulley, Natasha, 131, 138
Pullman, Philip, 135
  His Dark Materials, 147
Pynchon, Thomas, 4, 5, 86, 226
  Gravity's Rainbow, 19, 92, 257, 265
  Inherent Vice, 88
  V., 256

queer, 160–1, 168
queer fiction, 13–14
queer theory, 13, 159–60, 213
Quin, Ann, 7
Quinn, Julia, 219, *See Bridgerton* (TV series)

Rabinovitz, Rubin, 113
race, 57, 62, 77, 87, 109, 164, 171, 175–78, 182, 183–4, 187, 195, 219, 250–1
racial diversity, 218–19
realism, 118, 129, 133, 156, 218, 252, 257, 261
reality TV, 26
Reed, Ishmael, 4
Rees-Mogg, Jacob, 208, 213
religion, 148, 149, 152, 154
Rhimes, Shonda. *See Bridgerton* (TV series)
Rhys, Jean, 7
  Wide Sargasso Sea, 206, 210, 214
Richard and Judy Book Club, The, 133
Ricoeur, Paul, 207
Rigney, Anne, 194
Robbe-Grillet, Alain, 144
  Dans le labyrinthe, 256
Robinson Crusoe (Daniel Defoe), 37, 76, 85
Robinson, Alan, 215
romance, 13
Rowling, J. K., 140
  Diagon Alley, 132
Rudrum, David and Nicholas Stavris, 175
Rushdie, Salman, 5, 7, 9, 10, 11, 14, 15, 49, 131, 145, 148, 175, 241, 250–1, 256
  Midnight's Children, 1, 8, 9, 49, 108, 174, 177, 195, 229–30, 231, 257, 262
  The Satanic Verses, 23, 49, 73, 85, 145
Ryan, Marie-Laure, 260, 261
Ryman, Geoff
  253, 132

Saadi, Suhayl, 99
  Psychoraag, 101, 108–9, 175
Sahota, Sunjeev
  Ours are the Streets, 175
Saussure, Ferdinand de, 70
Saxton, Laura, 218
science fiction, 69, 231, 232–3
Scott, Walter, 98
Scottish Asian fiction, 108–9
Scottish postmodernism, 12
Sedgwick, Eve Kosofsky, 160
Self, Will, 5, 9, 15, 131, 135, 241, 246
  How the Dead Live, 150
  Shark, 250
  Umbrella, 250
self-consciousness. *See* metafiction
self-reflexive reading, 202
self-reflexivity. *See* metafiction
Selvon, Sam and George Lamming, 181
Seth, Vikram
  A Suitable Boy, 177
Sexual Offences Act 1967 (Wolfenden Report), 161
sexuality, 159–60
Shiller, Dana, 208
Simmonds, Posy, 131
simulation. *See* Baudrillard, Jean
Sinclair, Iain, 11, 132, 255
  Downriver, 72
  Lud Heat, 71
  White Chappell, Scarlet Tracings, 71, 72
slave narratives (eighteenth century), 183
Smith, Ali, 5, 13, 15, 99, 101, 147, 150–2, 156, 246
  Artful, 150–1
  Hotel World, 151–2, 177
  How to be Both, 14, 151, 193, 196–8, 199, 249–50
  The Accidental, 15, 100, 232, 235, 236–7
Smith, Zadie, 5, 11, 12, 14, 92–3, 95, 175, 177, 184–8, 250, 251–3
  'Two Directions for the Novel', 185
  NW, 31, 132, 185–6, 252–3, 268
  On Beauty, 184, 250
  The Autograph Man, 92–3, 184
  The Embassy of Cambodia, 187
  The Fraud, 211
  White Teeth, 74, 184, 185, 192–3
Soja, Edward, 66
space and spatiality, 66–79
  cities, 68
  London, 70–4, 79
  non-places, 74–7
  regional landscapes, 77–9
  transatlantic, the, 82–95

Spark, Muriel, 8, 9, 11, 12, 35, 36, 83, 84, 98
  Memento Mori, 152
  'Miss Pinkerton's Apocalypse', 86
  Robinson, 37
  The Abbess of Crewe, 21
  The Comforters, 6, 35, 37, 38, 102
  The Driver's Seat, 20
spectacle, 26, 27
speculative fiction, 13, 29, 137
Spivak, Gayatri, 21
Stace, Wesley
  Misfortune, 215
steampunk, 147, 210
Sterne, Laurence
  The Life and Opinions of Tristram Shandy, Gentleman, 132
Stevenson, Randall, 103, 109
Stewart, Stewart, 191
Strauss, Darin
  Change and Eng, 214
Stross, Charles, 140
suburbia, 76–7
surveillance, 27
Swift, Graham, 5, 11, 35, 39, 174, 255
  Last Orders, 82
  Waterland, 16, 23, 42, 77–8, 191, 258–9, 261, 266
Syal, Meera, 175

technology, 42, 88, 196
television, 26
temporality, 195
Tennant, Emma, 98
Thatcher, Margaret, 8, 23, 34, 39, 98, 107, 162, 181, 208, 210, 213
The Believer. See Eggers, Dave
The Waste Land (T. S. Eliot), 92
Thiong'o, Ngũgĩ wa
  A Grain of Wheat, 53–5, 58–63
Thomas, D. M., 8, 9, 256
  The White Hotel, 9, 257, 262
Thomas, Scarlett, 131
Thomson, Rupert
  Divided Kingdom, 27
  The Insult, 26
Thorpe, Adam, 11
  Ulverton, 78–9
Todd, Richard, 134
Toibin, Colm
  The Master, 250
Tolkien, J. R. R., 139, 147
  The Lord of the Rings, 136
totalisation, 224
transatlantic traditions in postmodern fiction, 11–12

transgender, 170, 215
transglossic, the (Shaw and Upstone), 176, 177
Tremain, Rose, 130, 138
  Restoration, 9
  The Road Home, 28
typographical innovations, 106

UK European Union membership referendum. *See* Brexit
Underwood, Ted
  Why Literary Periods Mattered, 212, 225
Unsworth, Barry
  Sacred Hunger, 9
Updike, John, 153, 176
Upstone, Sara, 182
Urry, John, 152
US global dominance, 57

Venturi, Robert, 224
Vermeulen, Pieter, 263
Vietnam War, the, 19, 21
Virilio, Paul, 145
virtual reality, 70
Vonnegut, Kurt, 4
  Slaughterhouse-Five, 19

Wallace, David Foster, 4, 6, 91, 226, 264
  'E Unibus Pluram: Television and U. S. Fiction', 93, 225
  Infinite Jest, 82, 91
  'Octet', 93
  The Pale King, 91
Warner, Alan, 98
Warner, Michael
  The Trouble with Normal, 161
Watergate scandal, 21
Waters, Sarah, 14, 15, 130, 168–9, 194, 216
  Affinity, 168, 206, 214, 215
  Fingersmith, 9, 169, 206, 211, 217
  Tipping the Velvet, 168, 206, 215
Waugh, Patricia, 85, 86, 121, 261, 262
  Metafiction: The Theory and Practice of Self-Conscious Fiction, 83
  Practising Postmodernism, Reading Modernism, 226
Welsh postmodernism, 12, 23
Welsh, Irvine, 98, 99, 109
  Trainspotting, 99, 101, 107–8
Wheatle, Alex, 251
White, Hayden, 207
Whyte, Christopher, 98
Wilde, Oscar, 169
Williams, Nigel
  Star Turn, 9

Williams, Raymond, 22–3
  Volunteers, 22
Wilson, Angus, 138
Wilson, Harold, 33
Winterson, Jeanette, 5, 9, 11, 13, 15, 68–9, 130, 140, 161, 169–70, 241, 256
  Oranges Are Not the Only Fruit, 163, 245
  Sexing the Cherry, 9, 68–9, 82, 169, 170, 195, 249, 262
  The Gap of Time, 14, 193, 200–1
  The Passion, 9, 68, 169, 170
  Why Be Happy When You Can Be Normal?, 245
  Written on the Body, 159
Wood, James, 150, 186
  'hysterical realism', 99, 185, 251
Woods, Patrick, 164
Woolf, Virginia, 85, 87, 94, 130, 131

Cambridge Companions To...

AUTHORS

Edward Albee edited by Stephen J. Bottoms

Margaret Atwood edited by Coral Ann Howells (second edition)

W. H. Auden edited by Stan Smith

Jane Austen edited by Edward Copeland and Juliet McMaster (second edition)

James Baldwin edited by Michele Elam

Balzac edited by Owen Heathcote and Andrew Watts

Beckett edited by John Pilling

Bede edited by Scott DeGregorio

Aphra Behn edited by Derek Hughes and Janet Todd

Saul Bellow edited by Victoria Aarons

Walter Benjamin edited by David S. Ferris

William Blake edited by Morris Eaves

Boccaccio edited by Guyda Armstrong, Rhiannon Daniels, and Stephen J. Milner

Jorge Luis Borges edited by Edwin Williamson

Brecht edited by Peter Thomson and Glendyr Sacks (second edition)

The Brontës edited by Heather Glen

Bunyan edited by Anne Dunan-Page

Frances Burney edited by Peter Sabor

Byron edited by Drummond Bone (second edition)

Albert Camus edited by Edward J. Hughes

Willa Cather edited by Marilee Lindemann

Catullus edited by Ian Du Quesnay and Tony Woodman

Cervantes edited by Anthony J. Cascardi

Chaucer edited by Piero Boitani and Jill Mann (second edition)

Chekhov edited by Vera Gottlieb and Paul Allain

Kate Chopin edited by Janet Beer

Caryl Churchill edited by Elaine Aston and Elin Diamond

Cicero edited by Catherine Steel

John Clare edited by Sarah Houghton-Walker

J. M. Coetzee edited by Jarad Zimbler

Coleridge edited by Lucy Newlyn

Coleridge edited by Tim Fulford (new edition)

Wilkie Collins edited by Jenny Bourne Taylor

Joseph Conrad edited by J. H. Stape

H. D. edited by Nephie J. Christodoulides and Polina Mackay

Dante edited by Rachel Jacoff (second edition)

Daniel Defoe edited by John Richetti

Don DeLillo edited by John N. Duvall

Charles Dickens edited by John O. Jordan

Emily Dickinson edited by Wendy Martin

John Donne edited by Achsah Guibbory

Dostoevskii edited by W. J. Leatherbarrow

Theodore Dreiser edited by Leonard Cassuto and Claire Virginia Eby

John Dryden edited by Steven N. Zwicker

W. E. B. Du Bois edited by Shamoon Zamir

George Eliot edited by George Levine and Nancy Henry (second edition)

T. S. Eliot edited by A. David Moody

Ralph Ellison edited by Ross Posnock

Ralph Waldo Emerson edited by Joel Porte and Saundra Morris

William Faulkner edited by Philip M. Weinstein

Henry Fielding edited by Claude Rawson

F. Scott Fitzgerald edited by Ruth Prigozy

F. Scott Fitzgerald edited by Michael Nowlin (second edition)

Flaubert edited by Timothy Unwin

E. M. Forster edited by David Bradshaw

Benjamin Franklin edited by Carla Mulford

Brian Friel edited by Anthony Roche

Robert Frost edited by Robert Faggen

Gabriel García Márquez edited by Philip Swanson

Elizabeth Gaskell edited by Jill L. Matus

Edward Gibbon edited by Karen O'Brien and Brian Young

Goethe edited by Lesley Sharpe

Günter Grass edited by Stuart Taberner

Thomas Hardy edited by Dale Kramer

David Hare edited by Richard Boon

Nathaniel Hawthorne edited by Richard Millington

Seamus Heaney edited by Bernard O'Donoghue

Ernest Hemingway edited by Scott Donaldson

Hildegard of Bingen edited by Jennifer Bain

Homer edited by Robert Fowler

Horace edited by Stephen Harrison
Ted Hughes edited by Terry Gifford
Ibsen edited by James McFarlane
Kazuo Ishiguro edited by Andrew Bennett
Henry James edited by Jonathan Freedman
Samuel Johnson edited by Greg Clingham
Ben Jonson edited by Richard Harp and Stanley Stewart
James Joyce edited by John Nash (third edition)
Kafka edited by Julian Preece
Keats edited by Susan J. Wolfson
Rudyard Kipling edited by Howard J. Booth
Lacan edited by Jean-Michel Rabaté
D. H. Lawrence edited by Anne Fernihough
Primo Levi edited by Robert Gordon
Lucian edited by Simon Goldhill
Lucretius edited by Stuart Gillespie and Philip Hardie
Machiavelli edited by John M. Najemy
David Mamet edited by Christopher Bigsby
Thomas Mann edited by Ritchie Robertson
Christopher Marlowe edited by Patrick Cheney
Andrew Marvell edited by Derek Hirst and Steven N. Zwicker
Ian McEwan edited by Dominic Head
Herman Melville edited by Robert S. Levine
Arthur Miller edited by Christopher Bigsby (second edition)
Milton edited by Dennis Danielson (second edition)
Molière edited by David Bradby and Andrew Calder
William Morris edited by Marcus Waithe
Toni Morrison edited by Justine Tally
Alice Munro edited by David Staines
Nabokov edited by Julian W. Connolly
Eugene O'Neill edited by Michael Manheim
George Orwell edited by John Rodden
Ovid edited by Philip Hardie
Petrarch edited by Albert Russell Ascoli and Unn Falkeid
Harold Pinter edited by Peter Raby (second edition)
Sylvia Plath edited by Jo Gill
Plutarch edited by Frances B. Titchener and Alexei Zadorojnyi

Edgar Allan Poe edited by Kevin J. Hayes
Alexander Pope edited by Pat Rogers
Ezra Pound edited by Ira B. Nadel
Mary Prince edited by Nicole N. Aljoe
Proust edited by Richard Bales
Pushkin edited by Andrew Kahn
Thomas Pynchon edited by Inger H. Dalsgaard, Luc Herman, and Brian McHale
Rabelais edited by John O'Brien
Rilke edited by Karen Leeder and Robert Vilain
Philip Roth edited by Timothy Parrish
Salman Rushdie edited by Abdulrazak Gurnah
John Ruskin edited by Francis O'Gorman
Sappho edited by P. J. Finglass and Adrian Kelly
Seneca edited by Shadi Bartsch and Alessandro Schiesaro
Shakespeare edited by Margareta de Grazia and Stanley Wells (second edition)
George Bernard Shaw edited by Christopher Innes
Shelley edited by Timothy Morton
Mary Shelley edited by Esther Schor
Sam Shepard edited by Matthew C. Roudané
Spenser edited by Andrew Hadfield
Laurence Sterne edited by Thomas Keymer
Wallace Stevens edited by John N. Serio
Tom Stoppard edited by Katherine E. Kelly
Harriet Beecher Stowe edited by Cindy Weinstein
August Strindberg edited by Michael Robinson
Jonathan Swift edited by Christopher Fox
J. M. Synge edited by P. J. Mathews
Tacitus edited by A. J. Woodman
Henry David Thoreau edited by Joel Myerson
Thucydides edited by Polly Low
Tolstoy edited by Donna Tussing Orwin
Anthony Trollope edited by Carolyn Dever and Lisa Niles
Mark Twain edited by Forrest G. Robinson
John Updike edited by Stacey Olster
Mario Vargas Llosa edited by Efrain Kristal and John King
Virgil edited by Fiachra Mac Góráin and Charles Martindale (second edition)
Voltaire edited by Nicholas Cronk
David Foster Wallace edited by Ralph Clare

Edith Wharton edited by Millicent Bell
Walt Whitman edited by Ezra Greenspan
Oscar Wilde edited by Peter Raby
Tennessee Williams edited by Matthew C. Roudané
William Carlos Williams edited by Christopher MacGowan
August Wilson edited by Christopher Bigsby
Mary Wollstonecraft edited by Claudia L. Johnson
Virginia Woolf edited by Susan Sellers (second edition)
Wordsworth edited by Stephen Gill
Richard Wright edited by Glenda R. Carpio
W. B. Yeats edited by Marjorie Howes and John Kelly
Xenophon edited by Michael A. Flower
Zola edited by Brian Nelson

TOPICS

The Actress edited by Maggie B. Gale and John Stokes
The African American Novel edited by Maryemma Graham
The African American Slave Narrative edited by Audrey A. Fisch
African American Theatre edited by Harvey Young
Allegory edited by Rita Copeland and Peter Struck
American Crime Fiction edited by Catherine Ross Nickerson
American Gothic edited by Jeffrey Andrew Weinstock
The American Graphic Novel edited by Jan Baetens, Hugo Frey, and Fabrice Leroy
American Horror edited by Stephen Shapiro and Mark Storey
American Literature and the Body edited by Travis M. Foster
American Literature and the Environment edited by Sarah Ensor and Susan Scott Parrish
American Literature of the 1930s edited by William Solomon
American Modernism edited by Walter Kalaidjian
American Poetry since 1945 edited by Jennifer Ashton
American Realism and Naturalism edited by Donald Pizer
American Short Story edited by Michael J. Collins and Gavin Jones
American Travel Writing edited by Alfred Bendixen and Judith Hamera
American Utopian Literature and Culture since 1945 edited by Sherryl Vint
American Women Playwrights edited by Brenda Murphy
Ancient Rhetoric edited by Erik Gunderson
Arthurian Legend edited by Elizabeth Archibald and Ad Putter
Australian Literature edited by Elizabeth Webby
The Australian Novel edited by Nicholas Birns and Louis Klee
The Beats edited by Stephen Belletto
The Black Body in American Literature edited by Cherene Sherrard-Johnson
Boxing edited by Gerald Early
British Black and Asian Literature (1945–2010) edited by Deirdre Osborne
British Fiction: 1980–2018 edited by Peter Boxall
British Fiction since 1945 edited by David James
British Literature of the 1930s edited by James Smith
British Literature of the French Revolution edited by Pamela Clemit
British Postmodern Fiction edited by Bran Nicol
British Romantic Poetry edited by James Chandler and Maureen N. McLane
British Romanticism edited by Stuart Curran (second edition)
British Romanticism and Religion edited by Jeffrey Barbeau
British Theatre, 1730–1830 edited by Jane Moody and Daniel O'Quinn
Canadian Literature edited by Eva-Marie Kröller (second edition)
The Canterbury Tales edited by Frank Grady
Children's Literature edited by M. O. Grenby and Andrea Immel

The City in World Literature edited by Ato Quayson and Jini Kim Watson

The Classic Russian Novel edited by Malcolm V. Jones and Robin Feuer Miller

Comics edited by Maaheen Ahmed

Contemporary African American Literature edited by Yogita Goyal

Contemporary Irish Poetry edited by Matthew Campbell

Creative Writing edited by David Morley and Philip Neilsen

Crime Fiction edited by Martin Priestman

Dante's 'Commedia' edited by Zygmunt G. Barański and Simon Gilson

Dracula edited by Roger Luckhurst

Early American Literature edited by Bryce Traister

Early Modern Women's Writing edited by Laura Lunger Knoppers

The Eighteenth-Century Novel edited by John Richetti

Eighteenth-Century Poetry edited by John Sitter

Eighteenth-Century Thought edited by Frans De Bruyn

Emma edited by Peter Sabor

English Dictionaries edited by Sarah Ogilvie

English Literature, 1500–1600 edited by Arthur F. Kinney

English Literature, 1650–1740 edited by Steven N. Zwicker

English Literature, 1740–1830 edited by Thomas Keymer and Jon Mee

English Literature, 1830–1914 edited by Joanne Shattock

English Melodrama edited by Carolyn Williams

English Novelists edited by Adrian Poole

English Poetry, Donne to Marvell edited by Thomas N. Corns

English Poets edited by Claude Rawson

English Renaissance Drama edited by A. R. Braunmuller and Michael Hattaway (second edition)

English Renaissance Tragedy edited by Emma Smith and Garrett A. Sullivan Jr.

English Restoration Theatre edited by Deborah C. Payne Fisk

Environmental Humanities edited by Jeffrey Cohen and Stephanie Foote

The Epic edited by Catherine Bates

Erotic Literature edited by Bradford Mudge

The Essay edited by Kara Wittman and Evan Kindley

European Modernism edited by Pericles Lewis

European Novelists edited by Michael Bell

Fairy Tales edited by Maria Tatar

Fantasy Literature edited by Edward James and Farah Mendlesohn

Feminist Literary Theory edited by Ellen Rooney

Fiction in the Romantic Period edited by Richard Maxwell and Katie Trumpener

The Fin de Siècle edited by Gail Marshall

Frankenstein edited by Andrew Smith

The French Enlightenment edited by Daniel Brewer

French Literature edited by John D. Lyons

The French Novel: From 1800 to the Present edited by Timothy Unwin

Gay and Lesbian Writing edited by Hugh Stevens

German Romanticism edited by Nicholas Saul

Global Literature and Slavery edited by Laura T. Murphy

Gothic Fiction edited by Jerrold E. Hogle

The Graphic Novel edited by Stephen Tabachnick

The Greek and Roman Novel edited by Tim Whitmarsh

Greek and Roman Theatre edited by Marianne McDonald and J. Michael Walton

Greek Comedy edited by Martin Revermann

Greek Lyric edited by Felix Budelmann

Greek Mythology edited by Roger D. Woodard

Greek Tragedy edited by P. E. Easterling

The Harlem Renaissance edited by George Hutchinson

The History of the Book edited by Leslie Howsam

Human Rights and Literature edited by Crystal Parikh

The Irish Novel edited by John Wilson Foster

Irish Poets edited by Gerald Dawe

The Italian Novel edited by Peter Bondanella and Andrea Ciccarelli

The Italian Renaissance edited by Michael Wyatt

Jewish American Literature edited by Hana Wirth-Nesher and Michael P. Kramer

The Latin American Novel edited by Efraín Kristal

Latin American Poetry edited by Stephen Hart

Latina/o American Literature edited by John Morán González

Latin Love Elegy edited by Thea S. Thorsen

Literature and Animals edited by Derek Ryan

Literature and the Anthropocene edited by John Parham

Literature and Climate edited by Adeline Johns-Putra and Kelly Sultzbach

Literature and Disability edited by Clare Barker and Stuart Murray

Literature and Food edited by J. Michelle Coghlan

Literature and the Posthuman edited by Bruce Clarke and Manuela Rossini

Literature and Religion edited by Susan M. Felch

Literature and Science edited by Steven Meyer

The Literature of the American Civil War and Reconstruction edited by Kathleen Diffley and Coleman Hutchison

The Literature of the American Renaissance edited by Christopher N. Phillips

The Literature of Berlin edited by Andrew J. Webber

The Literature of the Crusades edited by Anthony Bale

The Literature of the First World War edited by Vincent Sherry

The Literature of London edited by Lawrence Manley

The Literature of Los Angeles edited by Kevin R. McNamara

The Literature of New York edited by Cyrus Patell and Bryan Waterman

The Literature of Paris edited by Anna-Louise Milne

The Literature of World War II edited by Marina MacKay

Literature on Screen edited by Deborah Cartmell and Imelda Whelehan

Lyrical Ballads edited by Sally Bushell

Manga and Anime edited by Jaqueline Berndt

Medieval British Manuscripts edited by Orietta Da Rold and Elaine Treharne

Medieval English Culture edited by Andrew Galloway

Medieval English Law and Literature edited by Candace Barrington and Sebastian Sobecki

Medieval English Literature edited by Larry Scanlon

Medieval English Mysticism edited by Samuel Fanous and Vincent Gillespie

Medieval English Theatre edited by Richard Beadle and Alan J. Fletcher (second edition)

Medieval French Literature edited by Simon Gaunt and Sarah Kay

Medieval Romance edited by Roberta L. Krueger

Medieval Romance edited by Roberta L. Krueger (new edition)

Medieval Women's Writing edited by Carolyn Dinshaw and David Wallace

Modern American Culture edited by Christopher Bigsby

Modern British Women Playwrights edited by Elaine Aston and Janelle Reinelt

Modern French Culture edited by Nicholas Hewitt

Modern German Culture edited by Eva Kolinsky and Wilfried van der Will

The Modern German Novel edited by Graham Bartram

The Modern Gothic edited by Jerrold E. Hogle

Modern Irish Culture edited by Joe Cleary and Claire Connolly

Modern Italian Culture edited by Zygmunt G. Baranski and Rebecca J. West

Modern Latin American Culture edited by John King

Modern Russian Culture edited by Nicholas Rzhevsky

Modern Spanish Culture edited by David T. Gies

Modernism edited by Michael Levenson (second edition)

The Modernist Novel edited by Morag Shiach

Modernist Poetry edited by Alex Davis and Lee M. Jenkins

Modernist Women Writers edited by Maren Tova Linett

Narrative edited by David Herman

Narrative Theory edited by Matthew Garrett

Native American Literature edited by Joy Porter and Kenneth M. Roemer

Nineteen Eighty-Four edited by Nathan Waddell

Nineteenth-Century American Literature and Politics edited by John Kerkering

Nineteenth-Century American Poetry edited by Kerry Larson

Nineteenth-Century American Women's Writing edited by Dale M. Bauer and Philip Gould

Nineteenth-Century Thought edited by Gregory Claeys

The Novel edited by Eric Bulson

Old English Literature edited by Malcolm Godden and Michael Lapidge (second edition)

Performance Studies edited by Tracy C. Davis

Piers Plowman edited by Andrew Cole and Andrew Galloway

The Poetry of the First World War edited by Santanu Das

Popular Fiction edited by David Glover and Scott McCracken

Postcolonial Literary Studies edited by Neil Lazarus

Postcolonial Poetry edited by Jahan Ramazani

Postcolonial Travel Writing edited by Robert Clarke

Postmodern American Fiction edited by Paula Geyh

Postmodernism edited by Steven Connor

Prose edited by Daniel Tyler

The Pre-Raphaelites edited by Elizabeth Prettejohn

Pride and Prejudice edited by Janet Todd

Queer Studies edited by Siobhan B. Somerville

Renaissance Humanism edited by Jill Kraye

Robinson Crusoe edited by John Richetti

Roman Comedy edited by Martin T. Dinter

The Roman Historians edited by Andrew Feldherr

Roman Satire edited by Kirk Freudenburg

The Romantic Sublime edited by Cian Duffy

Romanticism and Race edited by Manu Samriti Chander

Science Fiction edited by Edward James and Farah Mendlesohn

Scottish Literature edited by Gerald Carruthers and Liam McIlvanney

Sensation Fiction edited by Andrew Mangham

Shakespeare and Contemporary Dramatists edited by Ton Hoenselaars

Shakespeare and Popular Culture edited by Robert Shaughnessy

Shakespeare and Race edited by Ayanna Thompson

Shakespeare and Religion edited by Hannibal Hamlin

Shakespeare and War edited by David Loewenstein and Paul Stevens

Shakespeare on Film edited by Russell Jackson (second edition)

Shakespeare on Screen edited by Russell Jackson

Shakespeare on Stage edited by Stanley Wells and Sarah Stanton

Shakespearean Comedy edited by Alexander Leggatt

Shakespearean Tragedy edited by Claire McEachern (second edition)

Shakespeare's First Folio edited by Emma Smith

Shakespeare's History Plays edited by Michael Hattaway

Shakespeare's Language edited by Lynne Magnusson with David Schalkwyk

Shakespeare's Last Plays edited by Catherine M. S. Alexander

Shakespeare's Poetry edited by Patrick Cheney

Sherlock Holmes edited by Janice M. Allan and Christopher Pittard

The Sonnet edited by A. D. Cousins and Peter Howarth

The Spanish Novel: From 1600 to the Present edited by Harriet Turner and Adelaida López de Martínez

Textual Scholarship edited by Neil Fraistat and Julia Flanders

Theatre and Science edited by Kristen E. Shepherd-Barr

Theatre History edited by David Wiles and Christine Dymkowski

Transnational American Literature edited by Yogita Goyal

Travel Writing edited by Peter Hulme and Tim Youngs

The Twentieth-Century American Novel and Politics edited by Bryan Santin

Twentieth-Century American Poetry and Politics edited by Daniel Morris

Twentieth-Century British and Irish Women's Poetry edited by Jane Dowson

The Twentieth-Century English Novel edited by Robert L. Caserio

Twentieth-Century English Poetry edited by Neil Corcoran

Twentieth-Century Irish Drama edited by Shaun Richards

Twentieth-Century Literature and Politics edited by Christos Hadjiyiannis and Rachel Potter

Twentieth-Century Russian Literature edited by Marina Balina and Evgeny Dobrenko

Utopian Literature edited by Gregory Claeys

Victorian and Edwardian Theatre edited by Kerry Powell

The Victorian Novel edited by Deirdre David (second edition)

Victorian Poetry edited by Joseph Bristow

Victorian Women's Poetry edited by Linda K. Hughes

Victorian Women's Writing edited by Linda H. Peterson

War Writing edited by Kate McLoughlin

Women's Writing in Britain, 1660–1789 edited by Catherine Ingrassia

Women's Writing in the Romantic Period edited by Devoney Looser

World Crime Fiction edited by Jesper Gulddal, Stewart King, and Alistair Rolls

World Literature edited by Ben Etherington and Jarad Zimbler

Writing of the English Revolution edited by N. H. Keeble

The Writings of Julius Caesar edited by Christopher Krebs and Luca Grillo

For EU product safety concerns, contact us at Calle de José Abascal, 56–1°,
28003 Madrid, Spain or eugpsr@cambridge.org.

www.ingramcontent.com/pod-product-compliance
Ingram Content Group UK Ltd.
Pitfield, Milton Keynes, MK11 3LW, UK
UKHW021824130825
461759UK00020B/379